Ordnance Survey

STREET ATLAS

Berkshire

Contents

PHILIP'S

First edition published 1990
First colour edition published 1996
Reprinted 1998, 1999 by

Ordnance Survey®   and George Philip Ltd, a division of
Romsey Road   Octopus Publishing Group Ltd
Maybush   2-4 Heron Quays
Southampton   London
SO16 4GU   E14 4JP

ISBN 0-540-06170-0 (hardback)
ISBN 0-540-06172-7 (wire-o)

© Crown copyright 1996
© George Philip Ltd 1996

Printed and bound in Spain by Cayfosa

Also available in various formats

- Bristol and Avon
- Buckinghamshire
- Birmingham and West Midlands
- Cannock, Lichfield Rugeley
- Cardiff, Swansea and Glamorgan
- Cheshire
- Derbyshire
- Derby and Belper
- Durham
- Edinburgh & East Central Scotland
- East Essex
- West Essex
- Glasgow & West Central Scotland
- Greater Manchester
- North Hampshire
- South Hampshire
- Hertfordshire
- East Kent
- West Kent
- Lancashire
- Merseyside
- Northwich, Winsford Middlewich
- Nottinghamshire
- Oxfordshire
- Peak District Towns
- Staffordshire
- Stafford, Stone Uttoxeter
- Surrey
- East Sussex
- West Sussex
- Tyne and Wear
- Warrington, Widnes Runcorn
- Warwickshire
- South Yorkshire
- West Yorkshire

◆ Colour regional atlases (hardback, spiral, wire-o, pocket) ◇ Colour local atlases (paperback)
◆ Black and white regional atlases (hardback, softback, pocket)

	Motorway
	Primary route (dual carriageway and single)
	A road (dual carriageway and single)
	B road (dual carriageway and single)
	Minor road (dual carriageway and single)
	Other minor road
	Road under construction
	County and unitary authority boundaries
	Railway
	Rural track, private road or narrow road in urban area
	Gate or obstruction to traffic (restrictions may not apply at all times or to all vehicles)
	Path, bridleway, byway open to all traffic, road used as a public path, dismantled railways, etc.
	The representation in this atlas of a road, track or path is no evidence of the existence of a right of way
174	**Adjoining page indicator**

	British Rail station
	Private railway station
	Bus, coach station
	Ambulance station
	Coastguard station
	Fire station
	Police station
+	**Accident and Emergency entrance to hospital**
H	**Hospital**
+	**Church, place of worship**
i	**Information Centre** (open all year)
P	**Parking**
□	**Post Office**
●	**Public convenience**
	Important buildings, schools, colleges, universities and hospitals
River Kennet	**Water name**
	Stream
	River or canal (minor and major)
	Water
	Tidal water
	Woods
	Houses

Acad	**Academy**		Mon	**Monument**
Cemy	**Cemetery**		Mus	**Museum**
C Ctr	**Civic Centre**		Obsy	**Observatory**
CH	**Club House**		Pal	**Royal Palace**
Coll	**College**		PH	**Public House**
Ex H	**Exhibition Hall**		Resr	**Reservoir**
Ind Est	**Industrial Estate**		Ret Pk	**Retail Park**
Inst	**Institute**		Sch	**School**
Ct	**Law Court**		Sh Ctr	**Shopping Centre**
L Ctr	**Leisure Centre**		Sta	**Station**
LC	**Level Crossing**		TH	**Town Hall/House**
Liby	**Library**		Trad Est	**Trading Estate**
Mkt	**Market**		Univ	**University**
Meml	**Memorial**		YH	**Youth Hostel**

0	¼	½	¾	1 mile
0	250 m	500 m	750 m	1 Kilometre

The scale of the maps is 5.52 cm to 1 km (3½ inches to 1 mile)

The small numbers around the edges of the maps identify the 1 kilometre National Grid lines

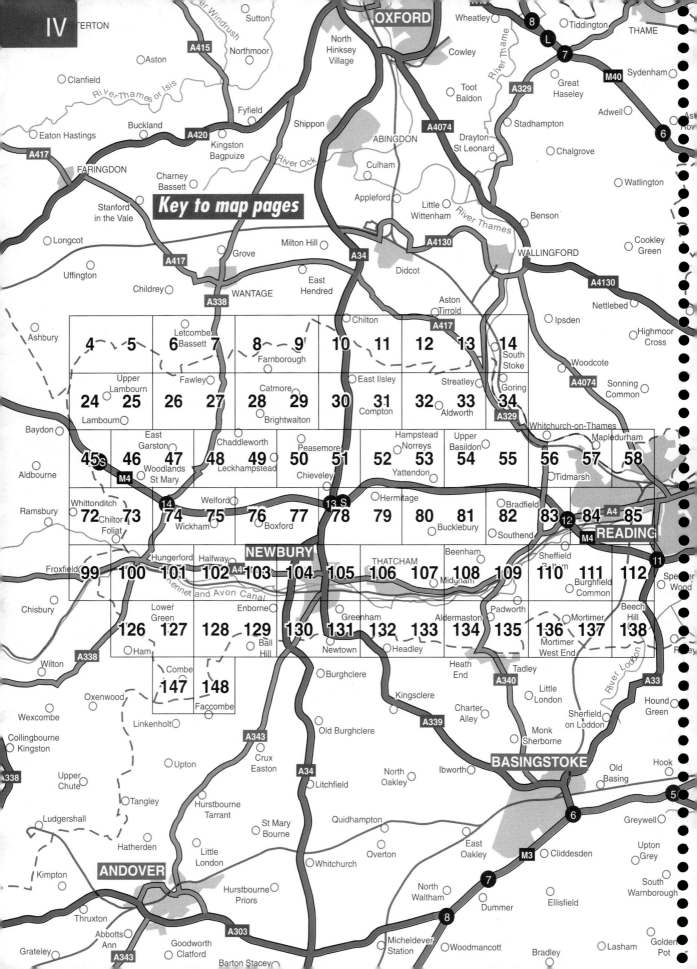

Key to map pages

OXFORD
THAME

Map grid numbers
4 | 5 | 6 | 7 | 8 | 9 | 10 | 11 | 12 | 13 | 14
24 | 25 | 26 | 27 | 28 | 29 | 30 | 31 | 32 | 33 | 34
45 | 46 | 47 | 48 | 49 | 50 | 51 | 52 | 53 | 54 | 55 | 56 | 57 | 58
72 | 73 | 74 | 75 | 76 | 77 | 78 | 79 | 80 | 81 | 82 | 83 | 84 | 85
99 | 100 | 101 | 102 | 103 | 104 | 105 | 106 | 107 | 108 | 109 | 110 | 111 | 112
126 | 127 | 128 | 129 | 130 | 131 | 132 | 133 | 134 | 135 | 136 | 137 | 138
147 | 148

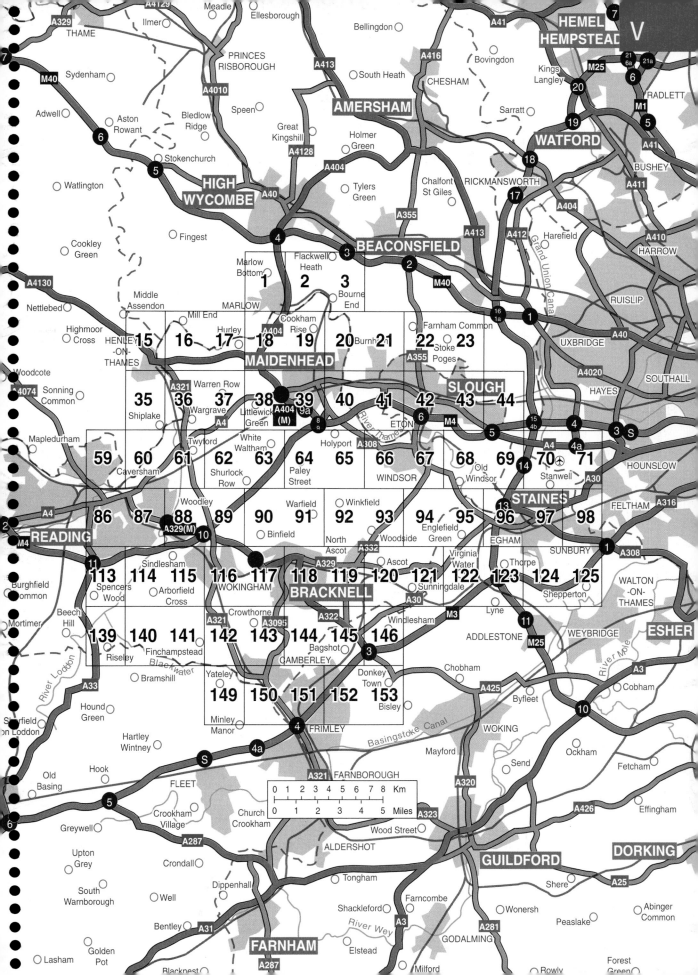

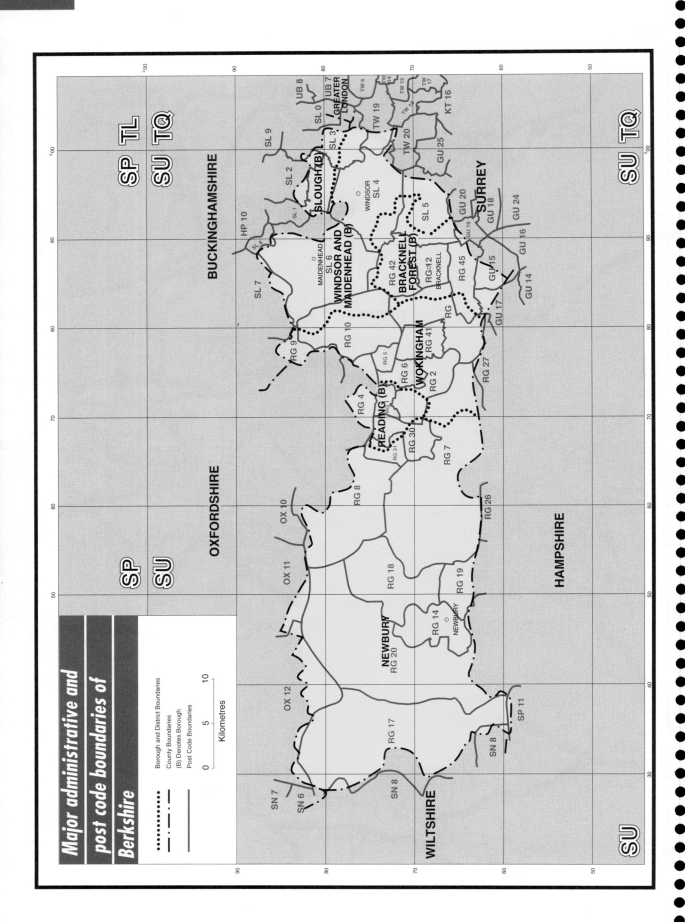

Major administrative and
post code boundaries of
Berkshire

Borough and District Boundaries
County Boundaries
(B) Denotes Borough
Post Code Boundaries

0   5   10
Kilometres

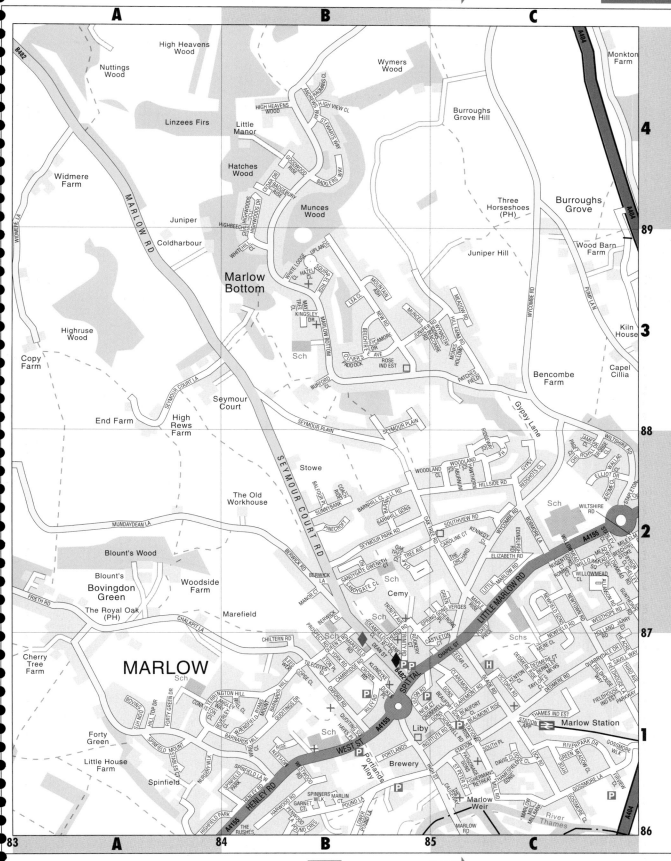

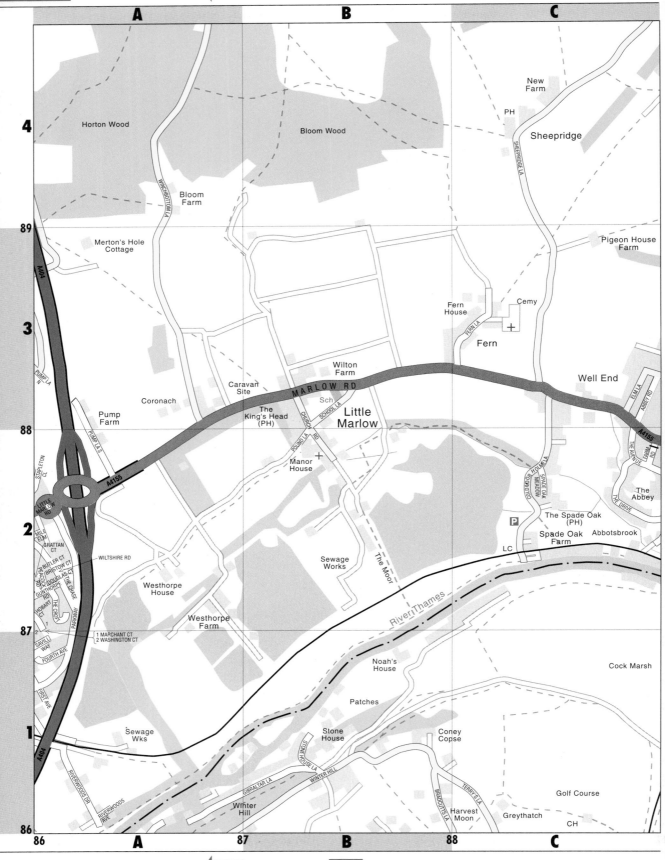

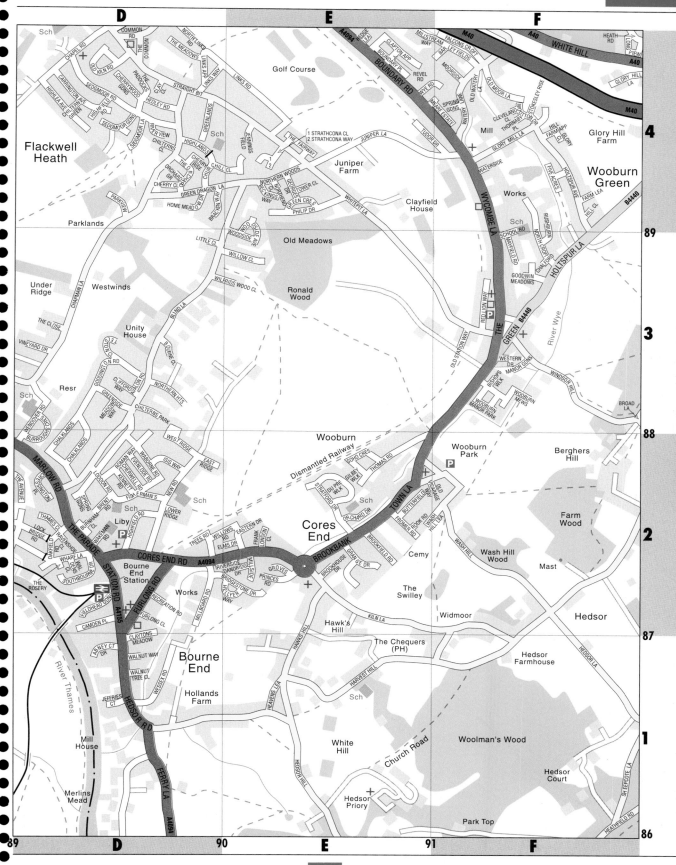

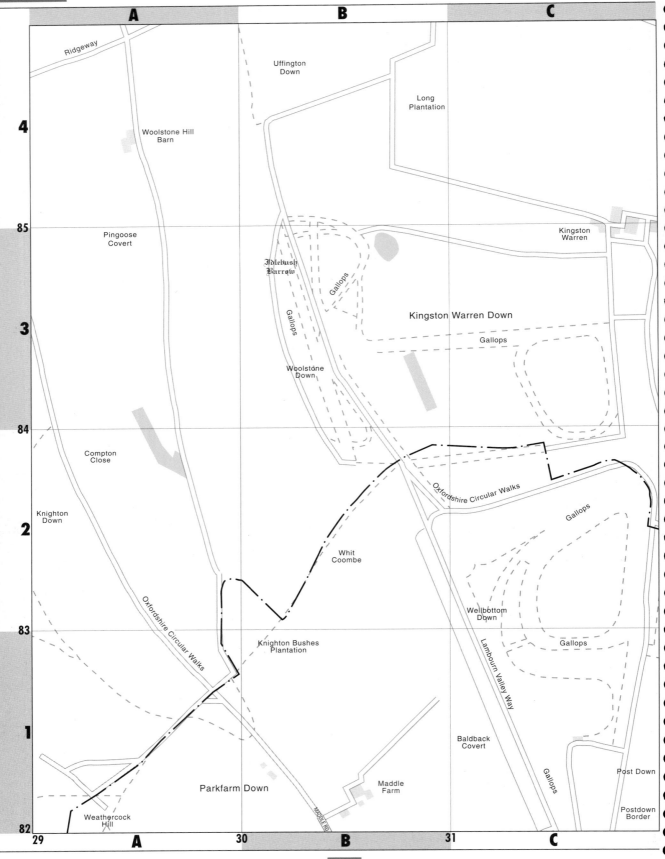

A   B   C

Ridgeway

Uffington
Down

Long
Plantation

4

Woolstone Hill
Barn

Kingston
Warren

85

Pingoose
Covert

Idlebush
Barrow

Gallops

Kingston Warren Down

3

Gallops

Gallops

Woolstone
Down

Gallops

84

Compton
Close

Oxfordshire Circular Walks

Gallops

Knighton
Down

2

Whit
Coombe

Wellbottom
Down

Gallops

Oxfordshire Circular Walks

83

Knighton Bushes
Plantation

Lambourn Valley Way

Gallops

1

Baldback
Covert

Post Down

Parkfarm Down

Maddle
Farm

Postdown
Border

MADDLE RD

Gallops

82

29   A   30   B   31   C

Weathercock
Hill

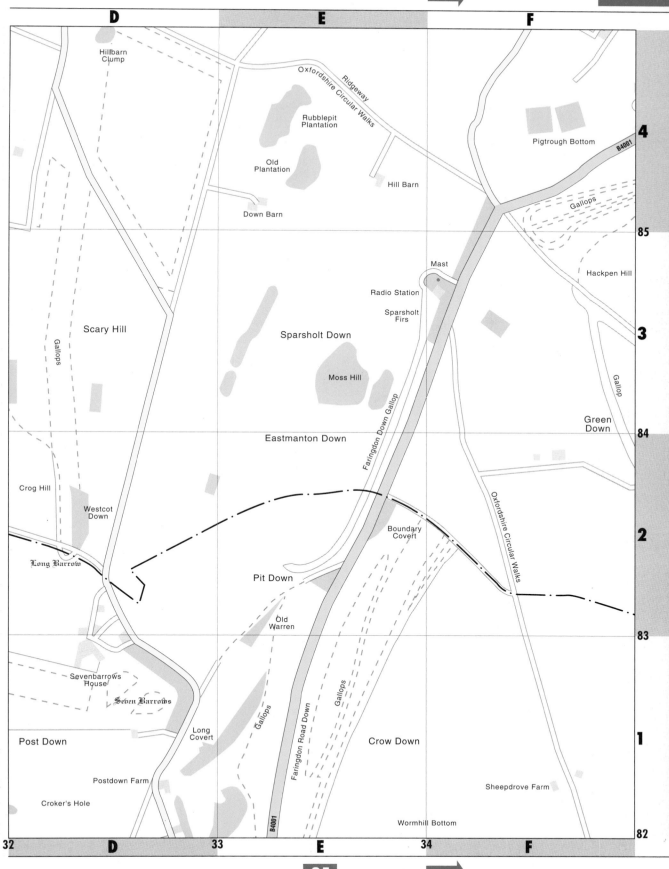

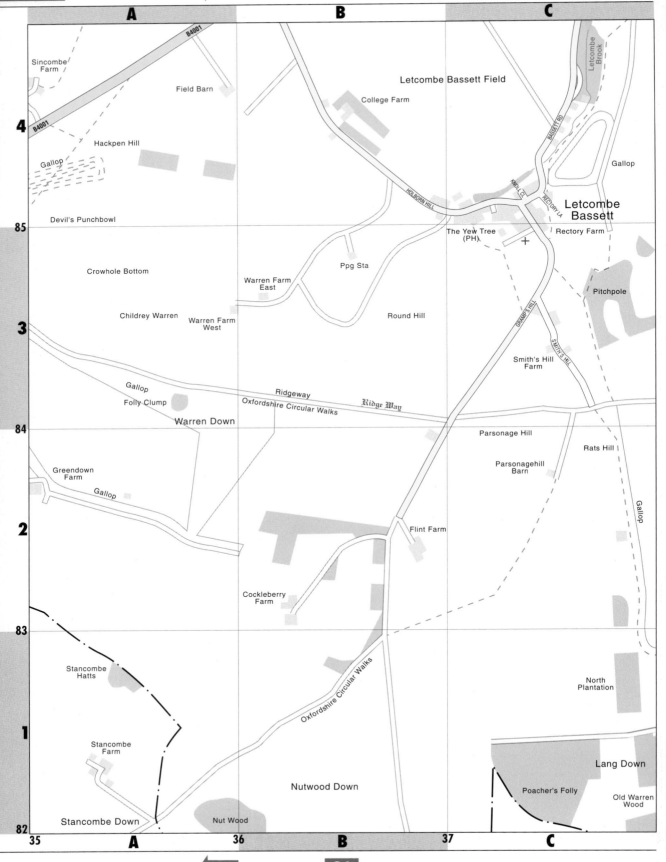

B4001

Sincombe Farm

Field Barn

4

Hackpen Hill

Gallop

Devil's Punchbowl

85

Crowhole Bottom

Childrey Warren

Warren Farm West

Warren Farm East

3

Gallop

Folly Clump

Ridgeway

Oxfordshire Circular Walks

Ridge Way

Warren Down

84

Greendown Farm

Gallop

2

Cockleberry Farm

83

Stancombe Hatts

1

Stancombe Farm

Stancombe Down

Nut Wood

Nutwood Down

Letcombe Bassett Field

College Farm

B4001

BASSETT RD

Letcombe Brook

Gallop

HOLBORN HILL

KNOLL CT

RECTORY LA

Letcombe Bassett

The Yew Tree (PH)

Rectory Farm

Ppg Sta

Round Hill

Pitchpole

GRAMP'S HILL

SMITH'S HILL

Smith's Hill Farm

Parsonage Hill

Rats Hill

Parsonagehill Barn

Gallop

Flint Farm

Oxfordshire Circular Walks

North Plantation

Lang Down

Poacher's Folly

Old Warren Wood

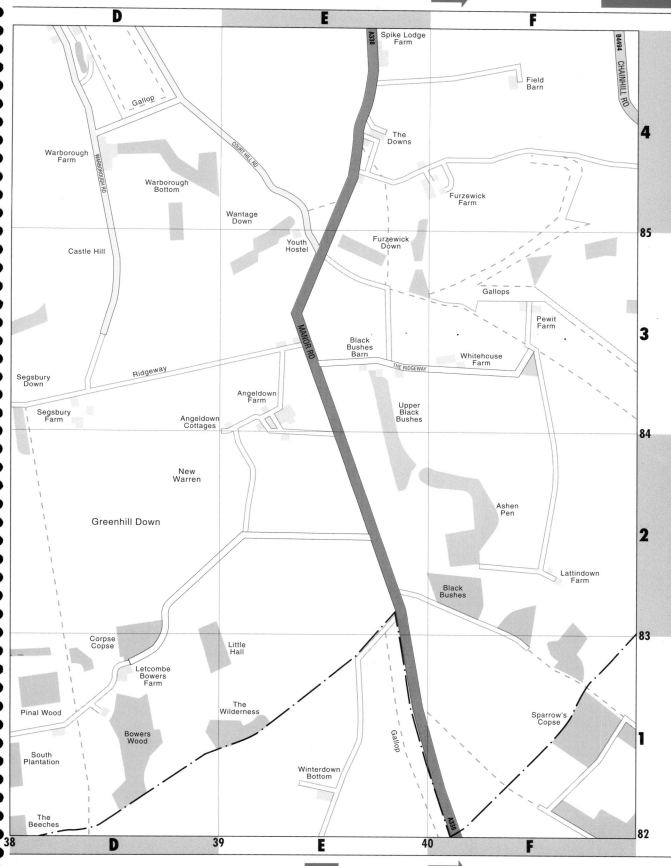

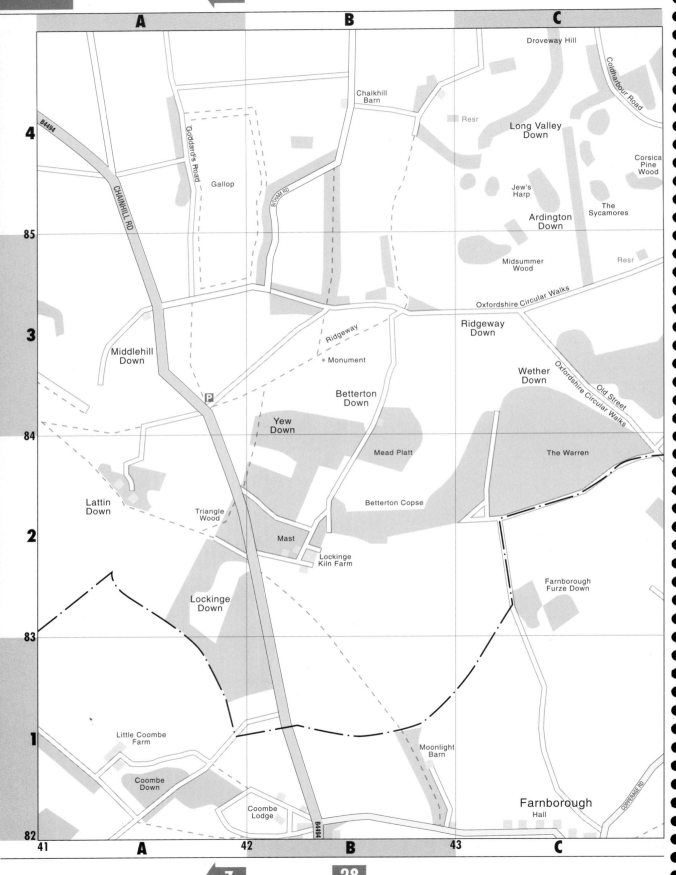

A   B   C

Droveway Hill

Coldharbour Road

B4494

Goddard's Road

Chalkhill
Barn

Resr

Long Valley
Down

Gallop

Corsica
Pine
Wood

BITHAM RD

CHAINHILL RD

Jew's
Harp

The
Sycamores

4

Ardington
Down

85

Midsummer
Wood

Resr

Oxfordshire Circular Walks

Ridgeway

Ridgeway
Down

3

Middlehill
Down

Monument

Wether
Down

Old Street

Oxfordshire Circular Walks

Betterton
Down

P

Yew
Down

84

Mead Platt

The Warren

Lattin
Down

Triangle
Wood

Betterton Copse

Mast

2

Lockinge
Kiln Farm

Farnborough
Furze Down

Lockinge
Down

83

Little Coombe
Farm

Moonlight
Barn

1

COPPERAGE RD

Coombe
Down

Farnborough

Coombe
Lodge

Hall

B4494

82
41   A   42   B   43   C

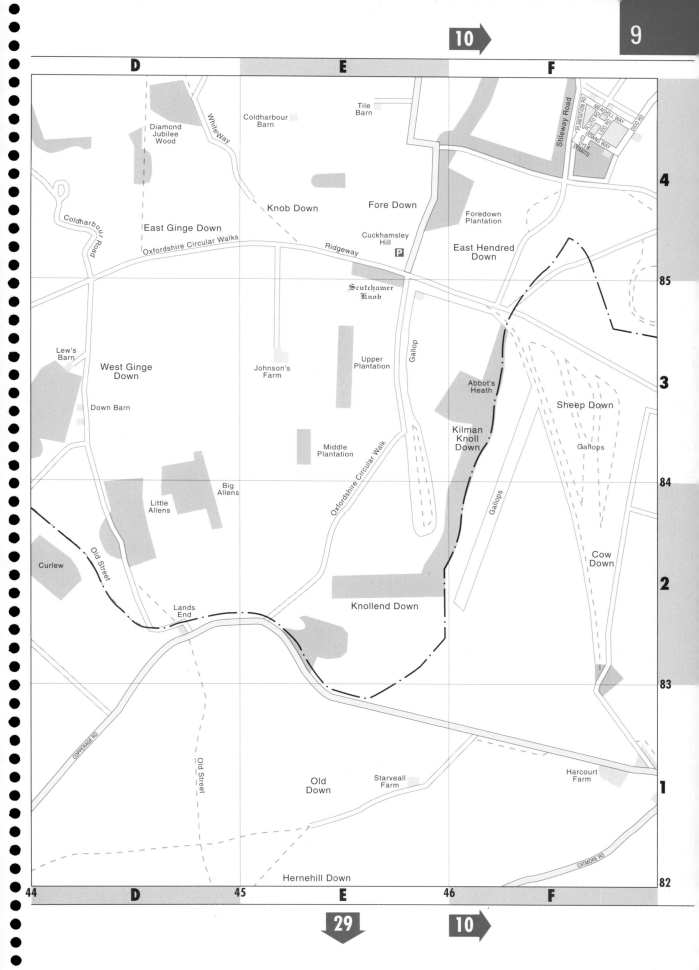

D   E   F

Stileway Road

PLANTATION RD
MEASHILL WAY
PLUTO RD
DOWNS WAY
LOST RD
DYER STRAITS
DUST RD

Tile
Barn

Coldharbour
Barn

Diamond Jubilee
Wood

WhiteWay

Knob Down

Fore Down

Foredown
Plantation

East Hendred
Down

4

Coldharbour Road

East Ginge Down

Oxfordshire Circular Walks

Ridgeway

Cuckhamsley
Hill

P

85

Scutchamer
Knob

Lew's
Barn

West Ginge
Down

Johnson's
Farm

Upper
Plantation

Gallop

Abbot's
Heath

Sheep Down

3

Down Barn

Kilman
Knoll
Down

Gallops

Middle
Plantation

Oxfordshire Circular Walk

84

Big
Allens

Little
Allens

Curlew

Old Street

Gallops

Cow
Down

2

Lands
End

Knollend Down

83

COPPERAGE RD

Old Street

Harcourt
Farm

1

Old
Down

Starveall
Farm

CATMORE RD

Hernehill Down

82

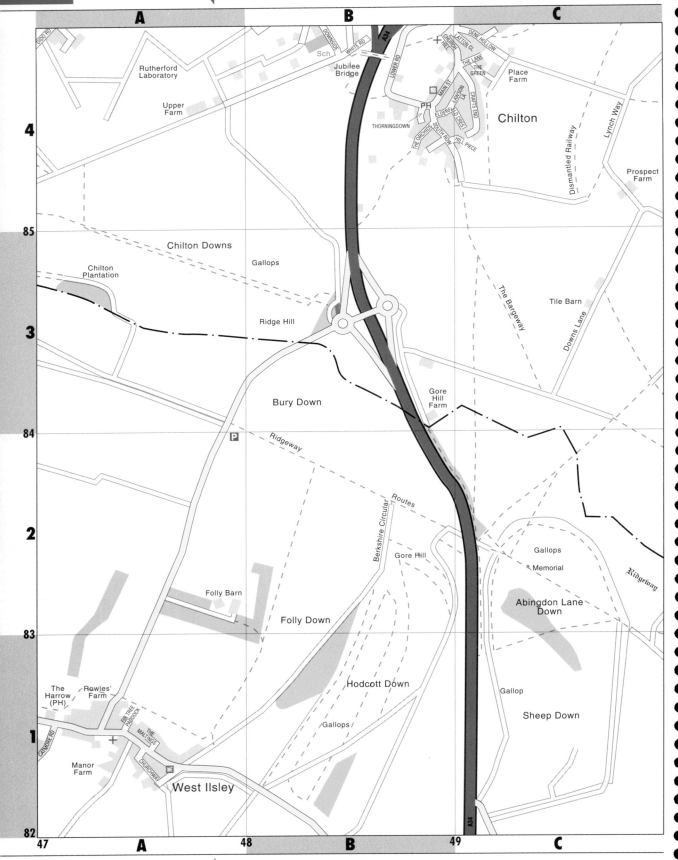

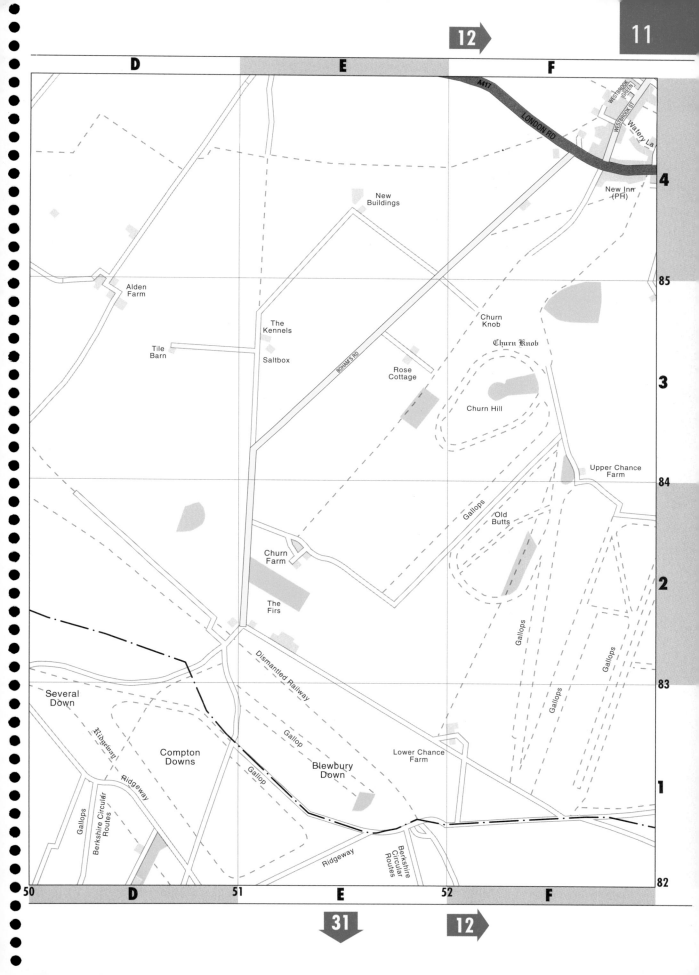

12

D
E
F

WESTBROOK GREEN
WESTBROOK ST
A417
LONDON RD
Watery La

New Inn
(PH)

4

New
Buildings

85

Alden
Farm

Churn
Knob

The
Kennels

Churn Knob

Tile
Barn

Saltbox

BOHAM'S RD

Rose
Cottage

Churn Hill

3

Churn
Farm

Gallops

Old
Butts

Upper Chance
Farm

84

The Firs

Gallops

2

Dismantled Railway

Gallops

Gallops

Gallops

83

Several
Down

Gallop

Lower Chance
Farm

Ridgeway

Compton
Downs

Gallop

Blewbury
Down

1

Gallops

Ridgeway

Berkshire Circular
Routes

Ridgeway

Berkshire
Circular
Routes

82

50
D
51
E
52
F

12

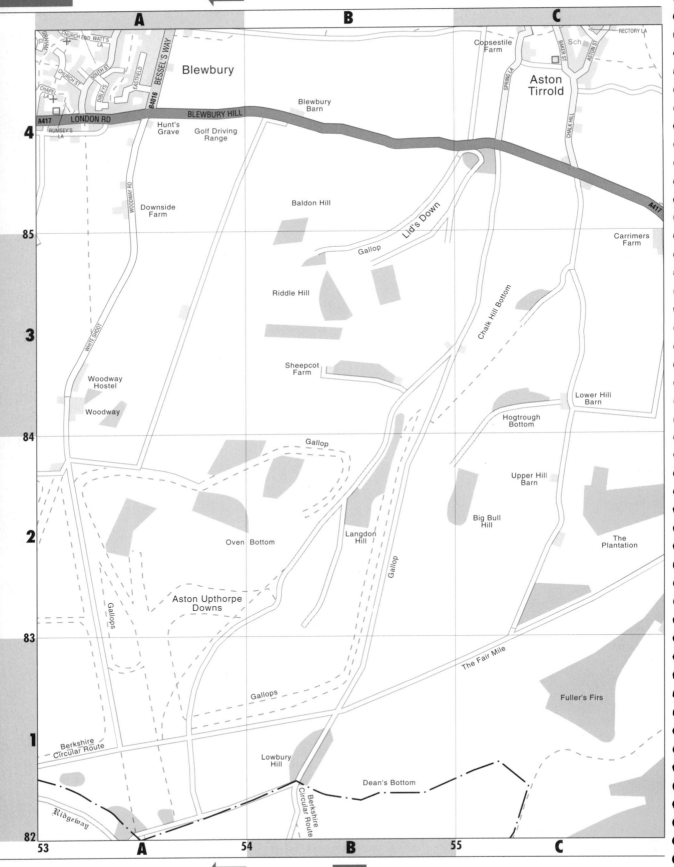

GRAHAM CL
CHURCH END
WATT'S LA
CHURCH ST
SOUTH ST
DIBLE'S
EASTFIELD
CHAPEL LA
BESSEL'S WAY
B4016
Blewbury
Copsestile Farm
RECTORY LA
Sch
BAKER ST
ASTON ST
SPRING LA
Aston Tirrold
A417
LONDON RD
RUMSEY'S LA
BLEWBURY HILL
Blewbury Barn
CHALK HILL
4
Hunt's Grave
Golf Driving Range
WOODWAY RD
Baldon Hill
Lid's Down
A417
Carrimers Farm
85
Downside Farm
Gallop
Chalk Hill Bottom
WHITE SHOOT
Riddle Hill
3
Sheepcot Farm
Lower Hill Barn
Woodway Hostel
Hogtrough Bottom
Woodway
84
Gallop
Upper Hill Barn
Big Bull Hill
The Plantation
2
Oven Bottom
Langdon Hill
Gallop
Gallops
Aston Upthorpe Downs
83
The Fair Mile
Gallops
Fuller's Firs
1
Berkshire Circular Route
Lowbury Hill
Dean's Bottom
Ridgeway
Berkshire Circular Route
82

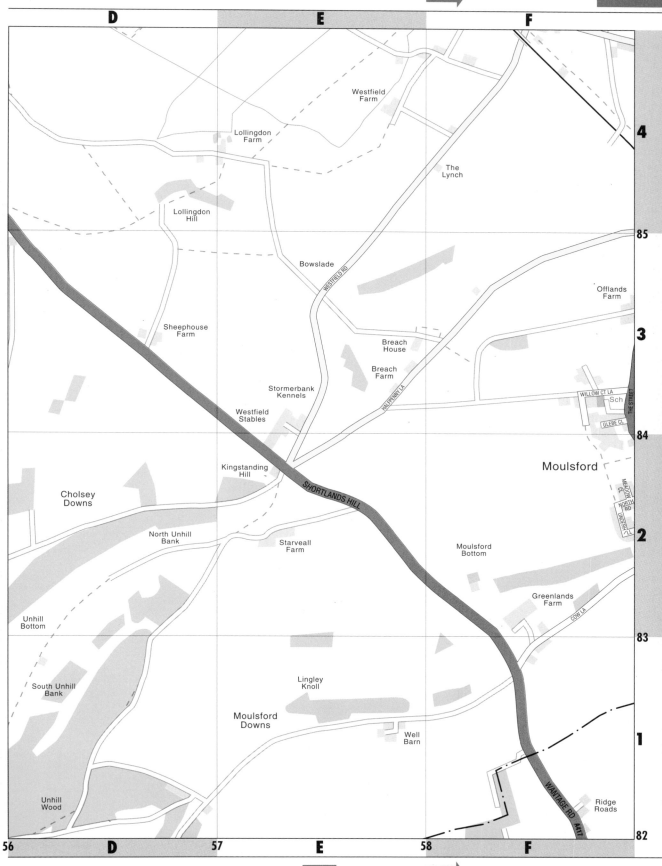

D E F

4

Westfield Farm

Lollingdon Farm

The Lynch

85

Lollingdon Hill

Bowslade

WESTFIELD RD

Offlands Farm

Sheephouse Farm

Breach House

3

Breach Farm

HALFPENNY LA

WILLOW CT LA

Sch

THE STREET

Stormerbank Kennels

Westfield Stables

GLEBE CL

84

Moulsford

MEADOW CL

Kingstanding Hill

SHORTLANDS HILL

NORTH RD

UNDERH LA

Cholsey Downs

North Unhill Bank

Starveall Farm

Moulsford Bottom

2

Greenlands Farm

COW LA

Unhill Bottom

83

South Unhill Bank

Lingley Knoll

Moulsford Downs

Well Barn

1

WANTAGE RD A417

Ridge Roads

Unhill Wood

82

56 D 57 E 58 F

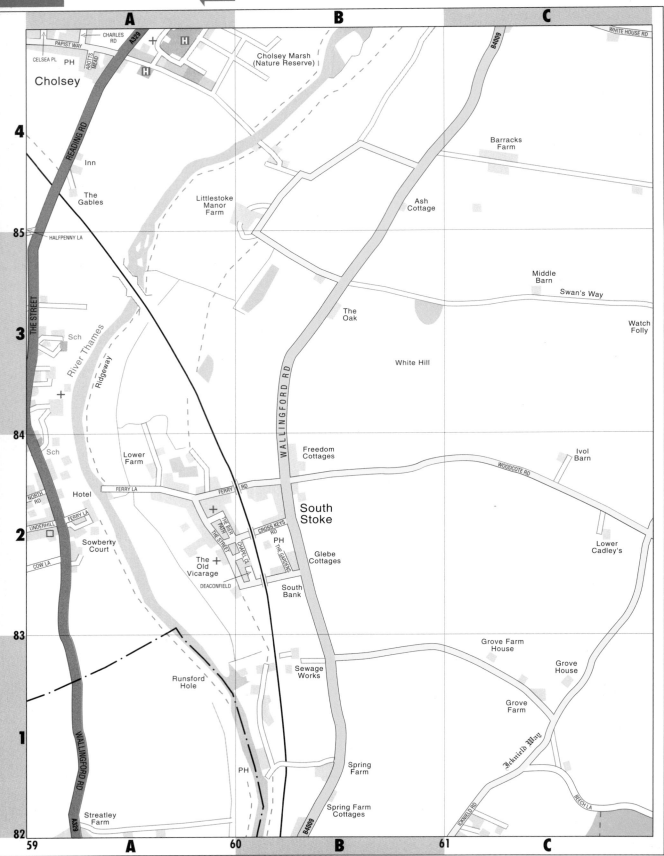

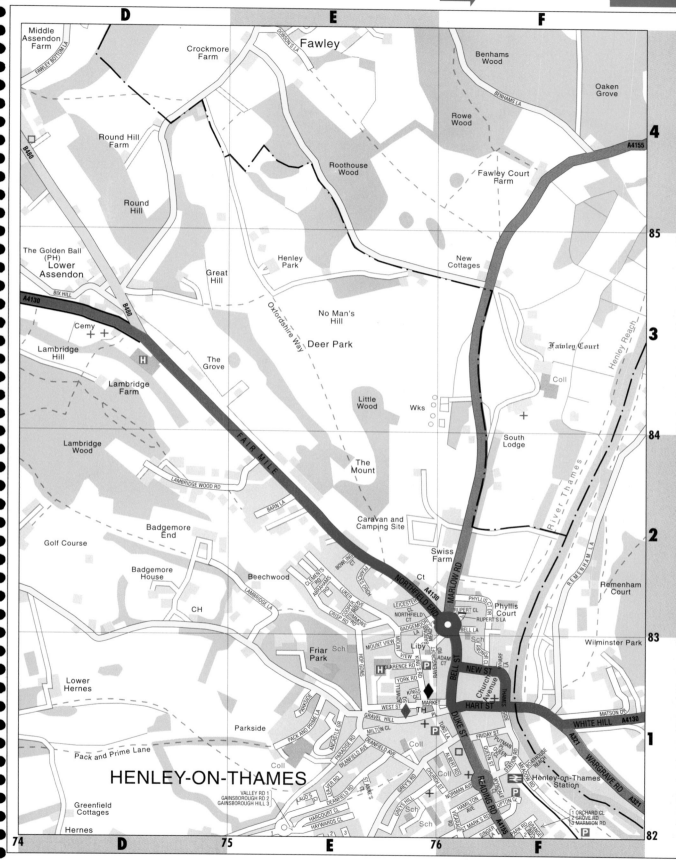

HENLEY-ON-THAMES

15

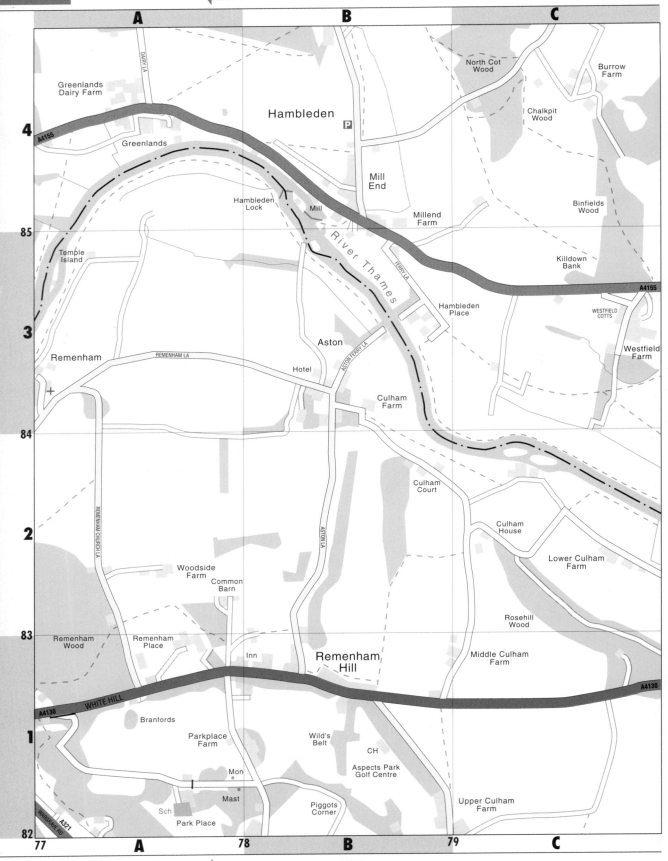

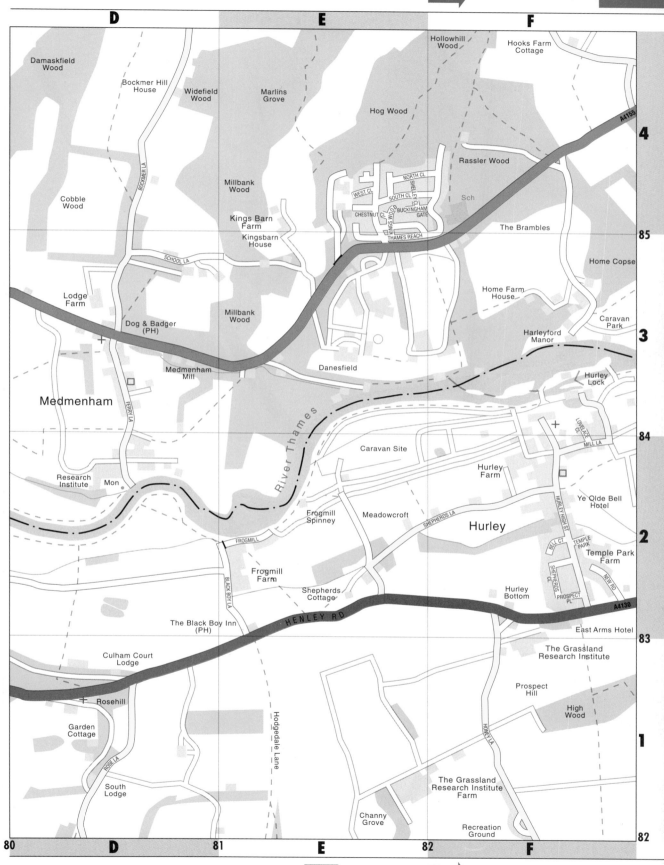

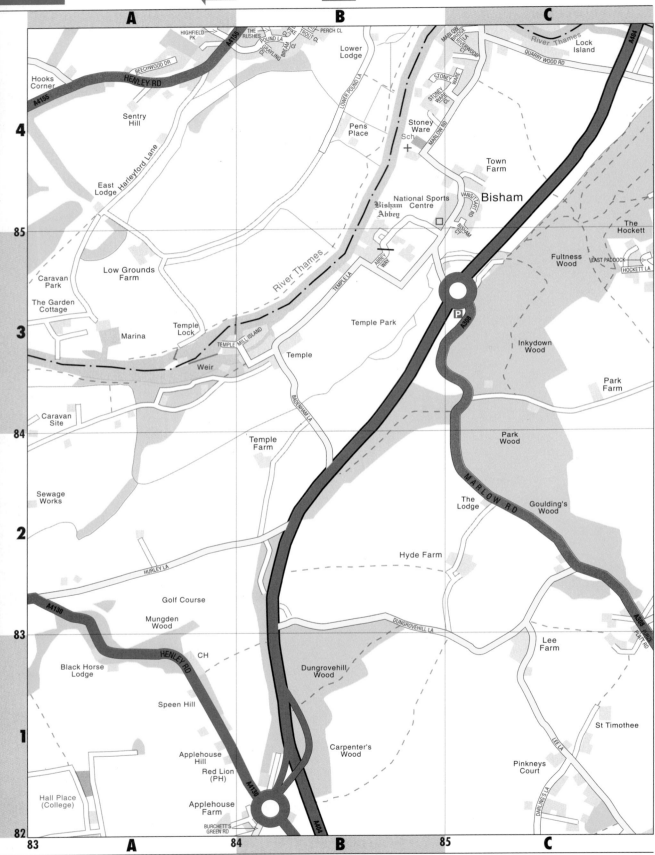

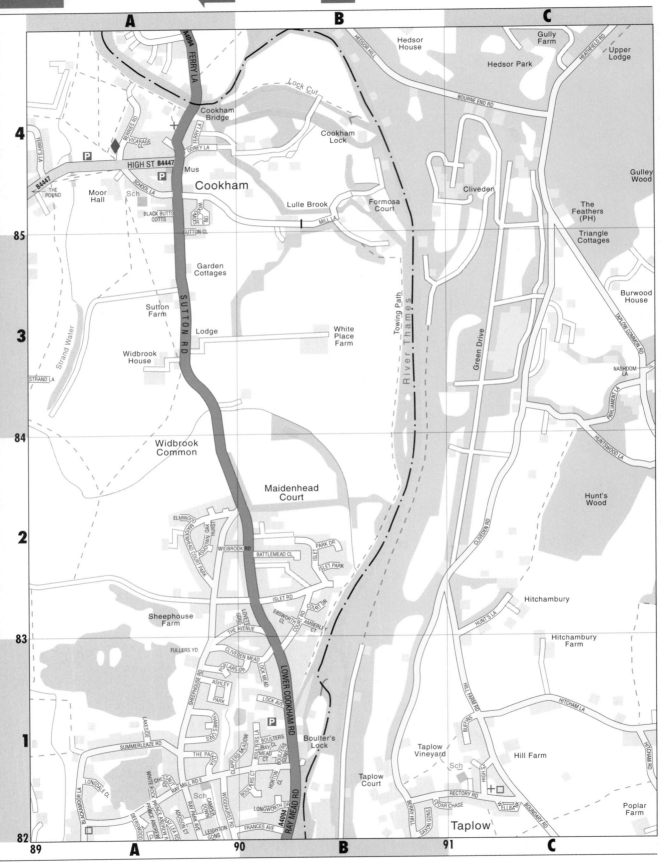

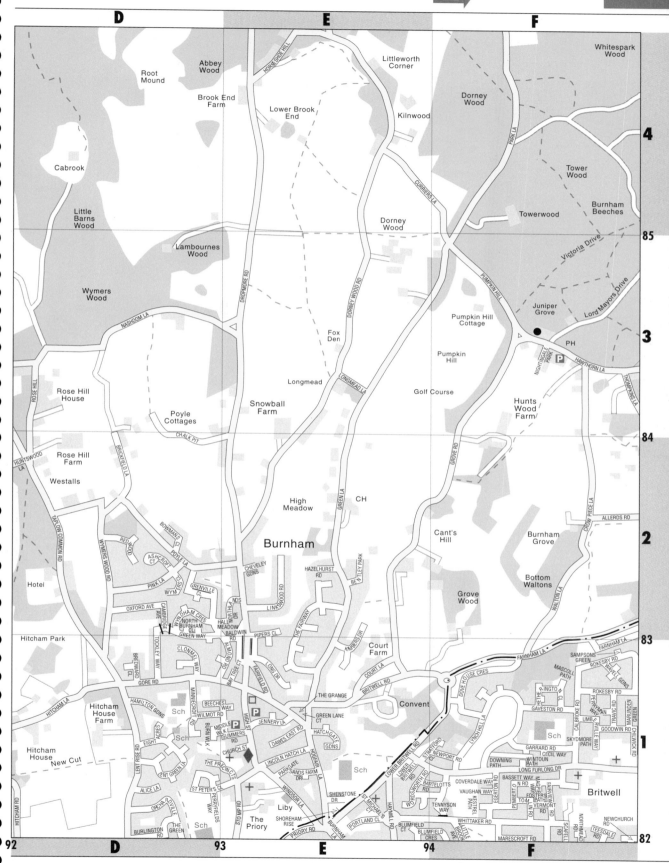

D · E · F

4
85
3
84
2
83
1
82

Whitespark Wood

Littleworth Corner

Dorney Wood

Tower Wood

Burnham Beeches

Root Mound

Abbey Wood

Brook End Farm

Lower Brook End

Kilnwood

Towerwood

Victoria Drive

Lord Mayors Drive

Cabrook

Little Barns Wood

Dorney Wood

Juniper Grove

PH

Lambournes Wood

PUMPKIN HILL

Pumpkin Hill Cottage

NIGHTINGALE PARK

HAWTHORN LA

THOMPKINS LA

Wymers Wood

NASHDOM LA

DROPMORE RD

DORNEY WOOD RD

Fox Den

Pumpkin Hill

P

Rose Hill House

ROSE HILL

Longmead

LONGMEAD LA

Golf Course

Hunts Wood Farm

Snowball Farm

Poyle Cottages

CHALK PIT

CURRIERS LA

GROVE RD

CROW PIECE LA

ALLERDS RD

Huntswood La

Rose Hill Farm

Westalls

BROOKFIELD LA

Burnham

High Meadow

GREEN LA

CH

Cant's Hill

Burnham Grove

Bottom Waltons

TAPLOW COMMON RD

WYMERS WOOD RD

RED WOOD

BOWMANS CL

POYLE LA

CHEVELEY GDNS

HAZELHURST RD

BEVERLEY PARK

LINKWOOD RD

THE FAIRWAY

Grove Wood

WALTON LA

Hotel

ASHCROFT CT

PINK LA

OXFORD AVE

GRENVILLE CL

NORTHLANDS DR

BALDWIN RD

PIPERS CL

KNIBBS RD

Court Farm

Hitcham Park

CLONMEL WAY

GORE RD

BREWARD CL

CAMBRIDGE AVE

TOCKLEY WAY

ODHAM CRES

NORTH BURNHAM CL

GREEN WAY

HALL MEADOW

BAY TREE CT

FAIRFIELD RD

LONG DR

THE GRANGE

BRITWELL RD

COURT LA

Convent

DOVE HOUSE CRES

FARNHAM LA

FARNHAM LA

Sampsons Green

ROKESBY RD

MASCOLL PATH

Hitcham La

Hitcham House Farm

HAMILTON GDNS

MINNECROFT RD

BEECHES WAY

WILMOT RD

BURN WLK

JENNERY LA

GREEN LANE CT

HATCH GATE GDNS

Sch

LYNCH HILL LA

HETHE

PINGTON

TRAVIC RD

SKYDMORE PATH

GAVESTON RD

CALBROKE RD

ROKESBY RD

FERMAN RD

RYVLLE PATH

MARLINDEN GDNS

Hitcham House

New Cut

LENT RISE RD

EIGHT ACRES

LENT GREEN LA

MIDDLE WLK

SUMMERS RD

CHURCH ST

DAWES EAST RD

LINCOLN HATCH LA

HOGFAIR LA

Sch

GARRARD RD

GOODWIN RD

CECIL WAY

DOWNING PATH

WINTOUN PATH

LONG FURLONG DR

UMB

Sch

ALICE LA

ORCHARDVILLE

ST PETER'S CL

PERRYFIELDS WAY

THE PRECINCT CS

PARKGATE

SANDS FARM DR

WINDSOR LA

SHENSTONE DR

STREATFORD CL

NEWPORT RD

LOWER BRITWELL RD

BARTELOTTS RD

COVERDALE WAY

BASSETT WAY

VAUGHAN WAY

FOSTERS PATH

KESTREL PATH

VERMONT RD

FARNHAM RD

Britwell

BURLINGTON RD

THE GREEN

Sch

STOMP RD

Liby

SHOREHAM RISE

The Priory

PRIORY RD

BURNHAM LA

PORTLAND CL

HAYMILL RD

ST MICHAEL'S LA

WORDSWORTH RD

TENNYSON WAY

PEMBER CL

EGERTON RD

WHITTAKER RD

BLUMFIELD CRES

MARESCROFT RD

SCAFELL RD

NORTHMEAD RD

TEESDALE RD

NEWCHURCH RD

CHISWICK RD

HITCHAM RD

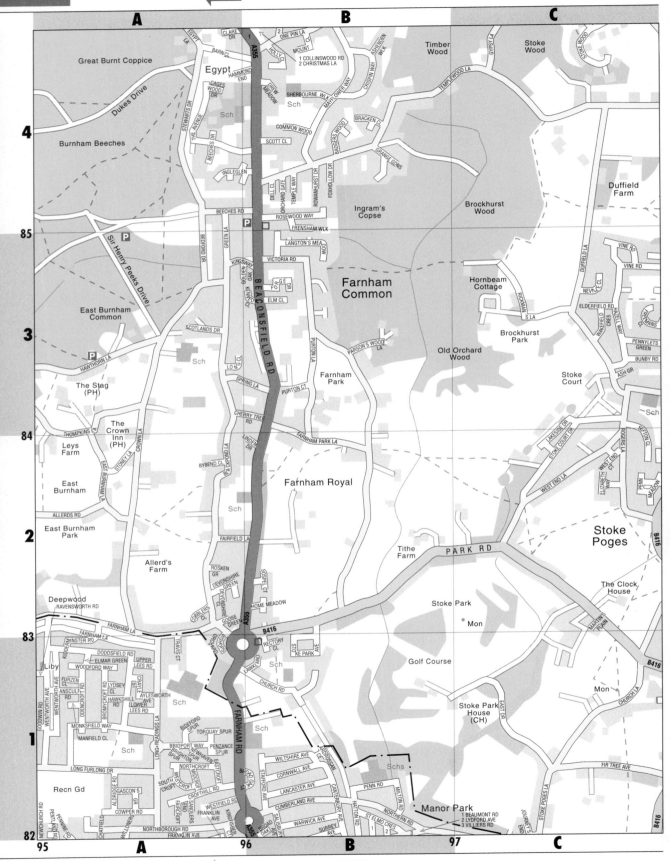

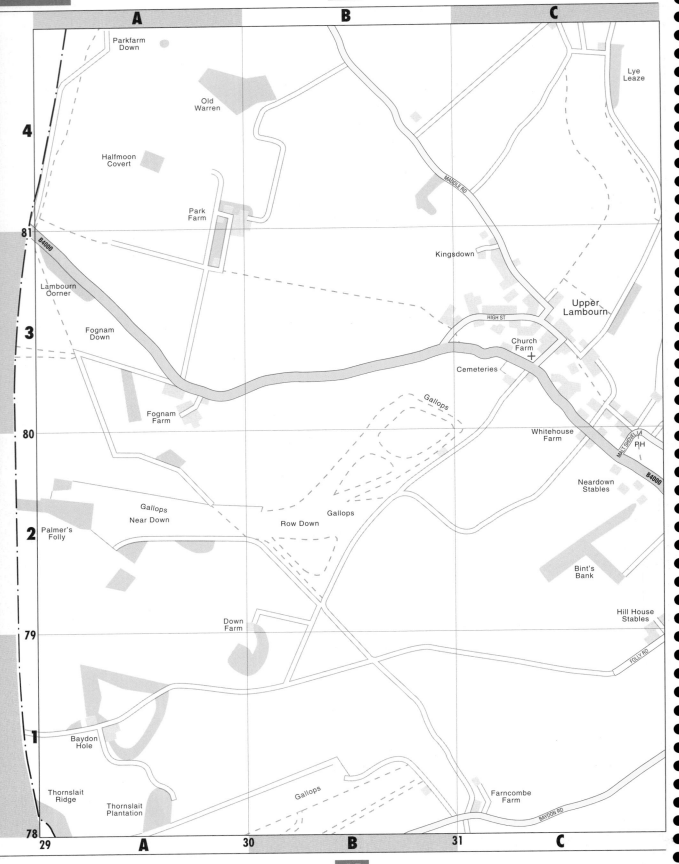

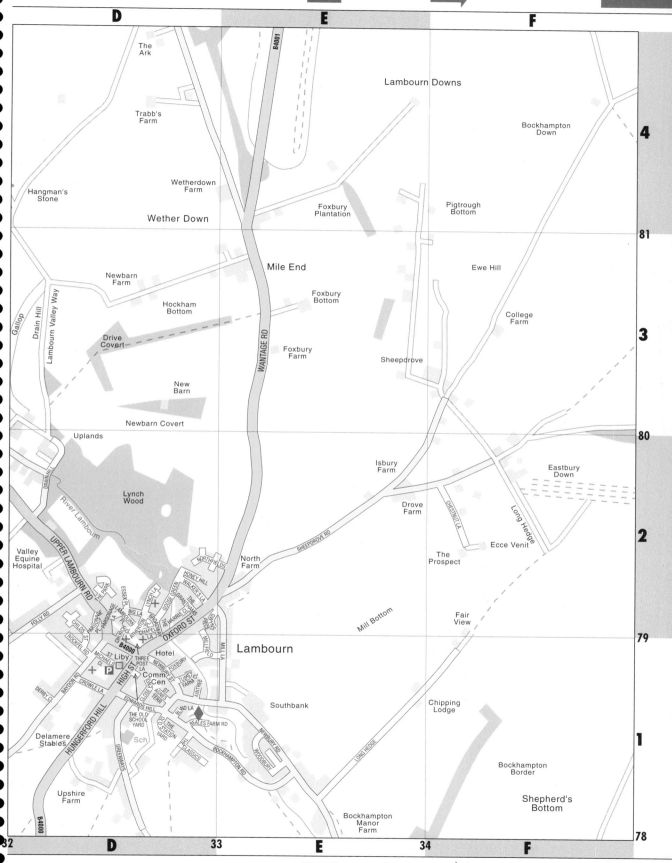

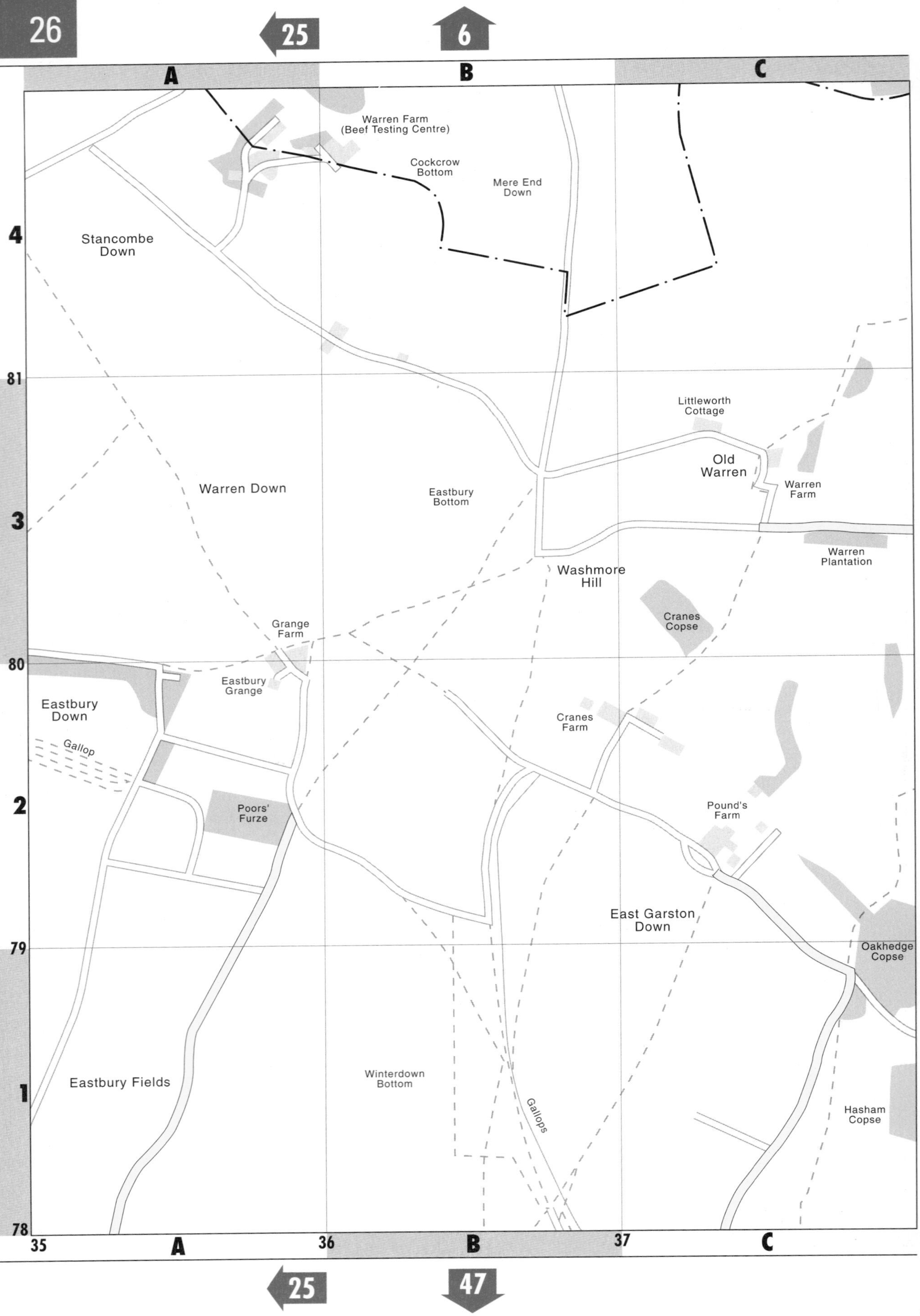

A   B   C

Warren Farm
(Beef Testing Centre)

Cockcrow
Bottom

Mere End
Down

4

Stancombe
Down

81

Littleworth
Cottage

Old
Warren

Warren
Farm

Warren Down

Eastbury
Bottom

3

Warren
Plantation

Washmore
Hill

Cranes
Copse

Grange
Farm

80

Eastbury
Grange

Cranes
Farm

Eastbury
Down

Gallop

Pound's
Farm

2

Poors'
Furze

East Garston
Down

79

Oakhedge
Copse

1

Eastbury Fields

Winterdown
Bottom

Gallops

Hasham
Copse

78

35   A   36   B   37   C

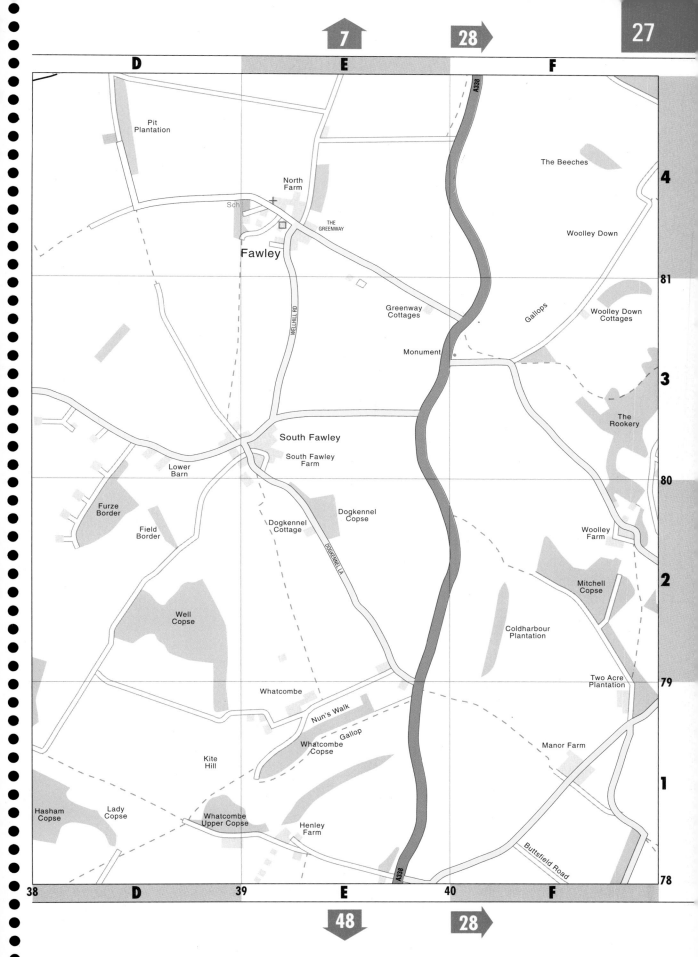

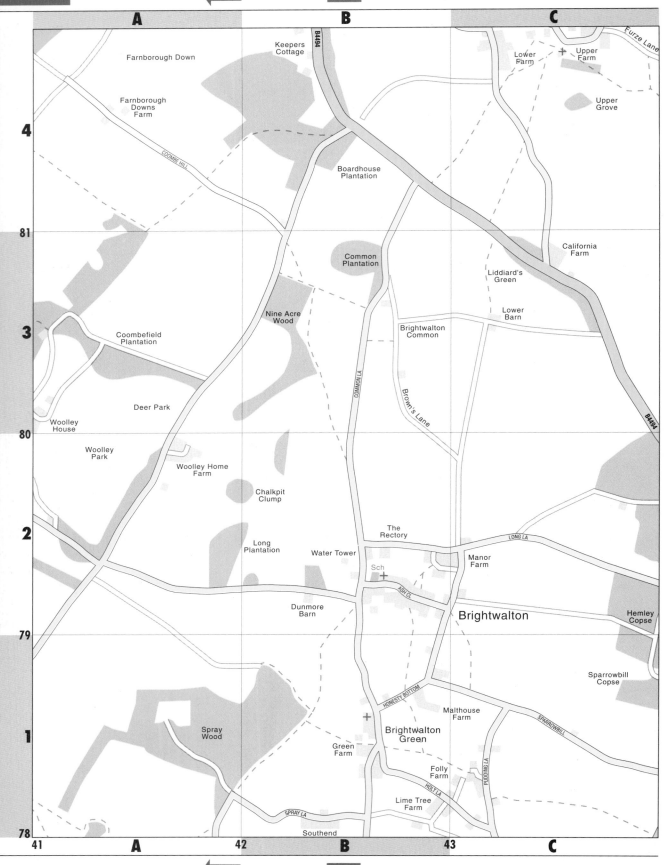

A   B   C

Keepers
Cottage

Farnborough Down

Lower
Farm

Upper
Farm

Furze Lane

Farnborough
Downs
Farm

Upper
Grove

4

COOMBE HILL

B4494

Boardhouse
Plantation

81

California
Farm

Common
Plantation

Liddiard's
Green

Nine Acre
Wood

Lower
Barn

Coombefield
Plantation

Brightwalton
Common

3

Deer Park

COMMON LA

Brown's Lane

B4494

Woolley
House

80

Woolley
Park

Woolley Home
Farm

Chalkpit
Clump

The
Rectory

2

LONG LA

Long
Plantation

Water Tower

Manor
Farm

Sch

ASH CL

Hemley
Copse

Dunmore
Barn

Brightwalton

79

Sparrowbill
Copse

HONESTY BOTTOM

Spray
Wood

Malthouse
Farm

SPARROWBILL

1

Green
Farm

Brightwalton
Green

PUDDING LA

Folly
Farm

HOLT LA

Lime Tree
Farm

SPRAY LA

78

Southend

41   A   42   B   43   C

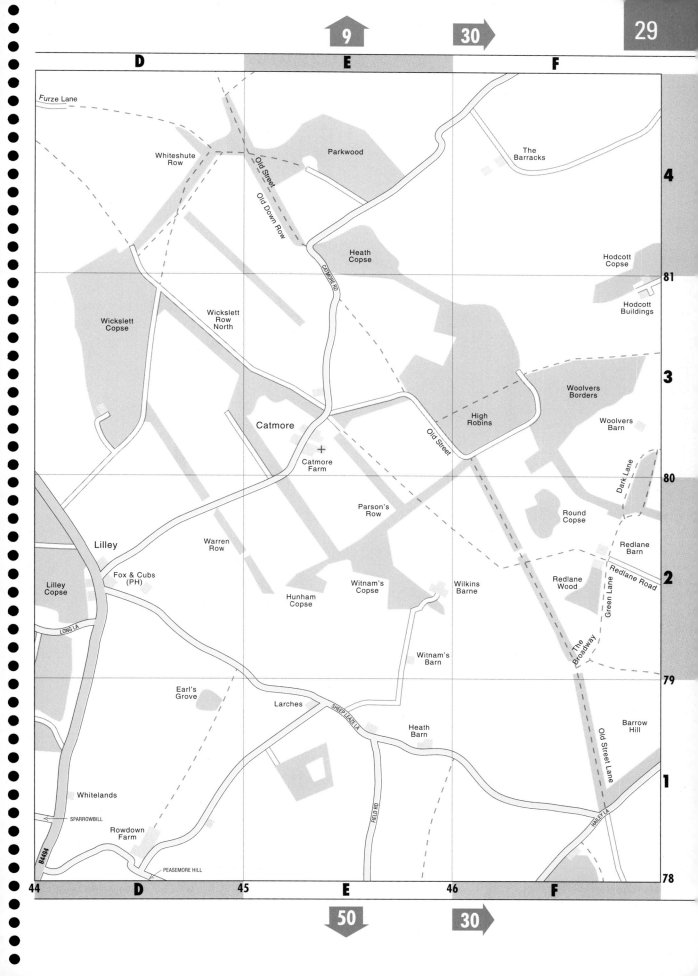

29
10

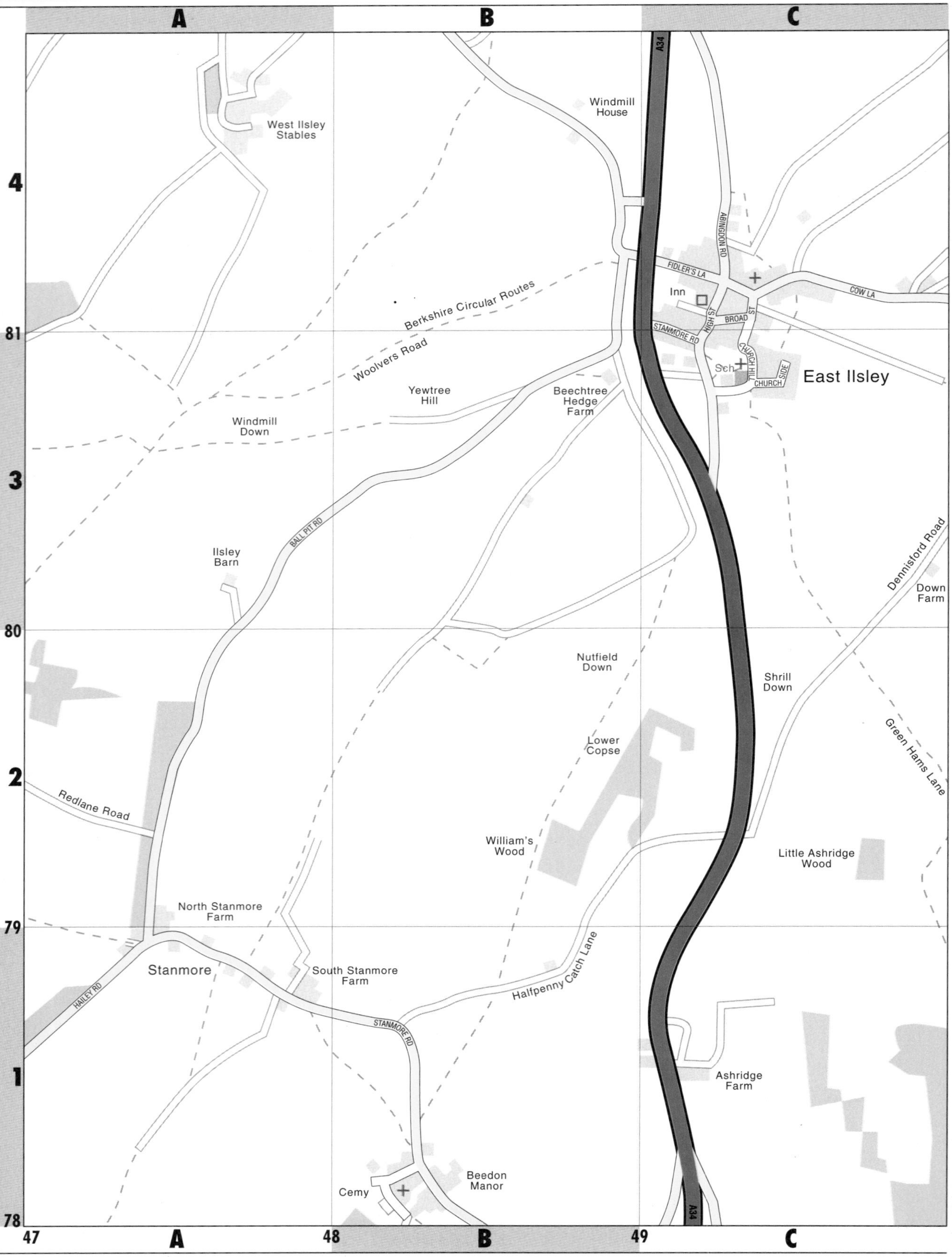

A
B
C

4

West Ilsley
Stables

Windmill
House

A34

ABINGDON RD

FIDLER'S LA

COW LA

Berkshire Circular Routes

Inn

HIGH ST

BROAD ST

STANMORE RD

81

Woolvers Road

Yewtree
Hill

Beechtree
Hedge
Farm

Sch

CHURCH HILL

CHURCH SIDE

East Ilsley

Windmill
Down

3

BALL PIT RD

Ilsley
Barn

Dennisford Road

Down
Farm

80

Nutfield
Down

Shrill
Down

Green Hams Lane

Lower
Copse

2

Redlane Road

William's
Wood

Little Ashridge
Wood

North Stanmore
Farm

79

HAILEY RD

Stanmore

South Stanmore
Farm

Halfpenny Catch Lane

STANMORE RD

Ashridge
Farm

1

A34

Cemy

Beedon
Manor

78

47
A
48
B
49
C

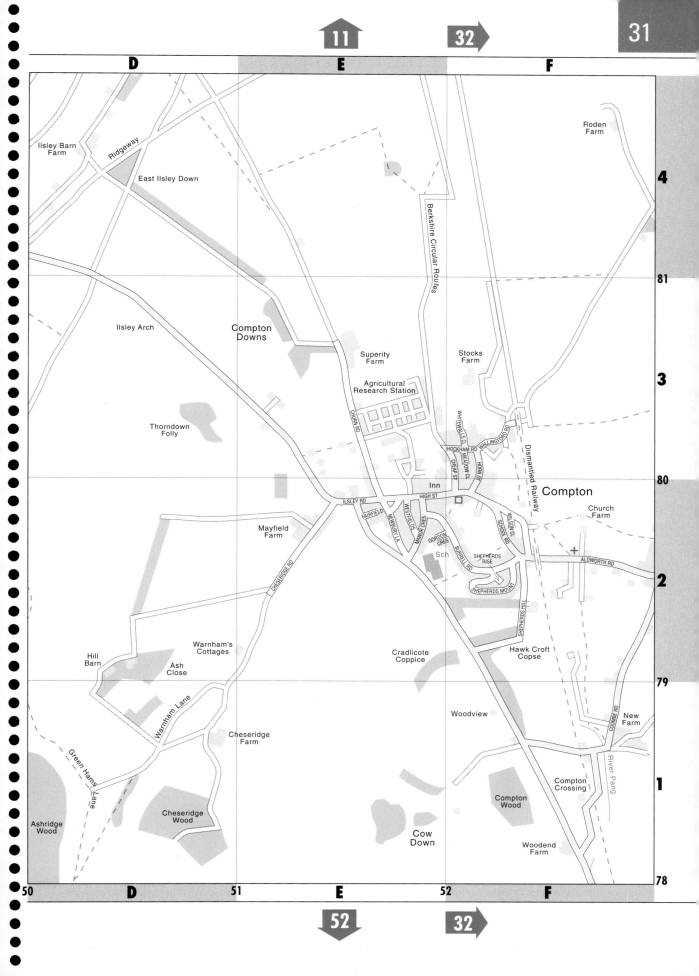

31
12

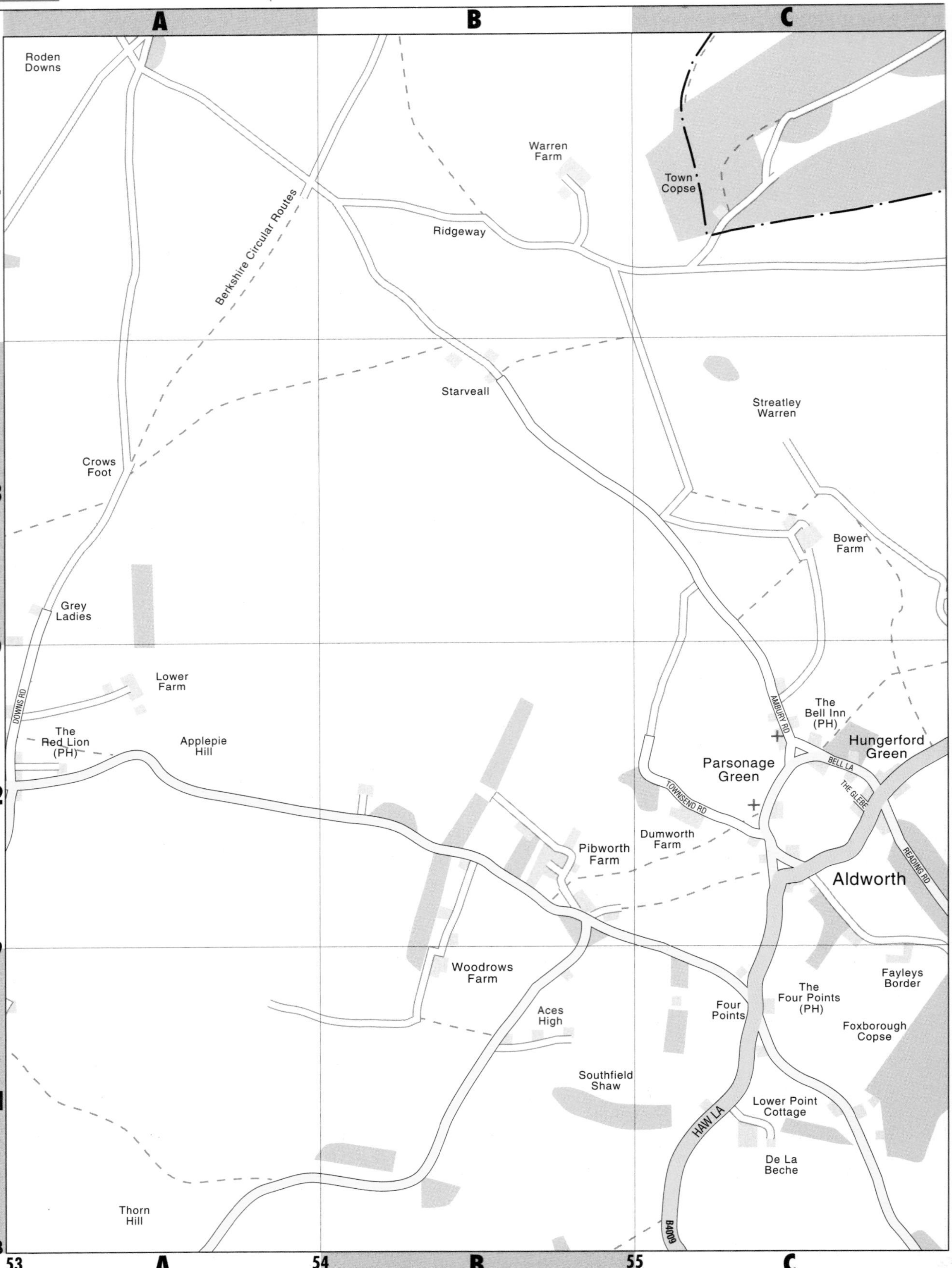

A **B** **C**

4

Roden
Downs

Warren
Farm

Town
Copse

Berkshire Circular Routes

Ridgeway

81

Starveall

Streatley
Warren

3

Crows
Foot

Bower
Farm

Grey
Ladies

80

DOWNS RD

Lower
Farm

The
Red Lion
(PH)

Applepie
Hill

AMBURY RD

The
Bell Inn
(PH)

Hungerford
Green

Parsonage
Green

BELL LA

THE GLEBE

2

TOWNSEND RD

Dumworth
Farm

Pibworth
Farm

Aldworth

READING RD

79

Woodrows
Farm

Four
Points

The
Four Points
(PH)

Fayleys
Border

Aces
High

Foxborough
Copse

Southfield
Shaw

HAW LA

Lower Point
Cottage

1

De La
Beche

Thorn
Hill

B4009

78

A **B** **C**
53   54   55

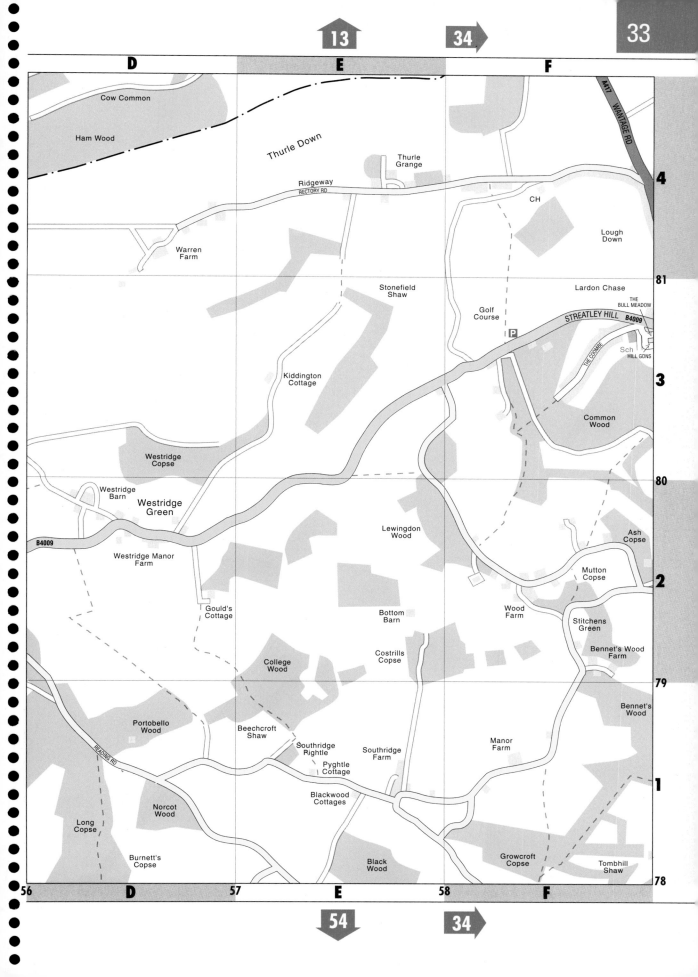

D
E
F

Cow Common

Ham Wood

Thurle Down

Thurle Grange

A417 WANTAGE RD

Ridgeway
RECTORY RD

CH

Lough Down

4

Warren Farm

Stonefield Shaw

Golf Course

Lardon Chase

THE BULL MEADOW

STREATLEY HILL B4009

81

P

THE COOMBE

Sch
HILL GDNS

Kiddington Cottage

3

Common Wood

Westridge Copse

Westridge Barn

Ash Copse

Westridge Green

B4009

Lewingdon Wood

Mutton Copse

80

Westridge Manor Farm

Wood Farm

2

Gould's Cottage

Bottom Barn

Stitchens Green

Bennet's Wood Farm

College Wood

Costrills Copse

79

Portobello Wood

Beechcroft Shaw

Bennet's Wood

READING RD

Southridge Pightle

Southridge Farm

Manor Farm

Pyghtle Cottage

1

Norcot Wood

Blackwood Cottages

Long Copse

Black Wood

Growcroft Copse

Tombhill Shaw

Burnett's Copse

78

56
D
57
E
58
F

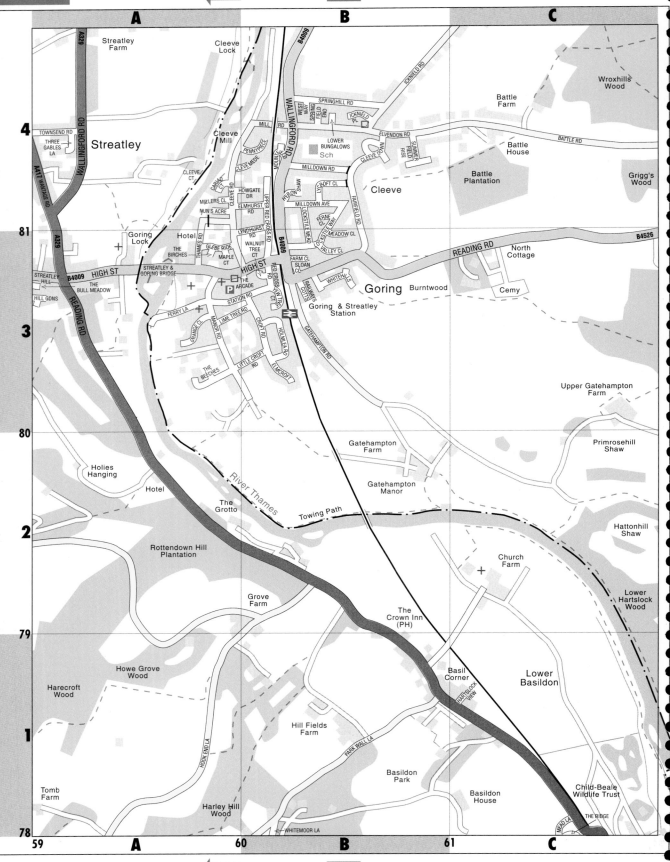

A   B   C

4
Streatley Farm
Cleeve Lock
A329
TOWNSEND RD
THREE GABLES LA
Streatley
Cleeve Mill
MILL RD
WALLINGFORD RD
CLEVE CT
PEMNYPIECE
B4009
CLEVE MEDE
CLEVE RD
GABRAD CT
SPRINGHILL RD
WEST WAY
SPRING FIELD END
ICKNIELD RD
Battle Farm
Wroxhills Wood
ICKNIELD PL
ELVENDON RD
Battle House
BATTLE RD
Battle Plantation
Grigg's Wood
LOWER BUNGALOWS
Sch
CLEEVE DOWN
SUMMER RISE

81
A417 WANTAGE RD
A329
Goring Lock
HOWGATE DR
ELMHURST RD
NUN'S ACRE
MILLERS CL
Hotel
THE BIRCHES
GLEBE RIDE
THAMES RD
MAPLE CT
WALNUT TREE CT
LYNDHURST RD
MILLDOWN RD
UPPER RED CROSS RD
SHAW
WILCON
MILLDOWN AVE
LOCKSTILE MEAD
FERNE CL
LOCKSTILE WAY
MEADOW CL
FAIRFIELD RD
VALLEY CL
FARM CL
SLOAN CL
Cleeve
North Cottage
READING RD
B4526

3
STREATLEY HILL
B4009
HIGH ST
THE BULL MEADOW
HILL GDNS
STREATLEY & GORING BRIDGE
HIGH ST
RED CROSS RD
STATION RD
THE ARCADE
P
FERRY LA
ORANGE CL
MANOR RD
LIME TREE RD
CROFT RD
HOLME LA RD
LITTLE CROFT RD
ELMCROFT
THE BEECHES
GATEHAMPTON RD
RAILWAY COTTS
WHITEHILLS
Goring & Streatley Station
Goring
Burntwood
Cemy

80
Holies Hanging
Hotel
The Grotto
River Thames
Towing Path
Gatehampton Farm
Gatehampton Manor
Upper Gatehampton Farm
Primrosehill Shaw

2
Rottendown Hill Plantation
Grove Farm
The Crown Inn (PH)
Church Farm
Hattonhill Shaw
Lower Hartslock Wood

79
Howe Grove Wood
Harecroft Wood
Basil Corner
HARTSLOCK VIEW
Lower Basildon

1
Tomb Farm
HOOK END LA
Harley Hill Wood
Hill Fields Farm
PARK WALL LA
Basildon Park
Basildon House
Child-Beale Wildlife Trust
MEAD LA
THE RIDGE

78
WHITEMOOR LA
59   A   60   B   61   C

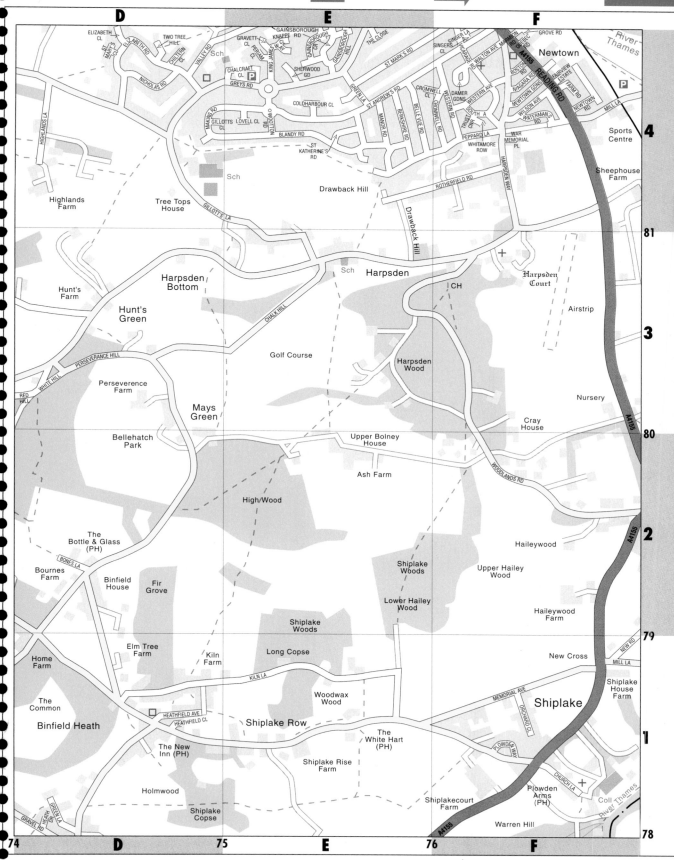

D · E · F

4 · 81 · 3 · 80 · 2 · 79 · 1 · 78

74 · D · 75 · E · 76 · F

River Thames

Newtown
READING RD
GROVE RD
A4155
Sports Centre
Sheephouse Farm

Highlands Farm
Tree Tops House
Drawback Hill
Drawback Hill
ROTHERFIELD RD
HARPSDEN WAY

Hunt's Farm
Harpsden Bottom
Sch
Harpsden
CH
Harpsden Court
Airstrip

Hunt's Green
CHALK HILL

PERSEVERANCE HILL
Golf Course
Harpsden Wood
Nursery
A4155

WHITE HILL
RED HILL
Perseverence Farm
Mays Green
Cray House

Bellehatch Park
Upper Bolney House
WOODLANDS RD

Ash Farm

High Wood
Haileywood
A4155

The Bottle & Glass (PH)
BONES LA
Shiplake Woods
Upper Hailey Wood

Bournes Farm
Binfield House
Fir Grove
Haileywood Farm

Lower Hailey Wood

Elm Tree Farm
Kiln Farm
Shiplake Woods
Long Copse
New Cross
MILL LA
NEW RD

Home Farm
KILN LA
Shiplake House Farm

The Common
HEATHFIELD AVE
HEATHFIELD CL
Woodwax Wood
MEMORIAL AVE
ORCHARD CL
Shiplake

Binfield Heath
Shiplake Row
PLOWDEN WAY

The New Inn (PH)
The White Hart (PH)

Holmwood
Shiplake Rise Farm
CHURCH LA
Plowden Arms (PH)
Coll Thames

Shiplake Copse
GRAVEL RD
HEATH DR
GREEN LA
Shiplakecourt Farm
A4155
Warren Hill
River Thames

Top street labels (Newtown area):
ELIZABETH CL
ST MARY'S CL
TWO TREE HILL
CHILTERN CL
ELIZABETH RD
VALLEY RD
GRAVETT CL
PERIAM CL
KING JAMES WAY
KNAPPE CL
GAINSBOROUGH RD
GAINSBOROUGH CRT
GAINSBOROUGH HILL
THE CLOSE
SINGERS LA
SINGERS CL
GARAGE RD
WALTON AVE
MARINERS
BOSTON RD
ST SECC
FAIRVIEW ESTATE
GROVE RD

NICHOLAS RD
Sch
CHALCRAFT CL
GREYS RD
SHERWOOD GD
GREEN LA
ST MARK'S RD
ST ANDREW'S RD
CROMWELL CL
CROMWELL RD
WESTERN RD
SOUTH A
WESTERN AVE
NIAGARA GDNS
NEWTOWN GDNS
WILSON AVE
NEWTOWN RD

MAKINS RD
GILLOTTS CL
LOVELL CL
O'WOOTTON
BLANDY RD
COLDHARBOUR CL
MANOR RD
BERKSHIRE RD
BELLE VUE RD
TRUST CRT
DAMER GDNS
PEPPARD RD
WHITMORE ROW
WATERMANS RD
MILL LA

GILLOTT'S LA
Sch
ST KATHERINE'S RD
WAR MEMORIAL PL
HARPSDEN WAY

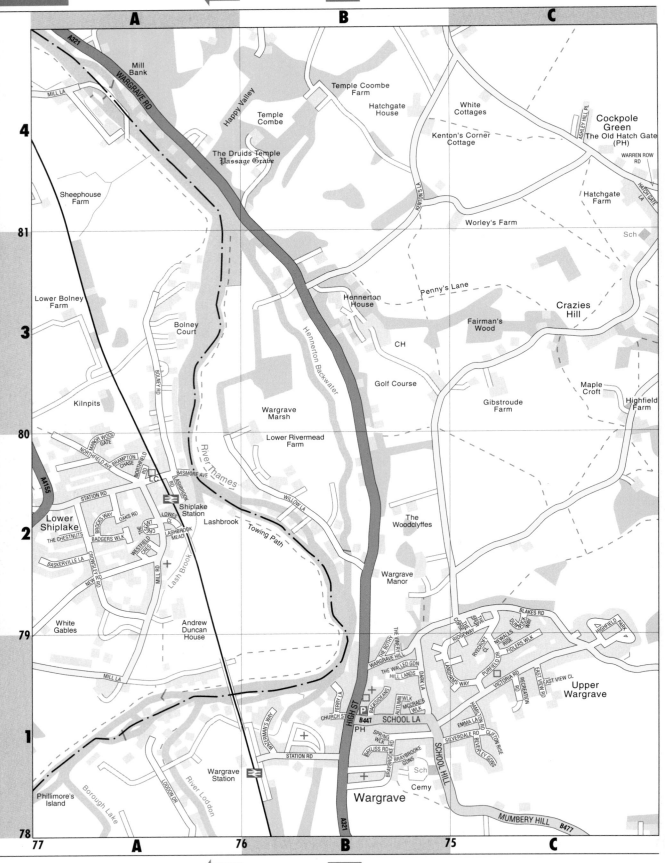

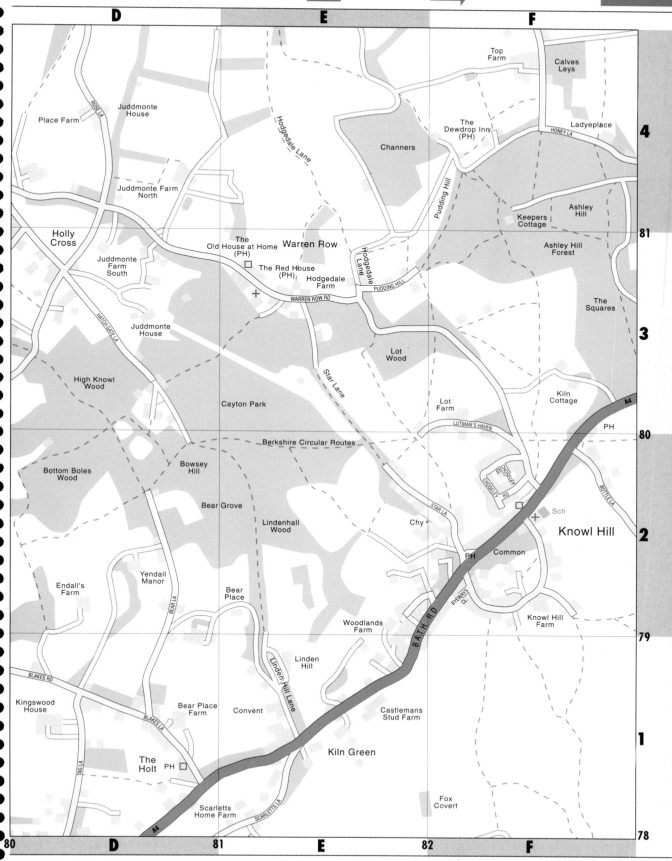

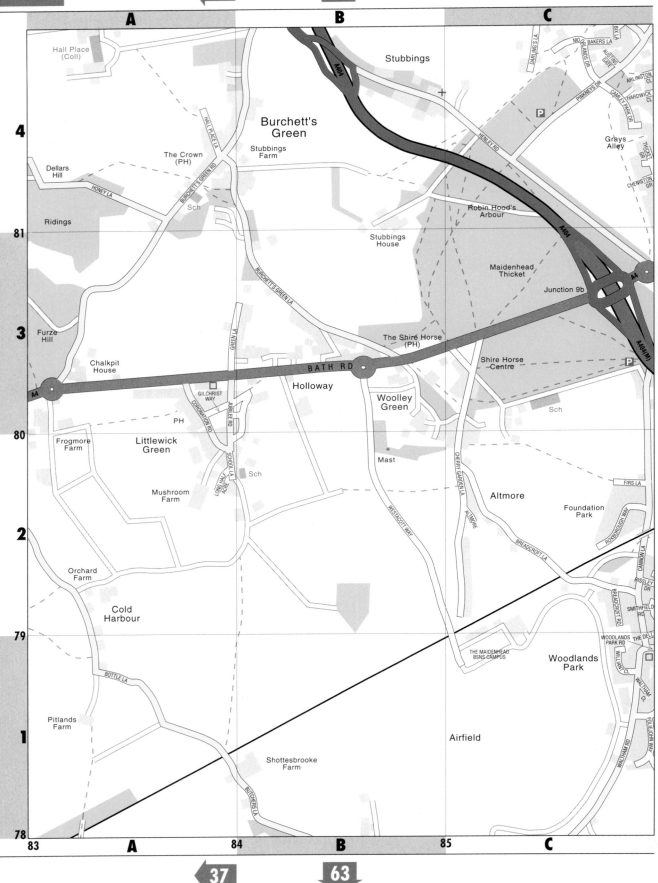

A B C

Hall Place (Coll)

Stubbings

DARLINGS LA

MO ORLANDS DR

BAKERS LA

AUSTINS GATE

BIX LA

ARLINGTON CL

PINKNEYS DR

CAMLEY PARK DR

HARDWICK CL

4

Burchett's Green

Stubbings Farm

HENLEY RD

P

Grays Alley

THICKET GR

The Crown (PH)

HALL PLACE LA

BURCHETT'S GREEN RD

Dellars Hill

HONEY LA

Sch

Robin Hood's Arbour

CHENISTON GR

Ridings

81

Stubbings House

Maidenhead Thicket

A404

BURCHETT'S GREEN LA

3

Furze Hill

GREEN LA

The Shire Horse (PH)

Shire Horse Centre

Junction 9b

A4(M)

A404

A4

Chalkpit House

BATH RD

P

AA

GILCHRIST WAY

Holloway

Woolley Green

Sch

Littlewick Green

CORONATION RD

JUBILEE RD

PH

Mast

Altmore

CHERRY GARDEN LA

ALTMORE

Sch

FIRS LA

80

Frogmore Farm

SCHOOL LA

LONG HALF ACRE

Sch

Mushroom Farm

Foundation Park

ROXBOROUGH WAY

CANNON LA

2

Orchard Farm

WESTSCOTT WAY

BREADCROFT LA

BISSLEY DR

BREADCROFT LA

SMITHFIELD RD

Cold Harbour

79

THE MAIDENHEAD BSNS CAMPUS

Woodlands Park

WOODLANDS PARK RD

THE DELL

WILLIAM CL

WALTHAM GL

BOTTLE LA

1

Pitlands Farm

Airfield

WALTHAM RD

FOLEJOHN WAY

Shottesbrooke Farm

BUTCHERS LA

78

83 A 84 B 85 C

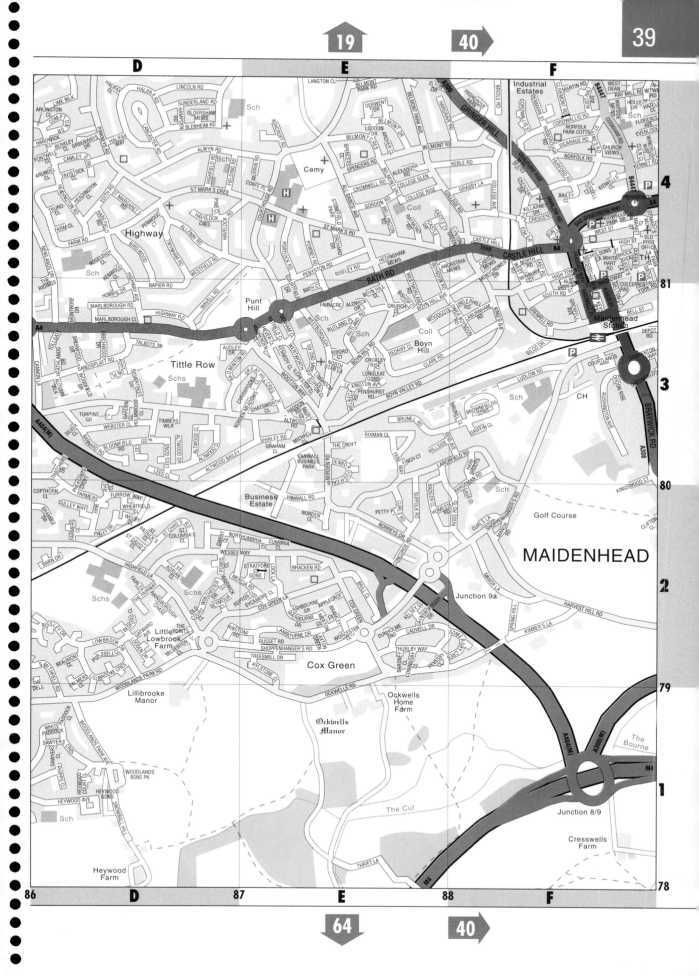

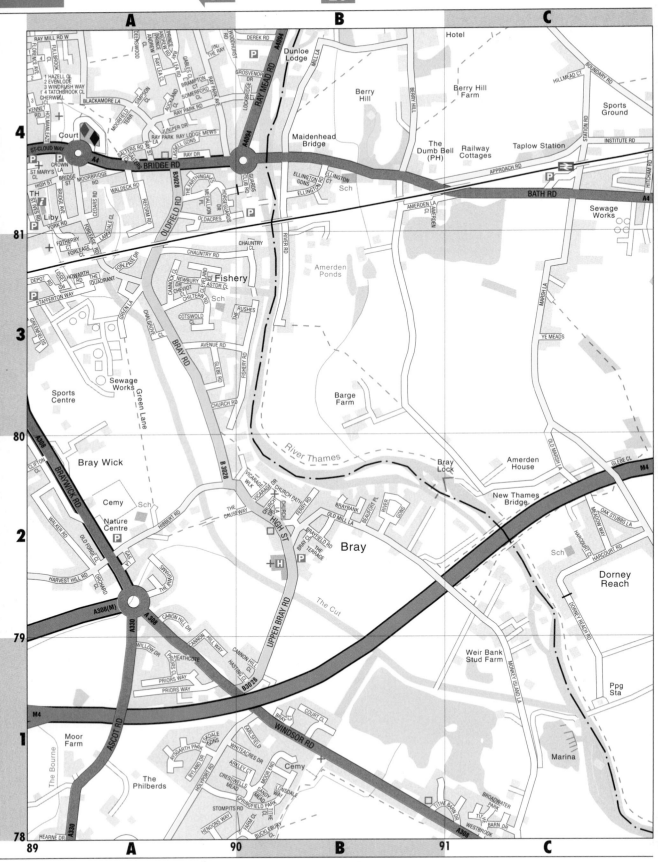

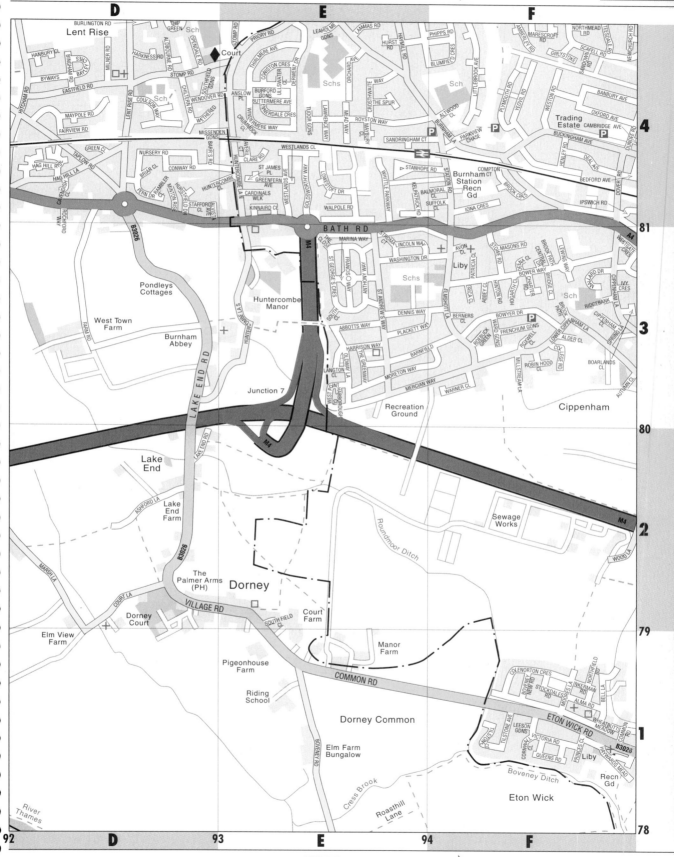

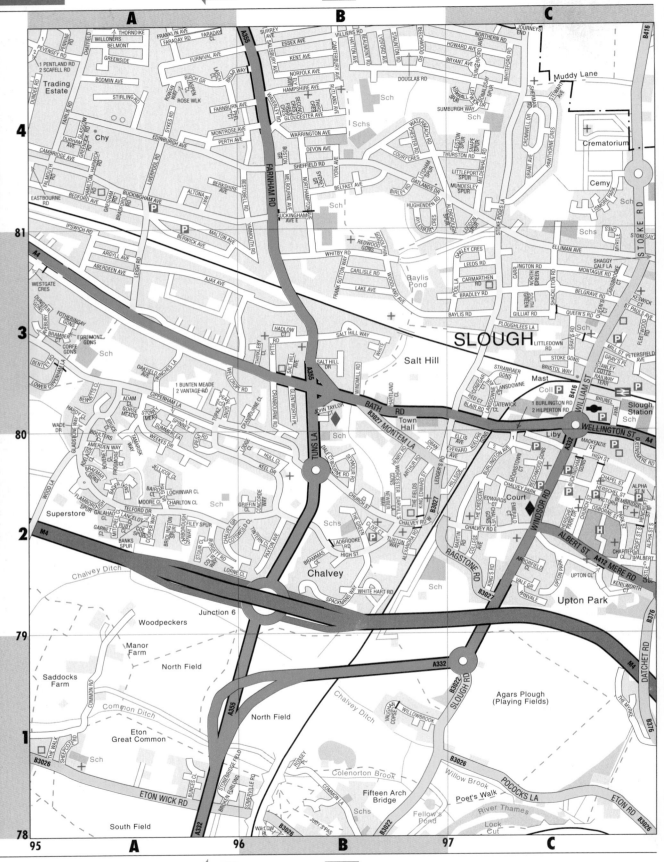

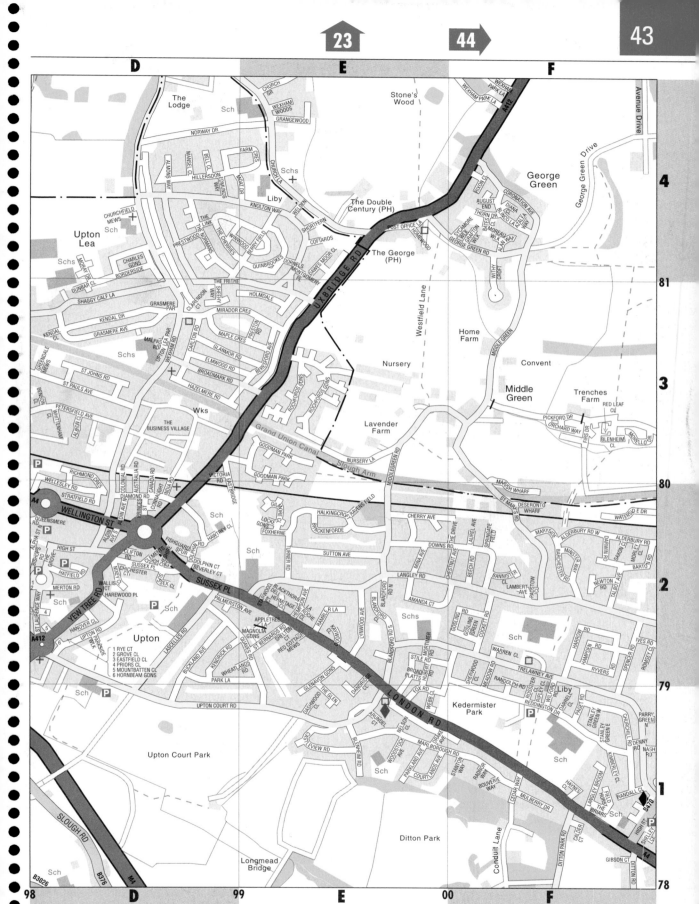

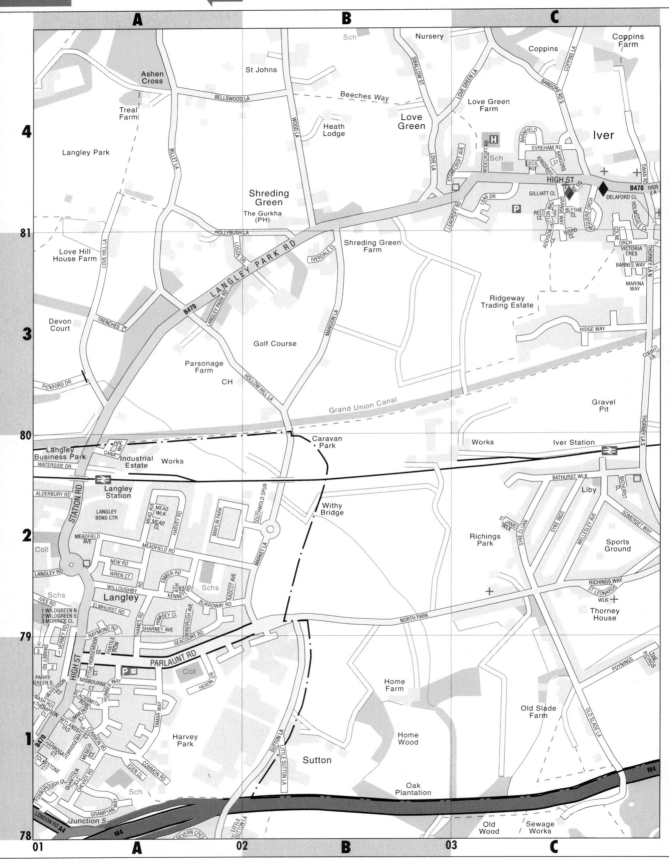

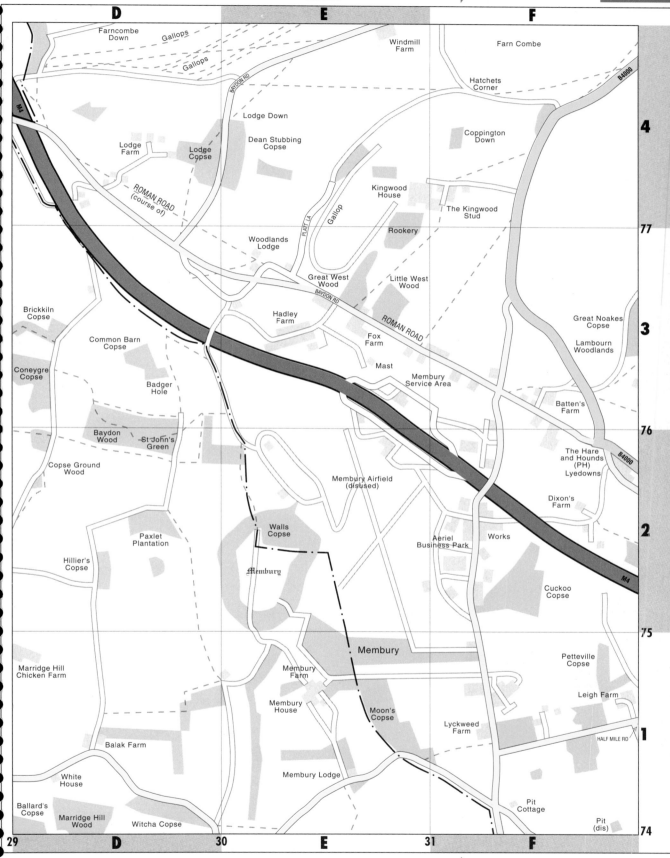

D   E   F

Farncombe Down
Gallops
Gallops

Windmill Farm

Farn Combe

B4000

Hatchets Corner

Lodge Down

Coppington Down

4

Dean Stubbing Copse

Lodge Farm

Lodge Copse

ROMAN ROAD (course of)

BAYDON RD

Kingwood House

The Kingwood Stud

PLATT LA

Gallop

Woodlands Lodge

Rookery

77

Great West Wood

Little West Wood

Brickkiln Copse

BAYDON RD

Hadley Farm

ROMAN ROAD

Great Noakes Copse

3

Common Barn Copse

Fox Farm

Lambourn Woodlands

Coneygre Copse

Badger Hole

Mast

Membury Service Area

Batten's Farm

Baydon Wood

St John's Green

76

Copse Ground Wood

The Hare and Hounds (PH) Lyedowns

B4000

Membury Airfield (disused)

Dixon's Farm

Paxlet Plantation

Walls Copse

Aeriel Business Park

Works

2

Hillier's Copse

Membury

Cuckoo Copse

M4

75

Membury

Petteville Copse

Marridge Hill Chicken Farm

Membury Farm

Leigh Farm

Membury House

Moon's Copse

Lyckweed Farm

HALF MILE RD

1

Balak Farm

White House

Membury Lodge

Pit Cottage

Ballard's Copse

Marridge Hill Wood

Witcha Copse

Pit (dis)

74

A | B | C

4
Hungerford Gap
Coppington Hill
Boldstart Farm
Boldstart Copse
White Shute
Thorn Hill
Thornhill Copse
Lambourn Valley Way
River Lambourn
The Hermitage
Hall
Manor Farm
Eastbury
The Plough (PH)
Hayfield Ct

77
Willis Farm
Ox Wood
Gifford's Copse
Cleeve Wood
Clapper Border

3
Dance's Cottage
Berry's Wood
Cleeve Hill
Lord's Wood
Alms Wood
Shrags Hill
Haycroft Hill

76
Rooksnest
Lambourn Woodlands
Danesfield Copse
Great Park Wood
Patch Copse
Pebblehill Copse
Household Copse
Straight La
Cymbalcroft Copse

2
Lyedown Copse
Hilldrop Farm
B4000
B4001
Stony Lane
Burgess's Farm
Watchcroft Copse
Leyatt Copse
Peaks Copse
Bushyleaze Border

75
M4
BAYDON RD
ROMAN ROAD
Hall
Eastbury Shute
May's Copse
Woodlands St Mary
Kimber's Border

1
Lye Farm Cottages
Half Mile Rd
Riverwood Border

74
Carols Acre
B4001
Breach Border
Holt Copse
M4

32 | 33 | 34

A | B | C

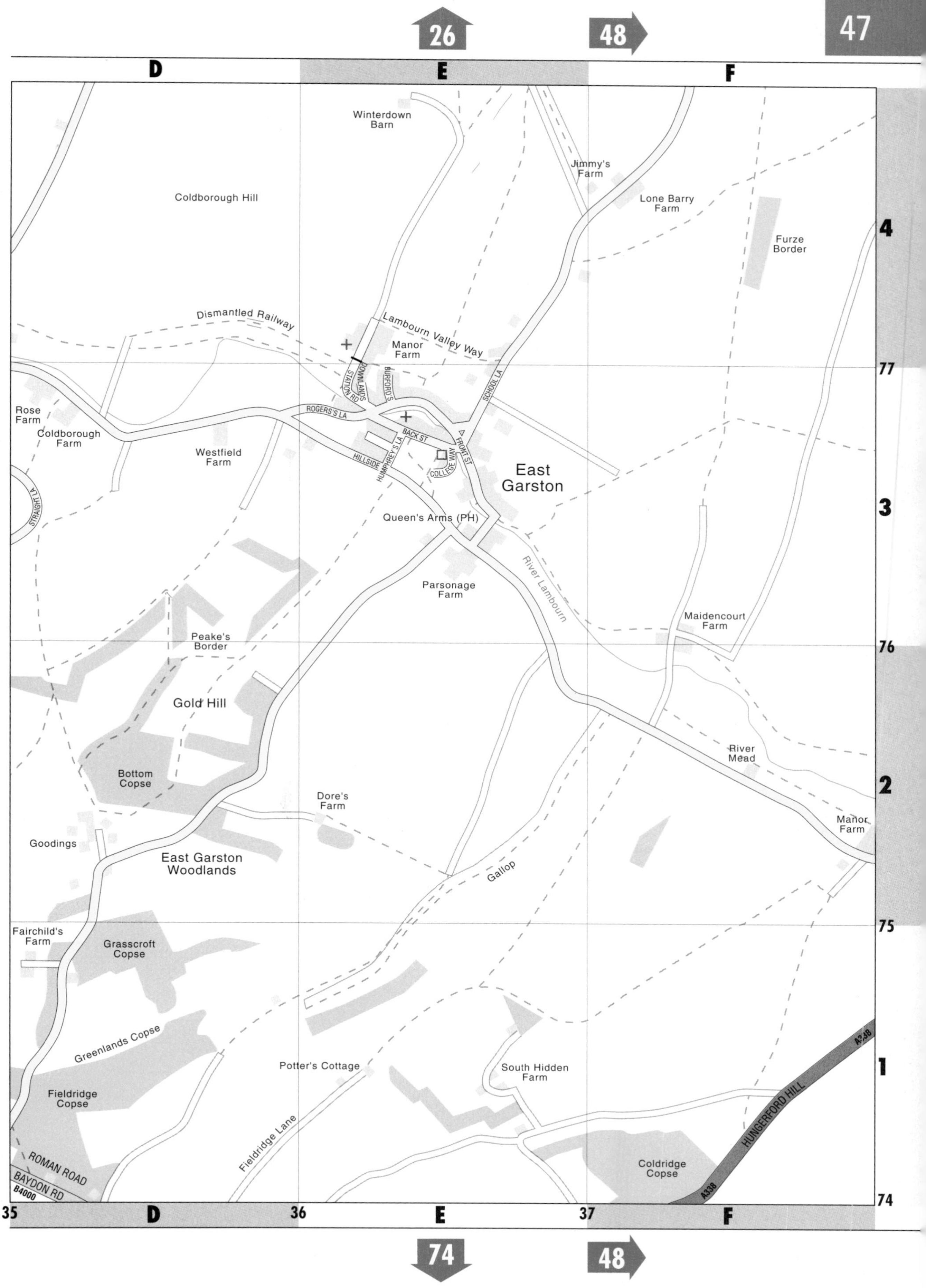

D E F

Winterdown
Barn

Jimmy's
Farm

Lone Barry
Farm

Furze
Border

4

Coldborough Hill

Dismantled Railway

Lambourn Valley Way

Manor
Farm

77

STATION RD

DOWNLANDS

BURFORD'S

SCHOOL LA

Rose
Farm

Coldborough
Farm

ROGERS'S LA

BACK ST

Westfield
Farm

HILLSIDE

HUMPHREY'S LA

COLLEGE

FRONT ST

East
Garston

STRAIGHT LA

3

Queen's Arms (PH)

River Lambourn

Parsonage
Farm

Maidencourt
Farm

76

Peake's
Border

Gold Hill

River
Mead

Bottom
Copse

Dore's
Farm

2

Goodings

Manor
Farm

East Garston
Woodlands

Gallop

75

Fairchild's
Farm

Grasscroft
Copse

Greenlands Copse

Potter's Cottage

South Hidden
Farm

1

A338

Fieldridge
Copse

Fieldridge Lane

HUNGERFORD HILL

ROMAN ROAD

BAYDON RD
B4000

Coldridge
Copse

A338

74

47 27

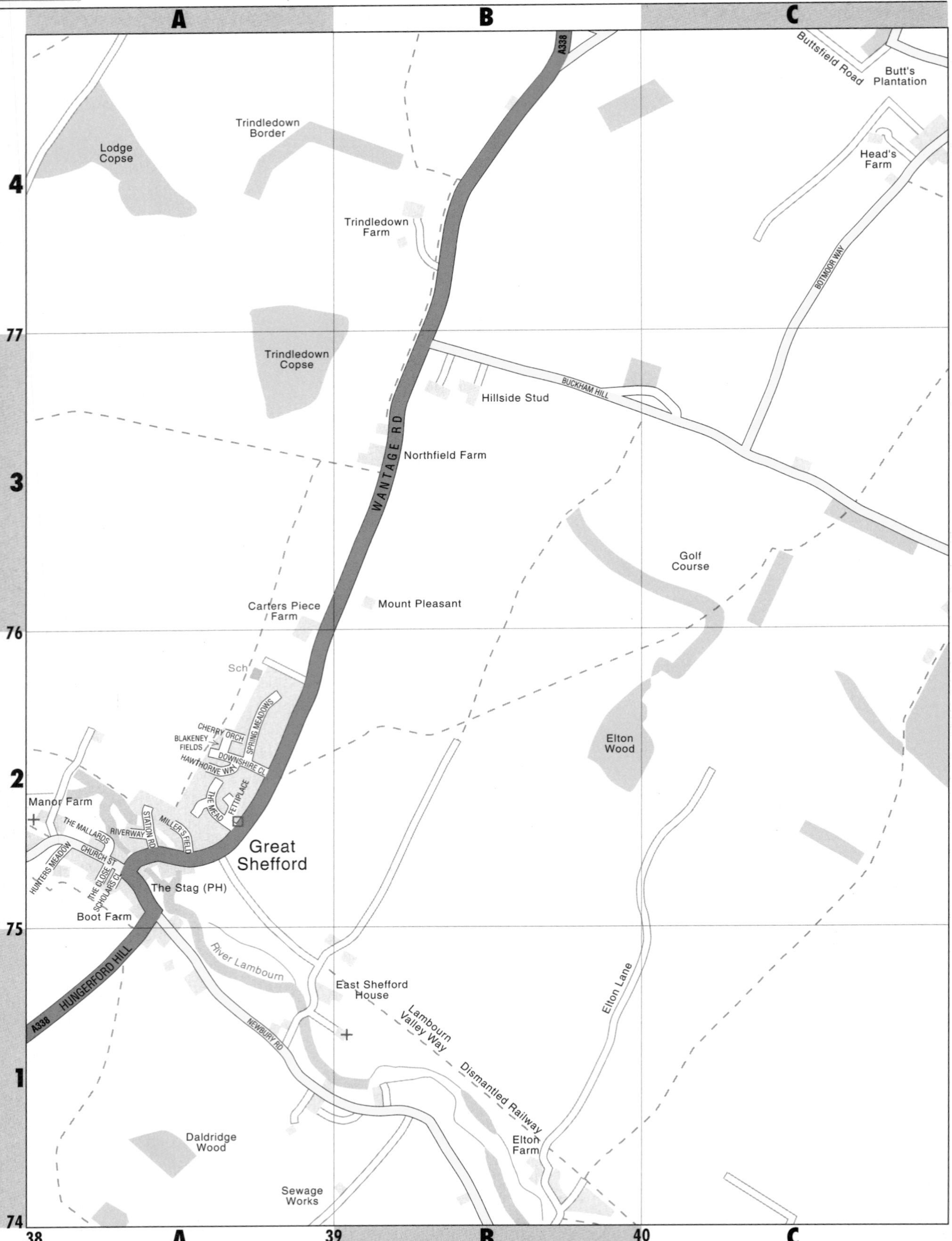

A B C

Buttsfield Road

Butt's
Plantation

Lodge
Copse

Trindledown
Border

Head's
Farm

4

Trindledown
Farm

BOTMOOR WAY

77

Trindledown
Copse

BUCKHAM HILL

Hillside Stud

WANTAGE RD

Northfield Farm

3

A338

Golf
Course

Carters Piece
Farm

Mount Pleasant

76

Sch

Elton
Wood

CHERRY ORCH
SPRING MEADOWS
BLAKENEY
FIELDS
DOWNSHIRE CL
HAWTHORNE WA

2

Manor Farm

THE MALLARDS
RIVERWAY
CHURCH ST
STATION RD
MILLER'S FIELD
THE MEAD
FETTIPLACE

Great
Shefford

HUNTERS MEADOW
THE CLOSE
SCHOLARS CL

The Stag (PH)

Boot Farm

75

River Lambourn

HUNGERFORD HILL

A338

NEWBURY RD

East Shefford
House

Elton Lane

Lambourn
Valley Way

Dismantled Railway

1

Daldridge
Wood

Elton
Farm

Sewage
Works

74

38 A 39 B 40 C

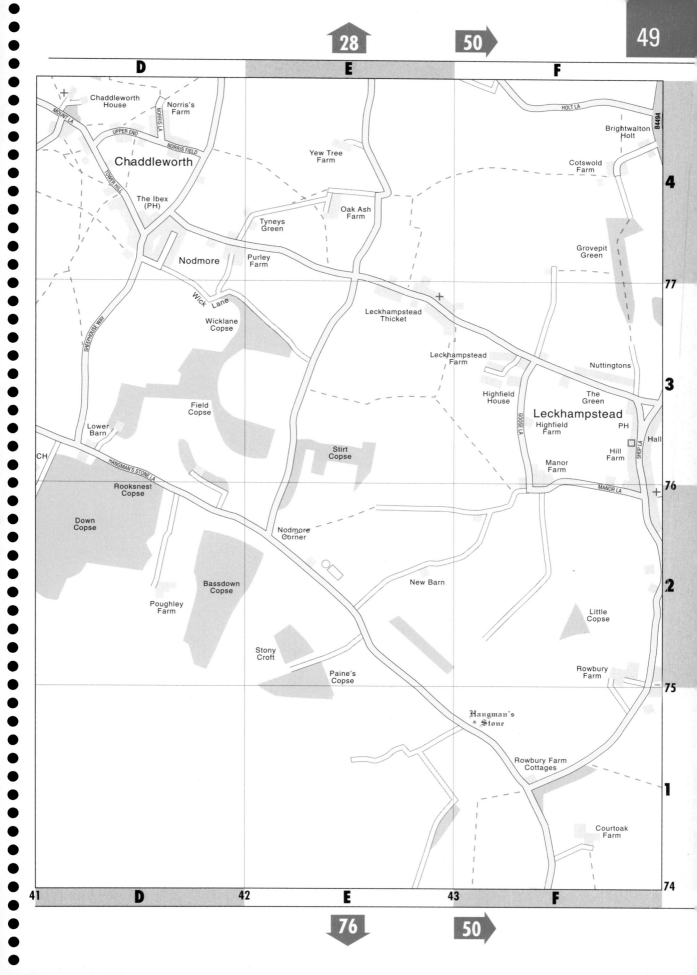

D · E · F

Chaddleworth
Chaddleworth House
Norris's Farm
MOUNT LA
NORRIS LA
UPPER END
NORRIS FIELD
TOWER HILL
The Ibex (PH)
Nodmore
Tyneys Green
Purley Farm
Yew Tree Farm
Oak Ash Farm

HOLT LA
Brightwalton Holt
B4494
Cotswold Farm

4

Grovepit Green

Wick Lane
Wicklane Copse
SHEEPHOUSE WAY

Leckhampstead Thicket

Leckhampstead Farm

Nuttingtons

77

Field Copse

Highfield House
The Green
Leckhampstead
PH
Highfield Farm
GOOSE LA
Hill Farm
SHOP LA
Hall

3

Lower Barn
CH
HANGMAN'S STONE LA
Rooksnest Copse

Stirt Copse

Manor Farm
MANOR LA

76

Down Copse

Nodmore Corner

New Barn

Little Copse

2

Bassdown Copse
Poughley Farm

Rowbury Farm

Stony Croft
Paine's Copse

75

Hangman's Stone

Rowbury Farm Cottages

1

Courtoak Farm

74

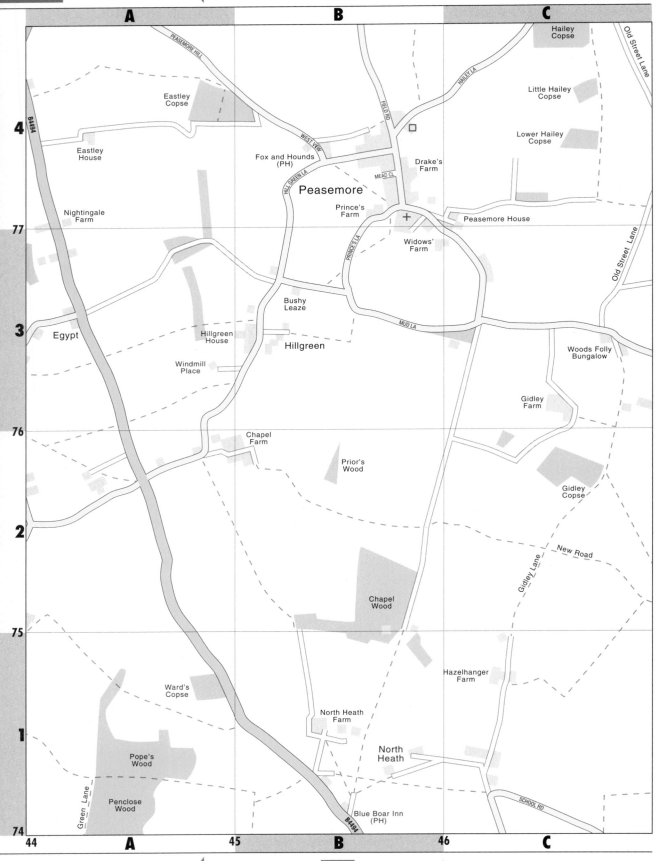

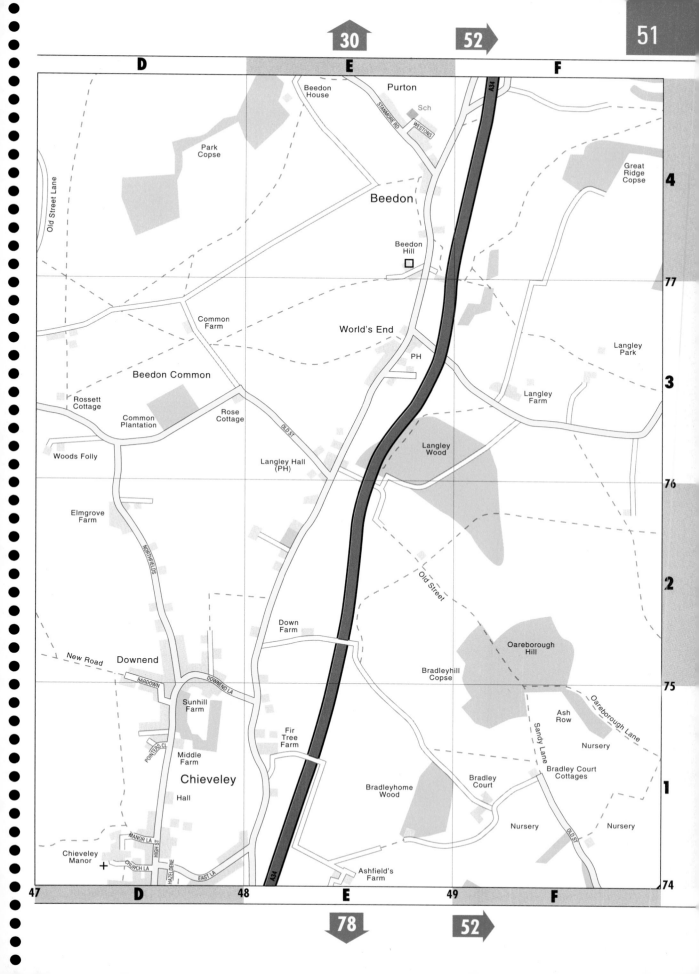

D   E   F

Beedon House
Purton
Sch
A34

Park
Copse

Great
Ridge
Copse

4

Old Street Lane

Beedon

Beedon Hill

77

Common
Farm

World's End

Langley
Park

PH

Beedon Common

Langley
Farm

3

Rossett
Cottage

Common
Plantation

Rose
Cottage

OLD ST

Woods Folly

Langley
Wood

Langley Hall
(PH)

76

Elmgrove
Farm

NORTHFIELDS

Old Street

2

Down
Farm

Oareborough
Hill

New Road

Downend

Bradleyhill
Copse

75

BARDOWN

DOWNEND LA

Sunhill
Farm

Ash
Row

Oareborough Lane

Sandy Lane

POINTERS CL

Fir
Tree
Farm

Nursery

Middle
Farm

Chieveley

Bradley Court
Cottages

Hall

Bradley
Court

Bradleyhome
Wood

1

MANOR LA

HIGH ST

HAZELDENE

Nursery

OLD ST

Nursery

Chieveley
Manor

CHURCH LA

EAST LA

A34

Ashfield's
Farm

74

47   D   48   E   49   F

A   B   C

4

Little Ridge
Copse

Northfield
Row

Banterwick
Farm

Perborough
Castle

Floodcross
Cottage

Milkhill
Farm

Uplands

Green Hams Lane

Ramsworth
Cottages

River Pang

77

Allen's
Row

New
Copse

Middle
Barn

Five
Ways

STATION HILL

WATER ST

THE CLOSE

SCOTTALLS LA

3

Oakhouse
Farm

Laycroft
Wood

Hampstead
Norreys

THE GUTTRISS

PENDALS CL

B4009

NEWBURY HILL

CHURCH ST

Bothampstead
Farm

Oakhouse
Cottages

Hollingsworth

Dismantled Railway

Sch

76

Park
Wood

Westbrook
Copse

Bothampstead

Trumpletts
Farm

Down
Wood

Malthouse

New
Cottages

Hatchgate
Cottages

The Thatched
Cottage

2

Eling

Elingpark
Copse

Eling
Farm

75

Four
Elms

1

Oareborough Lane

Pimbus
Shaw

EVERINGTON LA

Sand
Pit

Common
Barn
Cottages

Heather
Piece

Spring
Plantation

Everington
Hill

M4

Newhouse
Farm

B4009

Furze
Hill

M4

74

50   A   51   B   52   C

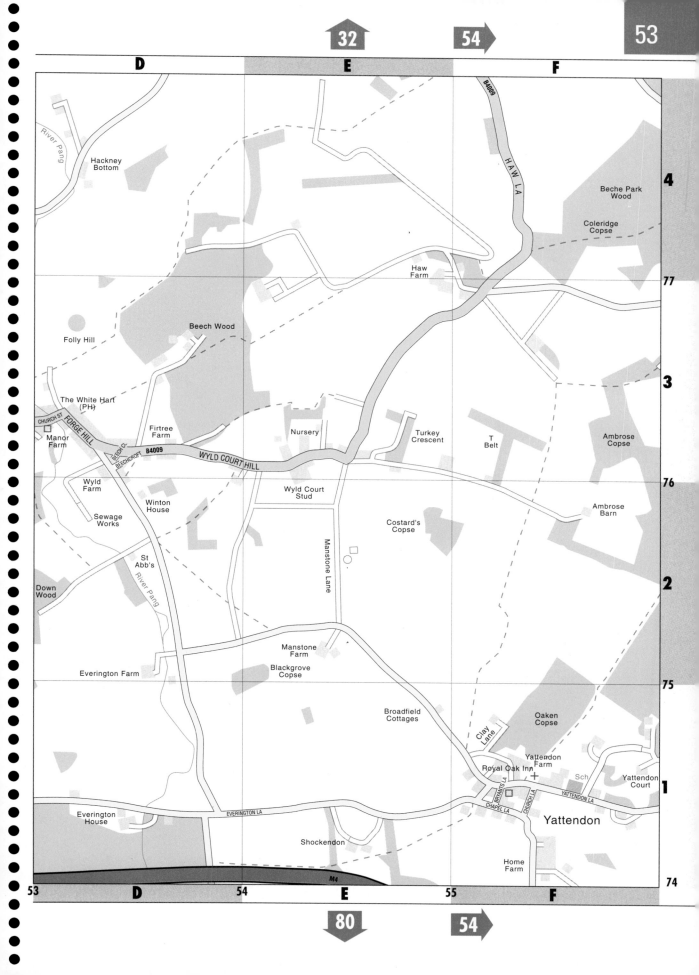

D
E
F

B4009

HAW LA

4

Hackney
Bottom

River Pang

Beche Park
Wood

Coleridge
Copse

Haw
Farm

77

Folly Hill

Beech Wood

The White Hart
(PH)

CHURCH ST
FORGE HILL

Manor
Farm

Firtree
Farm

BEECH CL
BEECHCROFT
B4009

WYLD COURT HILL

Nursery

Turkey
Crescent

T Belt

Ambrose
Copse

3

Wyld
Farm

Wyld Court
Stud

76

Winton
House

Ambrose
Barn

Sewage
Works

St
Abb's

Manstone Lane

Costard's
Copse

Down
Wood

River Pang

2

Everington Farm

Manstone
Farm

Blackgrove
Copse

75

Broadfield
Cottages

Oaken
Copse

Clay
Lane

Yattendon
Farm

Royal Oak Inn

Sch

Yattendon
Court

1

BRYANTS LA

CHAPEL LA

CHURCH LA

YATTENDON LA

Everington
House

EVERINGTON LA

M4

Shockendon

Yattendon

Home
Farm

74

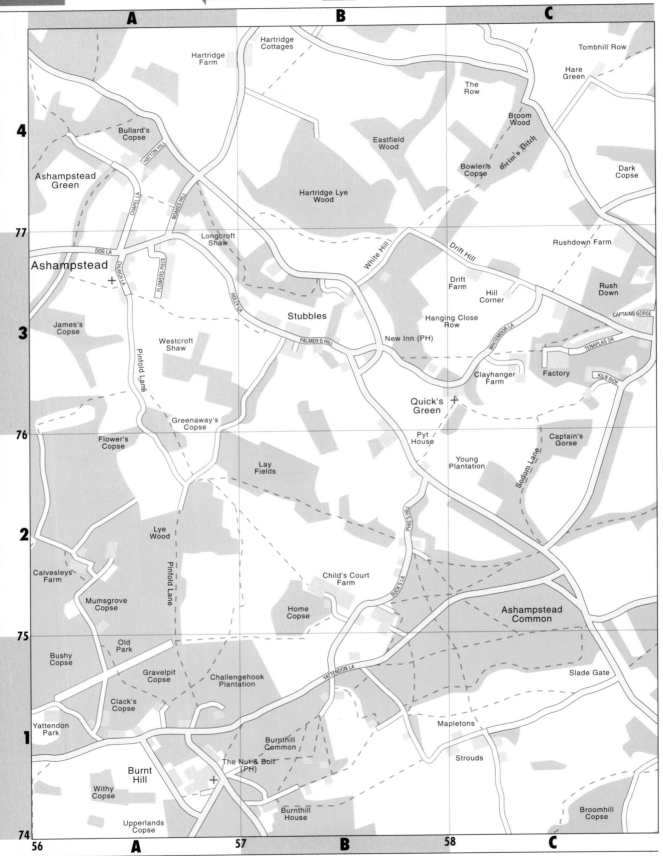
A

B

C

Hartridge
Cottages

Hartridge
Farm

Tombhill Row

The
Row

Hare
Green

Broom
Wood

Bullard's
Copse

4

Grim's Ditch

Eastfield
Wood

Ashampstead
Green

Bowler's
Copse

Dark
Copse

Hartridge Lye
Wood

77

Longcroft
Shaw

White Hill

Drift Hill

Rushdown Farm

Ashampstead

Drift
Farm

Rush
Down

Hill
Corner

CAPTAINS GORSE

James's
Copse

Stubbles

Hanging Close
Row

TENAPLAS DR

3

Westcroft
Shaw

PALMER'S HILL

New Inn (PH)

WHITEMOOR LA

Factory

KILN RIDE

Clayhanger
Farm

Quick's
Green

Pinfold Lane

Greenaway's
Copse

Captain's
Gorse

76

Flower's
Copse

Pyt
House

Young
Plantation

Sodom Lane

Lay
Fields

PYKE'S HILL

Lye
Wood

2

Child's Court
Farm

Pinfold Lane

SUCK'S LA

Calvesleys
Farm

Ashampstead
Common

Mumsgrove
Copse

Home
Copse

75

Old
Park

Bushy
Copse

Slade Gate

Gravelpit
Copse

Challengehook
Plantation

YATTENDON LA

Clack's
Copse

Mapletons

1

Yattendon
Park

Burpthill
Common

Strouds

The Nut & Bolt
(PH)

Burnt
Hill

Broomhill
Copse

Withy
Copse

Burnthill
House

Upperlands
Copse

74

56

A

57

B

58

C

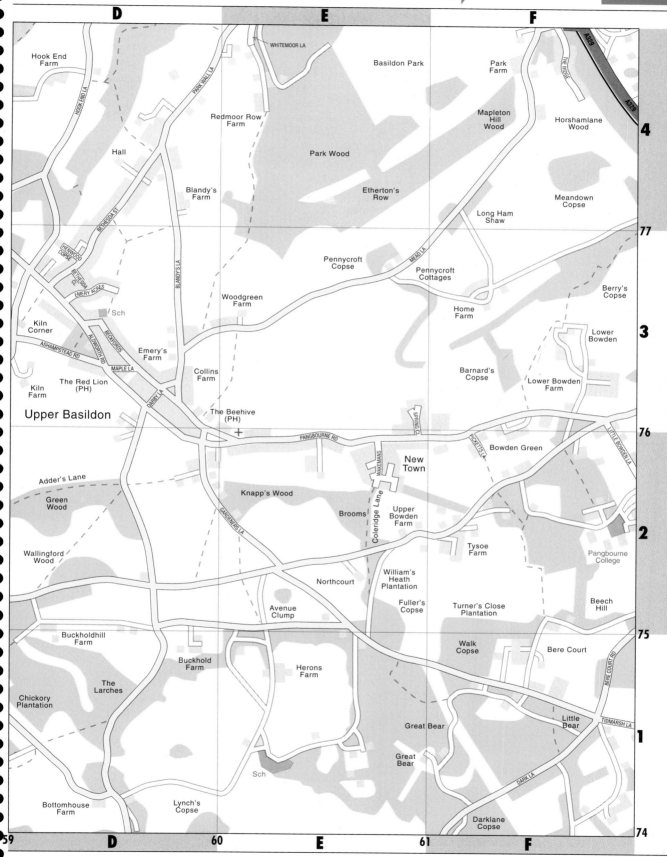

A329

Hook End
Farm

WHITEMOOR LA

Basildon Park

Park
Farm

THE RIDGE

HOOK END LA

PARK WALL LA

Redmoor Row
Farm

Mapleton
Hill
Wood

Horshamlane
Wood

4

Hall

Park Wood

Blandy's
Farm

Etherton's
Row

Meandown
Copse

Long Ham
Shaw

77

BETHESDA ST

HENWOOD
COPSE

MEAD LA

Pennycroft
Copse

Pennycroft
Cottages

Berry's
Copse

BETHESDA
CL

EMERY ACRES

Woodgreen
Farm

Home
Farm

Lower
Bowden

3

BLANDY'S LA

Sch

Kiln
Corner

BECKFORDS

Emery's
Farm

Barnard's
Copse

Lower Bowden
Farm

ASHAMPSTEAD RD

ALDWORTH RD

Collins
Farm

MAPLE LA

Kiln
Farm

The Red Lion
(PH)

DARBY LA

SPRING CL

PICKETS LA

LITTLE BOWDEN LA

Upper Basildon

The Beehive
(PH)

PANGBOURNE RD

Bowden Green

76

New
Town

WAKEMANS

Adder's Lane

Knapp's Wood

Upper
Bowden
Farm

Green
Wood

COLERIDGE LANE

Brooms

2

GARDENERS LA

Tysoe
Farm

Pangbourne
College

Wallingford
Wood

William's
Heath
Plantation

Northcourt

Fuller's
Copse

Turner's Close
Plantation

Beech
Hill

Avenue
Clump

75

Buckholdhill
Farm

Walk
Copse

Bere Court

BERE COURT RD

Buckhold
Farm

Herons
Farm

The
Larches

TIDMARSH LA

Chickory
Plantation

Little
Bear

Great Bear

1

Great
Bear

DARK LA

Bottomhouse
Farm

Lynch's
Copse

Sch

Darklane
Copse

74

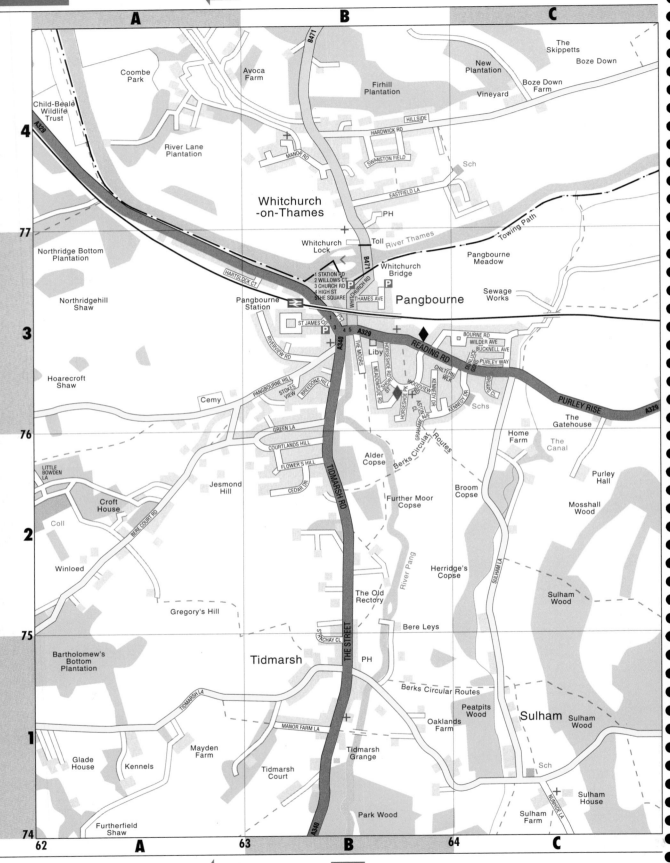

A   **B**   **C**

4

Child-Beale
Wildlife
Trust

Coombe
Park

Avoca
Farm

River Lane
Plantation

Firhill
Plantation

New
Plantation

The
Skippetts

Boze Down

Boze Down
Farm

Vineyard

HILLSIDE

HARDWICK RD

SWANSTON FIELD

Sch

MANOR RD

EASTFIELD LA

**Whitchurch
-on-Thames**

PH

77

Northridge Bottom
Plantation

HARTSLOCK CT

Whitchurch
Lock

Toll

River Thames

Towing Path

Pangbourne
Meadow

Whitchurch
Bridge

B471

Northridgehill
Shaw

Pangbourne
Station

1 STATION RD
2 WILLOWS CT
3 CHURCH RD
4 HIGH ST
5 THE SQUARE

CHURCH RD

THAMES AVE

Pangbourne

Sewage
Works

P

P

P

3

St James's

RIVERVIEW RD

A340

Liby

THE MOORS

A329

READING RD

HORSESHOE RD

MEADOWSIDE RD

DUKES LOCK RD

BOURNE RD

WILDER AVE

BUCKNELL AVE

PURLEY WAY

Hoarecroft
Shaw

Cemy

Pangbourne Hill

STOKES
VIEW

BREEDONS HILL

CHILTERN
WLK

WOODVIEW RD

KENNEDY DR

GRAHAME CL

ASTON AVE

KENNEDY DR

BRIARS CL

Schs

PURLEY RISE

The
Gatehouse

A329

76

GREEN LA

COURTLANDS HILL

FLOWER'S HILL

CEDAR DR

Alder
Copse

Berks Circular Routes

Home
Farm

The
Canal

Purley
Hall

LITTLE
BOWDEN LA

Croft
House

Coll

BERE COURT RD

Jesmond
Hill

Further Moor
Copse

Broom
Copse

Mosshall
Wood

2

Winloed

TIDMARSH RD

River Pang

Herridge's
Copse

SULHAM LA

Sulham
Wood

Gregory's Hill

The Old
Rectory

Bere Leys

75

Bartholomew's
Bottom
Plantation

STRACHAY CL

THE STREET

PH

Berks Circular Routes

Tidmarsh

Sulham

Sulham
Wood

TIDMARSH LA

MANOR FARM LA

Peatpits
Wood

Oaklands
Farm

Sch

1

Glade
House

Kennels

Mayden
Farm

Tidmarsh
Court

Tidmarsh
Grange

Sulham
Farm

NUNHIDE LA

Sulham
House

74

Furtherfield
Shaw

Park Wood

A340

62   **A**   **63**   **B**   **64**   **C**

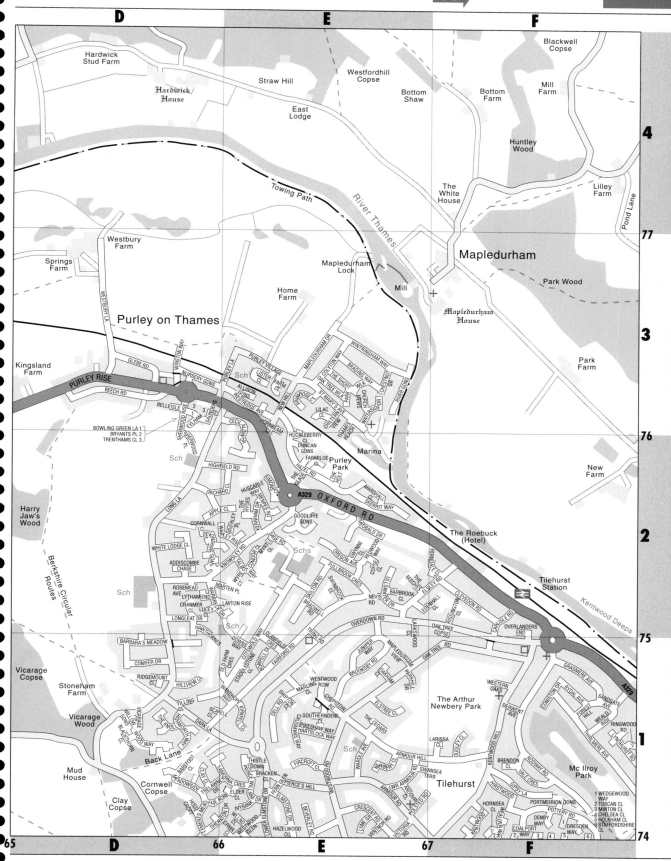

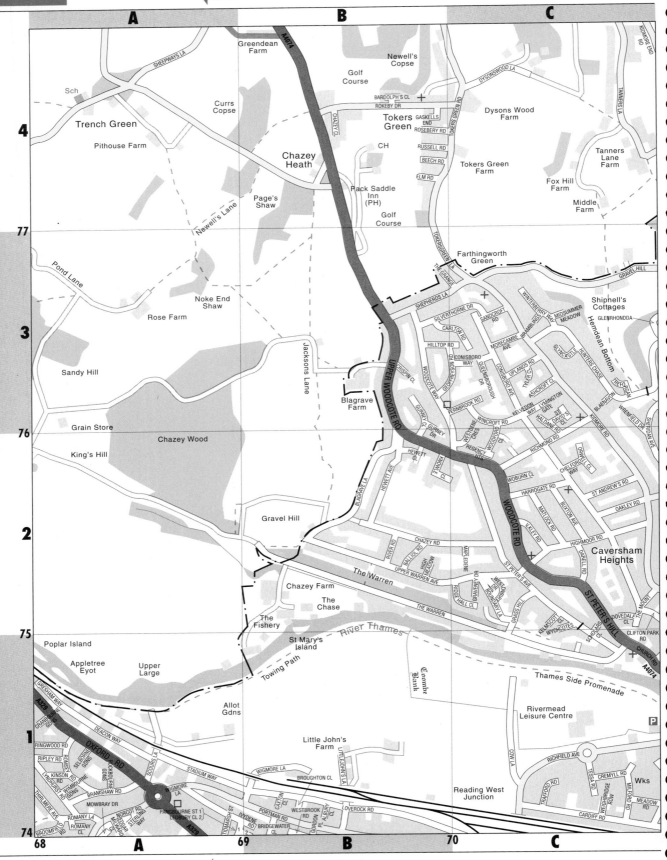

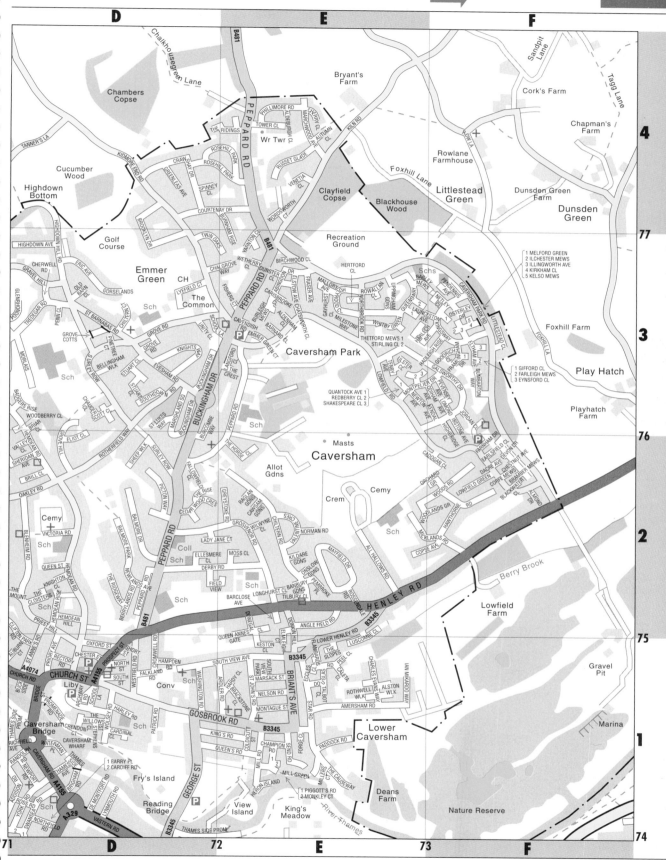

59
35

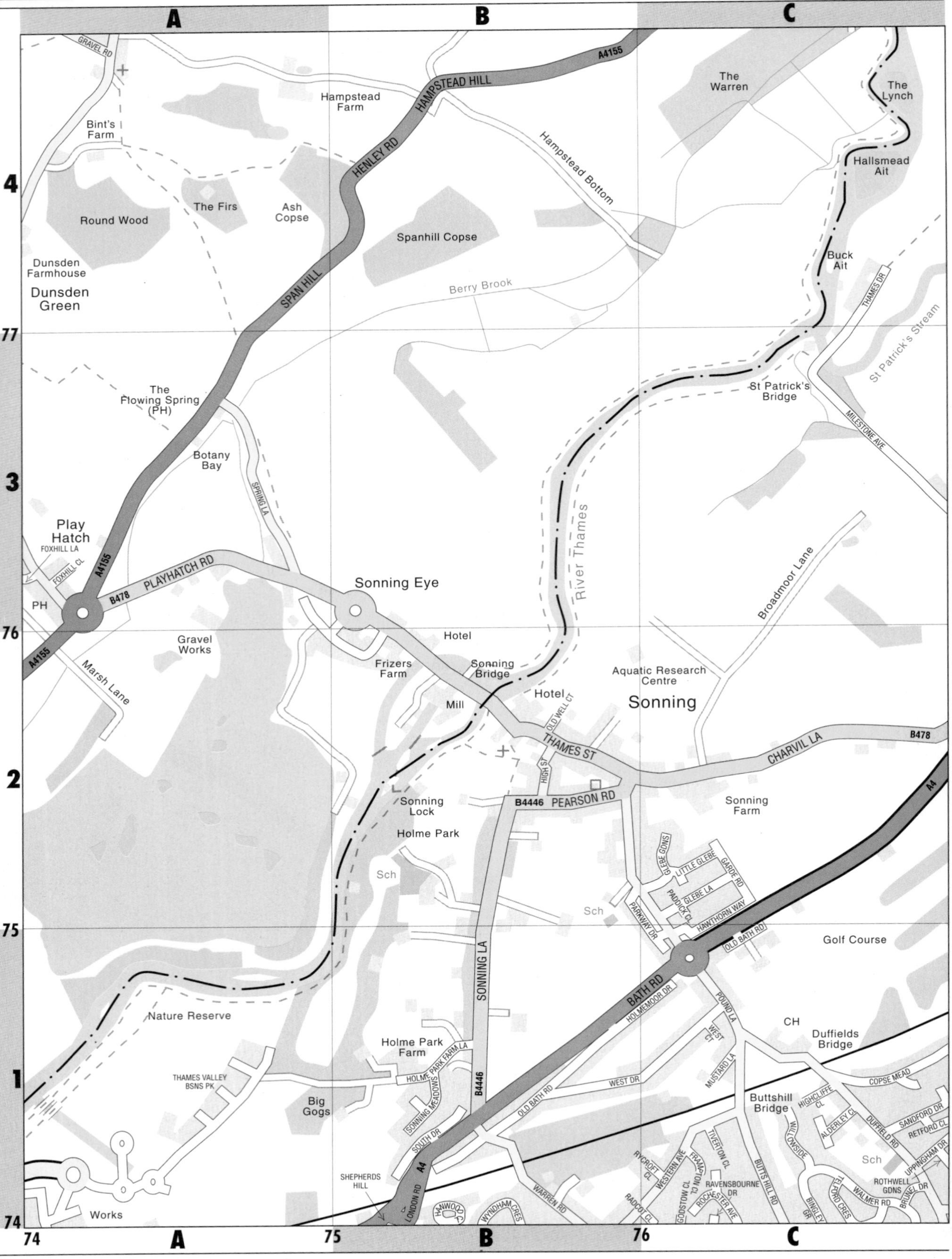

A   **B**   **C**

GRAVEL RD

A4155

Bint's Farm

Hampstead Farm

HAMPSTEAD HILL

Hampstead Hill

The Warren

The Lynch

4

Round Wood

The Firs

Ash Copse

HENLEY RD

Spanhill Copse

Hampstead Bottom

Hallsmead Ait

Dunsden Farmhouse

Dunsden Green

Berry Brook

Buck Ait

THAMES DR

SPAN HILL

77

St Patrick's Bridge

St Patrick's Stream

The Flowing Spring (PH)

MILLSTONE AVE

Botany Bay

SPRING LA

3

Play Hatch

FOXHILL LA

River Thames

Broadmoor Lane

FOXHILL CL

A4155

PLAYHATCH RD

Sonning Eye

B478

PH

Gravel Works

Hotel

76

A4155

Frizers Farm

Sonning Bridge

Hotel

Aquatic Research Centre

Sonning

CHARVIL LA

B478

Marsh Lane

Mill

OLD WELL CT

A4

THAMES ST

HIGH ST

2

Sonning Lock

PEARSON RD

B4446

Sonning Farm

Holme Park

SONNING LA

GLEBE GDNS

LITTLE GLEBE

GADGE RD

Sch

Sch

GLEBE LA

PADDOCK CL

HAWTHORN WAY

PARKWAY DR

75

Golf Course

Nature Reserve

BATH RD

HOLMEMOOR DR

POUND LA

OLD BATH RD

CH

Duffields Bridge

WEST CT

MUSTARD LA

COPSE MEAD

1

Holme Park Farm

HOLME PARK FARM LA

WEST DR

HIGHCLIFFE CL

SANDFORD DR

RETFORD CL

THAMES VALLEY BSNS PK

SONNING MEADOWS

B4446

WEST DR

Buttshill Bridge

WILTONSIDE

DUFFIELD CL

UPPINGHAM DR

Big Gogs

SOUTH DR

OLD BATH RD

TIVERTON CL

WESTERN AVE

RAVENSBOURNE DR

ROCHESTER AVE

BINGLEY

FLAND CRES

ROTHWELL GDNS

BRUNEL DR

Sch

SHEPHERDS HILL

LONDON RD

A4

WYNDHAM CRES

WARREN RD

RYCROFT CL

WESTERN CL

RADCOT CL

GOXSTOW CL

ALDERLEY CL

WALMER RD

74

Works

74   **A**   **75**   **B**   **76**   **C**

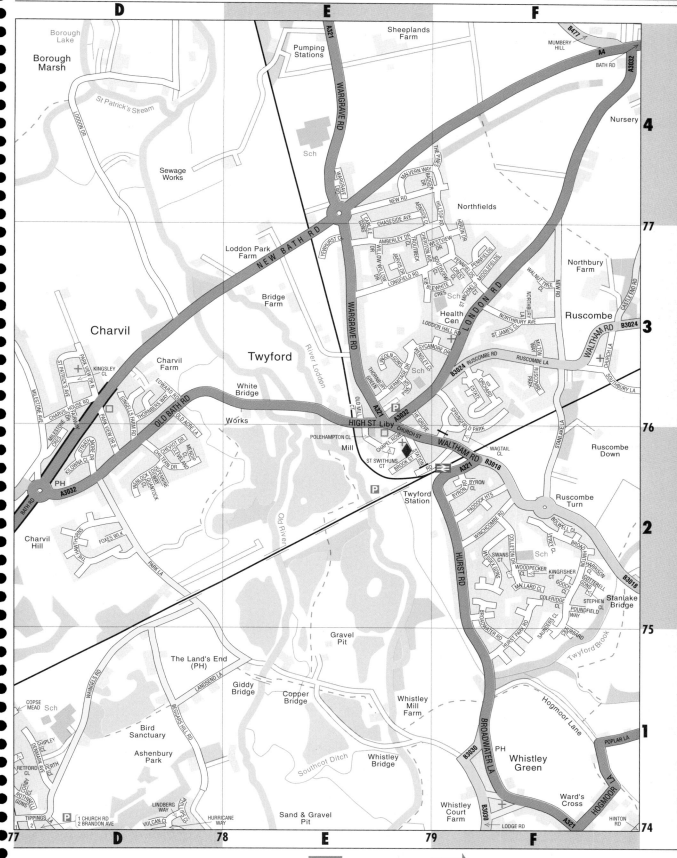

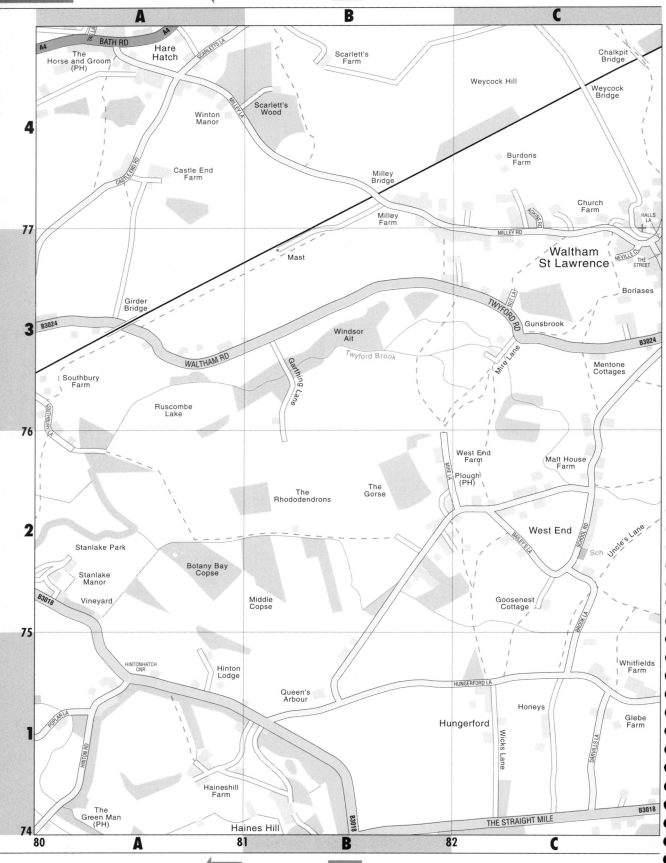

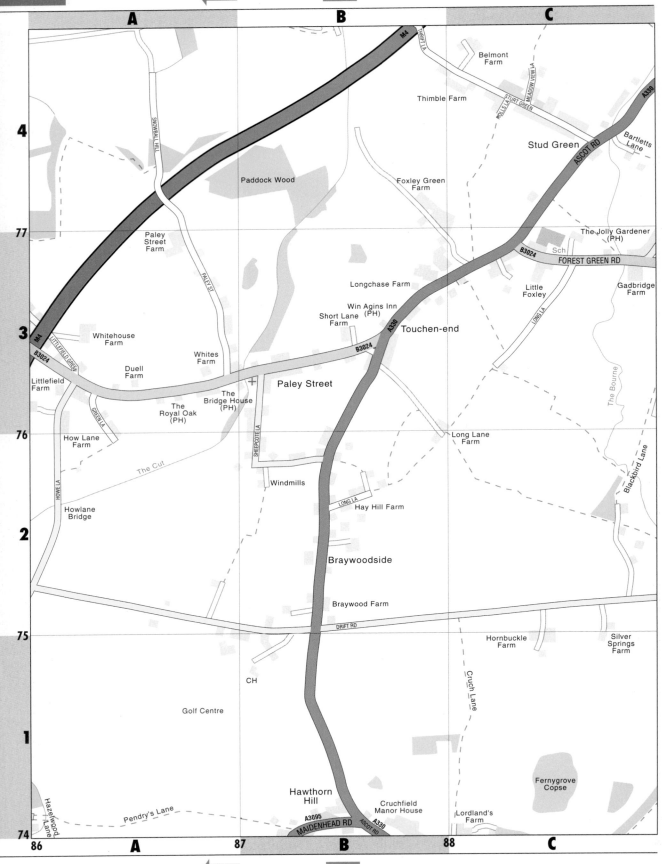

63 39

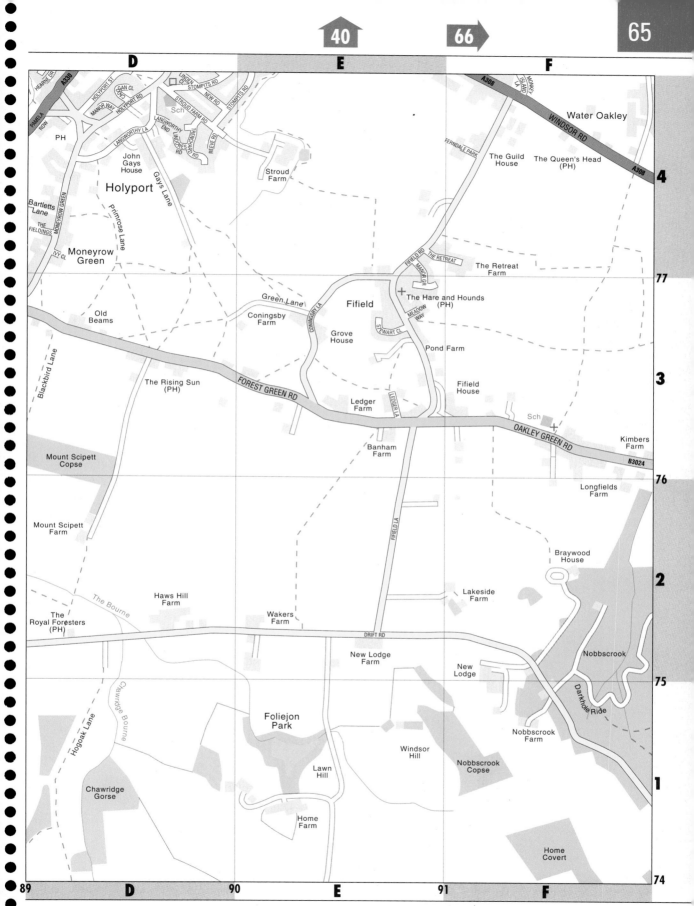

D   E   F

A330
HEARNE DR
PAMELA ROW
MOWBRAY GREEN
HOLYPORT ST
MANOR WAY
HOLYPORT RD
EGAN CL
LINDEN CL
STOMPITS RD
NEW RD
STROUD FARM RD
STOMPITS RD
Sch
LANGWORTHY END
LANGWORTHY LA
TRINGHAM RD
REEVE RD
INCHES RD

A308
MONKEY ISLAND LA
Water Oakley
WINDSOR RD
A308

PH
FERNDALE PARK
The Guild House
The Queen's Head (PH)

John Gays House
Stroud Farm

Holyport
Gays Lane

4

Bartletts Lane
THE FIELDINGS
Primrose Lane
IVY CL

Moneyrow Green

The Retreat Farm
FIELD RD
THE RETREAT
MANOR GR

77

Green Lane
Coningsby Farm
Fifield
MEADOW WAY
STEWART CL
The Hare and Hounds (PH)

Old Beams
Grove House
Pond Farm

Blackbird Lane
The Rising Sun (PH)
FOREST GREEN RD
Ledger Farm
LEDGER LA
Fifield House
3

Sch
OAKLEY GREEN RD
Kimbers Farm
B3024

Banham Farm

Mount Scipett Copse
Longfields Farm
76

Mount Scipett Farm
FIFIELD LA
Braywood House

The Bourne
Haws Hill Farm
Lakeside Farm
2

The Royal Foresters (PH)
Wakers Farm
Nobbscrook

DRIFT RD
New Lodge Farm
New Lodge
75

Hogoak Lane
Chawridge Bourne
Foliejon Park
Windsor Hill
Nobbscrook Farm
Darkhole Ride
Nobbscrook Copse

Lawn Hill
Chawridge Gorse
Home Farm
Home Covert
1

89   D   90   E   91   F   74

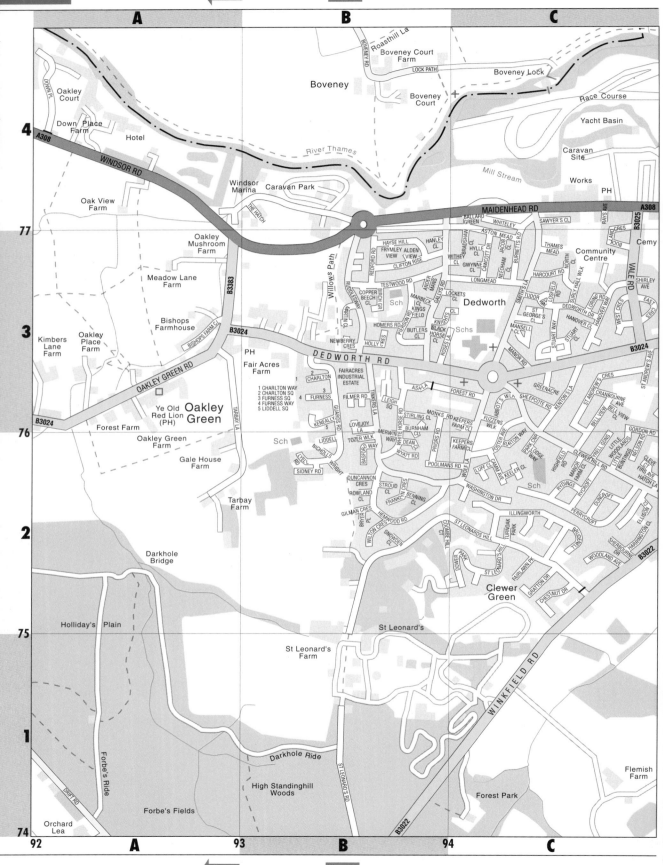

A

B

C

Roasthill La

Boveney Rd

Boveney Court Farm

LOCK PATH

Boveney Lock

Boveney

Boveney Court

Race Course

Yacht Basin

Oakley Court

Down Pl

River Thames

Caravan Site

Works

PH

4

A308

Down Place Farm

Hotel

Mill Stream

WINDSOR RD

Oak View Farm

Windsor Marina

Caravan Park

THE HATCH

MAIDENHEAD RD

A308

B3025

Oakley Mushroom Farm

77

BALLARD GREEN

WHITELEY

SAWYER'S CL

RAYS AVE

LAND CRES

BUCK

Cemy

HAYSE HILL

HANLEY CL

ASTON MEAD

BRADSHAW

JACOB CL

THAMES MEAD

Community Centre

VALE RD

SHIRLEY AVE

Meadow Lane Farm

B3383

REDFORD

FRYMLEY VIEW

HYLLE CL

ALDEN VIEW

WITHE CL

GWYNNE CL

CAWCOTT CL

BURNETTS RD

HARCOURT RD

NORTH

EAST

Bishops Farmhouse

CLIFTON RISE

TESTWOOD CL

LONGMEAD

ALVER

GALLS RD

SMITH LA

TUDOR

LOSFIELD RD

LORING RD

HANOVER WAY

WEST CRES

3

Kimbers Lane Farm

Oakley Place Farm

BISHOPS FARM CL

B3024

COPPER BEECH

BIRCH GR

Sch

MARBECK CL

KINGS FIELD

LOCKETS CL

ST GEORGE'S

DEDWORTH DR

HANOVER CL

Dedworth

Schs

HOMERS RD

PIERSON RD

BLACK HORSE CL

STUART WAY

STUART RD

Forest Farm

OAKLEY GREEN RD

PH

Fair Acres Farm

NEWBERRY CRES

HOLLY CL

BUTLERS CL

ROSE LA

MANSELL CL

MANOR RD

B3024

DEDWORTH RD

1 CHARLTON WAY

FAIRACRES INDUSTRIAL ESTATE

FOREST RD

GREENACRE

ST ANDREW'S CRES

CRANBOURNE AVE

2 CHARLTON SQ

1 CHARLTON

3

FILMER RD

ASH LA

SHEEPCOTE RD

KERTON LA

BELL VIEW CL

3 FURNESS SQ

2 CHARLTON

3 FURNESS

LEIGH SQ

TINKERS LA

FUZZENS WLK

ST ANDREW'S AVE

BELL VIEW

GORDON RD

4 FURNESS WAY

4 FURNESS

STIRLING CL

MONKS RD

KEEPERS FARM CL

ABBOTT'S WLK

FOSTER AVE

BURTON WAY

CLEVE CT

5 LIDDELL SQ

KENEALY RD

GUARDS RD

NELSON RD

76

B3024

Ye Old Red Lion (PH)

Oakley Green

TARBAY LA

Sch

LIDDELL

LOVEJOY LA

MERWIN WAY

BURNHAM CL

DEAN

PRIORS RD

KEEPERS FARM CL

PARK LODGE WAY

HIGHFIELD RD

MANOR FARM CL

CLEWER HILL RD

TYRELL CL

WOODLANDS

FIRS AVE

HATCH LA

TOZER WLK

LYELL RD

NICHOLL'S WRIGHT

WYATT RD

POOLMANS RD

WOLF LA

Sch

RYDINGS

Oakley Green Farm

SIDNEY RD

BASFORD WAY

DUNCANNON CRES

STROUD CL

WASHINGTON DR

LUFF CL

CALM AVE

KEELER CT

RYCROFT

PERRYCROFT

ELLISON CL

Gale House Farm

ROWLAND CL

FRANKLYN CRES

BENNING CL

ILLINGWORTH

BRIDGER

SHERBOURNE DR

HARRINGTON CL

2

Tarbay Farm

GILMAN CRES

BRYER PL

HEMWOOD RD

WILTON CRES

SNOWDON CL

TURNOAK PARK

WOODLAND AVE

B3022

Darkhole Bridge

COMBE HILL CT

ST LEONARDS HILL

FAIRLAWN PK

Clewer Green

GRATTON DR

CHESTNUT DR

75

Holliday's Plain

St Leonard's

ST LEONARD'S HILL

DOWER PARK

St Leonard's Farm

WINKFIELD RD

1

Forbe's Ride

ST LEONARD'S RD

Darkhole Ride

High Standinghill Woods

Forest Park

Flemish Farm

DRIFT RD

Forbe's Fields

B3022

74

Orchard Lea

92

A

93

B

94

C

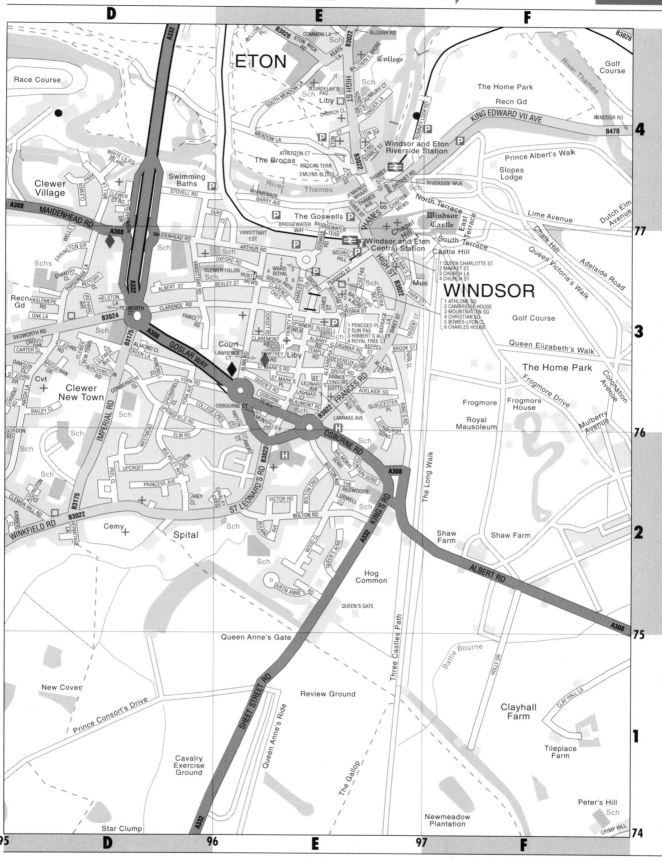

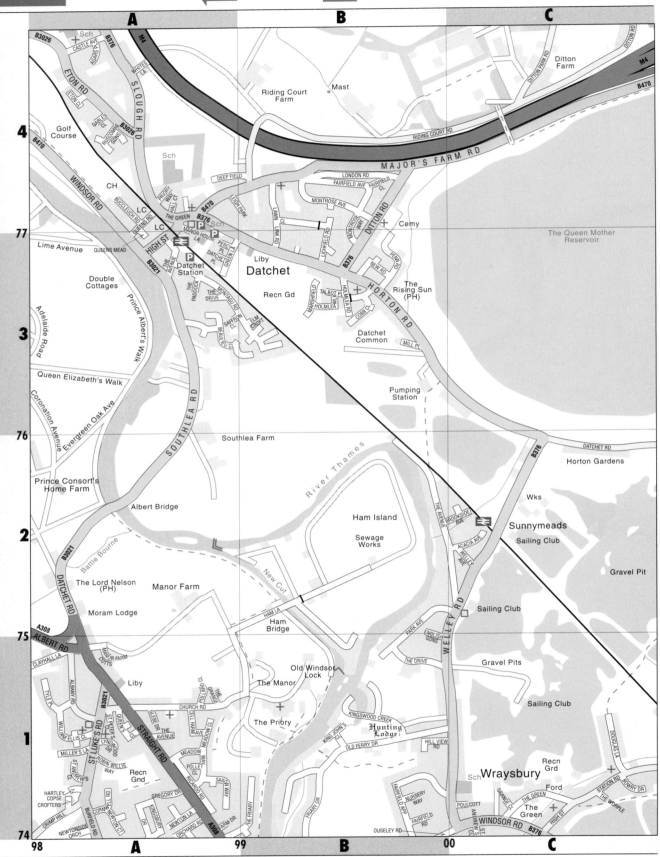

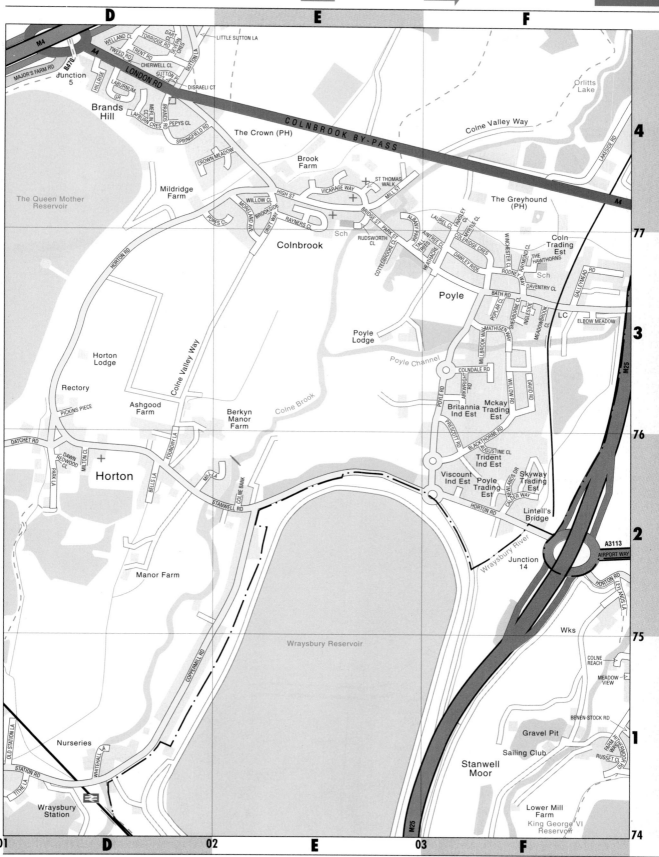

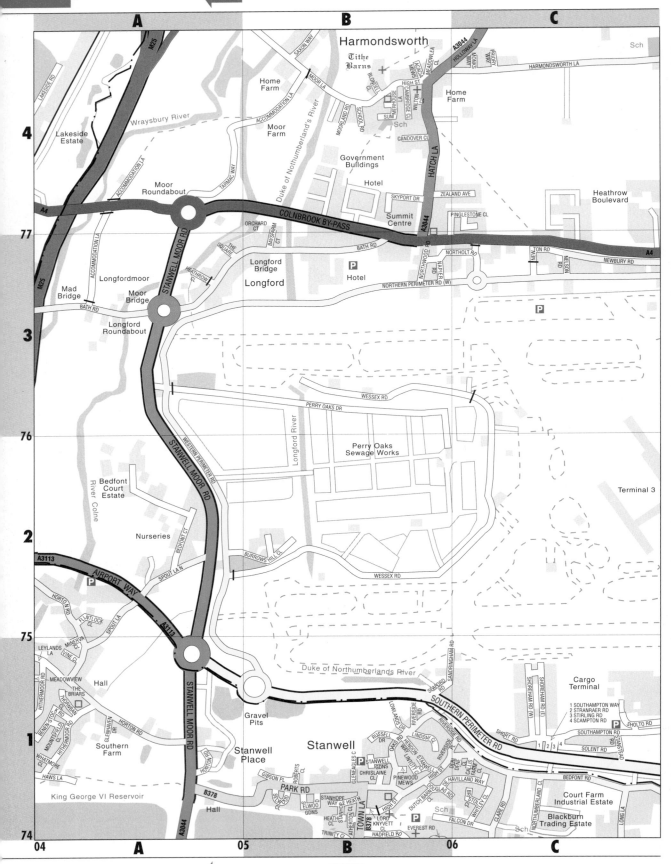

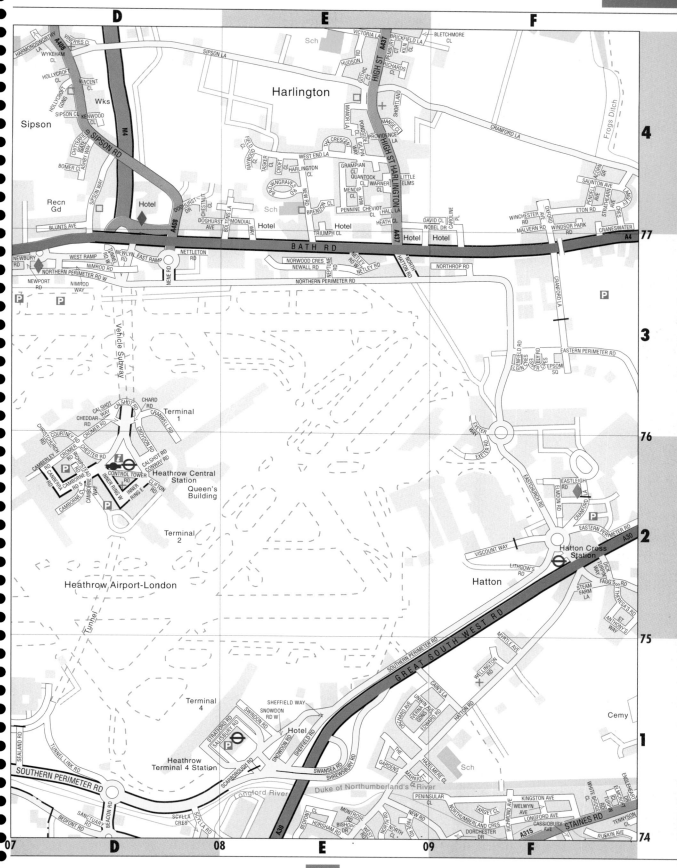

Harlington

Sipson

Heathrow Airport-London

Heathrow Central Station

Queen's Building

Terminal 1

Terminal 2

Terminal 4

Heathrow Terminal 4 Station

Hatton

Hatton Cross Station

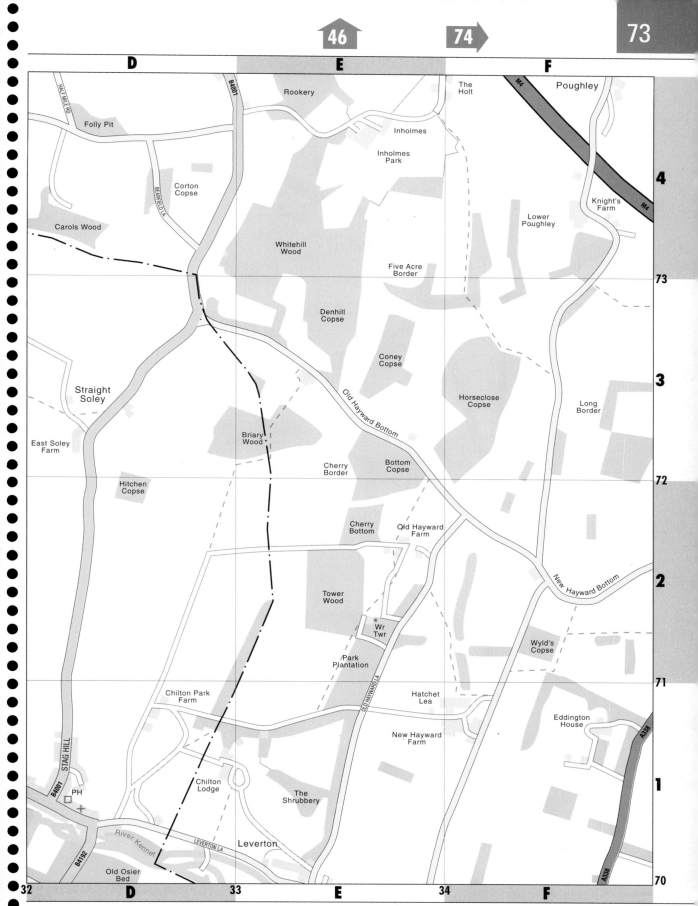

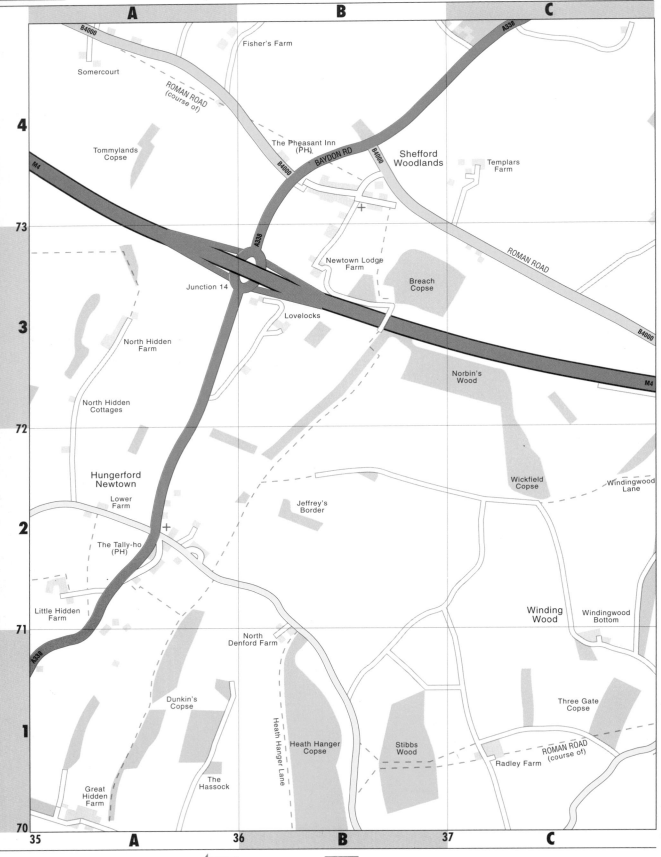

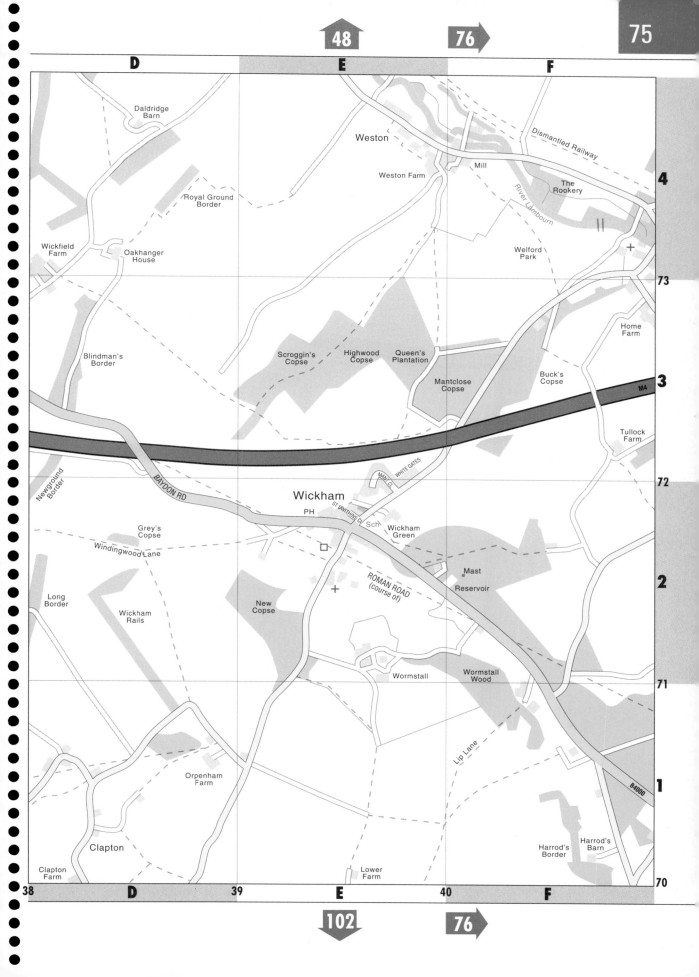

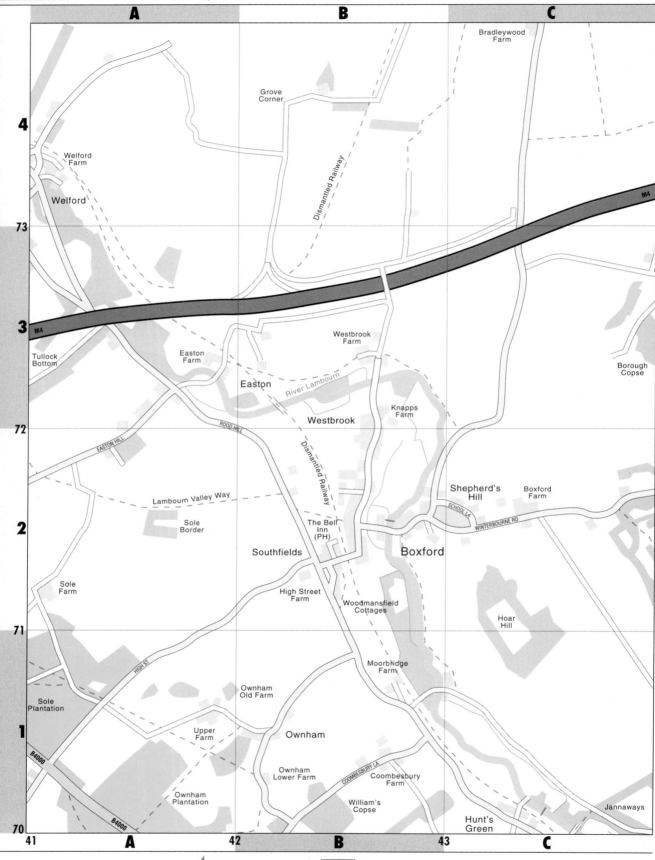

A   **B**   **C**

4

Bradleywood
Farm

Grove
Corner

Welford
Farm

Welford

73

M4

M4

3

M4

Tullock
Bottom

Easton
Farm

Westbrook
Farm

Borough
Copse

Easton

River Lambourn

Westbrook

Knapps
Farm

72

ROOD HILL

EASTON HILL

Lambourn Valley Way

Shepherd's
Hill

Boxford
Farm

Dismantled Railway

Sole
Border

The Bell
Inn
(PH)

SCHOOL LA

WINTERBOURNE RD

2

Southfields

Boxford

Sole
Farm

High Street
Farm

Woodmansfield
Cottages

Hoar
Hill

71

HIGH ST

Moorbridge
Farm

Sole
Plantation

Ownham
Old Farm

1

Upper
Farm

Ownham

B4000

Ownham
Lower Farm

COOMBESBURY LA

Coombesbury
Farm

Jannaways

Ownham
Plantation

William's
Copse

Hunt's
Green

70

B4000

41   **A**   42   **B**   43   **C**

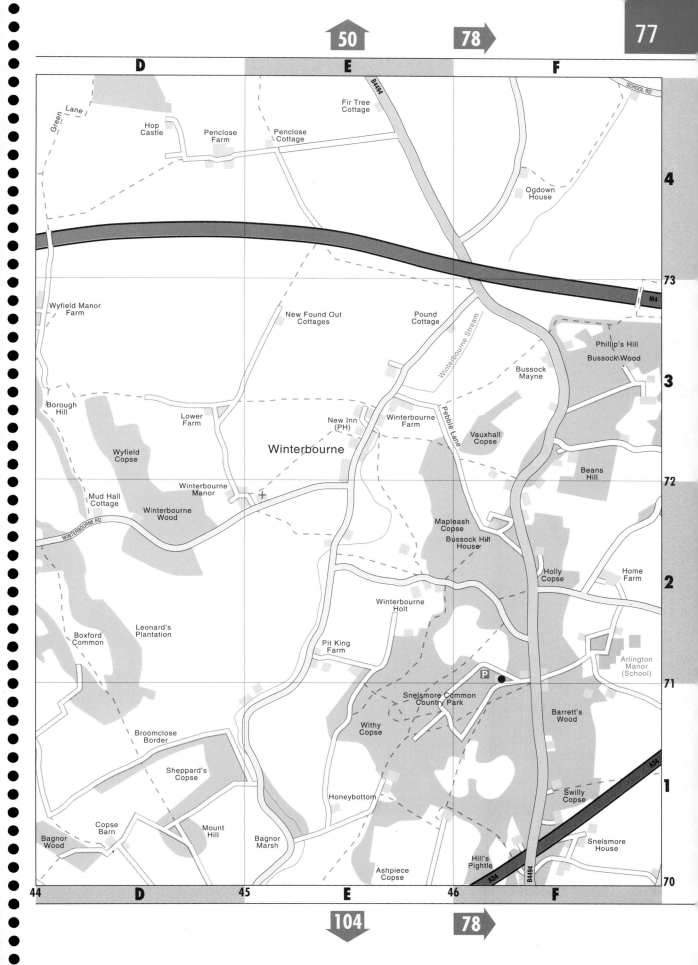

52
80

D   **E**   **F**

M4

Oare

MANOR LA

Chalkpit Piece

EVERINGTON LA

Birch Cottage

Rook's Copse

M4

Kiln Farm

COLYER CL

ORCHARD CL

Works

Little Hungerford

Windmill Farm

Common Firs

Box Wood

4

Roebuck Wood

CHAPEL LA

DEACONS LA

POND LA

Cuckoo Pits

HAMPSTEAD NORREYS RD

B4009

Spring Copse

DINES WAY

Hermitage

KILN CL

YATTENDON RD

Poundpit Piece

Parsons Piece

Well Lane

Box Cottage

NEWBURY RD

DOCTORS LA

BRIANT'S PIECE

New Plantation

States Hill Wood

Wellhouse Farm

73

PRIORS COURT RD

PH

LIPSCOMB CL

CHARLOTTE CL

Pheasant Hill Wood

WELLHOUSE LA

Long Grove

CRABTREE LA

Allen's Allotment

Wellhouse

3

LONG LA

Faircross Farm

Grimsbury Castle

MARLSTON RD

Fifield Farm

Fairfield Farm

Grimsbury Wood

Marlston Cottages

SLANTING HILL

Grimsbury Bank

Round Hill Wood

Adams Lane Copse

72

SANDY CL

RED SHUTE IND EST

B4009

The Common

Gravelly Pightles

Boar's Hole Farm

Brockhurst School (Marlston House)

SAWMILL RD

Longlane

RED SHUTE HILL

Money's Allotment

Fence Wood

Fence Lane

West Wood

2

Hangings Copse

Downe House School

WILLIS CL

Bucklebury Alley

Bushnell's Copse

Stonecroft Copse

71

Nothing Hill

HERMITAGE RD

Cold Ash Common

DROVE LA

Westrop Green

Hunters Hill Wood

Cold Ash Farm

Westrop Wood

Sermons Copse

Westrop Hill

Oaken Copse

1

FISHER'S LA

SEWELL CL

GORSE COTTAGE DR

WOODSIDE

ANNADALE

Westrop Farm

Malthouse Wood

Holly Farm House

Henwicklands Copse

THIRTOVER

Thirtover

ASHMORE GREEN RD

COLD ASH HILL

THE RIDGE

Sch

Salt's Copse

70

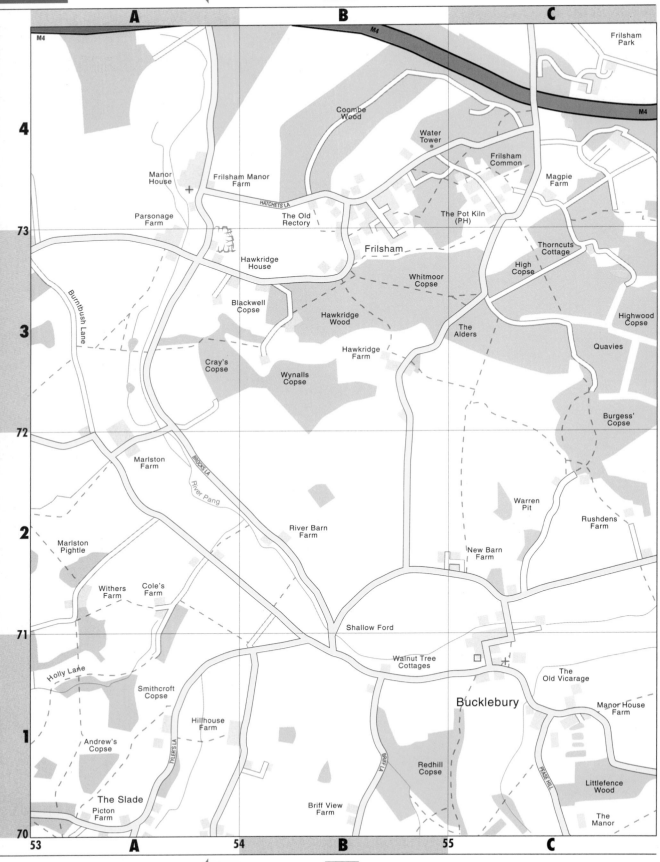

79
53

M4

A
B
C

M4

Frilsham
Park

4

Coombe
Wood

Water
Tower

Frilsham
Common

Magpie
Farm

Manor
House

Frilsham Manor
Farm

HATCHETS LA

The Pot Kiln
(PH)

The Old
Rectory

Parsonage
Farm

73

Frilsham

Thorncuts
Cottage

Hawkridge
House

Whitmoor
Copse

High
Copse

Blackwell
Copse

Hawkridge
Wood

Highwood
Copse

The
Alders

Quavies

Burntbush Lane

3

Cray's
Copse

Hawkridge
Farm

Wynalls
Copse

Burgess'
Copse

72

Marlston
Farm

BROCKS LA

River Pang

Warren
Pit

Rushdens
Farm

2

Marlston
Pightle

River Barn
Farm

New Barn
Farm

Withers
Farm

Cole's
Farm

71

Shallow Ford

Walnut Tree
Cottages

Holly Lane

The
Old Vicarage

Smithcroft
Copse

Bucklebury

Manor House
Farm

1

Hillhouse
Farm

TYLERS LA

Andrew's
Copse

BRIFF LA

Redhill
Copse

PEASE HILL

Littlefence
Wood

The Slade

Picton
Farm

Briff View
Farm

The
Manor

70

53
A
54
B
55
C

79
107

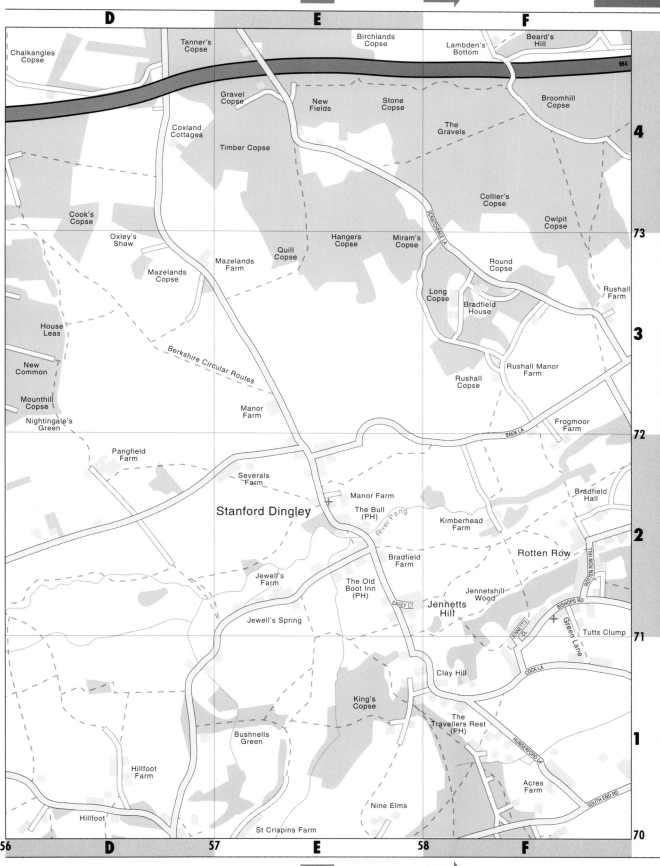

81
55

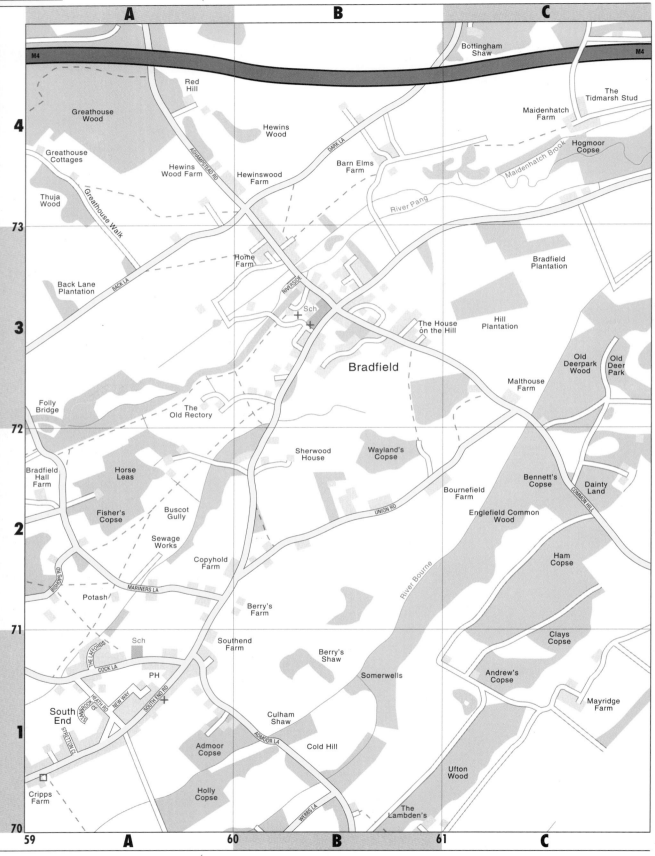

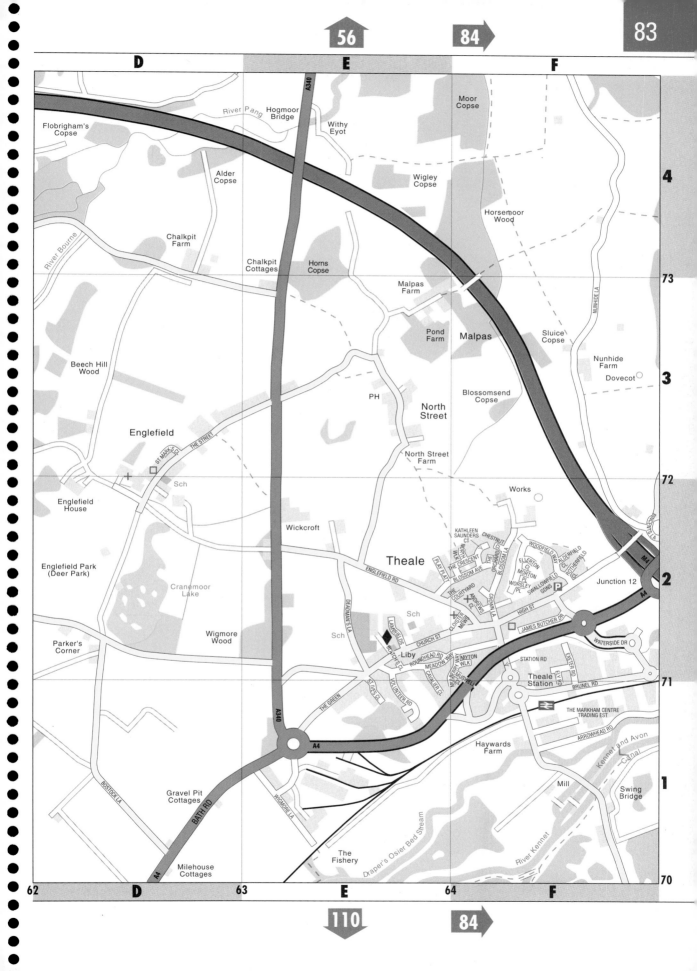

D   E   F

4

Flobrigham's Copse

River Pang   Hogmoor Bridge

Withy Eyot

Moor Copse

Wigley Copse

Alder Copse

Horsemoor Wood

River Bourne

Chalkpit Farm

Chalkpit Cottages

Horns Copse

NUNHIDE LA

73

Malpas Farm

Beech Hill Wood

Pond Farm   Malpas

Sluice Copse

Nunhide Farm

Dovecot

3

PH

North Street

Blossomsend Copse

Englefield

ST MARK'S CL   THE STREET

Sch

North Street Farm

72

Works

Englefield House

Wickcroft

KATHLEEN SAUNDERS CT   CHESTNUT

WOODFIELD WAY   ALDERFIELD

Theale

PLAY PLAT   THE CRESCENT   BLOSSOM AVE

THE ORCHARD   ELLERTON CL

MORTON PL   WORSLEY PL

ROTHERFIELD

PR'T'S LA

Junction 12

2

Englefield Park (Deer Park)

Cranemoor Lake

ENGLEFIELD RD

THE COURTYARD   ANDREWS CL

CROWN LA   SWALLOWFIELD GDNS

HIGH ST

JAMES BUTCHER DR

M4   A4

WATERSIDE DR

Parker's Corner

Wigmore Wood

DEADMAN'S LA

Sch

Sch

LAMBFIELDS   HEATON CL

CHURCH ST   CLOISTERS MEWS

Liby

ROUNDHEAD RD   MEADOW WAY

MYTON WLK

MULBERRY WAY   MUSTFIELD

STATION RD

EXETER RD   ELY RD

BRUNEL RD

71

THE GREEN   ST IVES CL   VOLUNTEER RD

CAVALIER CL

Theale Station

THE MARKHAM CENTRE TRADING EST

A340

A4

ARROWHEAD RD

Haywards Farm

Kennet and Avon Canal

1

BOSTOCK LA

Gravel Pit Cottages

BATH RD

WIGMORE LA

Mill

Swing Bridge

The Fishery

Draper's Osier Bed Stream

River Kennet

Milehouse Cottages

70

62   D   63   E   64   F

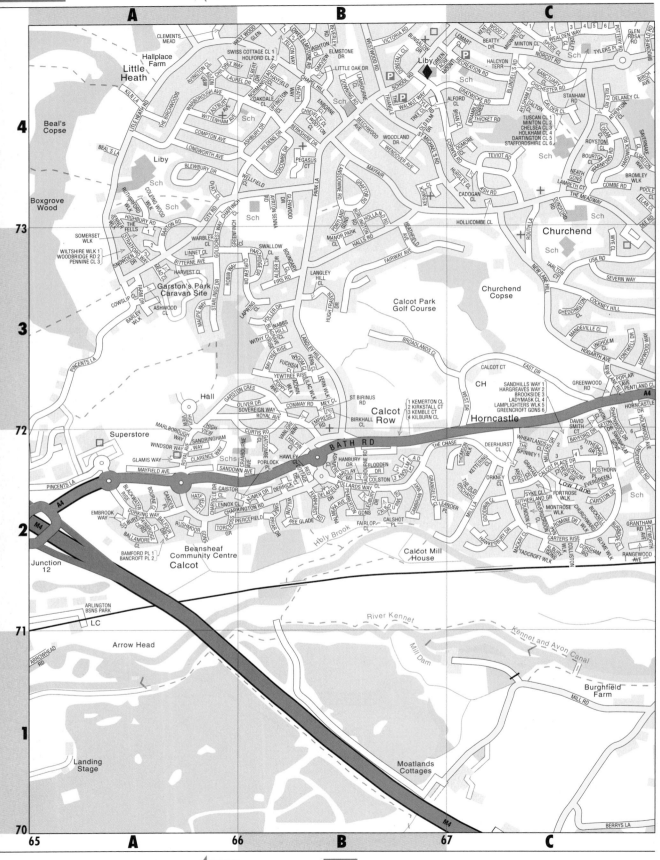

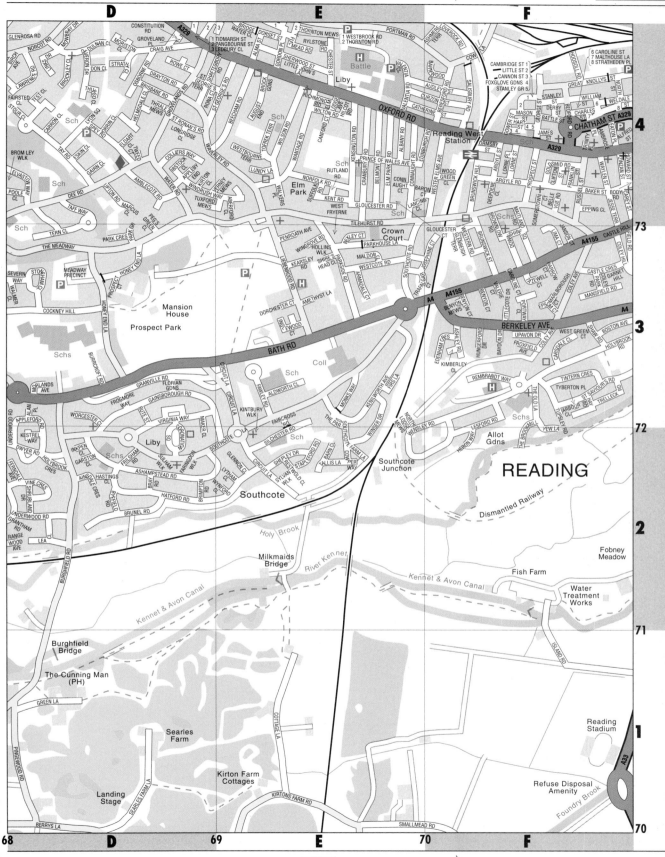

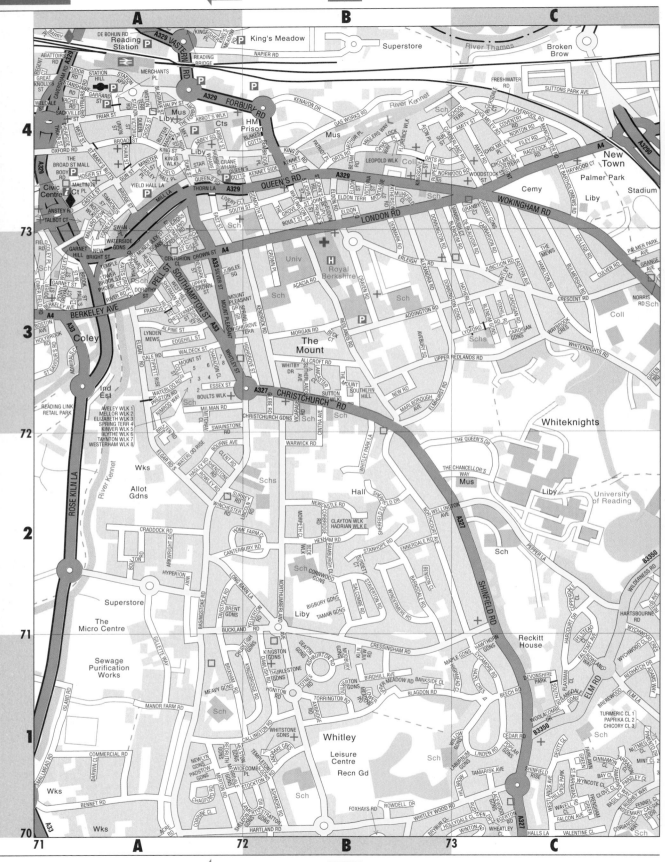

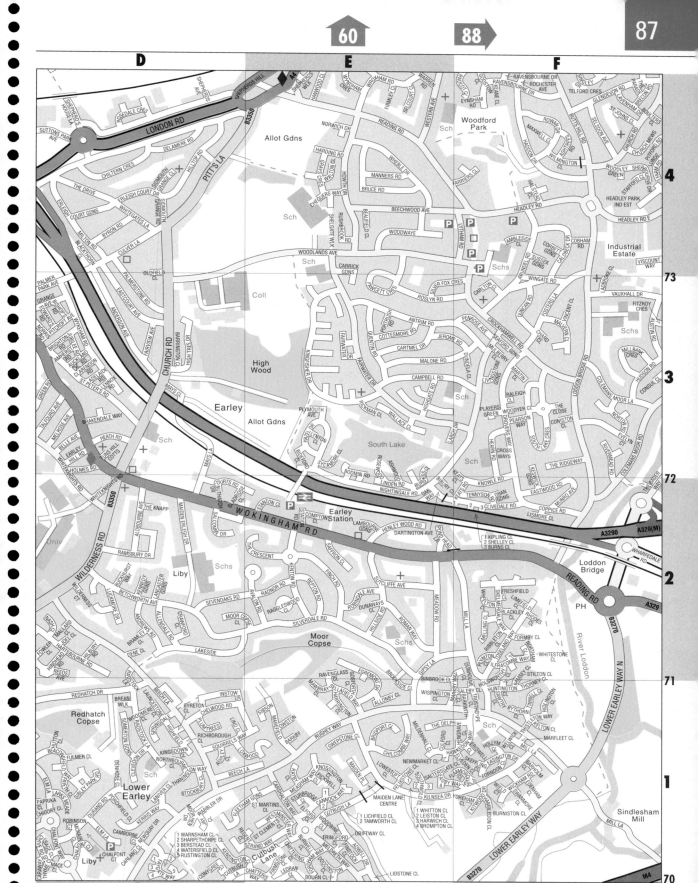

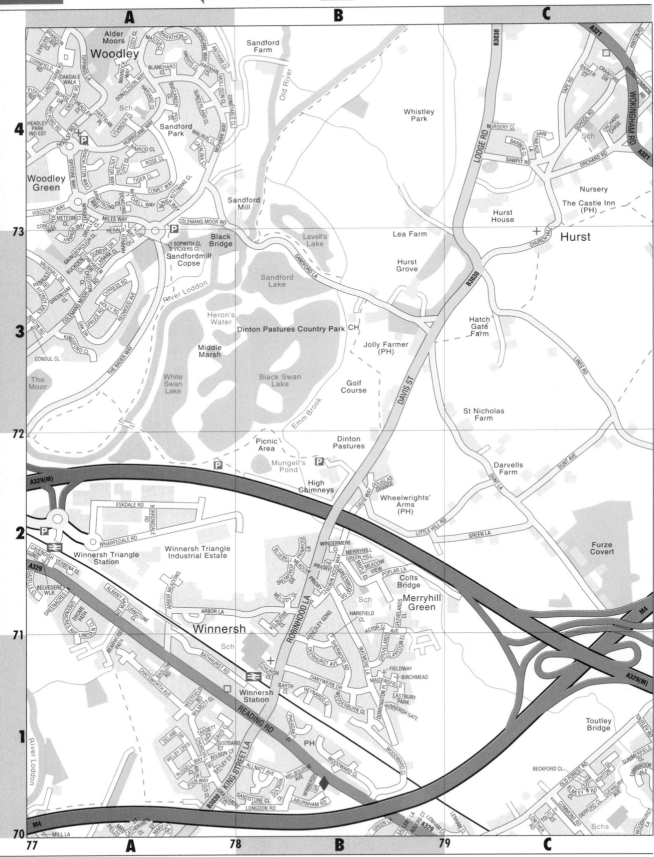

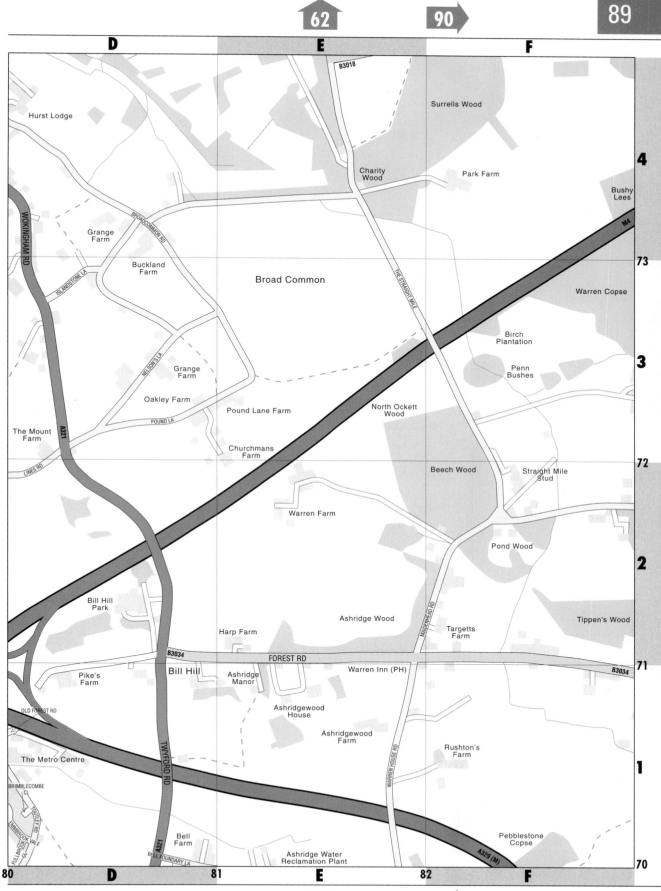

Hurst Lodge

Surrells Wood

Charity Wood

Park Farm

Bushy Lees

B3018

WOKINGHAM RD

BROADCOMMON RD

Grange Farm

Buckland Farm

Broad Common

M4

Warren Copse

ISLANDSTONE LA

NELSON'S LA

Grange Farm

Birch Plantation

Penn Bushes

THE STRAIGHT MILE

Oakley Farm

POUND LA

Pound Lane Farm

North Ockett Wood

The Mount Farm

A321

LINES RD

Churchmans Farm

Beech Wood

Straight Mile Stud

Warren Farm

Pond Wood

Bill Hill Park

Ashridge Wood

MAIDENHEAD RD

Targetts Farm

Tippen's Wood

Harp Farm

B3034

FOREST RD

Pike's Farm

Bill Hill

Ashridge Manor

Warren Inn (PH)

B3034

OLD FOREST RD

TWYFORD RD

Ashridgewood House

WARREN HOUSE RD

The Metro Centre

BRIMBLECOMBE CL

TOUTLEY RD

EMMBROOK VALE

FULLBROOK CRES

Ashridgewood Farm

Rushton's Farm

A321

BELL FOUNDARY LA

Bell Farm

Ashridge Water Reclamation Plant

A329 (M)

Pebblestone Copse

4

73

3

72

2

71

1

70

D

E

F

80

81

82

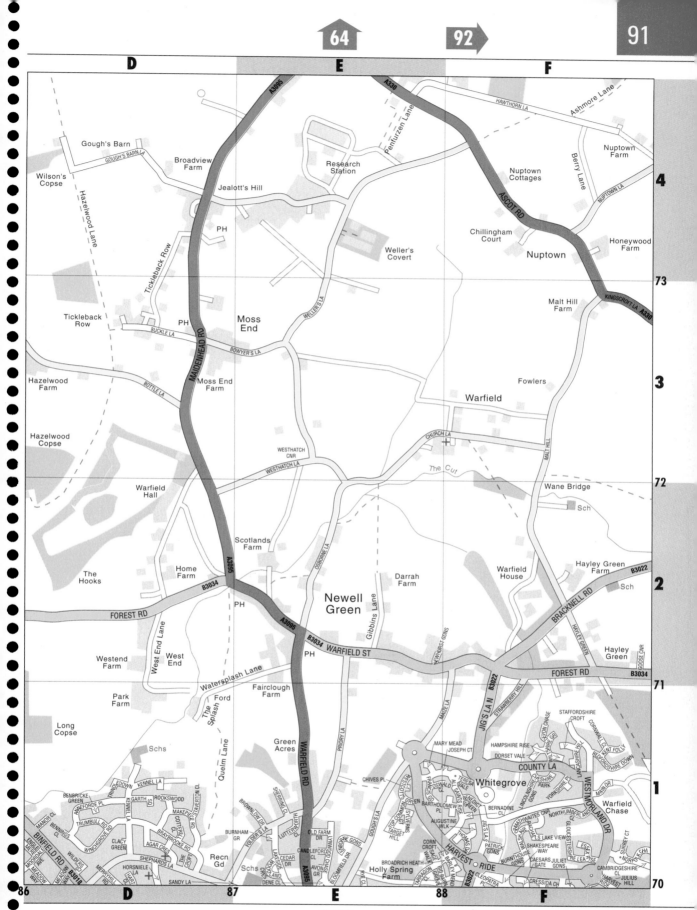

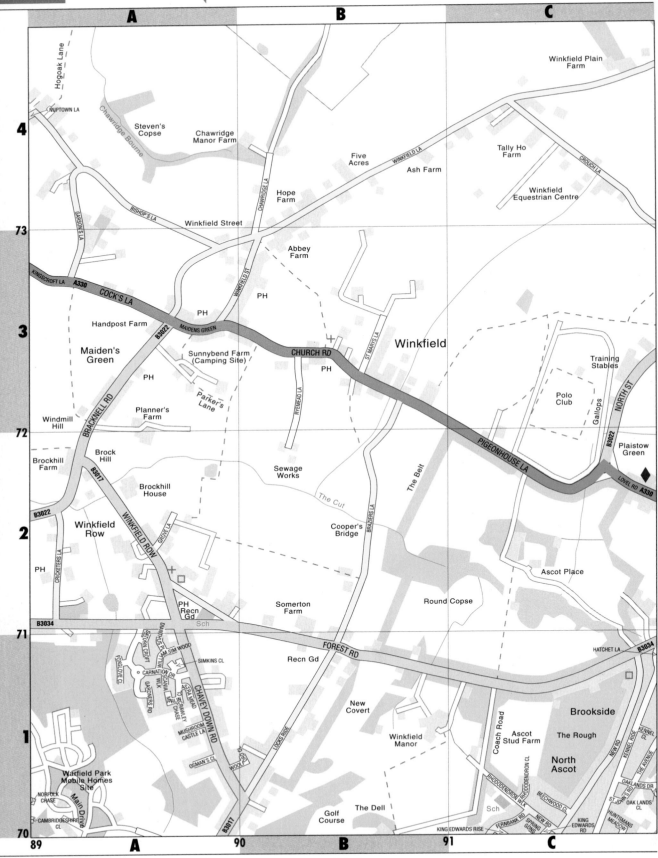

91
65

A B C

Hogoak Lane

Winkfield Plain
Farm

Nuptown La

4

Steven's
Copse

Chawridge
Manor Farm

Chawridge Bourne

Garson's La

Five
Acres

Winkfield La

Ash Farm

Tally Ho
Farm

Crouch La

Winkfield
Equestrian Centre

Bishop's La

Chawridge La

Hope
Farm

73

Winkfield Street

Winkfield St

Abbey
Farm

Kingscroft La   A330

COCK'S LA

Handpost Farm

B3022

MAIDENS GREEN

PH

PH

PH

Church Rd

PH

Winkfield

St Mary's La

Training
Stables

3

Maiden's
Green

Sunnybend Farm
(Camping Site)

Bracknell Rd

PH

Planner's
Farm

Parker's
Lane

Ryemead La

PH

Polo
Club

Gallops

North St

Windmill
Hill

72

Brockhill
Farm

Brock
Hill

B3017

Brockhill
House

Sewage
Works

The Cut

The Belt

Pigeonhouse La

B3022

Plaistow
Green

Lovel Rd   A330

B3022

Winkfield
Row

Winkfield Row

Grove La

Cooper's
Bridge

Brazers La

Ascot Place

2

PH

Crickers La

PH   Recn
Gd

Somerton
Farm

Round Copse

B3034

Sch

71

Forest Rd

Hatchet La   B3034

Dianthas Pl   Sim Wood

Satori Croft

Simkins Cl

Recn Gd

Foxglove Cl

Carnation Dr

Scavia La

Gardners Rd

Crawley Chase

Chavey Down Rd

Locks Ride

New
Covert

Winkfield
Manor

Coach Road

Ascot
Stud Farm

Brookside

The Rough

New Rd

Kennel Ride

Kennel Cl

1

Mushroom
Castle La

Osman's Cl

Woolford Cl

Warfield Park
Mobile Homes
Site

Norfolk
Chase

Main Drive

Cambridgeshire
Cl

B3017

Golf
Course

The Dell

North
Ascot

Rhododendron Wlk

Rhododendron Cl

Beechwood Cl

New Rd

Sch

King Edwards Rise

Fernbank Rd

Spring Gdns

King
Edwards
Rd

St Jo

Oaklands Dr

The Avenue

Oak Lands
Cl

Huntsmans
Meadow

King
Edwards
Rd

70

89   A   90   B   91   C

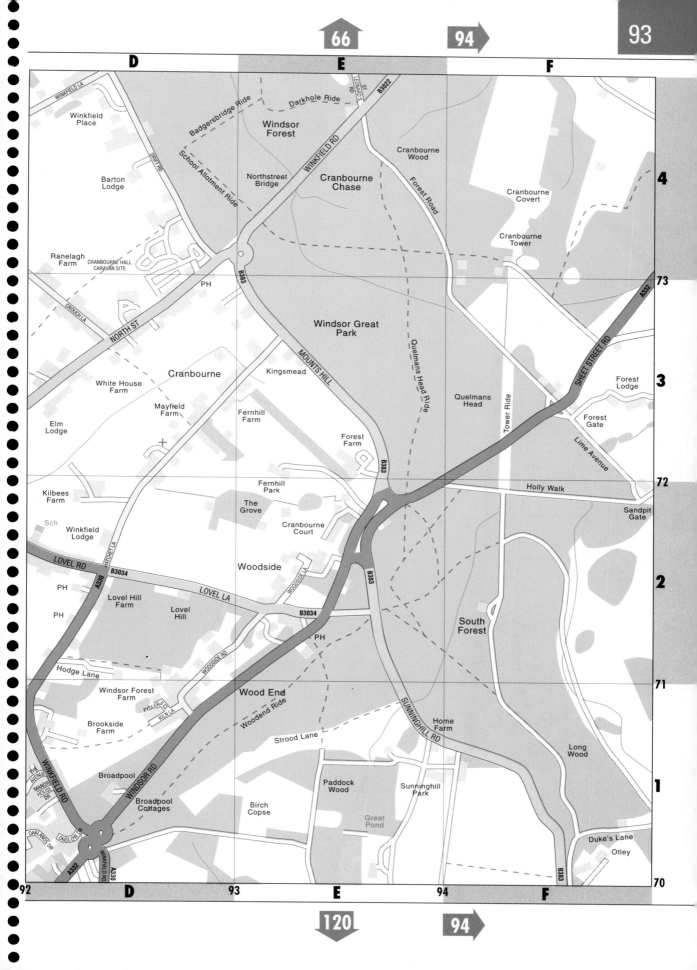

D

E

F

Winkfield La

Winkfield Place

Barton Lodge

DRIFT RD

Badgersbridge Ride

School Allotment Ride

Windsor Forest

Darkhole Ride

ST LEONARD'S

B3022

WINKFIELD RD

Northstreet Bridge

Cranbourne Chase

Cranbourne Wood

Forest Road

Cranbourne Covert

Cranbourne Tower

4

Ranelagh Farm

CRANBOURNE HALL CARAVAN SITE

PH

B383

Windsor Great Park

Quelmans Head Ride

A332

73

CROUCH LA

NORTH ST

Cranbourne

White House Farm

Kingsmead

MOUNTS HILL

Quelmans Head

Tower Ride

SHEET STREET RD

Forest Lodge

3

Elm Lodge

Mayfield Farm

Fernhill Farm

Forest Farm

Lime Avenue

Forest Gate

Kilbees Farm

Fernhill Park

The Grove

Cranbourne Court

B383

Holly Walk

72

Sch

Winkfield Lodge

HATCHET LA

Woodside

WOODSIDE LA

Sandpit Gate

LOVEL RD

B3034

A330

LOVEL LA

B3034

B383

2

PH

PH

Lovel Hill Farm

Lovel Hill

South Forest

Hodge Lane

WOODSIDE RD

PH

71

Windsor Forest Farm

PYDLER CT

KILN LA

Wood End

Woodend Ride

SUNNINGHILL RD

Home Farm

Brookside Farm

Strood Lane

Long Wood

THE AVENUE

WINKFIELD RD

WINDSOR RD

MANOR HOUSE DR

Broadpool

Broadpool Cottages

Birch Copse

Paddock Wood

Sunninghill Park

1

Great Pond

Duke's Lane

Otley

OAKLANDS DR

ONSLOW DR

A332

WINKFIELD RD

A330

B383

70

92

D

93

E

94

F

93
67

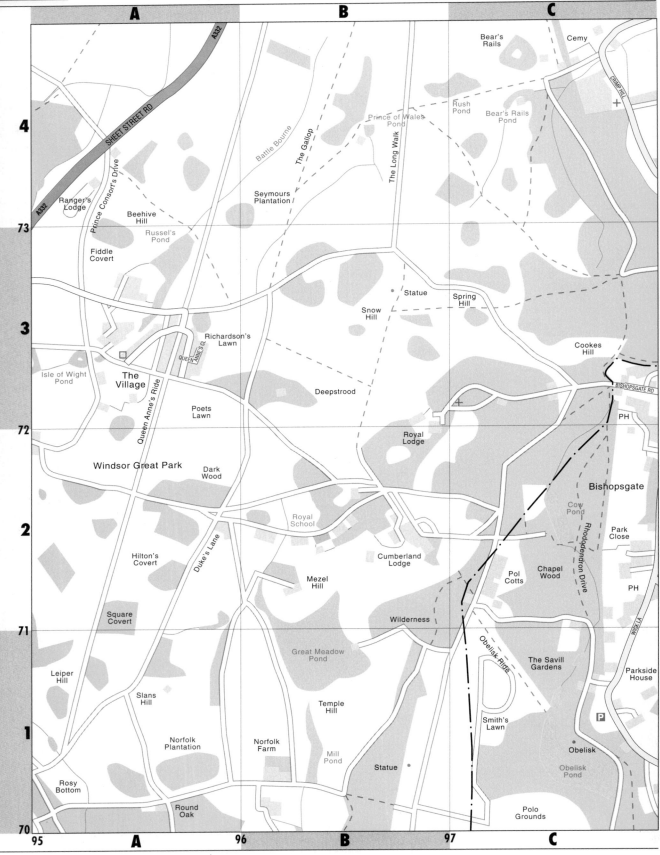

A B C

A32

SHEET STREET RD

Prince Consort's Drive

4

Ranger's
Lodge

Beehive
Hill

Fiddle
Covert

Russel's
Pond

Battle Bourne

The Gallop

Seymours
Plantation

Prince of Wales
Pond

The Long Walk

Bear's
Rails

Cemy

CRIMP HILL

Rush
Pond

Bear's Rails
Pond

+

73

Statue

Snow
Hill

Spring
Hill

Cookes
Hill

3

Richardson's
Lawn

QUEEN ANNE'S CL

The Village

Isle of Wight
Pond

Queen Anne's Ride

Poets
Lawn

Deepstrood

+

BISHOPSGATE RD

PH

72

Windsor Great Park

Dark
Wood

Royal
Lodge

Bishopsgate

Cow
Pond

Rhododendron Drive

Park
Close

Hilton's
Covert

Duke's Lane

Royal
School

Cumberland
Lodge

Pol
Cotts

Chapel
Wood

PH

WICK LA

2

Mezel
Hill

Square
Covert

Wilderness

Obelisk Ride

The Savill
Gardens

Parkside
House

71

Leiper
Hill

Slans
Hill

Great Meadow
Pond

Temple
Hill

Smith's
Lawn

P

1

Norfolk
Plantation

Norfolk
Farm

Mill
Pond

Statue

Obelisk

Obelisk
Pond

Rosy
Bottom

Round
Oak

Polo
Grounds

70

95 A 96 B 97 C

93
121

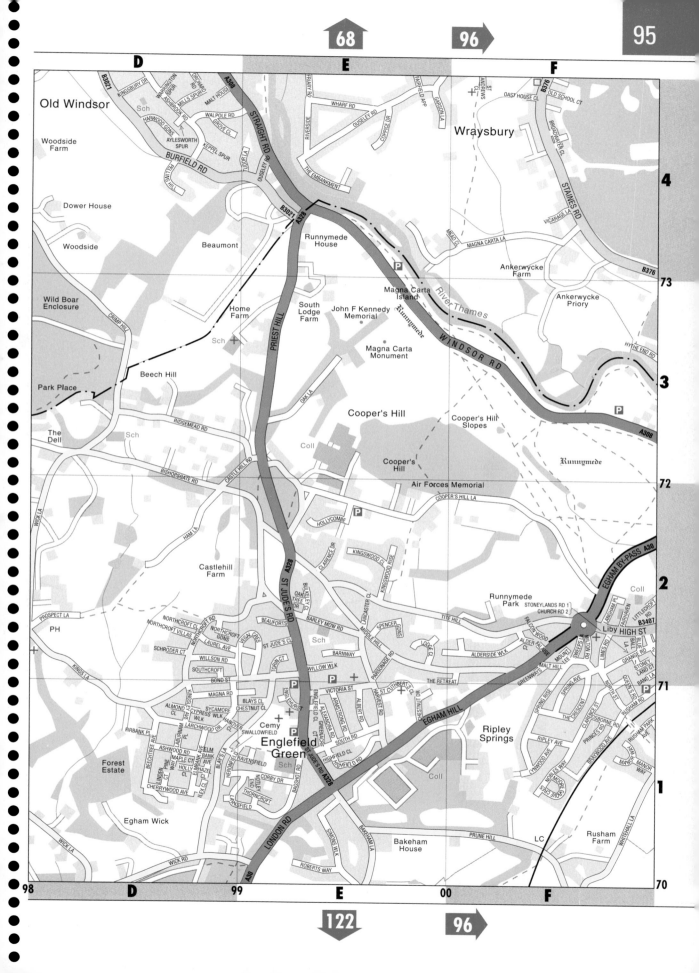

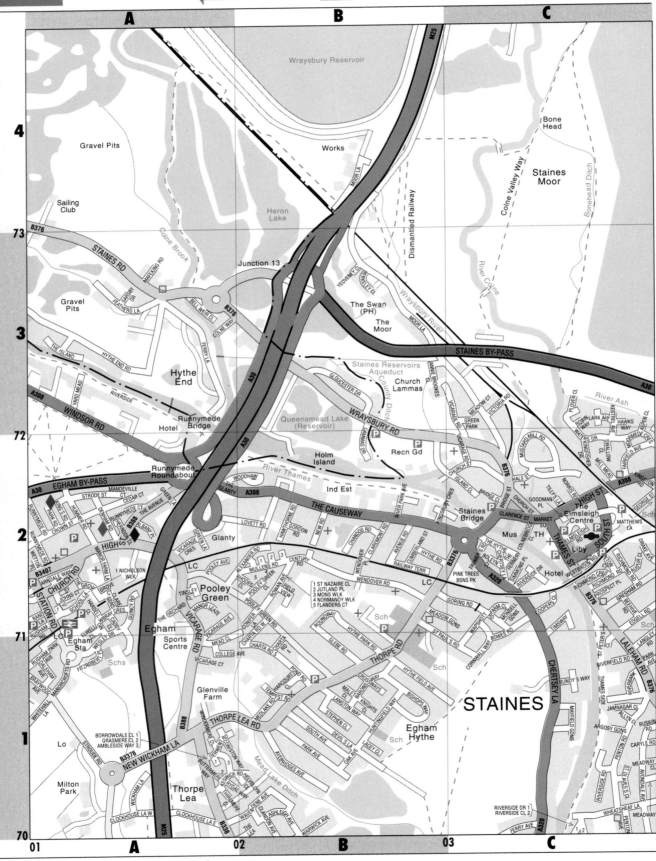

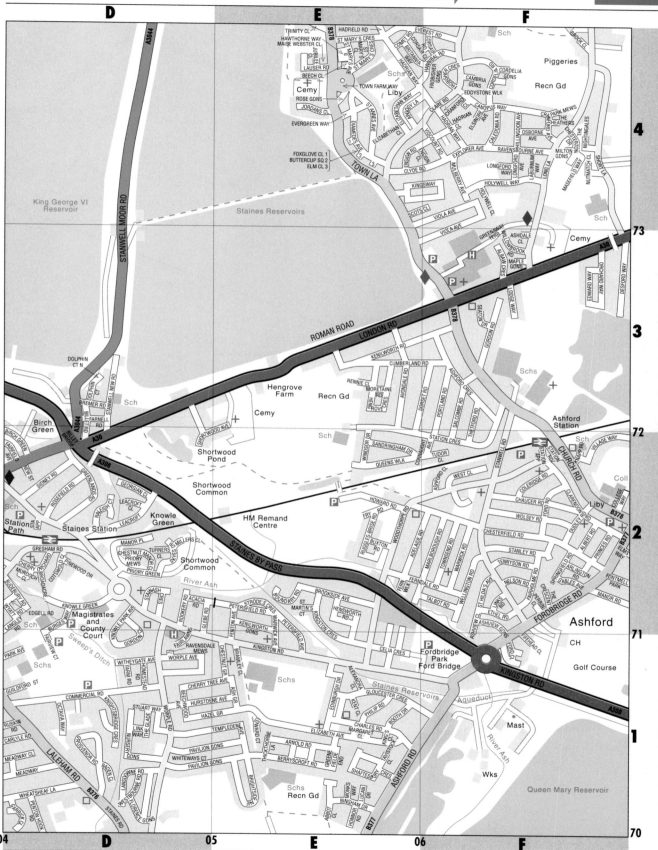

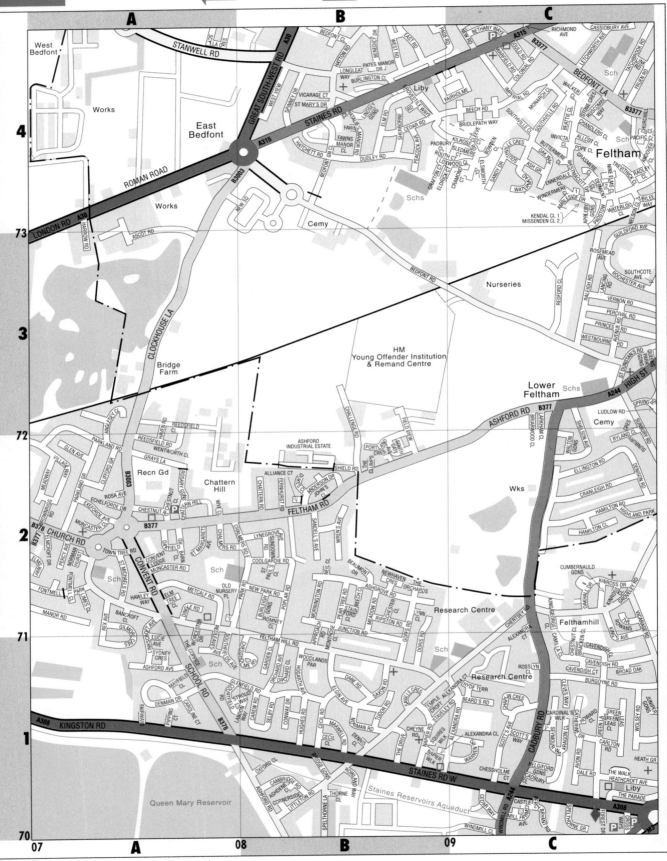

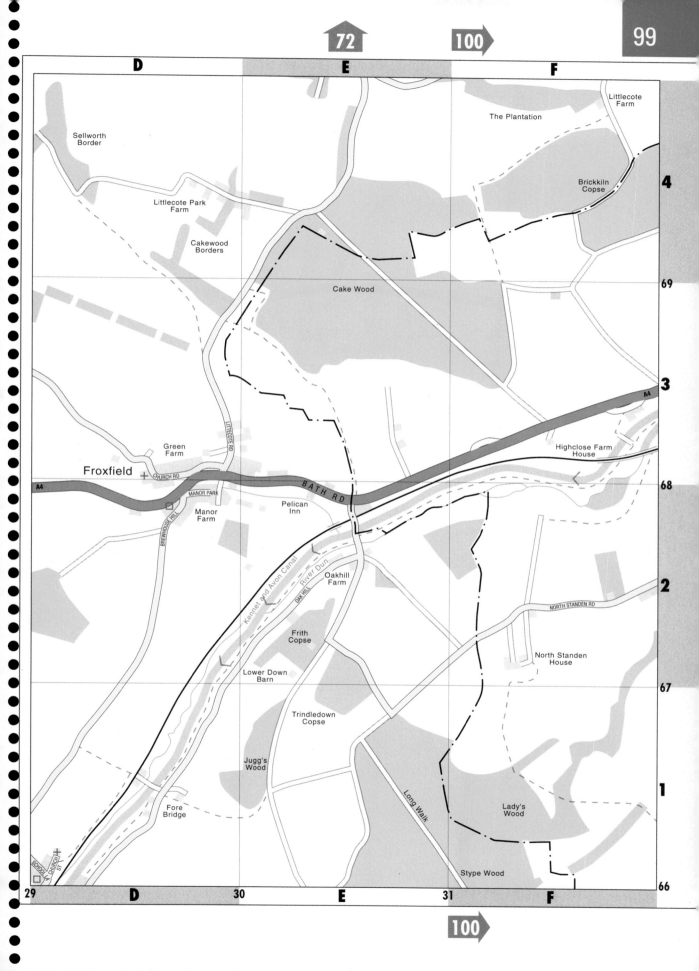

D E F

4
69
3
68
2
67
1
66

Sellworth Border

The Plantation

Littlecote Farm

Littlecote Park Farm

Brickkiln Copse

Cakewood Borders

Cake Wood

Green Farm

LITTLECOTE RD

Froxfield

CHURCH RD

A4

BATH RD

Highclose Farm House

A4

MANOR PARK

Manor Farm

Pelican Inn

BREWHOUSE HILL

Kennet and Avon Canal

River Dun

OAKHILL

Oakhill Farm

NORTH STANDEN RD

North Standen House

Frith Copse

Lower Down Barn

Trindledown Copse

Jugg's Wood

Long Walk

Lady's Wood

Fore Bridge

SCHOOL

CHURCH ST

Stype Wood

29 D 30 E 31 F

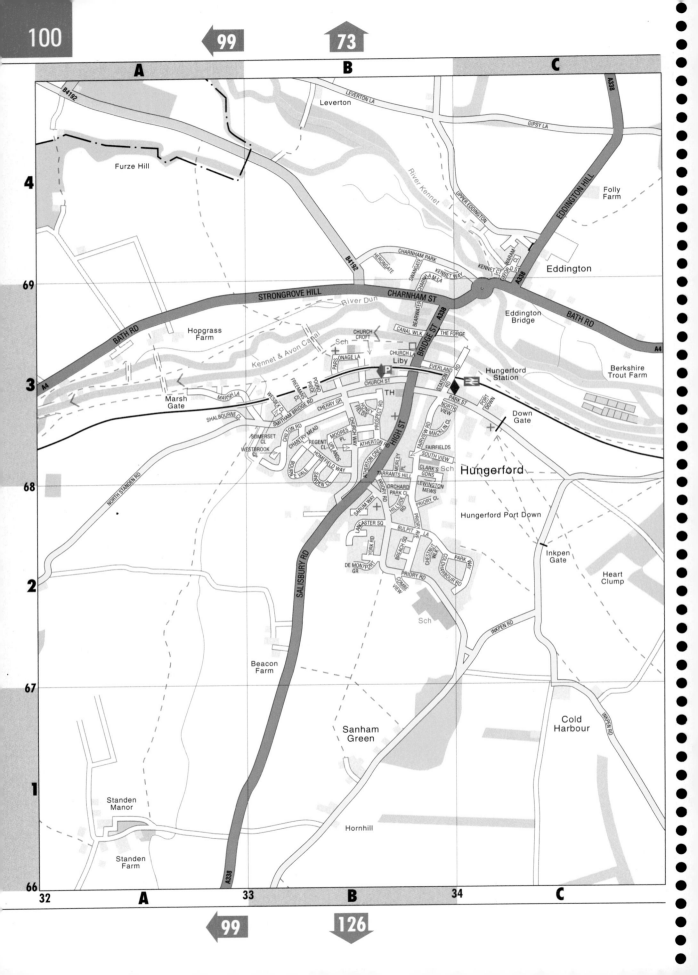

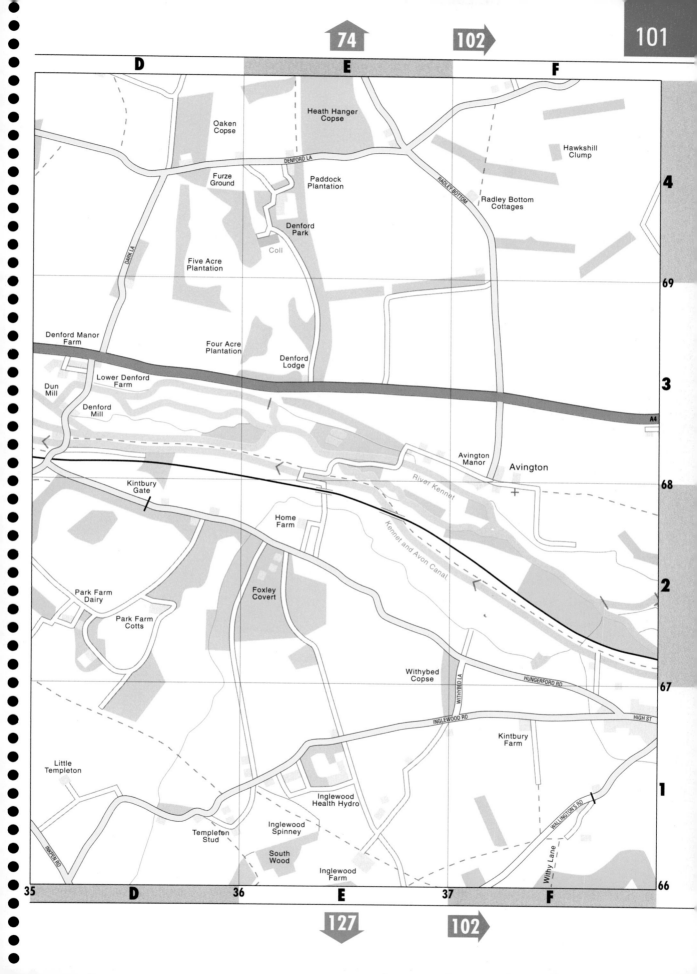

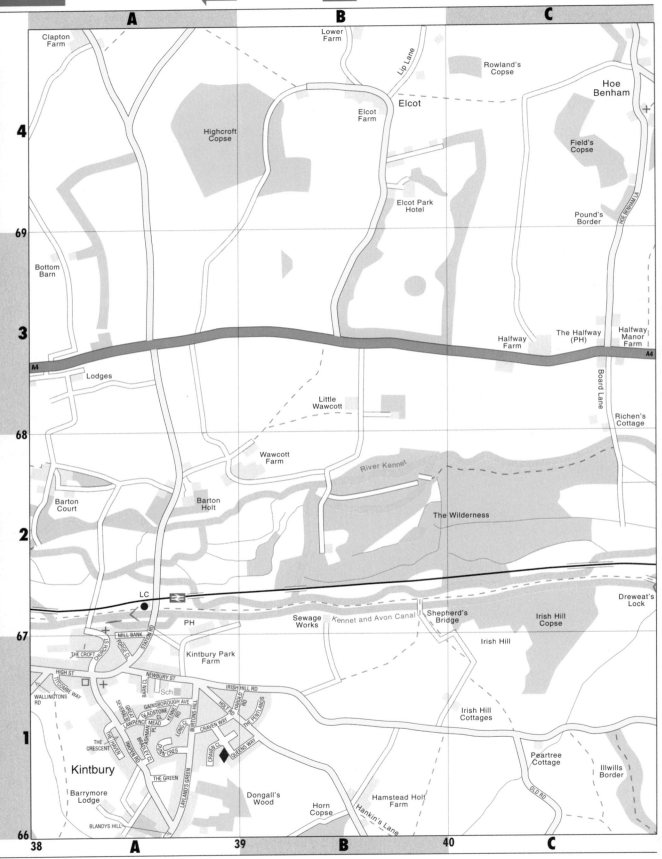

101
75

A   B   C

Clapton Farm

Lower Farm

Lip Lane

Rowland's Copse

Hoe Benham

Elcot

Elcot Farm

Field's Copse

4

Highcroft Copse

Elcot Park Hotel

Pound's Border

HOE BENHAM LA

69

Bottom Barn

3

Halfway Farm

The Halfway (PH)

Halfway Manor Farm

A4

A4

Lodges

Little Wawcott

Board Lane

Richen's Cottage

68

Wawcott Farm

River Kennet

Barton Court

Barton Holt

The Wilderness

2

LC

Dreweat's Lock

Sewage Works

Kennet and Avon Canal

Shepherd's Bridge

Irish Hill Copse

PH

67

Mill Bank

Kintbury Park Farm

Irish Hill

THE CROFT

CHURCH ST

FORBES CL

STATION RD

NEWBURY ST

Irish Hill Cottages

HIGH ST

BARN CL

Sch

IRISH HILL RD

WALLINGTONS RD

TITCOMBE WAY

GAINSBOROUGH AVE

GLADSTONE CL

GREAT SEVERALS

KENNET RD

LAWRENCE MEAD

HAROLD RD

HOLT RD

BURTONS HILL

THE PENTLANDS

1

LORD CL

CRAVEN WAY

THE HAVEN

BRADLEY CT

ASHMAN RD

UNION CRES

CRAVEN CL

QUEENS WAY

Peartree Cottage

OLD RD

Illwills Border

THE CRESCENT

INKPEN RD

Kintbury

THE GREEN

LAYLAND'S GREEN

Dongall's Wood

Hamstead Holt Farm

Barrymore Lodge

Horn Copse

Hankin's Lane

BLANDYS HILL

66

38   A   39   B   40   C

101
128

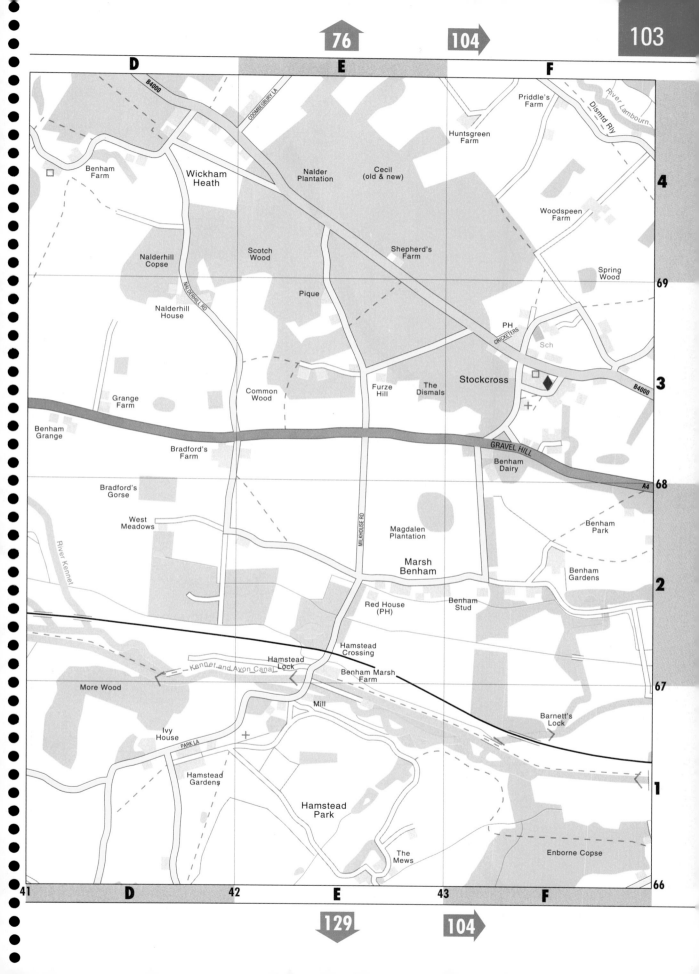

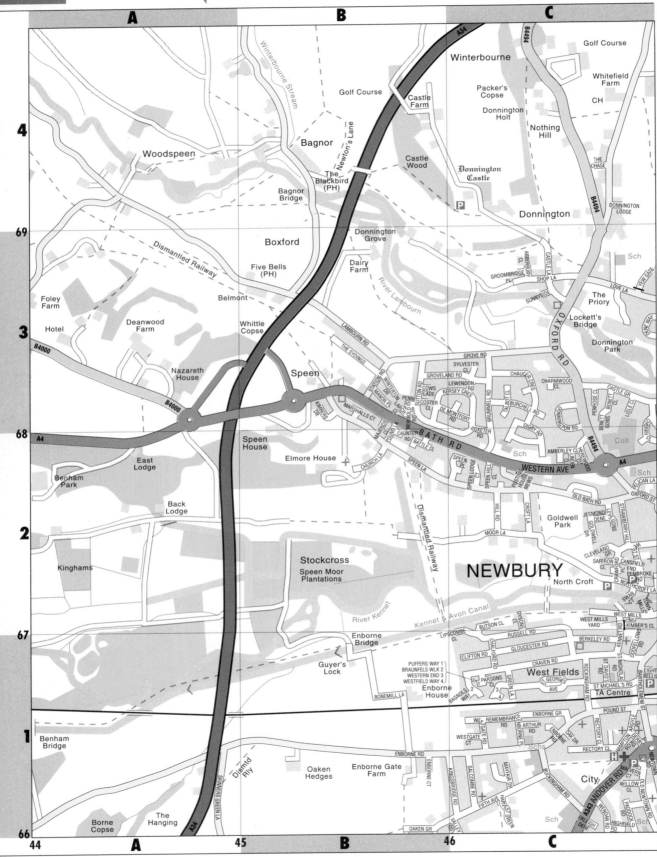

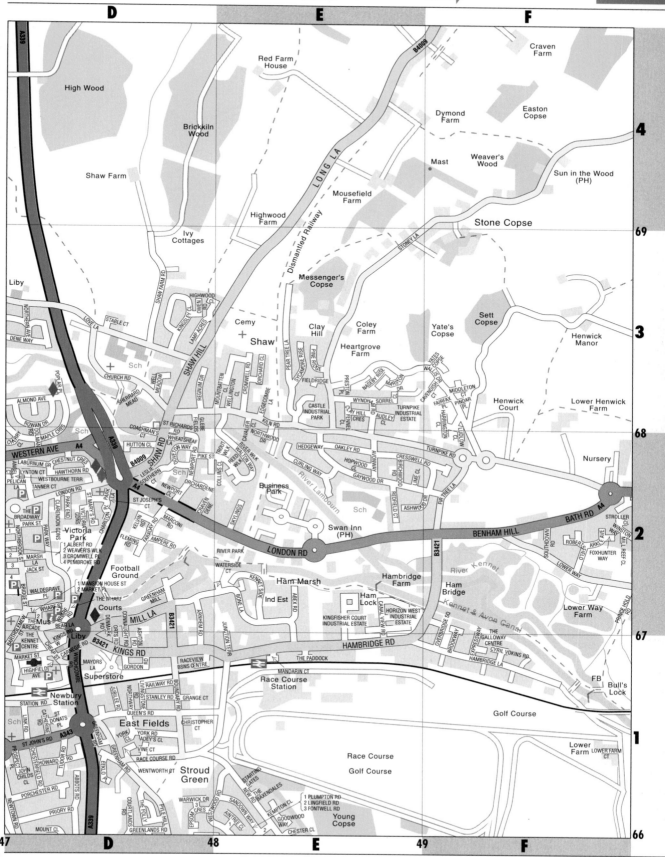

105
79

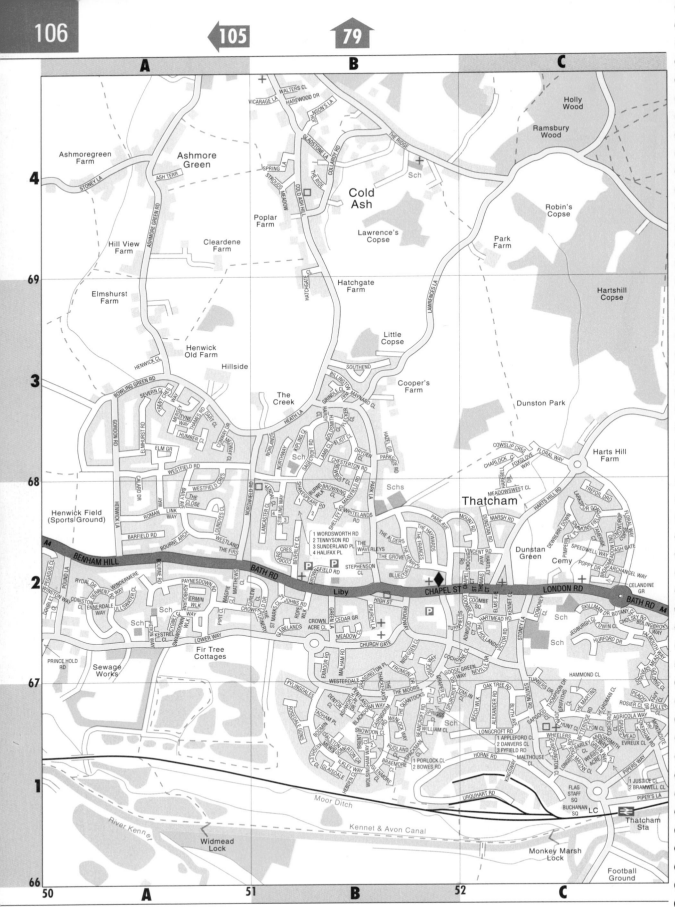

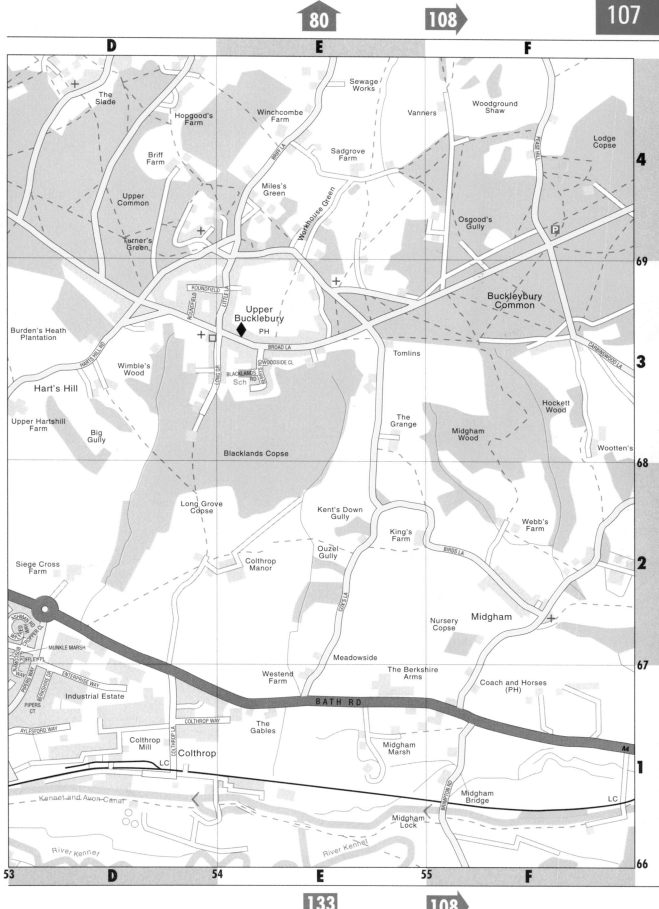

107   81

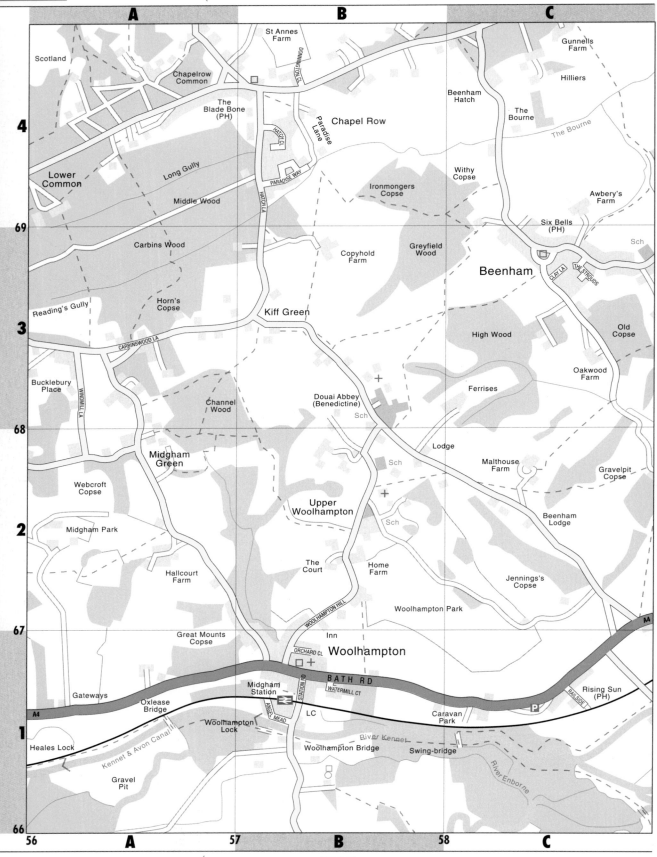

107   134

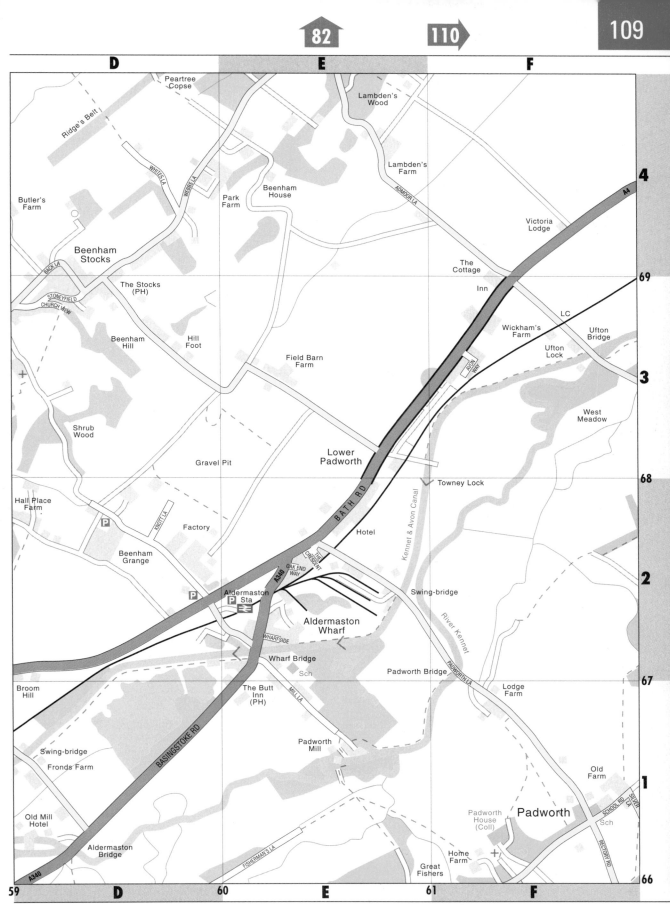

109
83

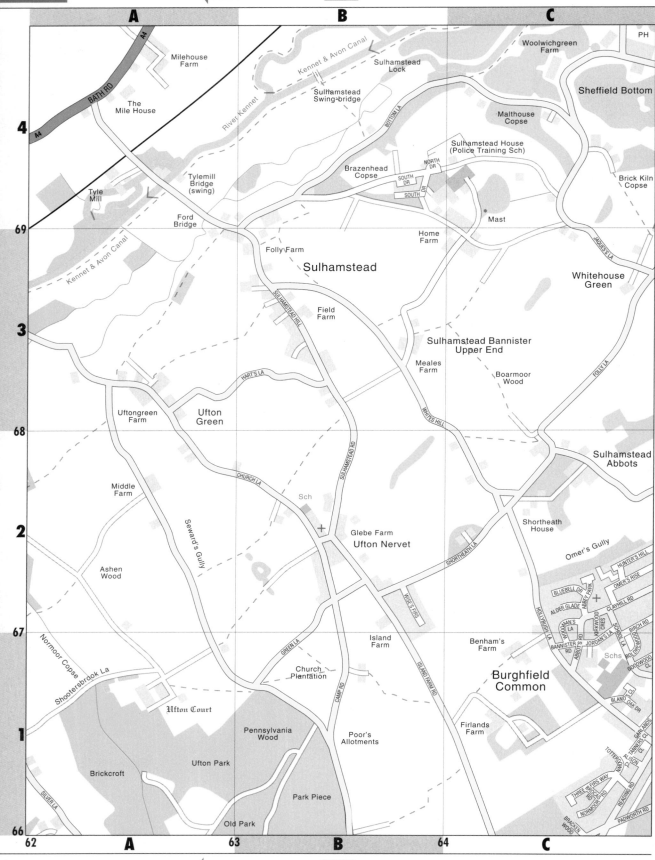

A B C

4

Milehouse Farm

BATH RD
A4
A4

The Mile House

Tyle Mill

River Kennet

Kennet & Avon Canal

Sulhamstead Lock

Sulhamstead Swing-bridge

Tylemill Bridge (swing)

Ford Bridge

Kennet & Avon Canal

Folly Farm

69

Sulhamstead

Field Farm

3

SULHAMSTEAD HILL

HART'S LA

Uftongreen Farm

Ufton Green

Middle Farm

CHURCH LA

Seward's Gully

Sch

Brazenhead Copse

NORTH DR
SOUTH DR
SOUTH

Sulhamstead House (Police Training Sch)

Malthouse Copse

Woolwichgreen Farm

PH

Sheffield Bottom

Brick Kiln Copse

Mast

Home Farm

Whitehouse Green

JAQUES'S LA

Sulhamstead Bannister Upper End

Meales Farm

WHITES HILL

Boarmoor Wood

FOLLY LA

68

Sulhamstead Abbots

Shortheath House

SHORTHEATH LA

Omer's Gully

HUNTER'S HILL

OMER'S RISE

2

Ashen Wood

SULHAMSTEAD RD

Glebe Farm
Ufton Nervet

Island Farm

WISE'S FIRS

Benham's Farm

BLUEBELL DR
ALDER GLADE
ABBEY PARK
CLAYHILL RD
KIRKWOOD CRES
BIRCH RD
SCHOOL LA

HOLYBUSH LA

WICKHAM'S LA
BANNISTER RD
JORDAN'S LA
ABBOTS
GOODWOOD CL
BOLBURYWOOD

Schs

67

Normoor Copse

Shootersbrook La

SILVER LA

Ufton Court

GREEN LA

Church Plantation

CAMP RD

ISLAND FARM RD

Burghfield Common

BLAND CL
OAK DR

GARLANDS
TOTTERDOWN
AL'SON
TANNERS CL

1

Brickcroft

Pennsylvania Wood

Ufton Park

Poor's Allotments

Park Piece

Firlands Farm

THREE FIRS WAY
READING RD
NORMOOR RD
PADWORTH RD
BRACKEL WOOD

Old Park

66

62 A 63 B 64 C

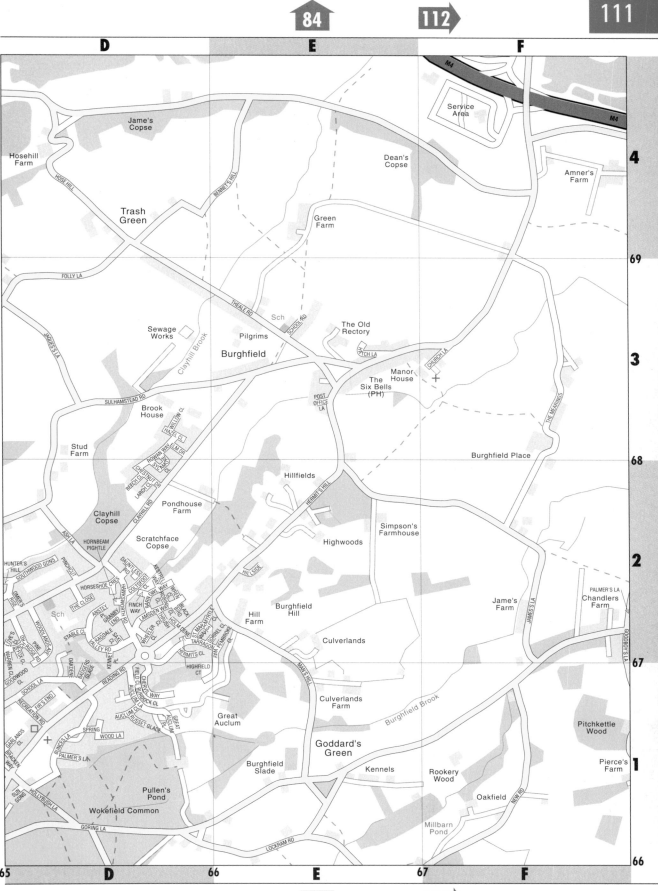

111
85

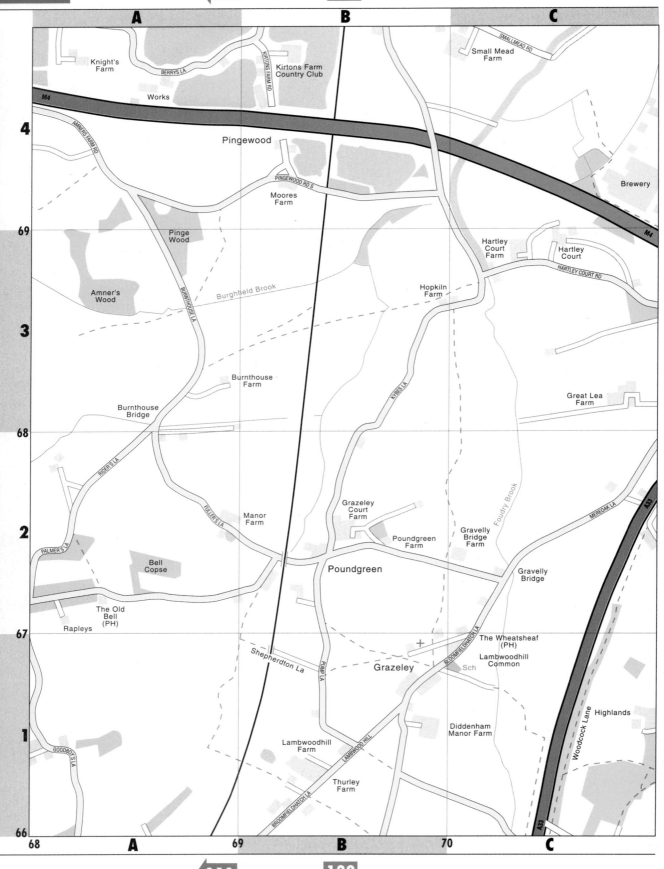

111
138

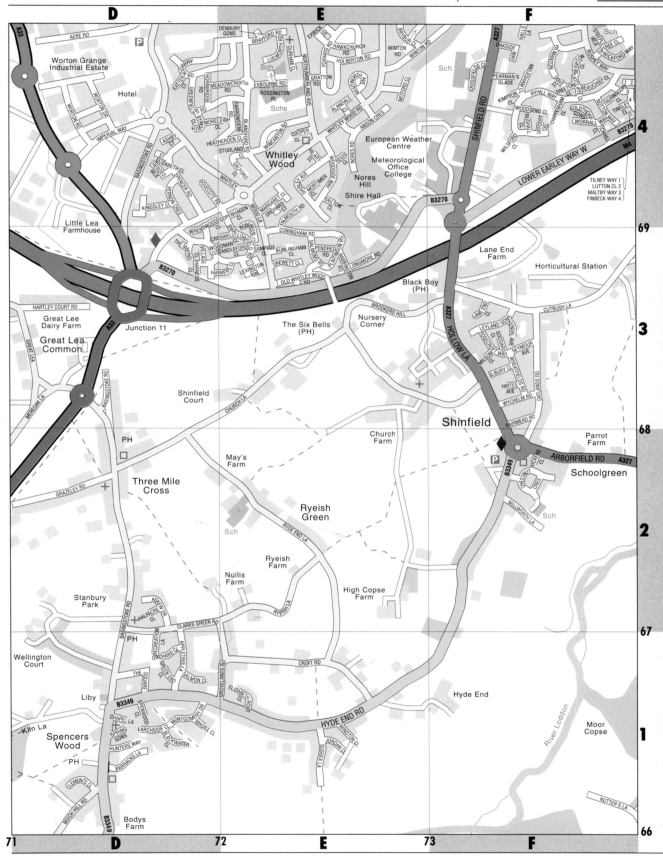

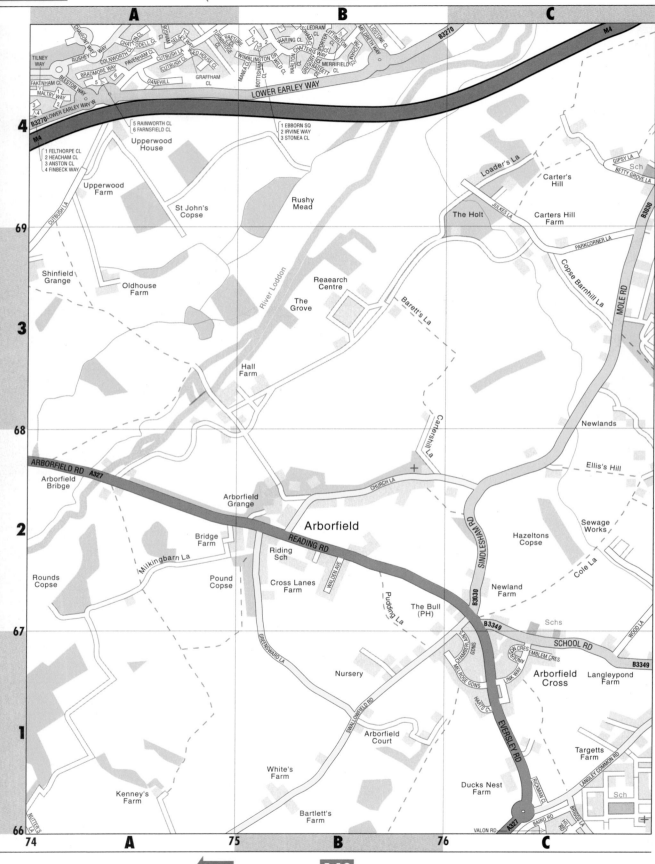

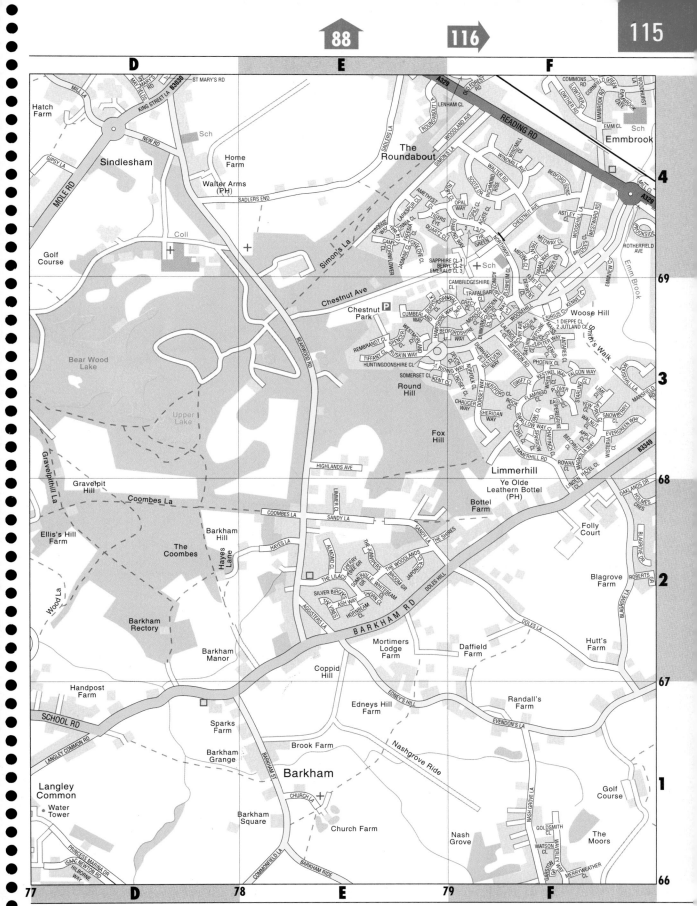

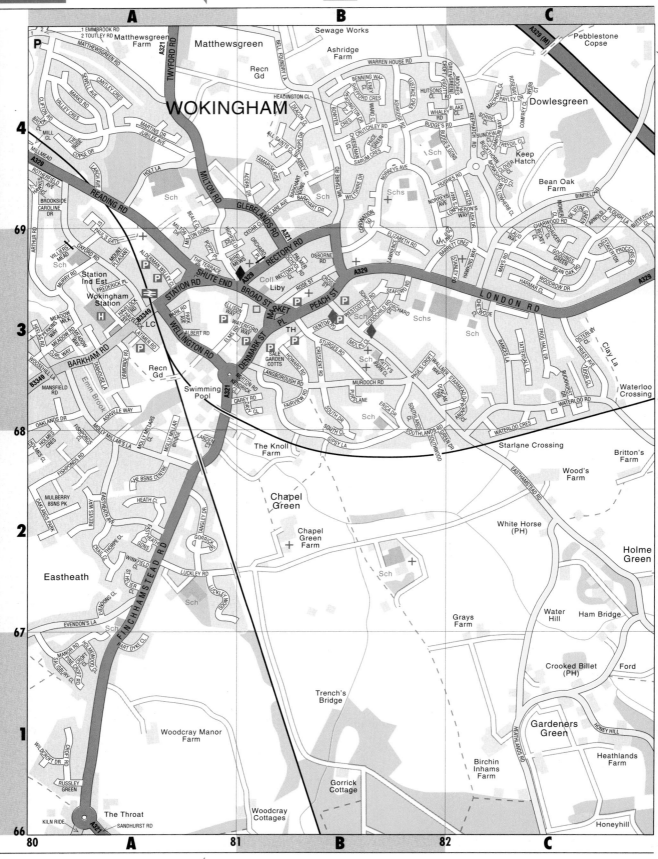

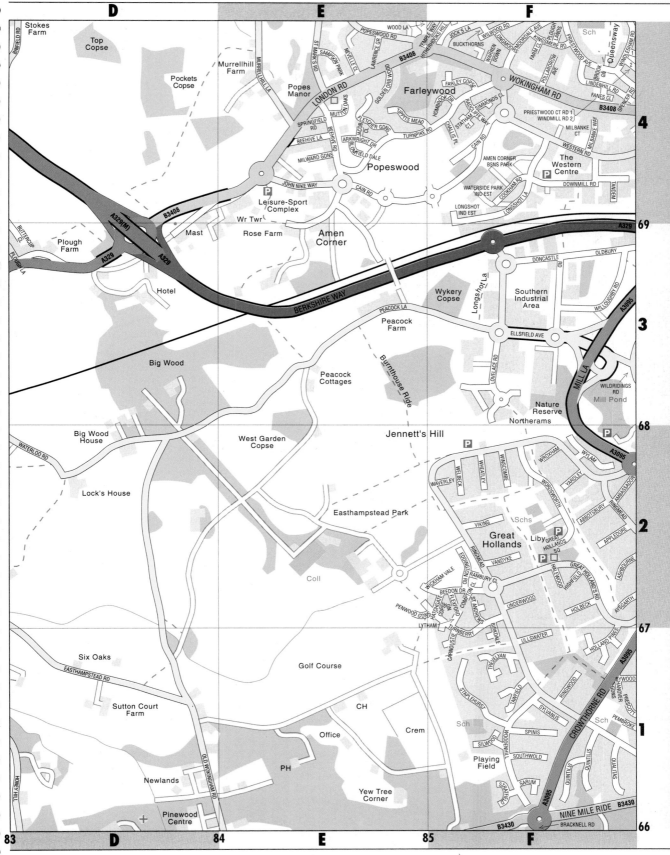

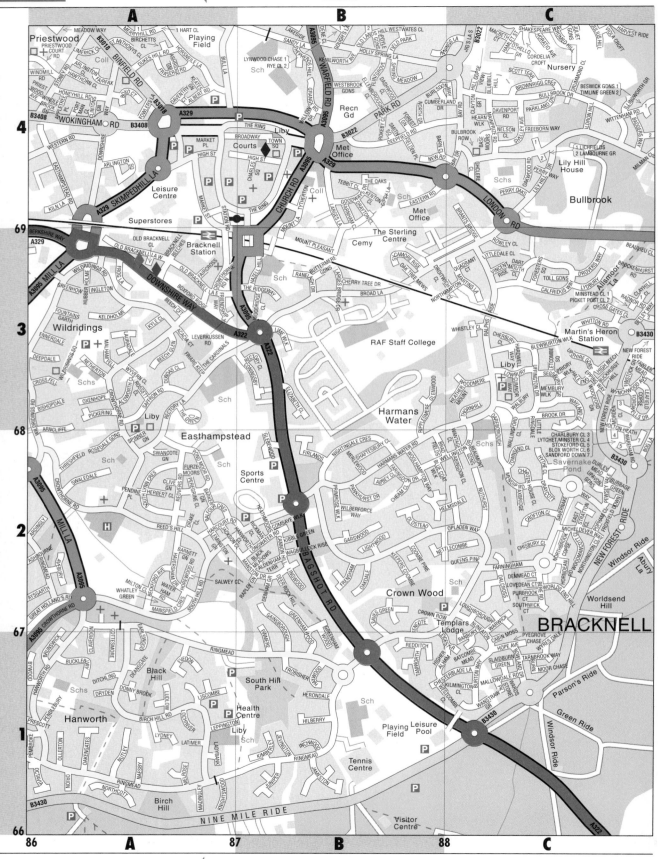

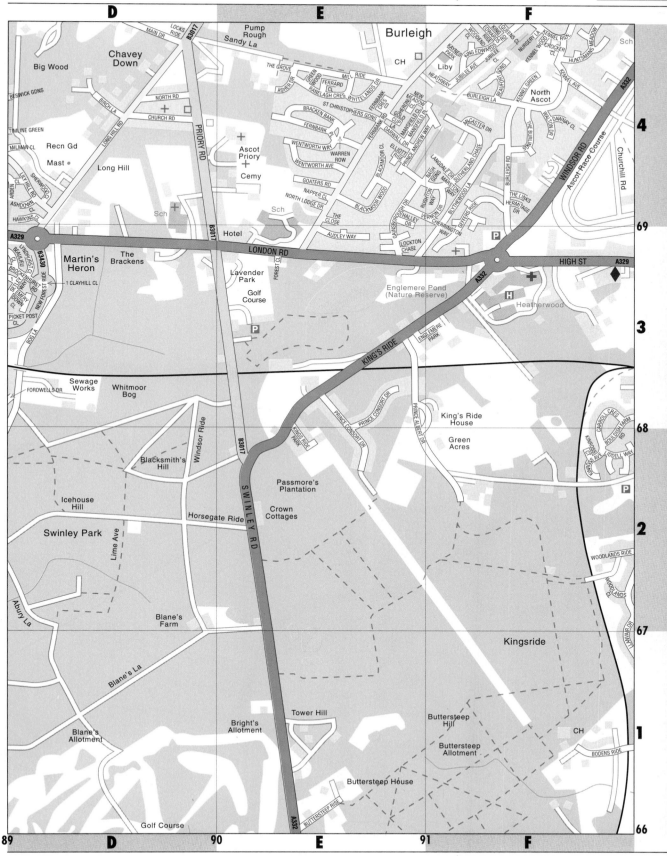

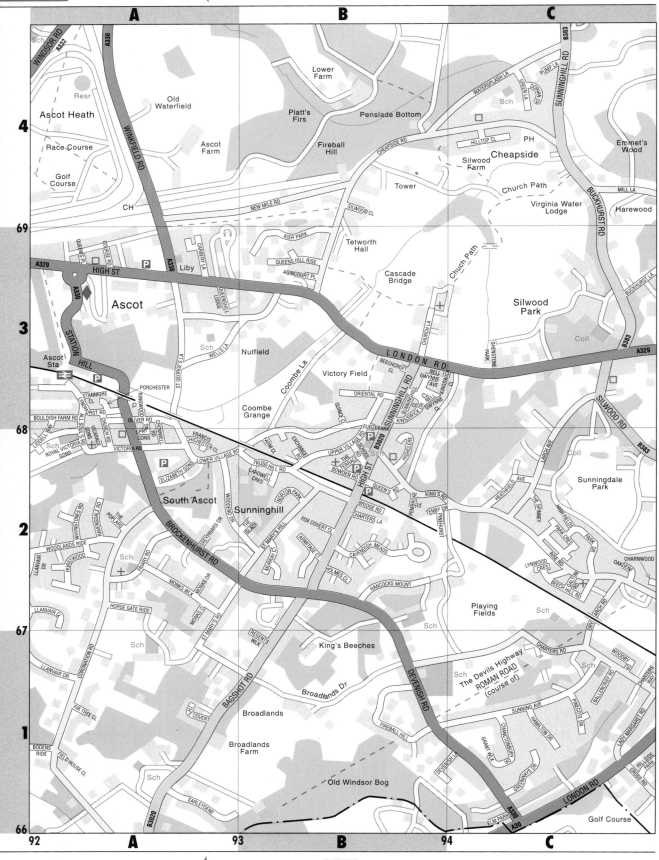

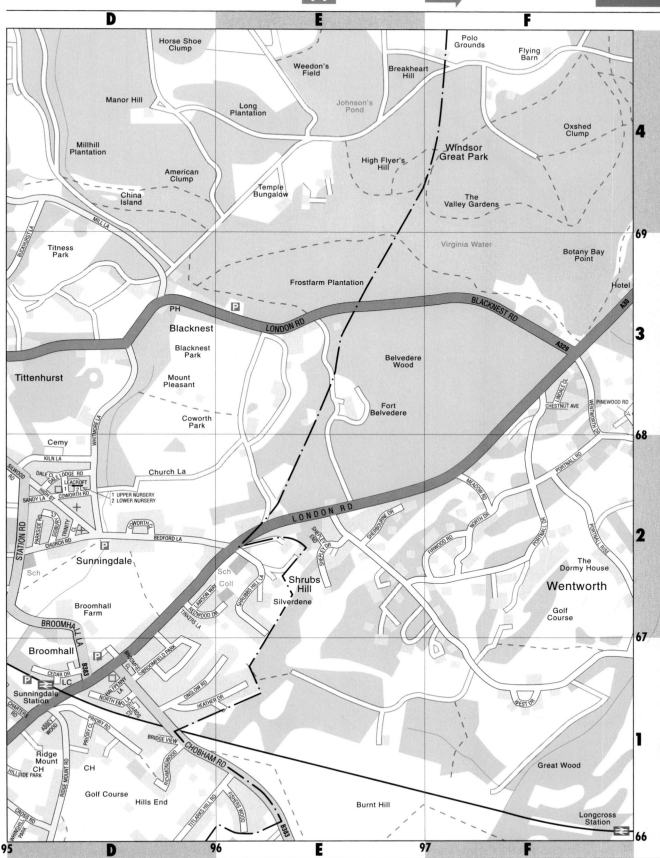

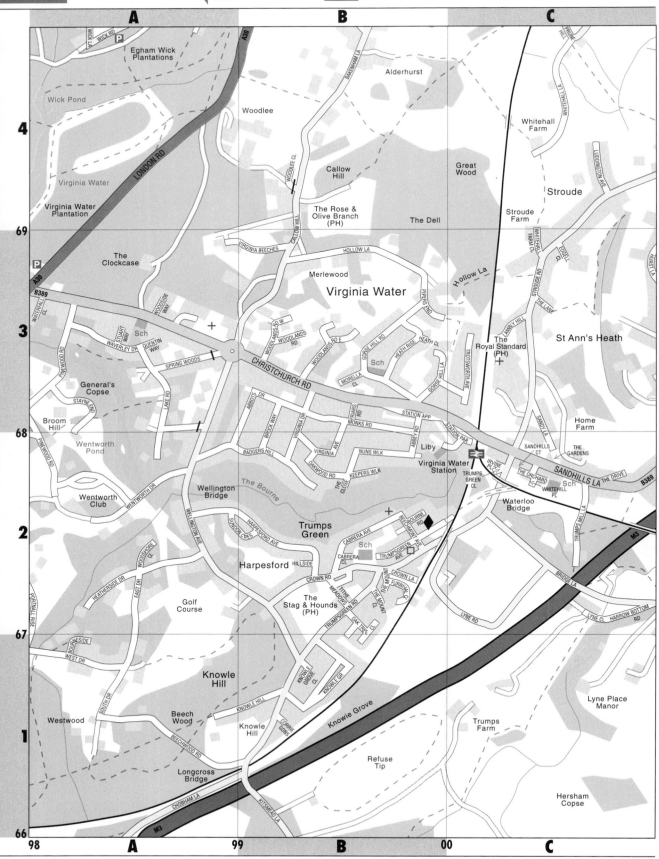

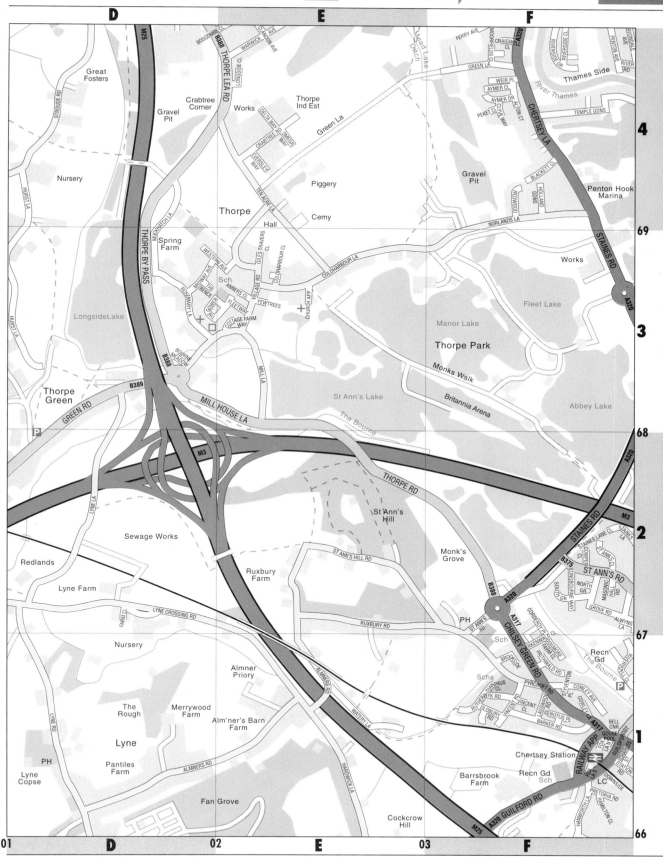

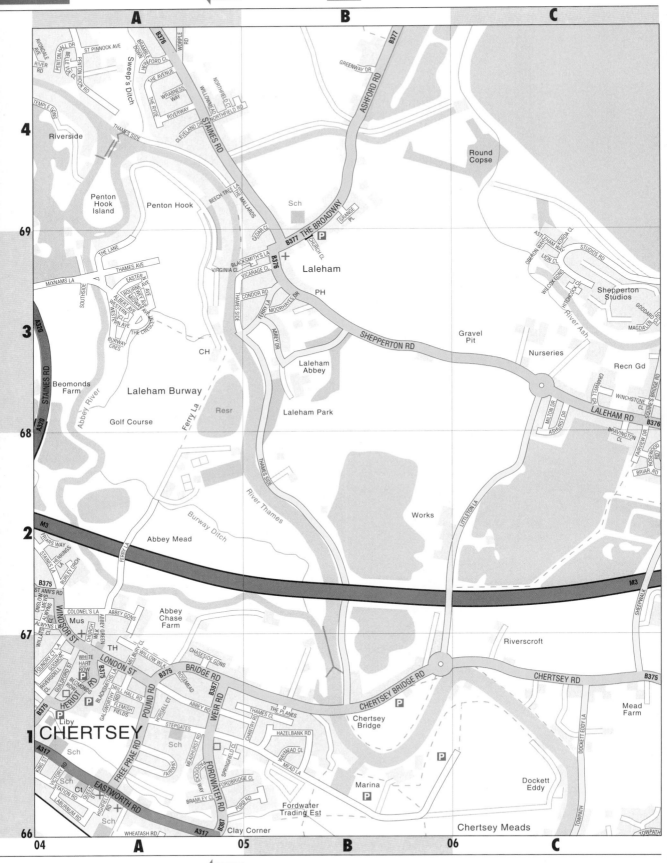

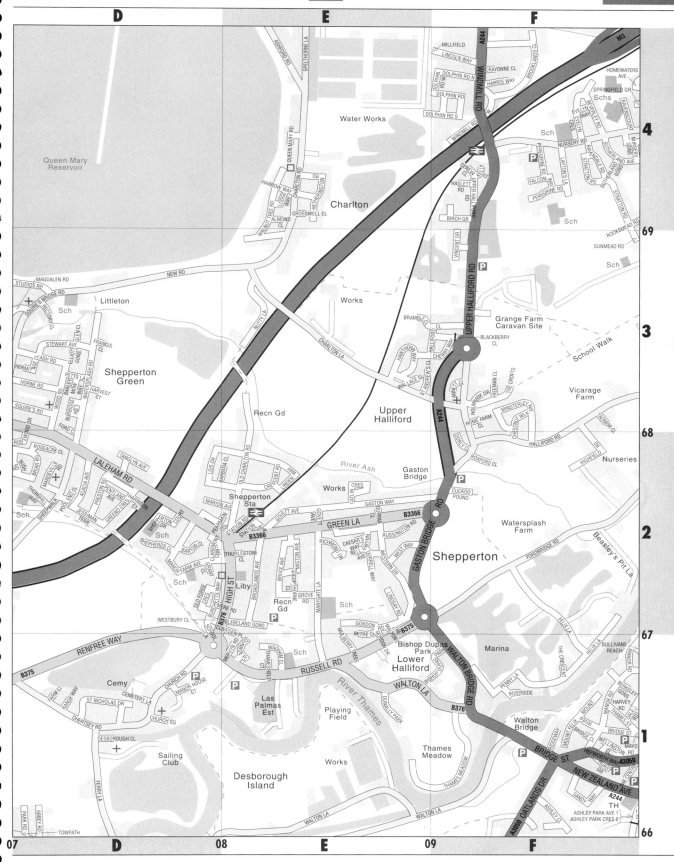

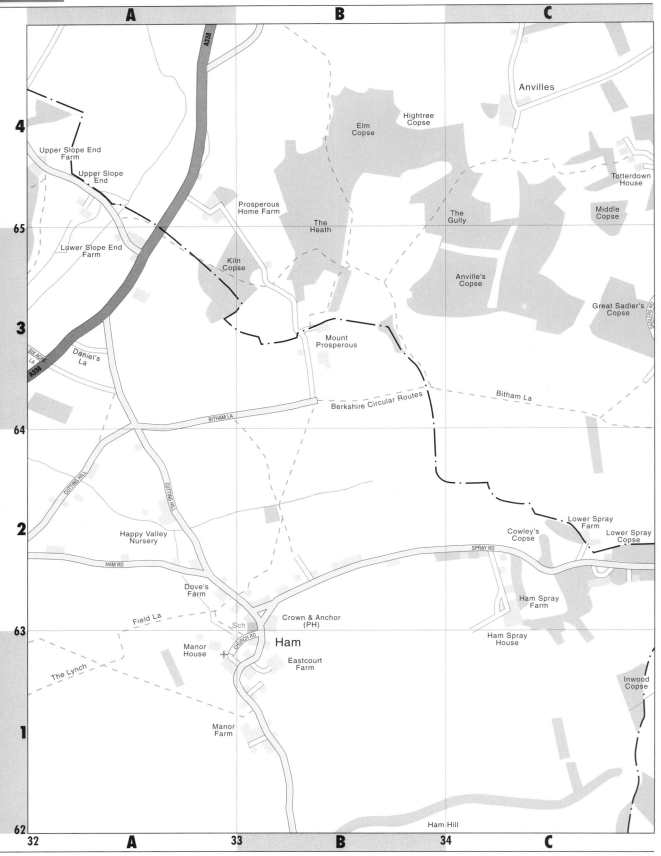

A   B   C

4

Anvilles

Hightree
Copse

Elm
Copse

Totterdown
House

Upper Slope End
Farm

Upper Slope
End

Prosperous
Home Farm

The
Gully

Middle
Copse

65

The
Heath

Lower Slope End
Farm

Kiln
Copse

Anville's
Copse

Great Sadler's
Copse

3

Daniel's
La

Mount
Prosperous

SIX ACRE LA

A338

Bitham La

64

BITHAM LA

Berkshire Circular Routes

CUTTING HILL

CUTTING HILL

2

Happy Valley
Nursery

Lower Spray
Farm

Cowley's
Copse

Lower Spray
Copse

SPRAY RD

HAM RD

Dove's
Farm

Ham Spray
Farm

Field La

Sch

Crown & Anchor
(PH)

63

CHURCH RD

Ham

Ham Spray
House

Manor
House

The Lynch

Eastcourt
Farm

Inwood
Copse

1

Manor
Farm

62

Ham Hill

32   A   33   B   34   C

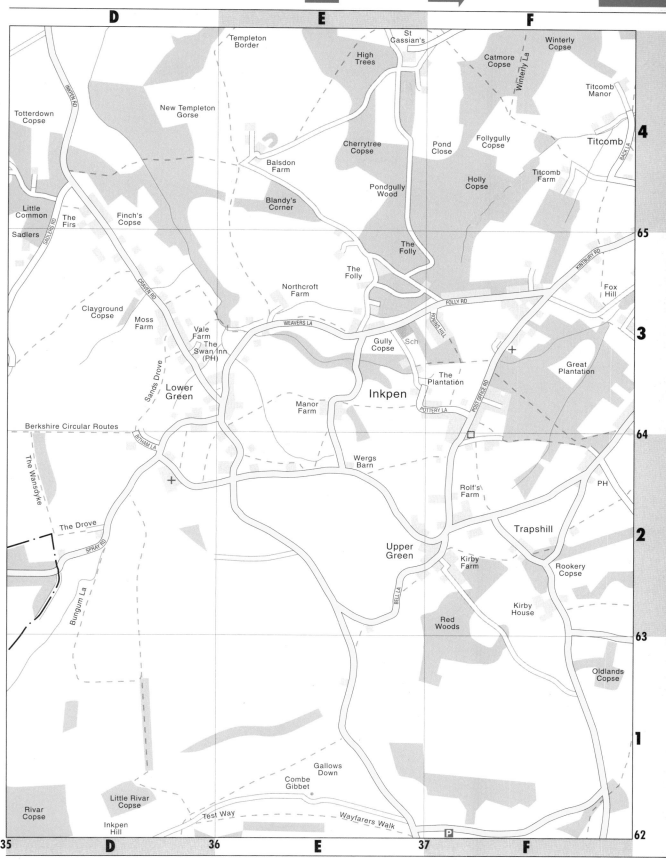

127
102

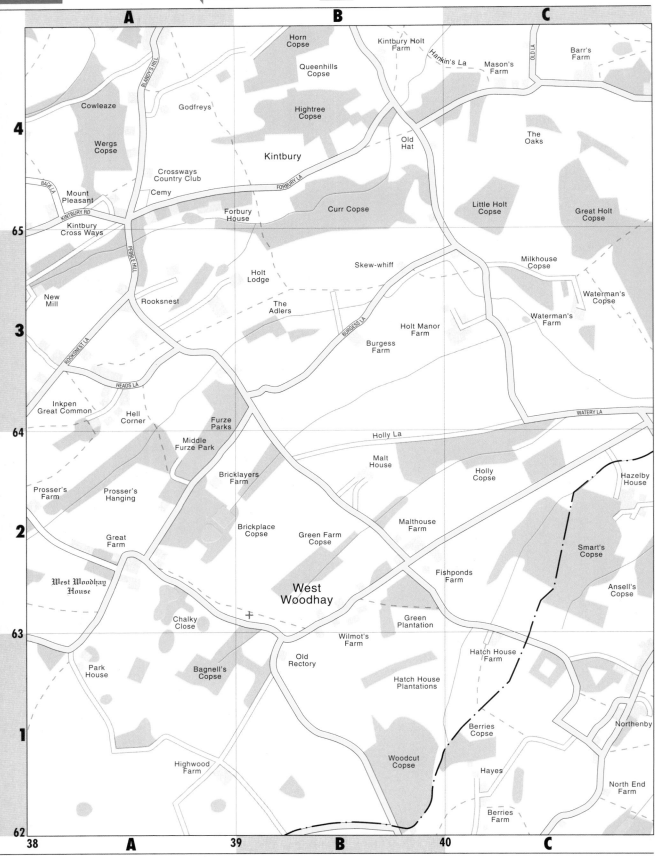

A B C

Horn Copse

Kintbury Holt Farm

Hankin's La

Mason's Farm

OLD LA

Barr's Farm

Queenhills Copse

Hightree Copse

4

Cowleaze

BLANDY'S HILL

Godfreys

Old Hat

The Oaks

Wergs Copse

Kintbury

Crossways Country Club

Cemy

FORBURY LA

BACK LA

Mount Pleasant

KINTBURY RD

Forbury House

Curr Copse

Little Holt Copse

Great Holt Copse

65

Kintbury Cross Ways

PEBBLE HILL

Skew-whiff

Milkhouse Copse

New Mill

Rooksnest

Holt Lodge

Waterman's Copse

The Adlers

BURGESS LA

Holt Manor Farm

Waterman's Farm

3

ROOKSNEST LA

Burgess Farm

HEADS LA

Inkpen Great Common

Hell Corner

Furze Parks

WATERY LA

64

Middle Furze Park

Holly La

Malt House

Holly Copse

Hazelby House

Prosser's Farm

Prosser's Hanging

Bricklayers Farm

Malthouse Farm

Smart's Copse

2

Great Farm

Brickplace Copse

Green Farm Copse

Ansell's Copse

West Woodhay House

West Woodhay

Fishponds Farm

Chalky Close

Green Plantation

63

Park House

Bagnell's Copse

Old Rectory

Wilmot's Farm

Hatch House Farm

Berries Copse

Northenby

Hatch House Plantations

1

Highwood Farm

Woodcut Copse

Hayes

North End Farm

Berries Farm

62

38 A 39 B 40 C

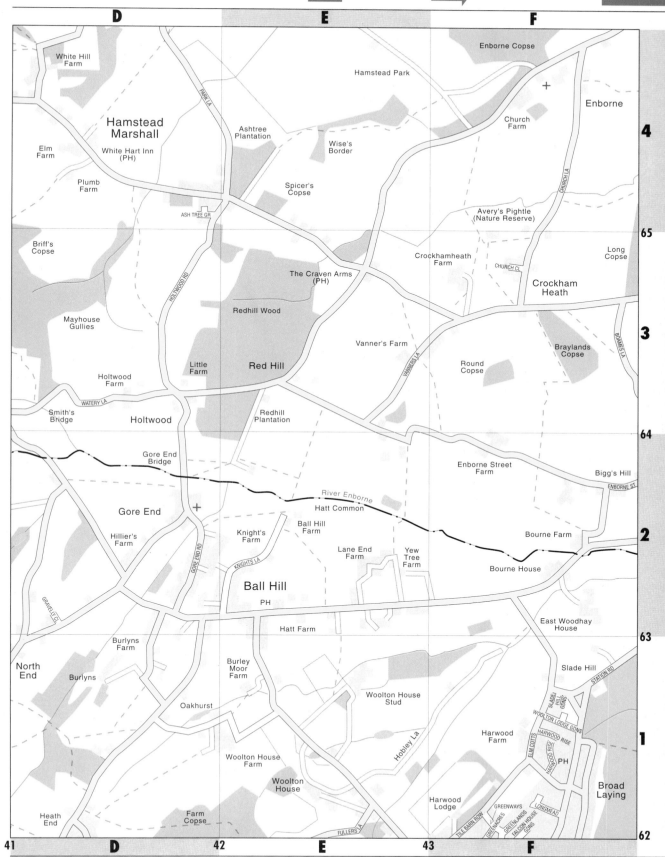

White Hill Farm

Enborne Copse

Hamstead Park

Enborne

PARK LA

Church Farm

4

Hamstead Marshall

Ashtree Plantation

Elm Farm

White Hart Inn (PH)

Wise's Border

Plumb Farm

Spicer's Copse

ASH TREE GR

Avery's Pightle (Nature Reserve)

65

Briff's Copse

HOLTWOOD RD

The Craven Arms (PH)

Crockhamheath Farm

CHURCH LA

Long Copse

CHURCH CL

Crockham Heath

Mayhouse Gullies

Redhill Wood

Vanner's Farm

Round Copse

Braylands Copse

BOAMES LA

3

Holtwood Farm

Little Farm

Red Hill

VANNERS LA

WATERY LA

Smith's Bridge

Holtwood

Redhill Plantation

64

Gore End Bridge

Enborne Street Farm

Bigg's Hill

ENBORNE ST

River Enborne

Gore End

Hatt Common

GORE END RD

Hillier's Farm

Knight's Farm

Ball Hill Farm

Lane End Farm

Yew Tree Farm

Bourne Farm

2

KNIGHTS LA

Bourne House

Ball Hill

PH

East Woodhay House

63

GRAVEL LA

Burlyns Farm

Hatt Farm

Slade Hill

STATION RD

North End

Burlyns

Burley Moor Farm

Woolton House Stud

SLADE HILL GDNS

WOOLTON LODGE GDNS

Harwood Farm

HARWOOD RISE

Oakhurst

HOBLEY LA

ELM COTTS

HARWOOD RISE

PH

1

Woolton House Farm

Woolton House

Broad Laying

Heath End

Farm Copse

FULLERS LA

Harwood Lodge

TILE BARN ROW

GREENMEADS

GREENWAYS

GREENLANDS

FALCON HOUSE GDNS

LONGMEAD

62

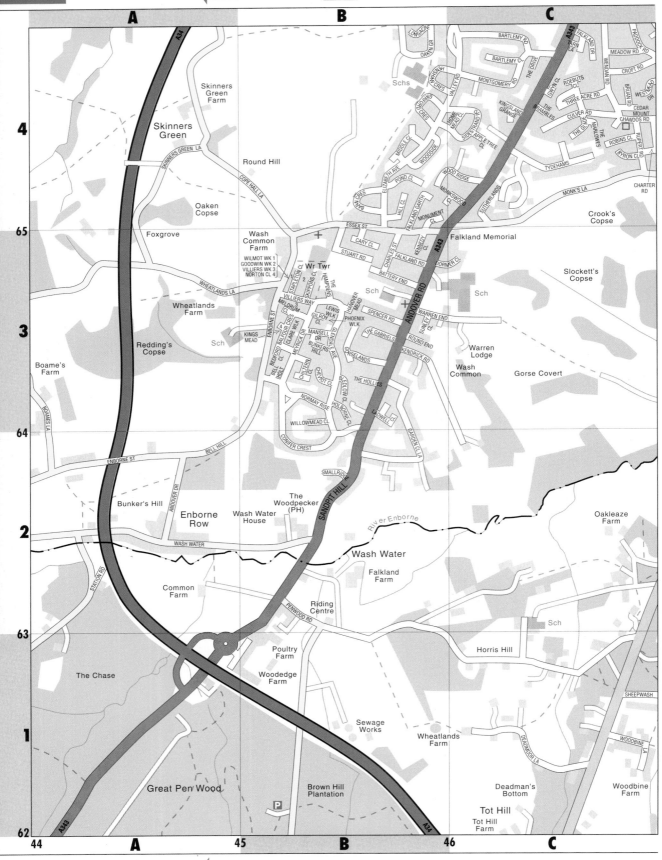

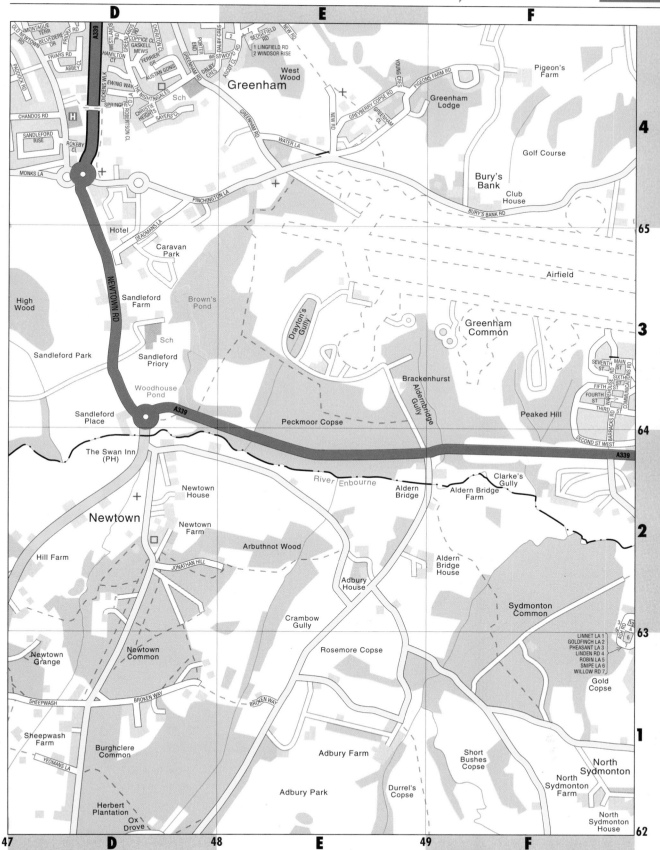

D
E
F

Pigeon's Farm

West Wood

Greenham

1 LINGFIELD RD
2 WINDSOR RISE

SEDGEFIELD RD
NEW RD

YOUNG CRES
PIGEONS FARM RD

GREYBERRY COPSE RD
GREENHAM CL

Greenham Lodge

4

WATER LA

Golf Course

GREENHAM RD

NEW RD

Bury's Bank

Club House

PINCHINGTON LA

BURY'S BANK RD

65

Hotel

Caravan Park

DEADMANS LA

Airfield

NEWTOWN RD

Sandleford Farm

Brown's Pond

High Wood

Drayton's Gully

Greenham Common

3

Sch

Sandleford Park

Sandleford Priory

Woodhouse Pond

Brackenhurst

Aldernbridge Gully

Peaked Hill

SEVENTH ST
MAIN ST
SIXTH ST
FIFTH ST
FOURTH ST
THIRD ST
WHARF RD
COMMUNICATIONS RD

A339

Sandleford Place

Peckmoor Copse

64

SECOND ST WEST

BARRACKS RD

A339

The Swan Inn (PH)

River Enbourne

Aldern Bridge

Aldern Bridge Farm

Clarke's Gully

Newtown House

Newtown

Newtown Farm

Arbuthnot Wood

Aldern Bridge House

2

Hill Farm

JONATHAN HILL

Adbury House

Sydmonton Common

Crambow Gully

LINNET LA 1
GOLDFINCH LA 2
PHEASANT LA 3
LINDEN RD 4
ROBIN LA 5
SNIPE LA 6
WILLOW RD 7

ASH RD
A2

63

Newtown Grange

Newtown Common

Rosemore Copse

Gold Copse

SHEEPWASH

BROKEN WAY

BROKEN WAY

Sheepwash Farm

Burghclere Common

YEOMANS LA

Short Bushes Copse

North Sydmonton

1

Adbury Farm

North Sydmonton Farm

Herbert Plantation

Ox Drove

Adbury Park

Durrel's Copse

North Sydmonton House

62

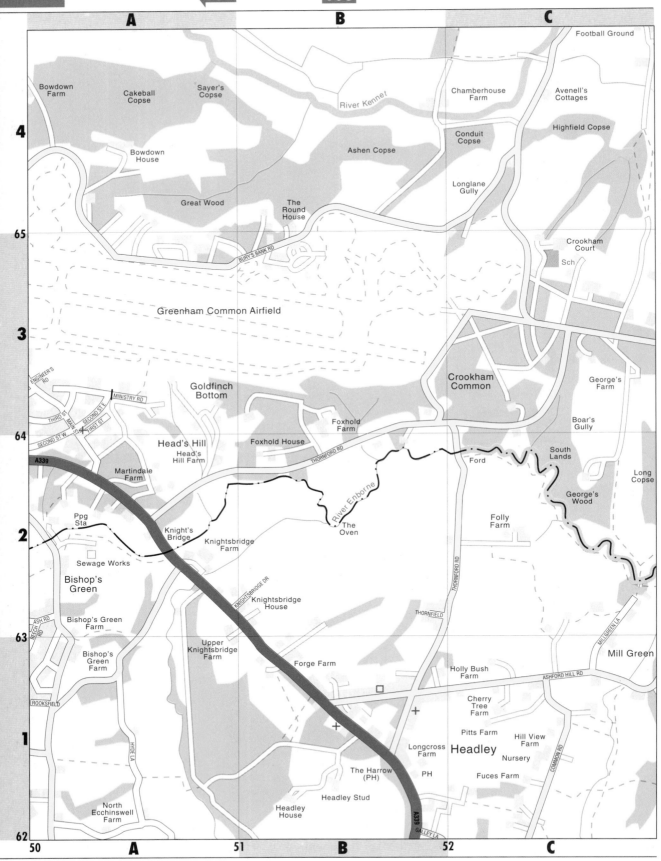

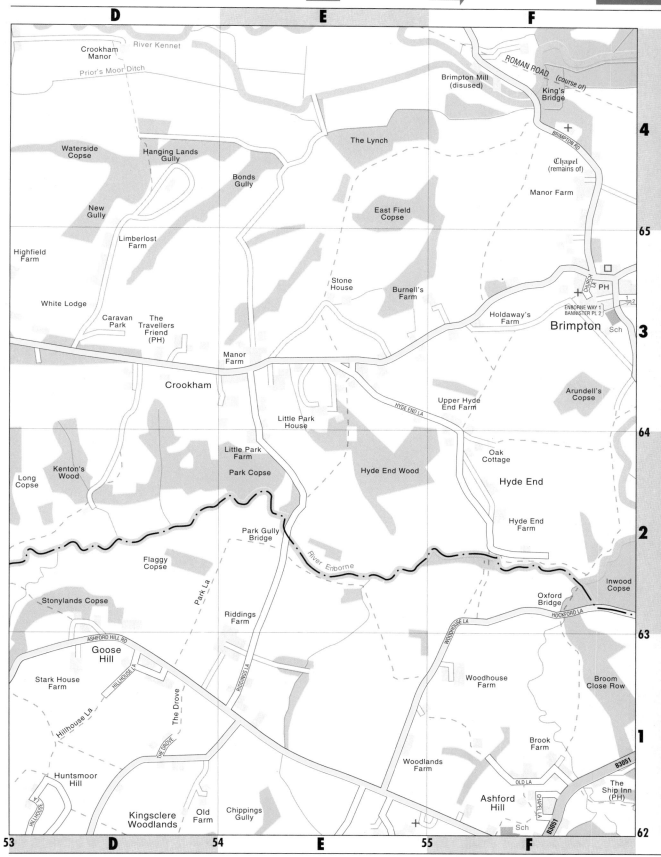

133 108

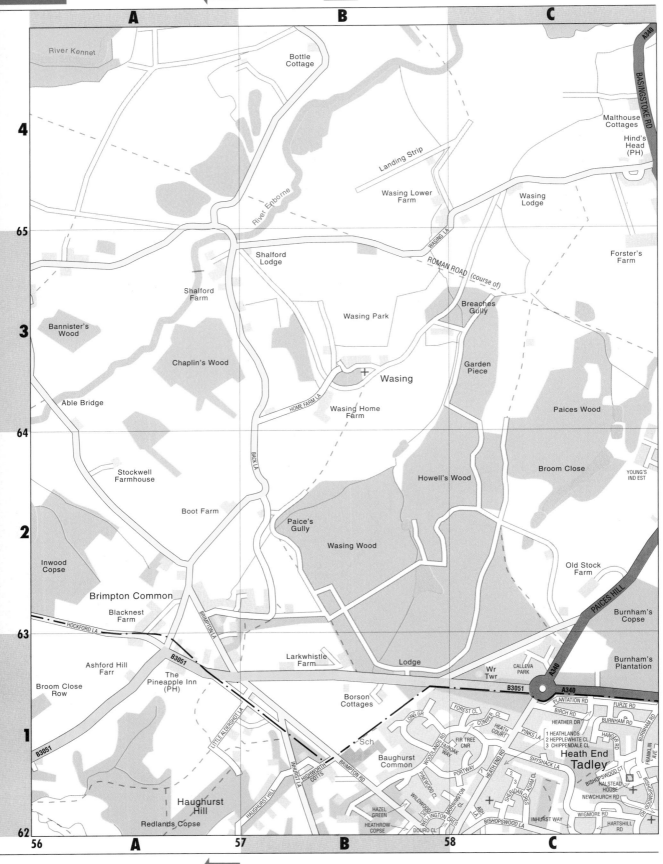

135 110

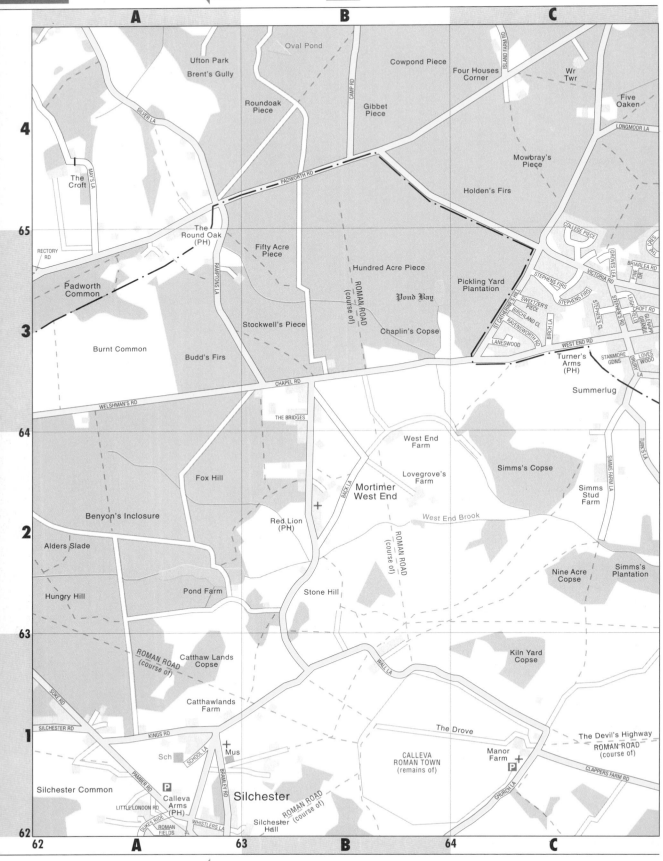

135

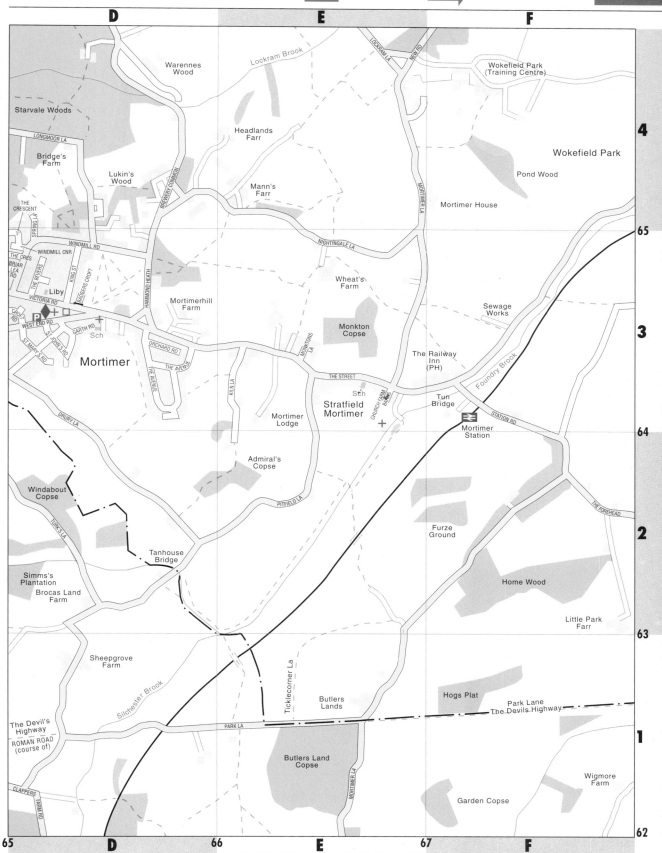

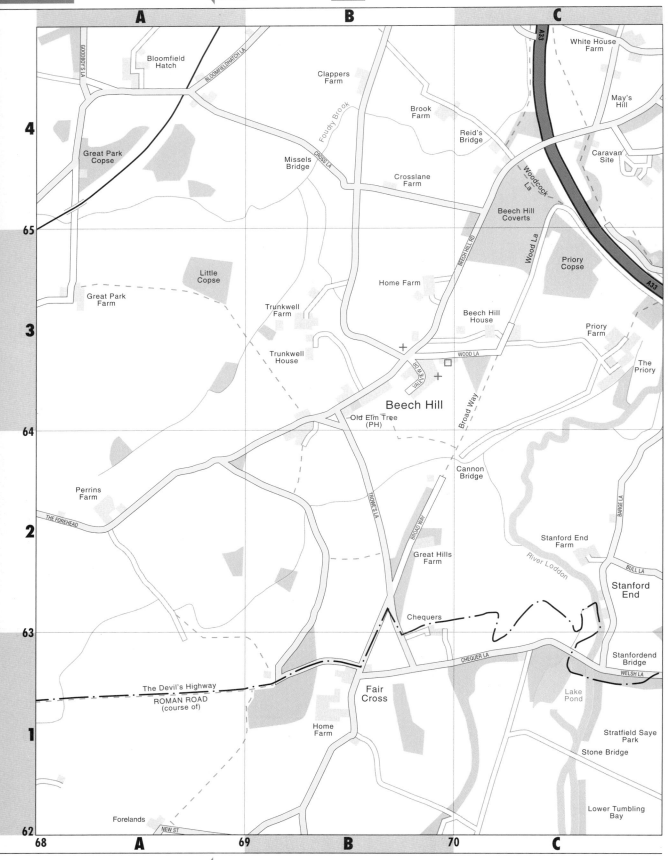

GOODBOY'S LA

Bloomfield
Hatch

BLOOMFIELDHATCH LA

Great Park
Copse

4

Clappers
Farm

Foudry Brook

CROSS LA

Brook
Farm

Reid's
Bridge

White House
Farm

A33

May's
Hill

Caravan
Site

Missels
Bridge

Crosslane
Farm

Woodcock La

Beech Hill
Coverts

65

Little
Copse

Home Farm

BEECH HILL RD

Priory
Copse

A33

Great Park
Farm

Trunkwell
Farm

Beech Hill
House

Wood La

Priory
Farm

3

Trunkwell
House

WOOD LA

WOOD LA

The
Priory

VALE'S LA

Beech Hill

Broad Way

Old Elm Tree
(PH)

64

Cannon
Bridge

Perrins
Farm

THE FOREHEAD

TROWE'S LA

BROAD WAY

Great Hills
Farm

Stanford End
Farm

River Loddon

BARGE LA

BULL LA

Stanford
End

2

Chequers

Stanfordend
Bridge

63

CHEQUER LA

WELSH LA

The Devil's Highway
ROMAN ROAD
(course of)

Fair
Cross

Lake
Pond

Home
Farm

Stratfield Saye
Park

Stone Bridge

1

Forelands

NEW ST

Lower Tumbling
Bay

62

68   **A**   69   **B**   70   **C**

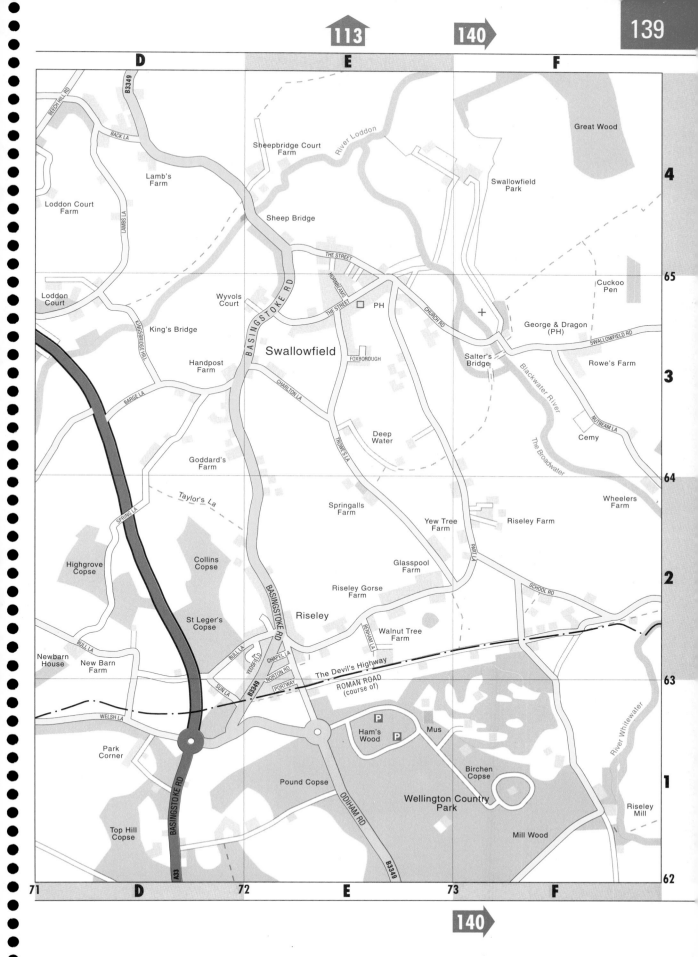

139
114

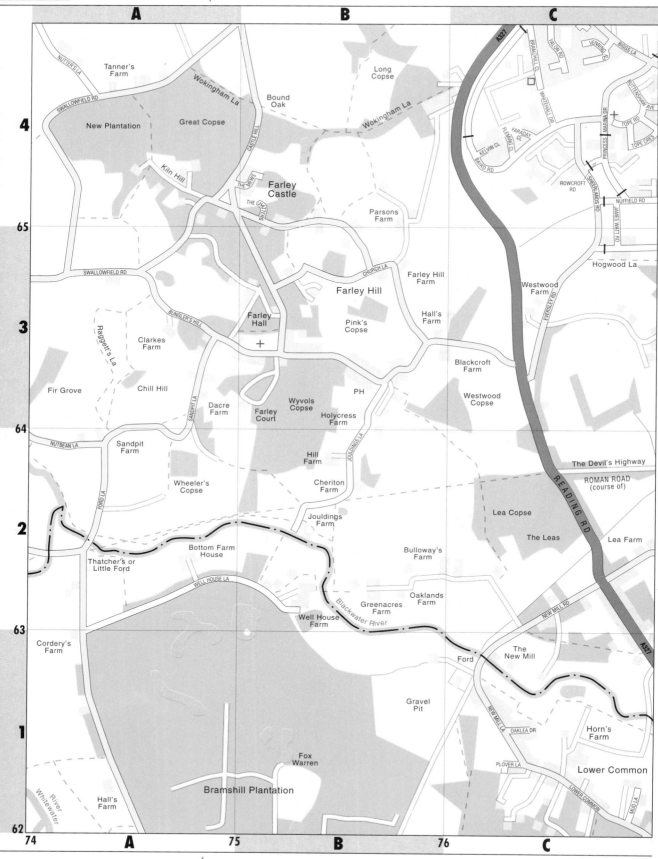

139

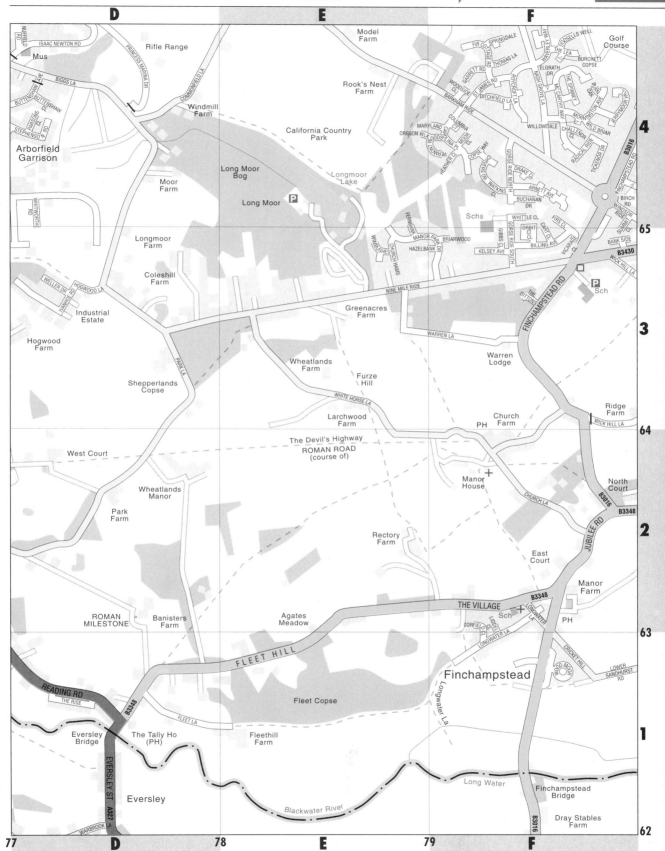

142

D   E   F

NUFFIELD RD
ISAAC NEWTON RD
Mus
Rifle Range
Model Farm

BIGGS LA
PRINCESS MARINA DR
COMMONFIELD LA
Windmill Farm
Rook's Nest Farm

BUTTENSHAW AVE
BUTTENSHAW CL
PARSONS CL
STEPHENSO RD
Arborfield Garrison
Moor Farm
California Country Park
Long Moor Bog
Longmoor Lake

FIR CO SPRINGDALE
GARRETT RD ST JAMES CL
COTTAGE RD THOMAS LA
WOODSIDE DITCHFIELD LA
BARKHAM RIDE
MARYLAND
COLUMBIA CT
CHRISTINA PL
OREGON WLK
VERADY CL
HEATHER CL
COPSE WAY
GORSE RIDE NORTH
VICKERS CL
THE LEA
DODSELLS WELL
POLYCROFT RD
NASH GROVE LA
MC CARTHY WAY
MORNINGTON AVE
WILLOWDALE
CHALLENOR CL
RADICAL RIDE
DRAKE CL
ARNETT AVE
BUCHANAN DR
Golf Course
BURCHETT COPSE
THE SPINNEY
ELGRATH DR
BIRCH DR
WILD BRIAR
TICKBOROUGH DR
LIGHTWOOD
B3016

WHITWORTH RD
WELLER DR
HOGWOOD LA
IVANHOE RD
Industrial Estate
Longmoor Farm
Coleshill Farm
Long Moor P
Schs
WHITTLE CL
GIBBS CL
GORSE RIDE SOUTH
KELSEY AVE
ORBIT CL
CART CL
BILLING AVE
FIRS CL
VICARAGE CL
BANK SIDE
WINDSOR RIDE
SUMMIT CL
BIRCH DR
65

Hogwood Farm
PARK LA
Shepperlands Copse
Greenacres Farm
NINE MILE RIDE
MANOR PARK DR
HAZELBANK
BRIARWOOD
FERNBANK
CHURCH HAMS
WIMBUSH WAY
THE DITTONS
FINCHAMPSTEAD RD
WICK HILL LA
B3430
P Sch
3

Wheatlands Farm
Furze Hill
WHITE HORSE LA
Larchwood Farm
WARREN LA
Warren Lodge
Church Farm
PH
Ridge Farm
WICK HILL LA
64

West Court
The Devil's Highway
ROMAN ROAD (course of)
Manor House +
CHURCH LA
North Court
B3016
B3348

Wheatlands Manor
Park Farm
Rectory Farm
East Court
Manor Farm
PH
JUBILEE RD
2

ROMAN MILESTONE
Banisters Farm
Agates Meadow
THE VILLAGE
Sch +
CORFIELD CL
LIDDELL CL
LONGWATER LA
LONGWATER LA
B3348
LONGWATER LA
Finchampstead
WOOD MOOR
CRICKET HILL
LOWER SANDHURST RD
63

READING RD
THE RISE
B3348
FLEET HILL
Fleet Copse
FLEET LA
Longwater La
1

EVERSLEY ST
A327
WARBROOK LA
Eversley Bridge
The Tally Ho (PH)
Eversley
Fleethill Farm
Blackwater River
Long Water
Finchampstead Bridge
B3016
Dray Stables Farm
62

77   D   78   E   79   F

142

141
116

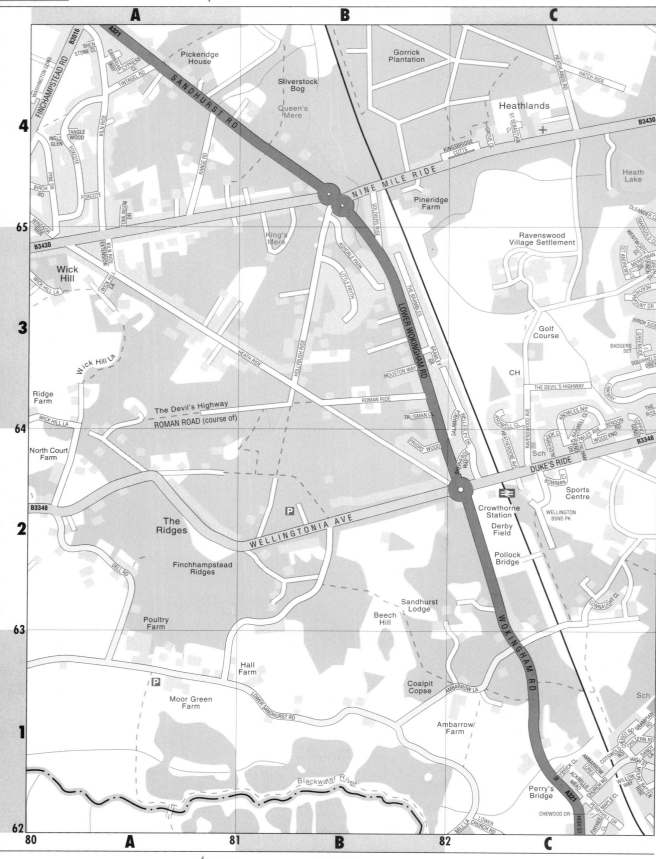

141
149

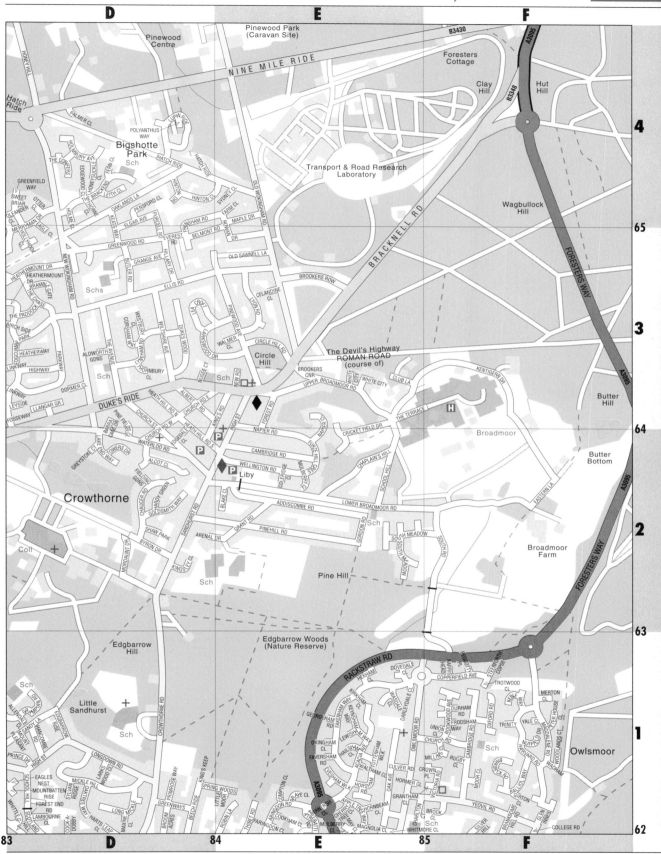

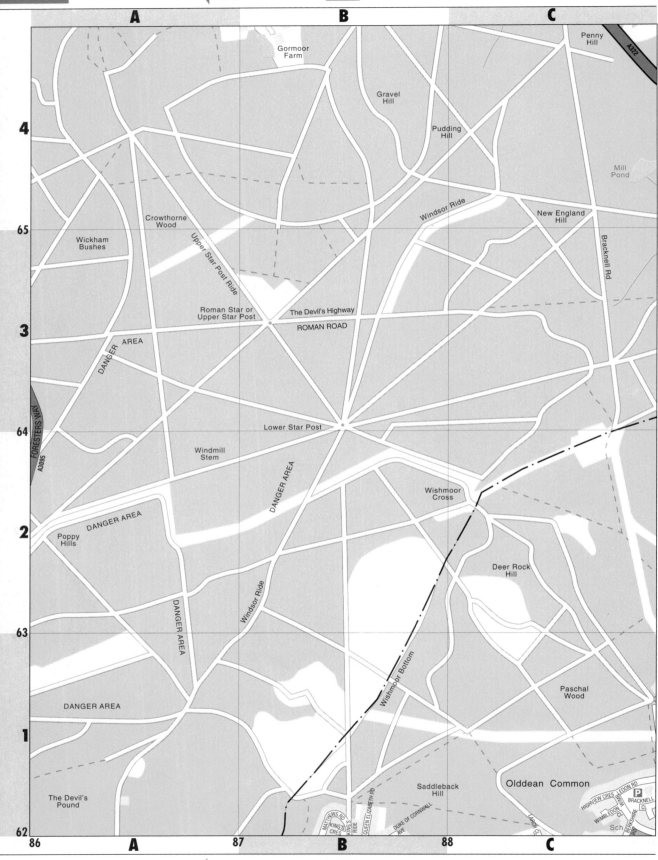

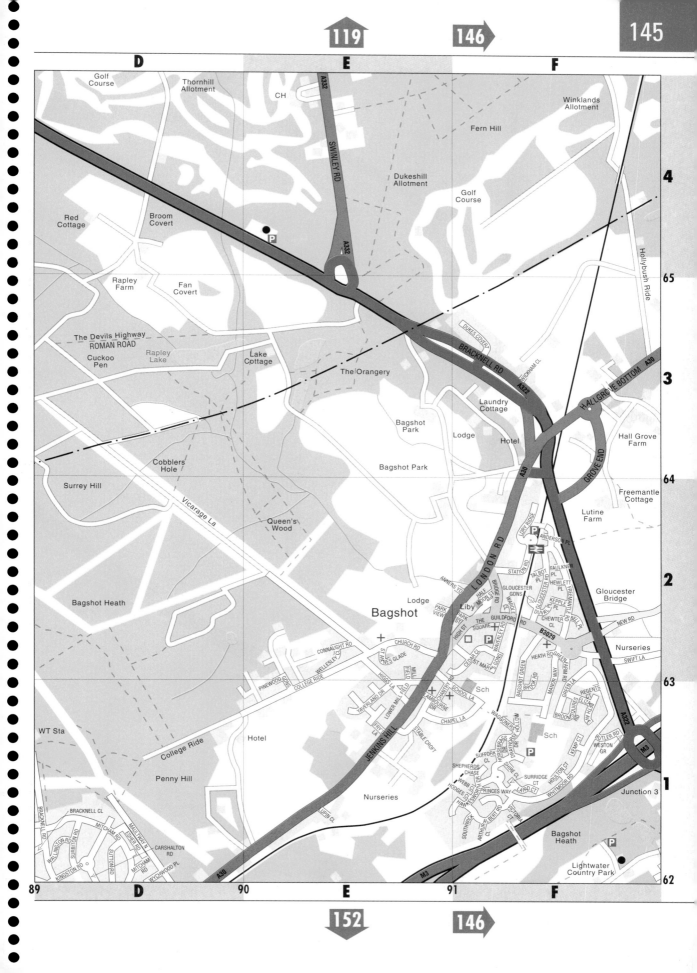

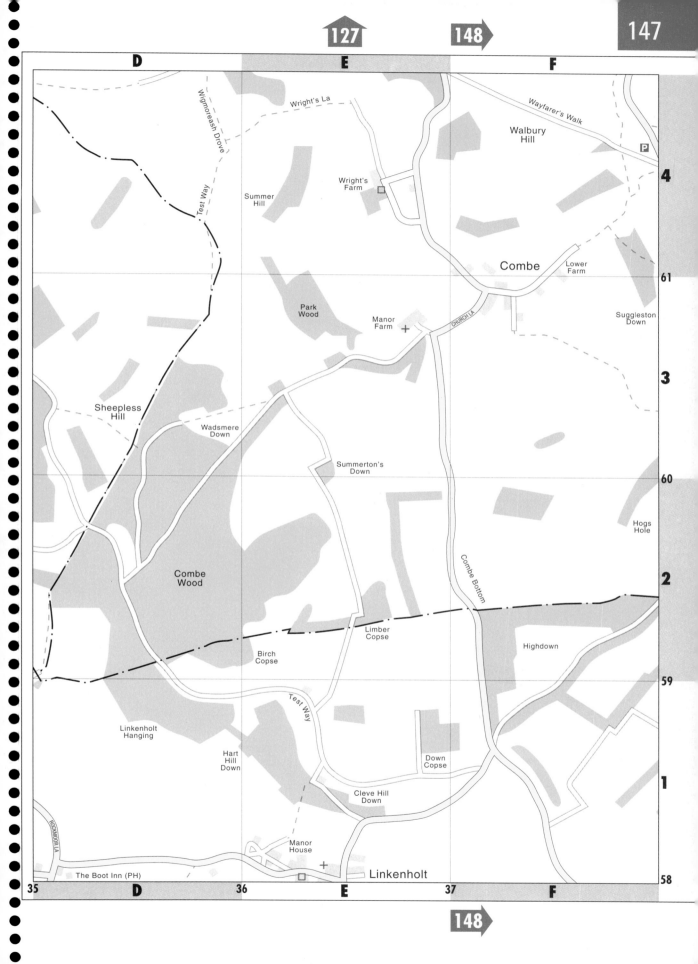

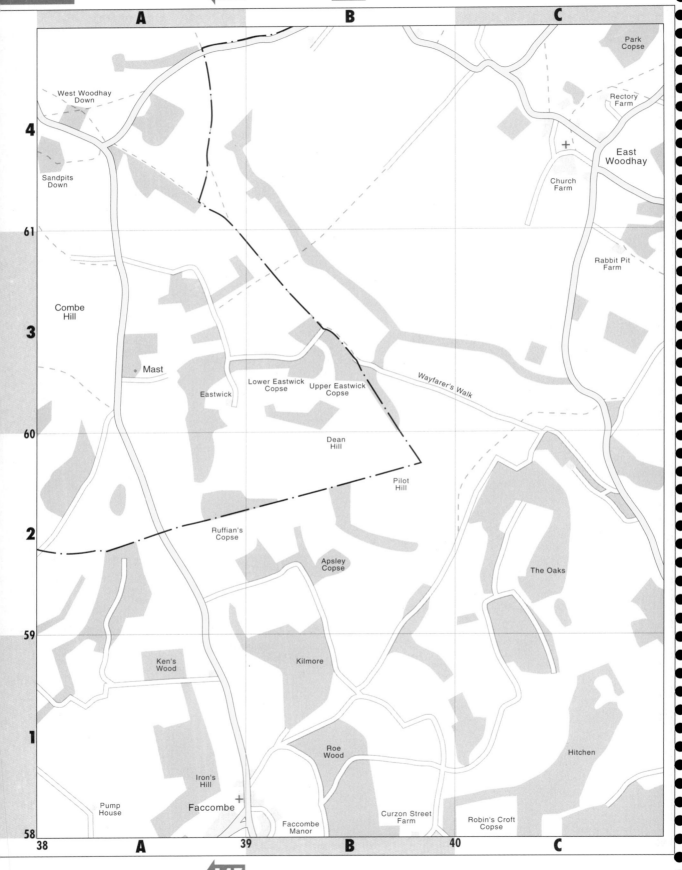

4

West Woodhay
Down

Park
Copse

Rectory
Farm

East
Woodhay

Sandpits
Down

Church
Farm

61

Rabbit Pit
Farm

Combe
Hill

3

Mast

Lower Eastwick
Copse

Upper Eastwick
Copse

Wayfarer's Walk

Eastwick

60

Dean
Hill

Pilot
Hill

The Oaks

2

Ruffian's
Copse

Apsley
Copse

59

Ken's
Wood

Kilmore

1

Roe
Wood

Hitchen

Iron's
Hill

Pump
House

Faccombe

Faccombe
Manor

Curzon Street
Farm

Robin's Croft
Copse

58

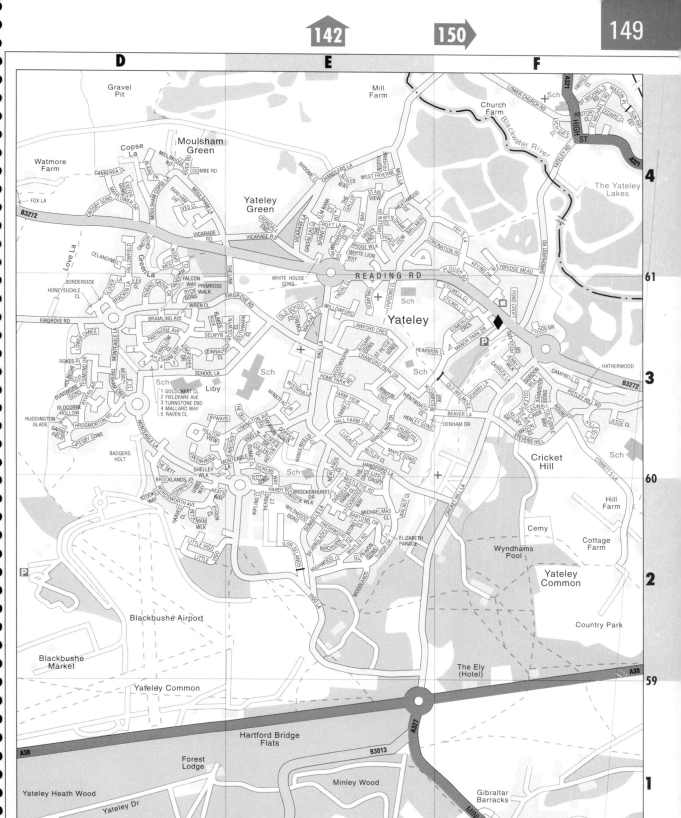

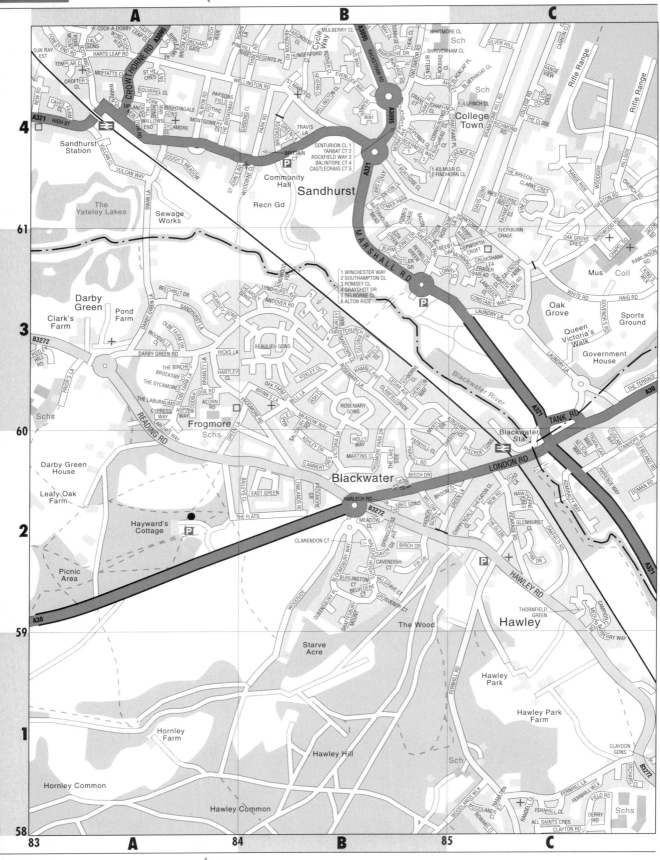

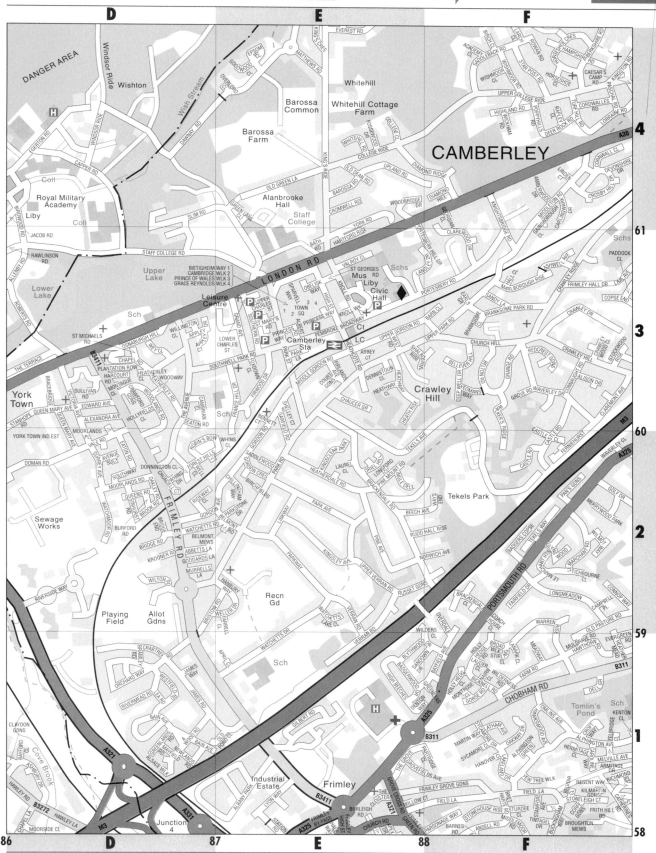

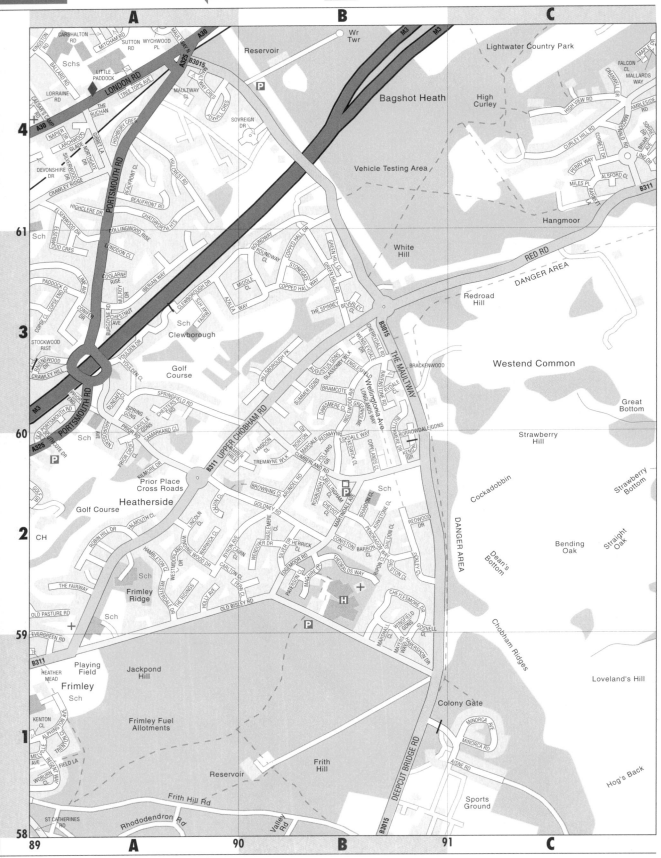

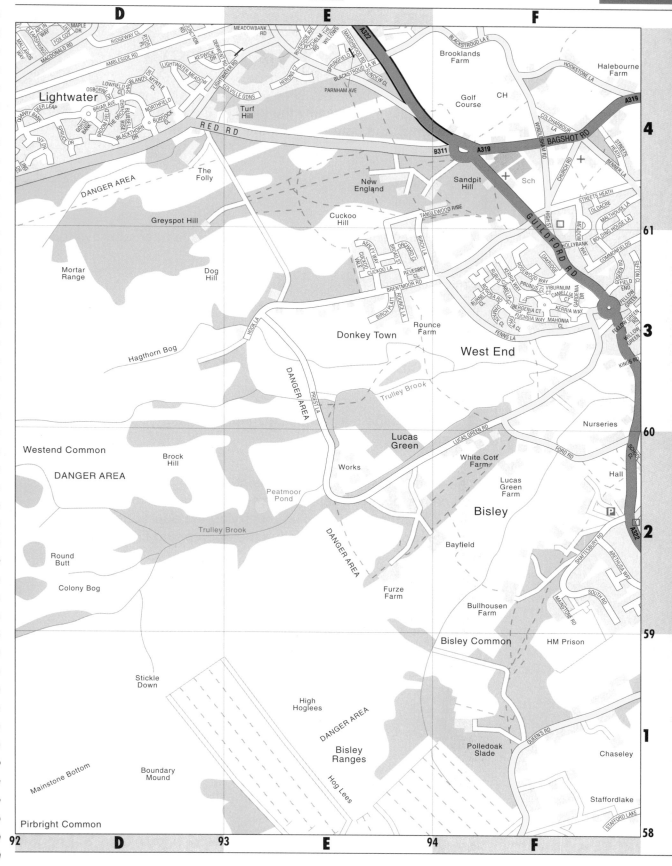

EXPLANATION OF THE STREET INDEX REFERENCE SYSTEM

Street names are listed alphabetically and show the locality, the page number and a reference to the square in which the name falls on the map page.

Example: Rushey Way. Read...RG6 87 E1

Rushey Way — This is the full street name, which may have been abbreviated on the map.

Read — This is the abbreviation for the town, village or locality in which the street falls.

RG6 — This is the Post Office Postcode District for the street name.

87 — This is the page number of the map on which the street name appears.

E1 — The letter and figure indicate the square on the map in which the centre of the street falls..The square can be found at the junction of the vertical column carrying the appropriate letter and the horizontal row carrying the appropriate figure.

ABBREVIATIONS USED IN THE INDEX
Road Names

Approach	App	Grove	Gr
Arcade	Arc	Heights	Hts
Avenue	Ave	Industrial Estate	Ind Est
Boulevard	Bvd	Junction	Junc
Buildings	Bldgs	Lane	La
Business Park	Bsns Pk	North	N
Broadway	Bwy	Orchard	Orch
By-Pass	By-Ps	Parade	Par
Causeway	Cswy	Passage	Pas
Circle	Circ	Place	Pl
Circus	Cir	Pleasant	Plea
Close	Cl	Precinct	Prec
Common	Comm	Promenade	Prom
Corner	Cnr	Road	Rd
Cottages	Cotts	South	S
Court	Ct	Square	Sq
Courtyard	Ctyd	Stairs	Strs
Crescent	Cres	Steps	Stps
Drive	Dri	Street,Saint	St
Drove	Dro	Terrace	Terr
East	E	Walk	Wlk
Embankment	Emb	West	W
Esplanade	Espl	Yard	Yd
Gardens	Gdns		

Key to abbreviations of Town, Village and Rural locality names used in the index of street names.

Abattoirs Rd. Read

159

Bosham Cl. Read

Budges Gdns. Woki

Bosham Cl. Read RG6 114 A4
Bosman Dr. Windl GU20 146 A3
Bostock La. Thea RG7 83 D1
Boston Ave. Read RG1 85 F3
Boston Gr. Slough SL1 42 B4
Boston Rd. Hen-O-T RG9 35 F4
Bosworth Gdns. Wood RG5 87 F2
Botany Cl. That RG19 106 C2
Bothy The. Warg RG10 36 B1
Botmoor Way. Chadd RG20 48 C4
Bottisham Cl. Winn RG6 114 B4
Bottle La. Binf RG42 91 D3
Bottle La. Know H SL6 38 A2
Bottle La. New G RG42 91 D3
Bottom La. Sulhd RG7 110 B4
Bouldish Farm Rd. Ascot SL5 119 F3
Boult St. Read RG1 86 B4
Boulters Cl. Maid SL6 20 B1
Boulters Cl. Slough SL1 42 A2
Boulters Cl. Wood RG5 87 F4
Boulters Ct. Maid SL6 20 B1
Boulters Gdns. Maid SL6 20 B1
Boulters La. Maid SL6 20 B1
Boulton Rd. Read RG2 86 A2
Boults Wlk. Read RG2 86 A3
Boundary Cl. Read RG31 84 B3
Boundary La. Caver RG4 58 C2
Boundary Pl. Woo G HP10 3 E4
Boundary Rd. Newb RG14 105 D1
Boundary Rd. Stai TW18 97 E2
Boundary Rd. Tapl SL6 40 C4
Boundary Rd. Woo G HP10 3 E4
Bourn Cl. Winn RG6 87 E1
Bourne Arch. That RG18 106 A2
Bourne Ave. Chert KT16 124 A3
Bourne Ave. Read RG2 86 A2
Bourne Ave. Wind SL4 67 E2
Bourne Cl. Bou E SL8 3 D3
Bourne Cl. Bur C RG31 84 A2
Bourne End Rd. Bou E SL6 20 C4
Bourne End Rd. Tapl SL6 20 C4
Bourne Meadow. Stai TW20 123 D3
Bourne Rd. Pangb RG8 56 C3
Bourne Rd. Slough SL1 42 B2
Bourne Rd. That RG19 106 A2
Bourne Rd. Went GU25 122 B2
Bourne Vale. Hung RG17 100 B3
Bourneside. Went GU25 122 A1
Bourton Cl. Read RG30 84 C4
Bouverie Way. Slough SL3 43 F1
Boveney Cl. Slough SL1 42 A2
Boveney New Rd. Eton SL4 41 F1
Boveney Rd. Dorn SL4 41 E1
Bovingdon Hts. Mar SL7 1 C1
Bowden Cl. Felt TW14 98 C4
Bowden Rd. Ascot SL5 120 B2
Bower Way. Slough SL1 41 F3
Bowes Rd. Stai TW18 96 C1
Bowes Rd. That RG19 106 B1
Bowfell Cl. Read RG31 57 E1
Bowland Drive. Brac RG12 118 C1
Bowling Ct. Hen-O-T RG9 15 E2
Bowling Green La. Pur O T RG8 57 D3
Bowling Green Rd. That RG18 106 A3
Bowman Ct. Woki RG45 142 C2
Bowmans Cl. Burn SL1 21 D2
Bowry Dr. Wray TW19 68 C1
Bowyer Cres. Woki RG40 116 B4
Bowyer Dr. Slough SL1 41 F3
Bowyers La. New G RG42 91 E3
Boxford Ridge. Brac RG12 118 A3
Boyd Ct. Brac RG42 118 A4
Boyn Hill Ave. Maid SL6 39 E3
Boyn Hill Cl. Maid SL6 39 E3
Boyn Hill Rd. Maid SL6 39 E3
Boyn Valley Rd. Maid SL6 39 E3
Boyndon Rd. Maid SL6 39 E4
Bracebridge. Camb GU15 151 D3
Bracken Bank. Burl SL5 119 E4
Bracken Cl. Ashf TW16 98 C1
Bracken Cl. Far C SL2 22 B4
Bracken Cl. Read RG31 57 E1
Bracken La. Yate GU17 149 D3
Bracken Rd. Maid SL6 39 E2
Bracken Way. Bur C RG7 111 D1
Bracken Way. Fla H HP10 3 D4
Brackendale Cl. Camb GU15 151 F2
Brackendale Rd. Camb GU15 151 E2
Brackenforde. Slough SL3 43 E2
Brackens The. Brac RG45 143 D4
Brackenwood. Bur C RG7 110 C1
Brackenwood. Camb GU15 152 B3
Brackenwood Dr. Tad RG26 135 D1
Bracknell Beeches. Brac RG12 118 A3
Bracknell Cl. Camb GU15 144 C1
Bracknell Rd. Bags GU19 145 F3
Bracknell Rd. Brac RG42 143 F4
Bracknell Rd. Camb GU15 145 D1
Bracknell Rd. New G RG42 92 A3
Bracknell Rd. Wink RG42 92 A3
Bradcutts La. Cook SL6 19 F4
Bradenham La. Bish SL7 18 B3
Bradfields. Brac RG12 118 B2
Bradford Rd. Slough SL1 42 A4
Brading Way. Pur O T RG8 57 E3
Bradley Cl. Kint RG17 102 A1
Bradley Rd. Slough SL1 42 C3
Bradmore Way. Read RG6 114 A4
Bradshaw Cl. Wind SL4 66 C3
Bradwell Rd. Read RG31 57 E2
Braemar Gdns. Slough SL1 42 A2
Braemore Cl. That RG19 106 B1
Brakendale Way. Read RG6 87 D3
Bramber Ct. Slough SL1 42 A3
Bramber Mews. Caver RG4 59 F2
Bramble Cl. Shepp TW17 125 E3
Bramble Cres. Read RG30 84 C4
Brambledown. Stai TW18 124 A4
Bramblegate. Crow RG45 143 D3
Brambles The. Brac RG45 142 B3
Bramblings. Caver RG4 58 C3
Bramcote. Camb GU15 152 B3
Bramley Cl. Chert KT16 124 A1
Bramley Cl. Maid SL6 39 E2
Bramley Cl. Read RG6 87 D2
Bramley Cl. Stai TW18 97 E1
Bramley Gr. Brac RG45 142 B3
Bramley La. Black GU17 150 A3
Bramley Rd. Camb GU15 151 D1
Bramley Rd. Silc RG7 136 A1
Bramling Ave. Yate GU17 149 D3
Brammas Cl. Slough SL1 42 B2
Brampton Chase. Shipl RG9 36 A2
Bramshaw Rd. Read RG30 58 A1
Bramshill Cl. Arbo RG2 140 C4
Bramwell Cl. That RG19 106 C1
Bran Cl. Read RG30 84 C4
Brandon Ave. Wood RG5 88 A4
Brandon Cl. Camb GU15 152 B2
Brands Rd. Slough SL3 69 D4
Branksome Cl. Camb GU15 151 F3
Branksome Hill Rd. Sand GU15 150 C4
Branksome Park Rd. Camb GU15 151 F3
Brants Bridge. Brac RG12 118 C3
Braunfels Wlk. Newb RG14 104 C1
Bravington Cl. Stai TW17 124 C2
Bray Cl. Maid SL6 40 B2
Bray Ct. Holy SL6 40 B1
Bray Rd. Maid SL6 40 A3
Bray Rd. Read RG30 85 D2
Braybank. Maid SL6 40 B2
Braybrooke Gdns. Warg RG10 36 B1
Braybrooke Rd. Brac RG42 91 D1
Braybrooke Rd. Warg RG10 36 B1
Braye Cl. Sand GU17 143 E1
Brayfield Rd. Maid SL6 40 B2
Brayford Rd. Read RG2 113 E4
Braywick Rd. Maid SL6 40 A3
Braywood Ave. Eng G TW20 96 A1
Braziers La. Wink RG42 92 B2
Breach Sq. Hung RG17 100 B2
Breadcroft La. Bur G SL6 38 C2
Breadcroft Rd. Whi Wa SL6 38 C2
Bream Cl. Mar SL7 18 B4
Brecon Rd. Wood RG5 87 F4
Bredon Rd. Woki RG41 88 C1
Bredward Cl. Burn SL1 21 D1
Breech The. Sand GU15 150 B4
Breedons Hill. Pangb RG8 56 B3
Bremer Rd. Stan TW18 97 D3
Brendon Cl. Harl UB7 71 E4
Brendon Cl. Read RG30 57 F1
Brent Cl. That RG19 106 B1
Brent Gdns. Read RG2 86 A2
Brent Rd. Bou E SL8 3 D2
Brentmoor Rd. West E GU24 153 E3
Brerewood. Read RG6 86 C1
Bret Harte Rd. Camb GU16 151 F1
Brewery Comm. Mort RG7 137 D4
Brewhouse Hill. Frox SN8 99 D2
Briants Ave. Caver RG4 59 E1
Briants Piece. Herm RG18 79 D3
Briar Ave. Light GU18 153 D4
Briar Cl. Burn SL6 41 D4
Briar Cl. Caver RG4 59 D3
Briar Dene. Maid SL6 19 E1
Briar Glen. Cook SL6 19 F3
Briar Rd. Stai TW17 125 D2
Briar Way. Slough SL2 42 A4
Briarlea Rd. Mort RG7 136 C3
Briars Cl. Pangb RG8 56 C3
Briars The. Slough SL3 43 F1
Briars The. Stan SL3 70 A1
Briarwood Cl. Felt TW13 98 C3
Briarwood. Woki RG40 141 F3
Brickfield La. Burn SL1 21 D2
Brickfield La. Harl UB7 71 E4
Bridge Ave. Cook SL6 19 F3
Bridge Ave. Maid SL6 40 A4
Bridge Ave.Maid SL6 40 A4
Bridge Cl. Shepp TW17 125 F1
Bridge Cl. Slough SL1 41 F3
Bridge Cl. Stai TW18 96 C2
Bridge End. Camb GU15 151 D2
Bridge Gdns. Stai TW15 98 B1
Bridge La. Went GU25 122 C2
Bridge Rd. Ascot SL5 120 B2
Bridge Rd. Bags GU19 145 F2
Bridge Rd. Camb GU15 151 D2
Bridge Rd. Chert KT16 124 A1
Bridge Rd. Maid SL6 40 A4
Bridge St. Caver RG4 59 D1
Bridge St. Hung RG17 100 B3
Bridge St. Iver SL3 69 E4
Bridge St. Maid SL6 40 A4
Bridge St. Newb RG14 105 D2
Bridge St. Read RG1 86 A4
Bridge St. Shepp TW17 125 F1
Bridge St. Stai TW18 96 C2
Bridge View. Went SL5 121 D1
Bridge Walk. Yate GU17 149 E4
Bridgeman Dr. Wind SL4 67 D3
Bridges Cl. Woki RG41 115 F4
Bridges The. Silc RG7 136 B3
Bridgestone Dr. Bou E SL8 3 E2
Bridgewater Cl. Read RG30 58 B1
Bridgewater Ct. Slough SL3 44 A1
Bridgewater Terr. Wind SL4 67 E3
Bridgewater Way. Wind SL4 67 E3
Bridle Cl. Maid SL6 19 F1
Bridle Rd. Maid SL6 19 F1
Bridlepath Way. Felt TW14 98 C4
Bridlington Spur. Slough SL1 42 A2
Bridport Cl. Read RG6 87 E1
Bridport Way. Slough SL2 22 A1
Brierley Pl. Pur O T RG31 57 E2
Briff La. Buck RG7 107 E4
Brigham Rd. Read RG1 59 D1
Brighton Rd. Read RG6 87 D3
Brighton Spur. Slough SL2 22 A1
Brightside Ave. Stai TW18 97 E1
Brill Cl. Caver RG4 59 D2
Brill Cl. Maid SL6 39 E2
Brill Cl. Mar SL7 1 B1
Brimblecombe Cl. Woki RG41 89 D1
Brimpton La. Brim RG7 134 A2
Brimpton Rd. Brim RG7 133 F4
Brimpton Rd. Read RG30 85 D2
Brimpton Rd. Tad RG26 134 B1
Brimpton Rd. Wool RG7 133 F4
Brinns La. Sand GU17 150 B3
Brisbane Rd. Read RG30 85 D4
Bristol Cl. Stan TW19 70 C1
Bristol Way. Slough SL1 42 C3
Bristow Ct. Mar SL7 2 A2
Bristow Rd. Camb GU15 151 D2
Bristow Rd. Camb GU15 151 E2
Britannia Way. Stan TW19 97 E4
Britten Rd. Read RG2 86 A3
Britwell Rd. Burn SL1 21 E1
Brixham Rd. Read RG2 86 A1
Broad Hinton. Twyf RG10 61 F2
Broad La. Bou E HP10 3 F3
Broad La. Brac RG12 118 B3
Broad La. Buck RG7 107 E3
Broad Oak. Ashf TW16 98 C1
Broad Oak Ct. Slough SL2 22 B1
Broad Oak. Slough SL2 22 B1
Broad Platts. Slough SL3 43 E2
Broad St. East I RG20 30 C4
Broad St. Read RG1 86 A4
Broad St. West E GU24 153 E3
Broad St. Woki RG40 116 B3
Broad Street Mall The. Read RG1 86 A4
Broad Way. Bee H RG7 138 B2
Broad Wlk. Camb GU16 151 F1
Broadacre. Stai TW18 97 D2
Broadcommon Rd. Hurst RG10 89 D4
Broadhalfpenny La. Tad RG26 135 E1
Broadlands Ave. Shepp TW17 125 E2
Broadlands Cl. Read RG31 84 B3
Broadley Gn. Windl GU20 146 B2
Broadmark Rd. Slough SL2 43 D3
Broadmeadow End. That RG18 106 C2
Broadmoor La. W St L RG10 63 D3
Broadmoor La. Whi Wa SL6 63 D3
Broadrich Heath. New G RG42 91 F1
Broadwater Cl. Wray TW19 95 F4
Broadwater La. Hurst RG10 61 F1
Broadwater Pk. Holy SL6 40 C1
Broadwater Pk. Holy SL6 40 C1
Broadwater Rd. Twyf RG10 61 F2
Broadway. Brac RG12 118 B4
Broadway. Maid SL6 39 F4
Broadway Rd. Light GU18 146 B1
Broadway. That RG19 106 B2
Broadway The. Lamb RG17 25 D2
Broadway The. Newb RG14 105 D2
Broadway The. Sand GU17 150 A4
Broadway The. Stai TW18 124 B4
Brocas Rd. Bur C RG7 110 C1
Brocas St. Eton SL4 67 E4
Brocas Terr. Eton SL4 67 E4
Brock Gdns. Read RG30 85 E4
Brock La. Maid SL6 39 F4
Brock Way. Vir W GU25 122 B3
Brockenhurst Dr. Yate GU17 149 E3
Brockenhurst Rd. Ascot SL5 120 A2
Brockenhurst Rd. Brac RG12 119 D3
Brocklands. Yate GU17 149 D2
Brockley Cl. Read RG30 85 D4
Brocks La. Buck RG7 & RG18 80 A2
Brocks Way. Shipl RG9 36 A2
Brocksby Cl. Black GU17 150 A3
Broken Furlong. Eton SL4 42 A1
Broken Way. Newt RG20 131 E1
Bromley Wlk. Read RG30 84 C4
Brompton Cl. Winn RG6 87 E1
Brompton Dr. Maid SL6 19 E1
Bromycroft Rd. Slough SL2 22 A1
Brook Cl. Sand GU15 143 F1
Brook Cl. Stan TW19 97 F4
Brook Cl. Woki RG41 116 A4
Brook Cres. Slough SL1 41 F4
Brook Dr. Brac RG12 118 C3
Brook Gn. Brac RG42 117 F4
Brook La. Hurst RG10 62 C2
Brook Path. Slough SL1 41 F3
Brook Path. Slough SL1 41 F3
Brook Rd. Bags GU19 145 F1
Brook Rd. Camb GU15 151 D2
Brook St. Twyf RG10 61 E2
Brook St W. Read RG1 86 A3
Brook St. Wind SL4 67 E3
Brookbank. Bou E HP10 3 E2
Brookdene Cl. Maid SL6 19 F1
Brooke Pl. Binf RG42 90 B2
Brookers Cnr. Crow RG45 143 E3
Brookers Hill. Read RG2 113 E3
Brookers Row. Brac RG45 143 D3
Brookfield Rd. Bou E HP10 3 E2
Brookhouse Dr. Bou E HP10 3 E2
Brooklands Cl. Stai TW16 125 F4
Brooklyn Dr. Caver RG4 59 D3
Brookmill The. Read RG1 85 F3
Brooks Rd. That RG18 106 C2
Brooksby Rd. Read RG31 57 E1
Brookside Ave. Stai TW19 97 E2
Brookside Ave. Wray TW19 68 C2
Brookside. Chert KT16 123 F1
Brookside Cl. Read RG6 87 E1
Brookside. Iver SL3 69 E4
Brookside. Read RG31 84 C2
Brookside. Sand GU17 150 B4
Brookside. Woki RG41 115 F4
Brookway. Newb RG14 105 E1
Broom Acres. Sand GU17 143 D1
Broom Cl. Black GU17 150 C2
Broom Cl. Read RG31 84 B3
Broom Field. Light GU18 153 D4
Broom Gr. Woki RG41 115 E2
Broom Hill. Cook SL6 19 F3
Broom Hill. Sto P SL2 23 D3
Broome Cl. Yate GU17 149 E4
Broomfield Cl. Went SL5 121 D1
Broomfield Pk. Went SL5 121 D1
Broomfield Rd. Read RG30 84 C4
Broomhall La. Sunn SL5 121 D2
Broomsquire Rd. Bags GU19 145 F1
Broughton Cl. Read RG30 58 B1
Broughton Mews. Camb GU16 151 F1
Brownfields Gdns. Maid SL6 39 F3
Browngraves Rd. Harl UB7 71 E4
Browning Cl. Camb GU15 152 B2
Browning Cl. That RG18 106 B2
Brownlow Dr. Brac RG42 91 E1
Brownlow Rd. Read RG1 85 F4
Brownrigg Cres. Brac RG12 118 C4
Brownrigg Rd. Ashf TW15 98 A2
Brownsfield Rd. That RG18 106 B2
Bruan Rd. Newb RG14 130 C4
Bruce Ave. Shepp TW17 125 E2
Bruce Cl. Slough SL1 42 A3
Bruce Rd. Wood RG5 87 E4
Bruce Wlk. Wind SL4 66 B3
Brudenell. Wind SL4 66 C2
Brummell Rd. Newb RG14 104 C3
Brunel Cl. Maid SL6 39 F3
Brunel Dr. Wood RG5 60 C1
Brunel Rd. Maid SL6 39 E3
Brunel Rd. Read RG30 85 D2
Brunel Rd. Thea RG7 83 F1
Brunel Way. Slough SL1 42 C3
Brunswick. Brac RG12 118 A1
Brunswick Hill. Read RG1 85 F4
Brunswick St. Read RG1 85 F3
Bruton Way. Brac RG12 118 C1
Bryant Ave. Slough SL2 42 C4
Bryants La. Yatt RG18 53 F1
Bryants Pl. Pur O T RG8 57 D3
Brybur Cl. Read RG2 113 E4
Bryer Pl. Wind SL4 66 B2
Bsns Centre The. Woki RG41 116 A2
Buccaneer Cl. Wood RG5 88 A4
Buccleuch Rd. Datch SL3 68 A4
Buchan The. Camb GU15 152 A4
Buchanan Dr. Woki RG40 141 F4
Buchanan Sq. That RG19 106 C1
Buck Side. Caver RG4 59 D1
Buckden Cl. Wood RG5 88 A3
Buckham Hill. Chadd RG17 & RG20 48 B3
Buckhurst Gr. Woki RG40 116 C3
Buckhurst Hill. Brac RG12 118 C3
Buckhurst La. Ascot SL5 121 D3
Buckhurst Rd. Ascot SL5 120 C4
Buckhurst Way. Read RG6 87 D2
Buckingham Ave E. Slough SL1 42 B4
Buckingham Ave. Slough SL1 42 A4
Buckingham Dr. Caver RG4 59 D3
Buckingham Gate. Medm SL7 17 E4
Buckingham Gdns. Slough SL1 42 C2
Buckingham Rd. Newb RG14 104 C1
Buckingham Way. Camb GU16 151 F1
Buckland Ave. Slough SL3 43 D2
Buckland Cres. Wind SL4 66 C3
Buckland Rd. Read RG2 86 A2
Buckle La. New G RG42 91 D3
Bucklebury. Brac RG12 118 A1
Bucklebury Cl. Holy SL6 40 B1
Bucknell Ave. Pangb RG8 56 C3
Bucknell Cl. Read RG31 84 C2
Buckthorn Cl. Woki RG40 116 C4
Budebury Rd. Stai TW18 97 D2
Budges Gdns. Woki RG40 116 C4

160

Budges Rd. Woki

Chalvey Gr. Slough

Budges Rd. Woki RG40 116 B4
Buffins. Tapl SL6 20 B1
Bulkeley Ave. Wind SL4 67 D2
Bulkeley Cl. Eng G TW20 95 E2
Bull La. Brac RG42 118 A4
Bull La. Swal RG7 139 D2
Bull Meadow The. Stre RG8 33 F3
Bullbrook Dr. Brac RG12 118 C4
Bullbrook Row. Brac RG12 118 C4
Bullfinch Cl. Sand GU15 150 C4
Bulmershe Rd. Read RG1 86 C3
Bulpit La. Hung RG17 100 B2
Bunby Rd. Sto P SL2 22 C3
Bunces Cl. Eton SL4 42 A1
Bunces La. Bur C RG7 111 D1
Bundys Way. Stai TW18 96 C1
Bungalow Dr. Read RG31 84 B4
Bunglers Hill. Swal RG7 140 A3
Bunkers Hill. Newb RG14 130 B3
Bunten Meade. Slough SL1 42 A3
Burbage Gn. Brac RG12 118 C2
Burbidge Cl. Read RG31 84 C2
Burbidge Rd. Stai TW17 125 D3
Burchell Rd. Newb RG14 104 C3
Burchett Copse. Woki RG40 141 F4
Burchetts Green La. Bur G SL6 38 B3
Burchetts Green Rd. Bur G SL6 38 A4
Burchetts Way. Shepp TW17 125 D2
Burcombe Way. Caver RG4 59 D2
Burcot Gdns. Maid SL6 19 F2
Burdett Ct. Read RG2 86 B2
Burdock Cl. Bur C RG7 111 D1
Burdock Cl. Light GU18 153 D4
Burfield Rd. Old W SL4 95 D4
Burford Cl. Mar B SL7 1 B3
Burford Gdns. Slough SL1 41 E4
Burford Rd. Camb GU15 151 D2
Burfords. East G RG17 47 E3
Burges Way. Stan TW18 97 D1
Burgess Cl. Wood RG5 87 E2
Burgess La. Kint RG20 128 B3
Burgett Rd. Slough SL1 42 A2
Burghead Cl. Sand GU15 150 B4
Burghfield Rd. Read RG30 85 D2
Burgoyne Rd. Ashf TW16 98 C1
Burgoyne Rd. Camb GU15 152 A3
Burleigh Gdns. Ashf TW15 98 B2
Burleigh La. Ascot SL5 119 F4
Burleigh Mews. Caver RG4 59 E3
Burleigh Rd. Ascot SL5 119 F4
Burleigh Rd. Camb GU16 151 E1
Burley Orch. Chert KT16 124 A2
Burley Way. Black GU17 150 B3
Burlingham Cl. Read RG2 113 E3
Burlings The. Ascot SL5 119 F4
Burlington Ave. Slough SL1 42 C2
Burlington Cl. Felt TW14 98 B4
Burlington Ct. Black GU17 150 B2
Burlington Rd. Burn SL1 41 D4
Burlington Rd. Read RG30 84 B4
Burlington Rd. Slough SL1 42 C2
Burlsdon Way. Brac RG12 118 C4
Burn Moor Chase. Brac RG12 118 C1
Burn Wlk. Burn SL1 21 D1
Burne-Jones Dr. Sand GU15 150 B3
Burnet Cl. West E GU24 153 F3
Burnetts Rd. Wind SL4 66 C3
Burney Bit. Silc RG26 135 F1
Burnham Cl. Bou E SL8 3 D2
Burnham Cl. Wind SL4 66 B3
Burnham Gr. Brac RG42 91 E1
Burnham La. Slough SL1 41 F4
Burnham Rd. Tad RG26 134 C1
Burnham Rise. Caver RG4 59 E3
Burniston Cl. Winn RG6 87 F1
Burns Cl. Wood RG5 87 F2
Burns Wlk. That RG18 106 B2
Burnt Oak. Cook SL6 19 F4
Burnt Oak. Woki RG40 141 F4
Burnt Pollard La. West E GU18 146 C1
Burnthouse Gdns. New G RG42 91 F1
Burnthouse La. Bur C RG30 112 A3
Burrcroft Rd. Read RG30 85 D3
Burrell Rd. Comp RG20 31 F2
Burroughs Cres. Bou E SL8 3 D2
Burroway Rd. Slough SL3 44 A2
Burrows Hill Cl. Stan TW6 70 B2
Burton Cl. Windl GU20 146 B2
Burton Way. Wind SL4 66 C2
Burtons Hill. Kint RG17 102 A1
Burway Cres. Chert KT16 124 A3
Burwell Cl. Winn RG6 87 E1
Burys Bank Rd. Gree RG19 132 A3
Burys Bank Rd. That RG19 132 A3
Bush Rd. Stai TW17 125 D2
Business Village The. Slough SL2 43 D3
Butchers La. Whi Wa SL6 63 E4
Bute St. Read RG30 85 D3
Butler Ct. Mar SL7 2 A2
Butler Rd. Bags GU19 145 F1
Butler Rd. Crow RG45 143 D3
Butlers Cl. Wind SL4 66 B3
Butson Cl. Newb RG14 104 C2
Buttenshaw Ave. Bark RG2 141 D4
Buttenshaw Cl. Bark RG2 141 D4
Butter Market. Read RG1 86 A4
Buttercup Cl. Woki RG40 116 C4
Buttercup Cl. Woki RG40 117 D3
Buttercup Sq. Stan TW19 97 E4
Butterfield. Bou E HP10 3 E2
Buttermere Ave. Slough SL1 41 E4
Buttermere Cl. Felt TW14 98 C4
Buttermere Dr. Camb GU15 152 B3
Buttermere Gdns. Brac RG12 118 B3
Buttermere Way. Stai TW20 96 A1
Buttersteep Rise. Brac SL5 119 E1
Butts Hill Rd. Wood RG5 87 F4
Buxton Ave. Caver RG4 58 C2
Buxton Rd. Ashf TW15 97 E2
Bybend Cl. Far C SL2 22 A2
Byefield Rd. Read RG30 85 D2
Byeways Cl. Warg RG10 37 F2
Byland Dr. Holy SL6 40 A1
Byreton Cl. Read RG6 87 D1
Byron Ave. Camb GU15 152 A2
Byron Cl. Mar SL7 1 C2
Byron Cl. Newb RG14 130 C4
Byron Cl. Twyf RG10 61 F2
Byron Cl. Yate GU17 149 D2
Byron Dr. Crow RG45 143 D2
Byron Rd. Read RG6 87 D4
Byron Rd. Twyf RG10 61 F2
Bythorn Cl. Winn RG6 87 F1
Byways. Burn SL1 41 D4
Byways. Yate GU17 149 D3
Bywood. Brac RG12 118 A1
Byworth Cl. Read RG2 113 D4

Cabin Moss. Brac RG12 118 C1
Cabrera Ave. Went GU25 122 B2
Cabrera Cl. Went GU25 122 B2
Cadbury Cl. Ashf TW16 98 C1
Cadbury Rd. Ashf TW16 98 C1
Caddy Cl. Eng G TW20 96 A2
Cadogan Cl. Caver RG4 59 F2
Cadogan Cl. Holy SL6 65 D4
Cadogan Cl. Read RG30 84 C4
Cadwell Dr. Maid SL6 39 E2
Caesars Camp Rd. Camb GU15 152 A4
Caesars Gate. New G RG42 91 F1
Caesars Way. Shepp TW17 125 E2
Cages Wood Dr. Far C SL2 22 A4
Cain Rd. Binf RG12 117 E4
Cain Rd. Brac RG12 117 F4
Cains La. Harm TW14 71 F1
Cairn Cl. Camb GU15 152 A2
Cairngorm Rd. That RG19 106 B1
Caistor Cl. Bur C RG31 84 A2
Calard Dr. That RG18 106 A3
Calbourne Dr. Bur C RG31 84 B2
Calbroke Rd. Slough SL2 21 F1
Calcot Ct. Read RG31 84 C3
Calcot Place Dr. Read RG31 84 C2
Caldbeck Dr. Wood RG5 87 F4
Calder Cl. Maid SL6 19 F1
Calder Cl. Read RG30 84 C4
Calder Ct. Maid SL6 19 E1
Calder Ct. Slough SL3 43 F1
Calder Way. Stan SL3 69 F2
Caldwell Rd. Windl GU20 146 B3
Caledonia Rd. Stan TW19 97 F4
Caleta Cl. Caver RG4 59 E1
Calfridus Way. Brac RG12 118 C3
Calleva Pk. Alde RG7 134 C1
Callington Rd. Read RG2 86 B1
Callins La. W St L RG10 63 D2
Callis Farm Cl. Stan TW19 70 C1
Callow Hill. Vir W GU25 122 B4
Calshot Pl. Bur C RG31 84 B2
Calshot Rd. Harm TW6 71 D3
Calshot Way. Harm TW6 71 D3
Calvin Cl. Camb GU15 152 A2
Camberley Rd. Harm TW6 71 D2
Camborne Cl. Crow RG6 143 D1
Camborne Cl. Harm TW6 71 D2
Camborne Cl. Read RG6 87 D1
Camborne Rd S. Harm TW6 71 D2
Camborne Way. Harm TW6 71 D2
Cambria Gdns. Stan TW19 97 F4
Cambrian Cl. Camb GU15 151 D3
Cambrian Way. Brac RG40 142 A4
Cambrian Way. Bur C RG31 84 B2
Cambridge Ave. Burn SL1 21 D2
Cambridge Ave. Slough SL1 42 A4
Cambridge Cl. Harm UB7 70 B4
Cambridge Rd. Crow RG45 143 D2
Cambridge Rd. Mar SL7 1 B1
Cambridge Rd. Sand GU15 143 F1
Cambridge Rd. Stai TW15 98 B1
Cambridge St. Read RG1 85 F4
Cambridge Wlk. Camb GU15 151 E3
Cambridgeshire Cl. New G RG42 91 F1
Cambridgeshire Cl. Woki RG41 115 F3
Camden Pl. Bou E SL8 3 D2
Camden Pl. Bur C RG31 84 A2
Camden Rd. Maid SL6 19 E1
Camellia Ct. West E GU24 153 F3
Camellia Way. Woki RG41 115 E4
Camilla Cl. Ashf TW16 98 C1
Camley Gdns. Maid SL6 39 D4
Camley Park Dr. Maid SL6 38 C4
Camm Ave. Wind SL4 66 C2
Camp Rd. Padw RG7 110 B1
Campbell Cl. Yate GU17 149 F3
Campbell Pl. Camb GU16 151 F2
Campbell Rd. Wood RG5 87 E3
Camperdown. Maid SL6 20 A1
Campion Cl. Black GU17 150 C2
Campion Way. Woki RG40 116 C4
Canada Rd. Slough SL1 43 D2
Canal View Rd. Newb RG14 105 E2
Canal Walk. Hung RG17 100 B3
Canal Way. Read RG1 86 B4
Canal Wharf. Slough SL3 44 A2
Canberra Cl. Yate GU17 149 D4
Canberra Rd. Harm TW6 71 D2
Candleford Cl. Brac RG12 91 E1
Candover Cl. Harm UB7 70 B4
Canford Ct. Read RG30 85 E4
Cannock Cl. Maid SL6 40 A3
Cannock Way. Wood RG6 87 E1
Cannon Cl. Sand GU15 150 C4
Cannon Court Rd. Cook SL6 19 E2
Cannon Court Rd. Maid SL6 19 E2
Cannon Hill. Brac RG12 118 B2
Cannon Hill Cl. Maid SL6 40 B1
Cannon La. Maid SL6 38 C2
Cannon La. Whi Wa SL6 38 C2
Cannon St. Read RG1 85 F4
Cannondown Rd. Cook SL6 19 F3
Canon Hill Dr. Maid SL6 40 A2
Canopus Way. Stan TW19 97 F4
Cansfield End. Newb RG14 104 C2
Canterbury Ave. Slough SL2 22 B1
Canterbury Rd. Read RG2 86 B2
Cantley Cres. Woki RG41 116 A4
Capper Rd. Camb GU15 151 D4
Captains Gorse. Upp B RG8 54 C3
Caraway Rd. Read RG6 87 D1
Carbery La. Ascot SL5 120 A3
Carbinswood La. Buck RG7 108 A3
Cardiff Rd. Read RG1 58 C1
Cardigan Gdns. Read RG1 86 C3
Cardigan Rd. Read RG1 86 C3
Cardinal Cl. Caver RG4 59 D1
Cardinals The. Brac RG12 118 A3
Cardinals Wlk. Ashf TW16 98 C1
Cardinals Wlk. Slough SL6 41 E4
Cardwell Cres. Ascot SL5 120 B2
Carew Rd. Ashf TW15 98 B1
Carey Cl. Wind SL4 67 D2
Carey Rd. Woki RG40 116 B3
Carey St. Read RG1 85 F4
Cariad Ct. Gori RG8 34 A4
Carisbrooke Cl. Caver RG4 59 E3
Carisbrooke Cl. Maid SL6 39 E3
Carisbrooke Ct. Slough SL1 42 C3
Carland Cl. Read RG6 87 D1
Carlile Gdns. Twyf RG10 61 E3
Carlingwark Dr. Camb GU15 151 F4
Carlisle Rd. Read RG31 57 F2
Carlisle Rd. Slough SL1 42 B3
Carlton Cl. Camb GU15 152 A2
Carlton Cl. Wood RG5 87 F3
Carlton Rd. Ashf TW16 98 C1
Carlton Rd. Caver RG4 58 C3
Carlton Rd. Slough SL2 43 D3
Carlyle Rd. Stai TW18 97 D1
Carmarthen Rd. Slough SL1 42 C3
Carnarvon Rd. Read RG1 86 C3
Carnation Dr. Burl RG42 92 A1
Carnegie Rd. Newb RG14 105 D1
Carnoustie. Brac RG12 117 F1
Carolina Pl. Woki RG40 141 F4
Caroline Ct. Ashf TW15 98 A1
Caroline Ct. Mar SL7 1 C2
Caroline Dr. Woki RG41 116 A4
Caroline Pl. Stan UB7 71 F4
Caroline St. Read RG1 85 F4
Caroline Way. Camb GU16 151 F1
Carrick Gdns. Wood RG5 87 E4
Carrick La. Yate GU17 149 F3
Carrington Ave. Fla H HP10 3 D4
Carrington Rd. Slough SL1 42 C3
Carroll Cres. Ascot SL5 119 F3
Carron Cl. Read RG30 85 D4
Carsdale Cl. Read RG1 85 F3
Carshalton Rd. Camb GU15 145 D1
Carshalton Way. Wood RG6 87 E1
Carston Gr. Read RG31 84 C2
Carter Cl. Wind SL4 67 D3
Carters Hill. Binf RG40 & RG42 90 A2
Carters Rise. Read RG31 84 C2
Cartmel Dr. Wood RG5 87 E3
Cary Cl. Newb RG14 130 B3
Casey Ct. Stan D RG7 81 E2
Cassia Dr. Read RG6 86 C1
Cassiobury Ave. Felt TW14 98 C4
Castle Ave. Datch SL3 68 A4
Castle Cl. Camb GU15 151 F2
Castle Cl. Stai TW16 98 C1
Castle Cres. Read RG1 85 F3
Castle Ct. Maid SL6 39 E4
Castle Dr. Maid SL6 39 E4
Castle End Rd. W St L RG10 62 A4
Castle Gr. Newb RG14 104 C3
Castle Hill. Maid SL6 39 F4
Castle Hill Rd. Eng G TW20 95 D3
Castle Hill Rd. Eng G TW20 95 E3
Castle Hill. Read RG1 85 F3
Castle Hill. Swal RG7 140 B4
Castle Hill Terr. Maid SL6 39 F4
Castle La. Wint RG14 104 C3
Castle Mews. Maid SL6 39 F4
Castle Rd. Camb GU15 151 F2
Castle St. Read RG1 86 A4
Castle St. Slough SL1 42 C2
Castlecraig Ct. Sand GU15 150 B4
Castleton Ct. Mar SL7 1 C1
Castleview Rd. Slough SL3 43 E1
Castor Ct. Yate GU17 149 D4
Caswall Cl. Binf RG42 90 B1
Caswall Ride. Yate GU17 149 F3
Catalina Cl. Wood RG5 88 A4
Catcliffe Way. Read RG6 113 F4
Catena Rise. Light GU18 146 A1
Catesby Gdns. Yate GU17 149 D3
Catherine Dr. Ashf TW16 98 C1
Catherine Rd. Newb RG14 105 D1
Catherine St. Read RG30 85 F4
Catlin Cres. Shepp TW17 125 E2
Catmore Rd. Farn RG20 29 E4
Catmore Rd. West I RG20 29 E4
Caunter Rd. Newb RG14 104 B2
Causeway The. Maid SL6 40 B2
Causeway The. Mar SL7 1 C1
Causeway The. Stai TW18 96 B2
Causmans Way. Read RG31 57 E1
Cavalier Cl. Newb RG14 105 E3
Cavalier Cl. Thea RG7 83 E1
Cavalry Cres. Wind SL4 67 E2
Cavendish Cl. Ashf TW16 98 C1
Cavendish Cl. Burn SL6 41 D4
Cavendish Ct. Ashf TW16 98 C1
Cavendish Ct. Black GU17 150 B2
Cavendish Ct. Newb RG14 105 F3
Cavendish Gdns. Winn RG41 88 A2
Cavendish Meads. Ascot SL5 120 B2
Cavendish Pk. Sand GU15 150 C3
Cavendish Rd. Ashf TW16 98 C1
Cavendish Rd. Caver RG4 59 E3
Caversham Park Rd. Caver RG4 59 F3
Caversham Rd. Caver RG1 59 D1
Caves Farm Cl. Sand GU17 150 A4
Cawcott Dr. Wind SL4 66 C3
Cawsham Gdns. Caver RG4 59 E2
Caxton Cl. Read RG30 58 B1
Cecil Aldin Dr. Pur O T RG31 57 E2
Cecil Cl. Ashf TW15 98 B1
Cecil Rd. Ashf TW15 98 B1
Cecil Rd. Iver SL0 44 C4
Cecil Way. Slough SL2 21 F1
Cedar Ave. Black GU17 150 B3
Cedar Chase. Tapl SL6 20 B1
Cedar Cl. Bags GU19 145 F2
Cedar Cl. Stai TW18 124 B3
Cedar Cl. Woki RG40 116 B3
Cedar Ct. Eng G TW20 96 A2
Cedar Ct. Mar SL7 1 C1
Cedar Dr. Brac RG42 91 E1
Cedar Dr. Cook SL6 19 F4
Cedar Dr. Mar B SL7 1 B4
Cedar Dr. Pangb RG8 56 B2
Cedar Dr. Windl SL5 121 D1
Cedar Gr. That RG19 106 B2
Cedar Mount. Newb RG14 130 C4
Cedar Rd. Felt TW14 98 B4
Cedar Rd. Read RG2 86 C1
Cedar Way. Slough SL3 43 F1
Cedar Way. Stai TW16 98 C1
Cedar Wood Cres. Caver RG4 59 D2
Cedars Cl. Sand GU17 149 F4
Cedars Rd. Maid SL6 40 A4
Cedars The. Read RG31 57 E1
Celandine Cl. Crow RG45 143 E3
Celandine Ct. Yate GU17 149 D4
Celandine Gr. That RG18 106 C2
Celia Cres. Stai TW15 97 E1
Cell Farm Ave. Old W SL4 68 A1
Celsea Pl. Chol OX10 14 A4
Cemetery La. Shepp TW17 125 D1
Central Dr. Slough SL1 41 F3
Centre The. Shepp TW17 125 F1
Centurion Cl. Read RG1 86 A3
Centurion Cl. Sand GU15 150 B4
Century Rd. Stai TW18 96 B2
Cerotus Pl. Chert KT16 123 F1
Chaffinch Cl. Read RG31 84 A4
Chaffinch Cl. Sand GU15 150 B4
Chaffinch Cl. Woki RG41 115 F3
Chagford Rd. Read RG2 86 A1
Chain St. Read RG1 86 A4
Chainhill Rd. Farn OX12 8 A4
Chalcraft Cl. Hen-O-T RG9 35 E4
Chalfont Cl. Read RG6 87 D1
Chalfont Ct. Read RG6 87 D1
Chalfont Way. Read RG6 87 D1
Chalford Rd. Newb RG14 104 C1
Chalford. Woo G HP10 3 F3
Chalgrove Cl. Maid SL6 40 A3
Chalgrove Way. Caver RG4 59 E3
Chalk Hill. Ast T OX11 12 C4
Chalk Hill. Shipl RG9 35 E3
Chalk Pit La. Burn SL1 21 D2
Chalkhousegreen La. Maples RG4 59 D4
Chalklands. Bou E SL8 3 D2
Chalkpit La. Mar SL7 1 A2
Challenge Rd. Felt TW15 98 B2
Challenor Cl. Woki RG40 141 F4
Challis Pl. Brac RG42 117 E4
Challow Ct. Maid SL6 19 E1
Chalmers Rd. Ashf TW15 98 A2
Chalmers Rd E. Ashf TW15 98 B2
Chalvey Gdns. Slough SL1 42 C2
Chalvey Gr. Slough SL1 42 A2

161

Chalvey Pk. Slough

Claremont Dr. Shepp

Chalvey Pk. Slough	SL1	42	C2
Chalvey Rd E. Slough	SL1	42	C2
Chalvey Rd W. Slough	SL1	42	B2
Chamberlains Gdns. Arbo	RG2	114	C1
Champion Rd. Caver	RG4	59	E1
Chancellors Way The. Read	RG6	86	C2
Chanctonbury Dr. Sunn	SL5	120	C1
Chandlers Cl. Felt	TW14	98	C4
Chandlers La. Yate	GU17	149	E4
Chandos Rd. Newb	RG14	131	D4
Chandos Rd. Stai	TW18	96	B2
Chantry Cl. Wind	SL4	67	D3
Chantry Mead. Hung	RG17	100	B3
Chantry Rd. Bags	GU19	145	E1
Chantry Rd. Chert	KT16	124	B1
Chapel Cl. Sou S	RG8	14	B2
Chapel Ct. That	RG18	106	C2
Chapel Hill. Read	RG31	84	B4
Chapel La. Asham	RG8	54	A4
Chapel La. Bags	GU19	145	E1
Chapel La. Binf	RG42	90	B1
Chapel La. Blew	OX11	12	A4
Chapel La. Camb	GU17	151	D1
Chapel La. Head	RG19	133	F1
Chapel La. Herm	RG18	78	C2
Chapel La. Herm	RG18	79	E4
Chapel La. Lamb	RG17	25	D2
Chapel La. Shin	RG7	113	D1
Chapel La. Silc	RG7	135	F3
Chapel La. Sto P	SL2	23	D3
Chapel La. Swal	RG7	139	E2
Chapel La. Yatt	RG18	53	F1
Chapel Rd. Camb	GU15	151	D3
Chapel Rd. Fla H	HP10	3	D4
Chapel Row. Twyf	RG27	61	E2
Chapel Sq. Sand	GU15	150	C3
Chapel St. Mar	SL7	1	C1
Chapel St. Slough	SL1	42	C2
Chapel St. That	RG18	106	B2
Chaplains Hill. Crow	RG45	143	E2
Chaplin Cres. Ashf	TW16	98	C1
Chapman La. Bou E	SL8	3	D3
Chapman La. Fla H	SL8	3	D3
Chapter Mews. Wind	SL4	67	E4
Charadon Cl. Read	RG2	86	A3
Chard Cl. Wood	RG5	87	F3
Chard Rd. Harm	TW6	71	D3
Charlbury Cl. Brac	RG12	118	C3
Charles Evans Way. Caver	RG4	59	E1
Charles Gdns. Slough	SL2	43	D4
Charles Rd. Chol	OX10	14	A4
Charles Rd. Stai	TW18	97	E1
Charles Sq. Brac	RG12	118	B4
Charles St. Chert	KT16	123	F1
Charles St. Newb	RG14	130	B3
Charles St. Read	RG1	85	F4
Charles St. Wind	SL4	67	D3
Charlock Cl. That	RG18	106	C3
Charlotte Cl. Herm	RG18	79	D3
Charlotte Way. Mar	SL7	1	C1
Charlton Cl. Slough	SL1	42	A2
Charlton Cl. Woki	RG40	141	F4
Charlton Ct. Sand	GU17	143	E1
Charlton La. Shepp	TW17	125	E3
Charlton La. Swal	RG7	139	E3
Charlton. Oak G	SL4	66	B3
Charlton Pl. Newb	RG14	105	D2
Charlton Rd. Stai	TW17	125	E4
Charlton Sq. Oak G	SL4	66	B3
Charlton Way. Oak G	SL4	66	B3
Charlville Dr. Bur C	RG31	84	A2
Charmwood Cl. Newb	RG14	104	C3
Charnham La. Hung	RG17	100	B4
Charnham Pk. Hello	RG17	100	B4
Charnham St. Hung	RG17	100	B3
Charnwood. Ascot	SL5	120	C2
Charrington Rd. Bur C	RG31	84	B2
Charta Rd (E). Stai	TW20	96	B1
Charta Rd (S). Stai	TW20	96	B1
Charta Rd (W). Stai	TW20	96	B2
Charter Cl. Slough	SL1	42	C2
Charter Rd. Newb	RG14	131	D4
Charter Rd. Slough	SL1	41	F3
Charterhouse Cl. Brac	RG12	118	C2
Charters La. Ascot	SL5	120	B2
Charters Rd. Sun	SL5	120	C1
Charters Rd. Windl	SL5	120	C1
Charters Way. Windl	SL5	120	C1
Charvil House Rd. Char	RG10	61	D3
Charvil La. Sonn	RG4	60	C2
Charwood Rd. Woki	RG40	116	C4
Chase Gdns. Binf	RG42	90	B2
Chase The. Bur C	RG31	84	B2
Chase The. Crow	RG45	143	D3
Chase The. Mar	SL7	2	A2
Chase The. Newb	RG14	104	C4
Chaseside Ave. Twyf	RG10	61	E4
Chaseside Gdns. Chert	KT16	124	A1
Chatfield. Slough	SL2	42	A4
Chatham St. Read	RG1	85	F4
Chatsworth Ave. Winn	RG41	88	A1
Chatsworth Cl. Caver	RG4	59	E3
Chatsworth Cl. Maid	SL6	39	E3
Chatsworth Hts. Camb	GU15	152	A4
Chatteris Way. Winn	RG6	114	B4
Chattern Hill. Ashf	TW15	98	A2
Chattern Rd. Ashf	TW15	98	B2
Chatters The. Swal	RG7	140	B4
Chatton Cl. Read	RG6	114	A4
Chaucer Cl. Caver	RG4	59	D3
Chaucer Cl. Woki	RG40	116	C3
Chaucer Cres. Newb	RG14	104	C3
Chaucer Gr. Camb	GU15	151	E3
Chaucer Rd. Ashf	TW15	97	F2
Chaucer Rd. Crow	RG45	143	D2
Chaucer Way. Woki	RG41	115	F3
Chauntry Cl. Maid	SL6	40	B3
Chauntry Rd. Maid	SL6	40	A3
Chavey Down Rd. Burl	RG42	92	A1
Chawridge La. Wink	SL4	92	B4
Chazey Cl. Maple	RG4	58	B4
Chazey Rd. Caver	RG4	58	B2
Cheam Cl. Brac	RG12	118	B2
Cheap St. Comp	RG20	31	F3
Cheap St. Newb	RG14	105	D1
Cheapside Rd. Ascot	SL5	120	B4
Cheapside. Read	RG1	86	A4
Cheddar Rd. Harm	TW6	71	D3
Cheddington Cl. Read	RG30	84	C3
Cheeseman Cl. Woki	RG40	116	B4
Chelford Way. Caver	RG4	58	C2
Chelsea Cl. Read	RG30	84	C4
Chelwood Dr. Sand	GU17	142	C1
Chelwood Rd. Read	RG6	87	D1
Cheney Cl. Binf	RG42	90	B1
Cheniston Gr. Maid	SL6	38	C4
Chepstow Rd. Read	RG31	57	E1
Chequer La. Bee H	RG7	138	C1
Chequers Orch. Iver	SL0	44	C4
Chequers Way. Wood	RG5	87	E4
Cherbury Cl. Brac	RG12	118	C3
Cherington Gate. Maid	SL6	19	D1
Cherington Way. Ascot	SL5	119	F4
Cheriton Ave. Twyf	RG10	61	E3
Cheriton Cl. Newb	RG14	131	D4
Cheriton Way. Black	GU17	150	B3
Cherries The. Slough	SL2	43	D4
Cherry Ave. Slough	SL3	43	E2
Cherry Cl. Caver	RG4	59	E4
Cherry Cl. Fla H	HP10	3	D4
Cherry Cl. Newb	RG14	104	C2
Cherry Garden La. Bur G	SL6	38	C2
Cherry Gr. Hung	RG17	100	B3
Cherry Orch. Gr She	RG17	48	A2
Cherry Orch. Stai	TW18	97	D2
Cherry Orch. Sto P	SL2	23	D3
Cherry Rise. Fla H	HP10	3	D4
Cherry Tree Ave. Stai	TW18	97	D1
Cherry Tree Cl. Sand	GU17	143	E1
Cherry Tree Dr. Brac	RG12	118	B3
Cherry Tree Gr. Woki	RG41	115	E2
Cherry Tree La. Fulm	SL3	23	F3
Cherry Tree Rd. Far C	SL2	22	B3
Cherry Way. Shepp	TW17	125	F3
Cherrydale Rd. Camb	GU15	152	B3
Cherrygarden La. Whi Wa	SL6	63	F4
Cherrywood Ave. Eng G	TW20	95	D1
Cherrywood Gdns. Fla H	HP10	3	D4
Chertsey Bridge Rd. Shepp	TW17	124	B1
Chertsey La. Stai	TW18	96	C1
Chertsey Rd. Felt	TW13	98	C2
Chertsey Rd. Shepp	TW17	124	C1
Chertsey Rd. Windl	GU20	146	C3
Chervil Way. Bur C	RG7	111	D1
Cherwell Cl. Maid	SL6	40	A4
Cherwell Cl. Slough	SL3	69	D4
Cherwell Rd. Bou E	SL8	3	D2
Cherwell Rd. Caver	RG4	59	D3
Cheseridge Rd. Comp	RG20	31	E2
Cheshire Ct. Slough	SL1	43	D2
Chessholme Ct. Ashf	TW16	98	C1
Chessholme Rd. Ashf	TW15	98	B1
Chester Cl. Ashf	TW15	98	B2
Chester Cl. Newb	RG14	105	E1
Chester Rd. Harm	TW6	71	D2
Chester Rd. Slough	SL1	42	B4
Chester St. Caver	RG4	59	D1
Chester St. Read	RG30	85	E4
Chesterblade La. Brac	RG12	118	C1
Chesterfield Rd. Ashf	TW15	97	F2
Chesterfield Rd. Newb	RG14	105	D1
Chesterman St. Read	RG1	86	A3
Chesters Rd. Camb	GU15	152	A3
Chesterton Dr. Stan	TW19	97	D1
Chesterton Rd. That	RG18	106	B3
Chestnut Ave. Camb	GU15	152	A3
Chestnut Ave. Caver	RG4	59	F2
Chestnut Ave. Slough	SL3	43	F2
Chestnut Ave. Went	GU25	121	F3
Chestnut Cl. Ashf	TW15	98	A2
Chestnut Cl. Ashf	TW15	98	C1
Chestnut Cl. Black	GU17	150	C3
Chestnut Cl. Eng G	TW20	95	E1
Chestnut Cl. Harl	UB7	71	D4
Chestnut Cl. Maid	SL6	20	A1
Chestnut Cl. Medm	SL7	17	E4
Chestnut Cl. Thea	RG7	83	F2
Chestnut Cres. Newb	RG14	105	D2
Chestnut Cres. Shin	RG2	113	F2
Chestnut Dr. Bur C	RG30	111	D2
Chestnut Dr. Eng G	TW20	95	E1
Chestnut Dr. Wind	SL4	66	C2
Chestnut Gr. Pur O T	RG8	57	E3
Chestnut Gr. Stai	TW18	97	E1
Chestnut La. Lamb	RG17	25	F2
Chestnut Manor Cl. Stai	TW18	97	D2
Chestnut Rd. Ashf	TW15	98	A2
Chestnut Wlk. Hung	RG17	100	B2
Chestnut Wlk. Shepp	TW17	125	F3
Chestnuts The. Shipl	RG9	36	A2
Chetwode Cl. Woki	RG40	116	C3
Cheveley Gdns. Burn	SL1	21	E2
Cheviot Cl. Camb	GU15	152	B2
Cheviot Cl. Hart	UB7	71	E4
Cheviot Cl. Maid	SL6	40	A3
Cheviot Cl. Newb	RG14	130	B3
Cheviot Dr. Char	RG10	61	D2
Cheviot Rd. Sand	GU17	142	C1
Cheviot Rd. Slough	SL3	44	A1
Chewter Cl. Bags	GU19	145	F2
Chewter La. Windl	GU20	146	A3
Cheylesmore Dr. Camb	GU16	152	B2
Cheyne Rd. Ashf	TW15	98	B1
Chichester Ct. Slough	SL1	43	D2
Chichester Rd. Read	RG30	84	C4
Chicory Cl. Read	RG6	87	D1
Chieveley Cl. Read	RG31	84	B4
Chilcombe Way. Read	RG6	87	E1
Child St. Lamb	RG17	25	D1
Childrey Way. Read	RG31	84	B4
Chillingham Way. Camb	GU15	151	E2
Chilsey Green Rd. Chert	KT16	123	F1
Chiltern Cl. Hen-O-T	RG9	35	D4
Chiltern Cl. Newb	RG14	130	B3
Chiltern Cres. Read	RG6	87	D4
Chiltern Ct. Caver	RG4	59	D3
Chiltern Dr. Char	RG10	61	D2
Chiltern Gn. Fla H	HP10	3	D4
Chiltern Rd. Burn	SL1	41	D4
Chiltern Rd. Caver	RG4	59	E2
Chiltern Rd. Maid	SL6	40	A3
Chiltern Rd. Mar	SL7	1	B1
Chiltern Rd. Sand	GU17	142	C1
Chiltern View. Pur O T	RG8	57	E3
Chiltern Wlk. Pangb	RG8	56	C3
Chilterns Cl. Fla H	HP10	3	D4
Chilterns Pk. Bou E	SL8	3	D3
Chilton Way. Hung	RG17	100	B3
Chilwick Rd. Slough	SL2	21	F1
Chippendale Cl. Black	GU17	150	C2
Chippendale Cl. Tad	RG26	134	C1
Chippenham Cl. Read	RG6	113	F4
Chipstead Rd. Harm	TW6	71	D2
Chisbury Cl. Brac	RG12	118	C2
Chitterfield Gate. Harm	UB7	71	D4
Chittering Cl. Winn	RG6	87	E1
Chive Rd. Read	RG6	87	D1
Chivers Dr. Woki	RG40	141	F4
Chives Pl. New G	RG42	91	F1
Chobham La. Went	GU25	122	A1
Chobham Rd. Camb	GU16	151	F1
Chobham Rd. Went	SL5	121	D1
Choke La. Cook	SL6	19	D2
Cholmeley Pl. Read	RG1	86	C4
Cholmeley Rd. Read	RG1	86	C4
Cholmeley Terr. Read	RG1	86	C4
Cholsey Rd. That	RG19	106	C2
Choseley Cl. Know H	RG10	37	F2
Choseley Rd. Know H	RG10	37	F2
Chrislaine Cl. Stan	TW19	70	B1
Christchurch Dr. Black	GU17	150	B3
Christchurch Gdns. Read	RG2	86	B3
Christchurch Rd. Harm	TW6	71	D2
Christchurch Rd. Read	RG2	86	B3
Christchurch Rd. Vir W	GU25	122	B3
Christie Cl. Light	GU18	146	B1
Christie Hts. Newb	RG14	131	D4
Christie Wlk. Yate	GU17	149	E2
Christmas La. Far C	SL2	22	B4
Christopher Ct. Newb	RG14	105	D1
Chudleigh Gdns. Read	RG2	86	B1
Church App. Stai	TW20	123	E3
Church Cl. Eton	SL4	67	E4
Church Cl. Ham M	RG20	129	F3
Church Cl. Lamb	RG17	25	D2
Church Cl. Maid	SL6	39	E3
Church Cl. Stai	TW18	124	B3
Church Cl. Winn	RG41	88	B1
Church Croft. Hung	RG17	100	B3
Church Dr. Maid	SL6	40	B2
Church End La. Read	RG30	84	C4
Church Farm Barns. Mort	RG7	137	E3
Church Gate. That	RG19	106	B2
Church Gr. Slough	SL3	43	E4
Church Hams. Woki	RG40	141	E3
Church Hill. Binf	RG42	90	B3
Church Hill. Camb	GU15	151	F3
Church Hill. Chil	OX11	10	B4
Church Hill. East I	RG20	30	C3
Church Hill. Hurst	RG10	88	C3
Church La. Arbo	RG2	114	B2
Church La. Ascot	SL5	120	B3
Church La. Asham	RG8	54	A3
Church La. Bark	RG40	115	E1
Church La. Binf	RG42	90	B2
Church La. Brim	RG7	133	F3
Church La. Bur C	RG30	111	F3
Church La. Chiev	RG20	51	D1
Church La. Combe	RG17	147	F3
Church La. Finch	RG40	141	F2
Church La. Ham M	RG20	129	F4
Church La. Hung	RG17	100	B3
Church La. Maid	SL6	40	B2
Church La. New G	RG42	91	E3
Church La. Newb	RG14	104	B2
Church La. Padw	RG7	110	B2
Church La. Read	RG2	113	E3
Church La. Shipl	RG9	35	F1
Church La. Silc	RG7	136	C1
Church La. Slough	SL3	43	E4
Church La. Sto P	SL2	22	C1
Church La. Swal	RG7	140	B3
Church La. That	RG19	106	B2
Church La. Twyf	RG10	61	F3
Church La. Wind	SL4	67	E3
Church La. Yatt	RG18	53	F1
Church Mews. Pur O T	RG8	57	E3
Church Mews. Wood	RG5	87	F4
Church Path. Maid	SL6	40	B2
Church Rd. Alde	RG7	135	D4
Church Rd. Ascot	SL5	120	A3
Church Rd. Ashf	TW15	97	F2
Church Rd. Bags	GU19	145	E2
Church Rd. Brac	RG12	118	B4
Church Rd. Burl	SL5	119	D4
Church Rd. Camb	GU16	151	E1
Church Rd. Caver	RG4	59	D1
Church Rd. Cook	SL6	19	D3
Church Rd E. Crow	RG45	143	D3
Church Rd. Eng G	TW20	96	A2
Church Rd. Far C	SL2	22	B1
Church Rd. Frox	SN8	99	D3
Church Rd. Ham	TW10	126	A1
Church Rd. Lit M	SL7	2	B3
Church Rd. Maid	SL6	40	A3
Church Rd. Newb	RG14	105	D3
Church Rd. Old W	SL4	68	A1
Church Rd. Pangb	RG8	56	B3
Church Rd. Read	RG6	87	D3
Church Rd. Sand	GU15	143	F1
Church Rd. Sand	GU15	150	C4
Church Rd. Shepp	TW17	125	D1
Church Rd. Silc	RG26	135	F1
Church Rd. Sunn	SL5	121	D2
Church Rd. Swal	RG7	139	E3
Church Rd W. Crow	RG45	143	D2
Church Rd. West E	GU24	153	F4
Church Rd. Windl	GU20	146	B2
Church Rd. Wink	SL4	92	B3
Church Rd. Wood	RG5	87	F4
Church Side. East I	RG20	30	C3
Church Sq. Shepp	TW17	125	D1
Church St. Blew	OX11	12	A4
Church St. Burn	SL1	21	E1
Church St. Caver	RG4	59	D1
Church St. Crow	RG45	143	D3
Church St. Frox	SN8	99	D1
Church St. Gr She	RG17	48	A2
Church St. Hamp N	RG18	52	C3
Church St. Hen-O-T	RG9	15	E1
Church St. Hung	RG17	100	B3
Church St. Kint	RG17	102	A1
Church St. Read	RG1	86	A3
Church St. Slough	SL1	42	B2
Church St. Slough	SL1	42	C2
Church St. Stai	TW18	96	C2
Church St. Thea	RG7	83	F2
Church St. Twyf	RG10	61	E2
Church St. Warg	RG10	36	B1
Church St. Wind	SL4	67	E3
Church View. Been	RG7	109	D3
Church View. Whi Wa	SL6	63	F4
Church View. Yate	GU17	149	E3
Church Views. Maid	SL6	39	F4
Church Way. Hung	RG17	100	B3
Church Wlk. Chert	KT16	124	A2
Churchfield Mews. Slough	SL2	43	D4
Churchill Cl. Felt	TW14	98	C4
Churchill Cl. Fla H	HP10	3	D4
Churchill Cl. Fla H	HP10	3	E4
Churchill Cres. Yate	GU17	149	E3
Churchill Dr. Mar	SL7	1	C2
Churchill Dr. Winn	RG41	88	A1
Churchill Rd. Slough	SL3	43	F1
Churchward Wlk. Read	RG31	84	C2
Churchway. West I	RG20	10	A1
Churn Rd. Comp	RG20	31	E3
Cinnamon Cl. Read	RG6	86	C1
Cintra Ave. Read	RG2	86	B3
Cippenham Cl. Slough	SL1	41	F3
Cippenham La. Slough	SL1	42	A3
Circle Hill Rd. Crow	RG45	143	E3
Circuit La. Read	RG30	85	E3
City Rd. Read	RG31	84	A4
Clacy Gn. Brac	RG42	91	D1
Clandon Ave. Stai	TW20	96	B1
Clanfield Cres. Read	RG31	57	E1
Clanfield Ride. Black	GU17	150	B3
Clappers Farm Rd. Silc	RG7	136	C1
Clappers Meadow. Maid	SL6	20	B1
Clapps Gate Rd. Silc	RG26	135	F1
Clapton App. Woo G	HP10	3	E4
Clare Ave. Woki	RG40	116	B4
Clare Dr. Far C	SL2	22	A4
Clare Gdns. Eng G	TW20	96	A2
Clare Rd. Maid	SL6	39	E3
Clare Rd. Slough	SL6	41	E4
Clare Rd. Stan	TW19	70	C1
Clare Rd. Stan	TW19	97	F4
Clare Wlk. Newb	RG14	130	B3
Claredon Cl. Winn	RG41	88	B1
Clarefield Cl. Maid	SL6	19	D1
Clarefield Dr. Maid	SL6	19	D1
Clarefield Rd. Maid	SL6	19	D1
Claremont Ave. Camb	GU15	151	F3
Claremont Dr. Shepp	TW17	125	D2

162

Claremont Gdns. Mar

Coworth Rd. Sunn

Claremont Gdns. Mar SL7 1 C1
Claremont Rd. Mar SL7 1 C1
Claremont Rd. Stai TW18 96 B2
Claremont Rd. Wind SL4 67 E3
Clarence Cres. Wind SL4 67 E3
Clarence Dr. Eng G TW20 95 E2
Clarence Rd. Hen-O-T RG9 15 E1
Clarence Rd. Wind SL4 67 D3
Clarence St. Eng G TW20 95 F1
Clarence St. Stai TW18 96 C2
Clarence Way. Read RG31 84 A2
Clarendon Ct. Black GU17 150 B2
Clarendon Ct. Slough SL2 43 D3
Clarendon Gdns. Newb RG14 105 D2
Clarendon Rd. Ashf TW15 97 F2
Clarendon Rd. Read RG6 87 D3
Clares Green Rd. Shin RG7 113 D2
Clarewood Dr. Camb GU15 151 F3
Clarke Cres. Sand GU15 150 C4
Clarks Gdns. Hung RG17 100 B3
Classics The. Lamb RG17 25 D1
Claverdon. Brac RG12 118 A1
Clay Cl. Fla H HP10 3 D4
Clay Cl. Pur O T RG31 57 D1
Clay Hill Cres. Newb RG14 105 E3
Clay La. Been RG7 108 C3
Claydon Gdns. Camb GU17 151 D1
Clayhall La. Old Wind SL4 67 F1
Clayhill Cl. Brac RG12 119 D3
Clayhill Rd. Bur C RG7 111 D2
Clayton Gr. Brac RG12 118 C4
Clayton Rd. Black GU14 150 C1
Clayton Wlk. Read RG2 86 B2
Claytons Meadow. Bou E SL8 3 D2
Clearsprings. Camb GU18 153 D4
Clearsprings. Light GU18 146 A1
Cleeve Ct. Felt TW14 98 C4
Cleeve Down. Gori RG8 34 B4
Cleeve Rd. Gori RG8 34 A4
Clements Cl. Shin RG7 113 D1
Clements Cl. Slough SL1 43 D2
Clements Mead. Sulh RG31 57 D1
Clements Rd. Hen-O-T RG9 15 E2
Clent Rd. Read RG2 86 A2
Cleopatra Pl. New G RG42 91 F1
Cleve Ct.Stre RG8 34 A4
Cleve Ct. Wind SL4 66 C2
Clevedon Dr. Read RG6 87 D1
Clevedon Rd. Read RG31 57 F2
Clevehurst Cl. Sto P SL2 23 D3
Cleveland. Char RG10 61 D2
Cleveland Cl. Maid SL6 40 A3
Cleveland Cl. Woo G HP10 3 F4
Cleveland Dr. Stai TW18 124 A4
Cleveland Gr. Newb RG14 104 C2
Clevemede. Gori RG8 34 B4
Cleves Way. Ashf TW16 98 C1
Clewborough Dr. Camb GU15 152 A3
Clewer Ave. Wind SL4 67 D3
Clewer Ct Rd. Wind SL4 67 D4
Clewer Fields. Wind SL4 67 D3
Clewer Hill Rd. Wind SL4 66 C2
Clewer New Town. Wind SL4 67 D3
Clewer Pk. Wind SL4 67 D4
Clifford Gr. Ashf TW15 98 A2
Clifford Way. Bou E SL8 3 D3
Clifton Cl. Maid SL6 40 A2
Clifton Rd. Harm TW6 71 D2
Clifton Rd. Newb RG14 104 C1
Clifton Rd. Slough SL1 43 D2
Clifton Rd. Woki RG41 116 A4
Clifton Rise. Warg RG10 36 C1
Clifton Rise. Wind SL4 66 B3
Clifton St. Read RG1 85 F4
Clintons Gn. Brac RG42 118 A4
Clive Ct. Slough SL1 42 B2
Clive Gn. Brac RG12 118 A2
Clivedale Rd RG5 87 F2
Clivedale Rd. Wood RG5 87 F2
Cliveden Mead. Maid SL6 20 B1
Cliveden Pl. Shepp TW17 125 E2
Cliveden Rd. Tapl SL6 20 C2
Clivemont Rd. Maid SL6 39 F4
Clockhouse La. Ashf TW15 98 A3
Clockhouse La E. Stai TW20 96 A1
Clockhouse La. Felt TW14 98 A3
Clockhouse La W. Eng G TW20 96 A1
Cloister Mews. Thea RG7 83 F2
Cloisters The. Camb GU16 151 E1
Cloisters The. Caver RG4 59 D2
Clonmel Way. Burn SL1 21 D1
Close End. Lamb RG17 25 D1
Close The. Bou E SL8 3 D3
Close The. Bur C RG7 111 D2
Close The. Burl SL5 119 E4
Close The. Gr She RG17 48 A2
Close The. Hamp N RG18 52 C3
Close The. Hen-O-T RG9 35 E4
Close The. Light GU18 146 A1
Close The. Sand GU15 150 C4
Close The. Slough SL1 41 E3
Close The. That RG18 106 A2
Close The. Vir W GU25 122 B2
Close The. Wood RG5 87 F3
Clough Dr. Herm RG18 78 C3
Clove Cl. Read RG6 86 C1
Clover Cl. Woki RG40 116 C4
Clover La. Yate GU17 149 D3
Club La. Crow RG45 143 E3
Clumps The. Felt TW15 98 B2
Clyde Rd. Stan TW19 97 F4
Clyve Way. Stai TW18 123 F4
Coach House Cl. Camb GU16 151 F2
Coach Ride. Mar SL7 1 B2
Coachmans Ct. Newb RG14 105 D2
Coalport Way. Read RG30 57 F1
Cobb Cl. Datch SL3 68 B3
Cobbetts La. Yate GU17 149 F3
Cobblers Cl. Far C SL2 22 A2
Cobham Rd. Wood RG5 87 F4
Cochrane Cl. That RG19 106 C2
Cochrane Pl. Windl GU20 146 B3
Cock La. Brad RG7 82 A1
Cock-a-Dobby. Sand GU17 143 D1
Cockett Rd. Slough SL3 43 F2
Cockney Hill. Read RG30 84 C3
Cocks La. New G RG42 92 A3
Cocks La. Wink RG42 92 A3
Cody Cl. Read RG5 88 A4
Coe Spur. Slough SL1 42 A2
Coftards. Slough SL2 43 E4
Cold Ash Hill. Cold A RG18 106 B4
Coldharbour Cl. Hen-O-T RG9 35 E4
Coldharbour Cl. Stai TW20 123 E3
Coldharbour La. Stai TW20 123 E3
Coldharbour La. West E GU24 153 F4
Coldharbour Rd. Hung RG17 100 B2
Coldicutt St. Caver RG4 59 E1
Coldmoorholme La. Bou E SL8 2 C2
Colemans Moor La. Wood RG5 87 F3
Colemans Moor Rd. Wood RG5 88 A3
Colenorton Cres. Eton SL4 41 F1
Coleridge Ave. Yate GU17 149 F3
Coleridge Cl. Crow RG45 143 E2
Coleridge Cl. Twyf RG10 61 F2
Coleridge Cres. Stan SL3 69 F3
Coleridge Rd. Ashf TW15 97 F2
Coley Ave. Read RG1 85 F3
Coley Hill. Read RG1 85 F3
Coley Park Rd. Read RG1 85 F3
Coley Pl. Read RG1 86 A3
Colin Way. Slough SL1 42 A2
Collaroy Rd. Cold A RG18 106 B4
College Ave. Maid SL6 39 F4
College Ave. Slough SL1 42 C2
College Ave. Stai TW20 96 A1
College Cl. Camb GU15 151 E4
College Cres. Sand GU15 150 C4
College Cres. Wind SL4 67 E3
College Glen. Maid SL6 39 E4
College Piece. Mort RG7 136 C3
College Rd. Maid SL6 39 F4
College Rd. Read RG6 86 C3
College Rd. Slough SL1 41 F3
College Ride. Bags GU19 145 E1
College Ride. Camb GU15 151 E4
College Rise. Maid SL6 39 E4
College Way. Ashf TW15 97 F2
College Way. East G RG17 47 E3
College Way. East G RG17 47 E3
Colleton Dr. Twyf RG10 61 F2
Collier Cl. Maid SL6 19 F1
Colliers Way. Read RG30 85 D4
Collingwood Rise. Camb GU15 152 A4
Collingwood Wlk. Read RG31 84 A4
Collins Cl. Newb RG14 105 E2
Collins Dr. Herm RG18 78 C3
Collinswood Rd. Far C SL2 22 B4
Collis St. Read RG2 86 A3
Colliston Wlk. Read RG31 84 C2
Collum Green Rd. Sto P SL2 23 D4
Coln Cl. Maid SL6 39 F4
Colnbrook By-Pass. Iver SL3 69 E4
Colnbrook By-Pass. Slough SL3 69 E4
Colndale Rd. Stan SL3 69 F3
Colne Bank. Hort SL3 69 E2
Colne Orchard. Iver SL0 44 C4
Colne Way. Wray TW19 96 A3
Colnebridge Cl. Stai TW18 96 C2
Colnworth Cl. Read RG6 114 A4
Colonels La. Chert KT16 124 A2
Colonial Rd. Felt TW14 98 C4
Colonial Rd. Slough SL1 43 D2
Colston Cl. Bur C RG31 84 B2
Colthrop La. That RG19 107 D1
Colthrop Way. That RG19 107 D1
Coltsfoot Cl. Bur C RG7 111 D2
Columbia Ct. Woki RG40 141 F4
Colville Gdns. Light GU18 153 E4
Colwyn Cl. Yate GU17 149 E3
Colyer Cl. Herm RG18 79 E4
Colyton Way. Pur O T RG8 57 E3
Combe Rd. Read RG30 84 C4
Combe View. Hung RG17 100 B2
Combermere Cl. Wind SL4 67 D3
Comet Rd. Stan TW19 97 E4
Comet Way. Wood RG5 88 A4
Comfrey Cl. Woki RG40 116 C4
Commercial Rd. Read RG2 86 A1
Commercial Rd. Stai TW18 97 D1
Common Hill. Brad RG7 82 C2
Common La. Brig RG20 28 B3
Common La. Eton SL4 42 B1
Common Rd. Dorn SL4 41 E1
Common Rd. Eton SL4 42 A1
Common Rd. Fla H HP10 3 D4
Common Rd. Head RG19 132 C1
Common Rd. Slough SL3 44 A1
Common The. Fla H HP10 3 D4
Common Wood. Far C SL2 22 B4
Commonfield La. Bark RG40 141 D4
Commonfields. West E GU24 153 F3
Commons Rd. Woki RG41 88 C1
Communications Rd. Gree RG19 131 F3
Compton Ave. Read RG31 57 D3
Compton Cl. Brac RG12 117 F2
Compton Cl. Read RG6 87 E2
Compton Cl. Sand GU17 143 E1
Compton Ct. Slough SL1 41 F4
Compton Dr. Maid SL6 39 D4
Comsaye Wlk. Brac RG12 118 B2
Concorde Rd. Maid SL6 39 E2
Concorde Way. Slough SL1 42 B2
Concorde Way. Wood RG5 88 A4
Condor Cl. Sulh RG31 57 E2
Condor Rd. Stai TW18 124 B3
Conegar Ct. Slough SL1 42 C3
Congreve Cl. Alde RG7 135 D4
Conifer Cl. Tad RG26 134 C1
Conifer Crest. Newb RG14 130 B2
Conifer Dr. Camb GU15 152 A3
Conifer Dr. Sulh RG31 57 D1
Conifer La. Stai TW20 96 B2
Conifers The. Brac RG45 143 D4
Coningham Rd. Read RG2 113 E3
Coningsby. Brac RG12 118 B3
Coningsby Cl. Maid SL6 39 E2
Coningsby La. Holy SL6 65 E3
Conisboro Ave. Caver RG4 58 C3
Conisboro Way. Caver RG4 58 C3
Coniston Cl. Camb GU15 152 B2
Coniston Cl. That RG19 106 A2
Coniston Cl. Wood RG5 87 F3
Coniston Cres. Slough SL1 41 E4
Coniston Ct. Light GU12 146 A1
Coniston Dr. Read RG30 57 F1
Coniston Way. Stai TW20 96 A1
Connaught Ave. Ashf TW15 97 F2
Connaught Cl. Crow RG45 142 C2
Connaught Cl. Maid SL6 19 F1
Connaught Cl. Read RG30 85 E4
Connaught Cl. Yate GU17 149 D3
Connaught Rd. Bags GU19 145 E2
Connaught Rd. Camb GU15 151 F3
Connaught Rd. Newb RG14 105 D2
Connaught Rd. Read RG30 85 E4
Connaught Rd. Slough SL1 43 D2
Conniston Cl. Mar SL7 1 A1
Connop Way. Camb GU16 151 F2
Constable Cl. Wood RG5 88 A4
Constable Way. Sand GU15 150 C3
Constitution Rd. Read RG30 85 D4
Consul Cl. Wood RG5 88 A3
Control Tower Rd. Harm TW6 71 D2
Convent Lodge. Ashf TW15 98 A2
Convent Rd. Ashf TW15 98 A2
Convent Rd. Wind SL4 67 D3
Conway Dr. Ashf TW15 98 B1
Conway Dr. That RG18 106 A3
Conway Rd. Burn SL6 41 D4
Conway Rd. Harm TW6 71 D2
Conway Rd. Read RG31 84 B3
Conway Rd. Slough SL6 41 D4
Conygree Cl. Read RG6 87 D1
Cookham Cl. Sand GU17 143 E1
Cookham Dean Bottom La.
Cook SL6 19 E4
Cookham Rd. Brac RG12 117 F4
Cookham Rd. Maid SL6 19 F1
Cookham Rd. Maid SL6 19 F2
Coolarne Rise. Camb GU15 152 A3
Coolgardie Rd. Ashf TW15 98 B2
Coombe Ct. That RG19 106 C2
Coombe Hill Ct. Wind SL4 66 B2
Coombe Hill. Farn OX12 28 A4
Coombe Pine. Brac RG12 118 B2
Coombe Rd. Comp RG20 31 F2
Coombe Rd. Yate GU17 149 D4
Coombe Sq. That RG19 106 C2
Coombe The. Stre RG8 33 F3
Coombes La. Woki RG41 115 E2
Coombesbury La. Box RG20 76 B1
Cooper Cl. Read RG2 113 E4
Cooper Rd. Hen-O-T RG9 15 E2
Cooper Rd. Windl GU20 146 B2
Cooper Way. Slough SL1 42 A2
Coopers Cl. Stai TW18 96 C2
Coopers Cres. That RG18 106 B2
Coopers Hill La. Eng G TW20 95 E2
Cope Hall La. Ham M RG14 130 B4
Copelands Cl. Camb GU15 152 B2
Copenhagen Cl. Read RG2 113 E4
Copped Hall Dr. Camb GU15 152 B3
Copped Hall Way. Camb GU15 152 B3
Copper Beech Cl. Wind SL4 66 B3
Copperage Rd. Farn OX11 9 D1
Copperdale Cl. Read RG6 86 C2
Coppermill Rd. Hort TW19 69 D1
Coppermill Rd. Wray TW19 69 D1
Coppice Cl. Newb RG14 131 D4
Coppice Dr. Wray TW19 95 E4
Coppice Gdns. Crow RG45 142 C3
Coppice Gdns. Yate GU17 149 E3
Coppice Gn. Brac RG42 90 C1
Coppice Rd. Wood RG5 87 F2
Coppice The. Ashf TW15 98 A1
Coppins La. Iver SL0 44 C4
Copse Ave. Caver RG4 59 F2
Copse Cl. Camb GU15 152 A3
Copse Cl. Mar SL7 1 B1
Copse Cl. Read RG31 57 E2
Copse Dr. Woki RG41 116 A4
Copse End. Camb GU15 152 A3
Copse Mead. Wood RG5 60 C1
Copse The. Warg RG10 36 C2
Copse Way. Woki RG40 141 F4
Copthorn Cl. Maid SL6 39 D2
Copthorne Cl. Shepp TW17 125 E2
Copthorne Dr. Light GU18 146 A1
Corbett Dr. Camb GU18 152 C4
Corbett Gdns. Wood RG5 87 F4
Corbridge Rd. Read RG2 86 B2
Corby Cl. Wood RG5 61 D1
Corby Dr. Eng G TW20 95 E1
Cordelia Croft. Brac RG42 118 C4
Cordelia Gdns. Stan TW19 97 F4
Cordelia Rd. Stan TW19 97 F4
Corderoy Cl. That RG19 106 C1
Corderoy Pl. Chert KT16 123 F2
Cordwalles Rd. Camb GU15 151 F4
Cordwallis Rd. Maid SL6 39 F4
Cordwallis St. Maid SL6 39 F4
Cores End Rd. Bou E SL8 3 D2
Corfe Gdns. Camb GU16 151 F1
Corfe Gdns. Slough SL1 42 A3
Corfe Mews. Caver RG4 59 F2
Corfe Pl. Maid SL6 39 E4
Corfield Cl. Finch RG40 141 F2
Coriander Way. Read RG6 86 C1
Cormorant Pl. Sand GU15 150 C4
Cornbunting Cl. Sand GU15 150 B4
Cornerside. Ashf TW15 98 B1
Cornfield Gn. Woki RG41 115 F4
Cornfield Rd. Wood RG5 88 A4
Cornfields. Yate GU17 149 D2
Cornflower Cl. Woki RG41 115 E4
Cornwall Ave. Slough SL2 22 B1
Cornwall Cl. Camb GU15 151 F4
Cornwall Cl. Eton SL4 41 F1
Cornwall Cl. Maid SL6 19 F1
Cornwall Cl. Pur O T RG31 57 D2
Cornwall Cl. Woki RG41 115 E3
Cornwall Way. Stai TW18 96 C1
Cornwell Rd. Old W SL4 68 A1
Cornwood Gdns. Read RG2 86 B2
Coronation Ave. Slough SL3 43 F4
Coronation Rd. Ascot SL5 120 A1
Coronation Rd. Bish SL6 38 A3
Coronation Rd. Brac SL5 120 A1
Coronation Rd. Yate GU17 149 F4
Coronation Sq. Read RG30 85 D2
Coronation Sq. Woki RG40 116 B4
Corrie Gdns. Went GU25 122 B1
Corrine Cl. Read RG2 86 A1
Corsair Cl. Stan TW19 97 F4
Corsair Rd. Stan TW19 97 F4
Corsham Rd. Read RG31 84 C2
Corsham Way. Crow RG45 143 D3
Corwen Rd. Read RG30 84 C4
Coster Cl. Newb RG14 104 B3
Cotswold Cl. Maid SL6 40 A3
Cotswold Cl. Slough SL1 42 B2
Cotswold Cl. Stai TW18 97 D2
Cotswold Rd. Sand GU17 142 C1
Cotswold Way. Read RG31 57 E1
Cottage Farm Way. Stai TW20 123 E3
Cottage La. Bur C RG30 85 E1
Cotterell Cl. Brac RG42 91 D1
Cotterell Gdns. Twyf RG10 61 F2
Cottesbrooke Cl. Stan SL3 69 E3
Cottesmore. Brac RG12 118 A1
Cottesmore Rd. Wood RG5 87 E3
Coulson Way. Burn SL1 41 D4
County La. New G RG42 91 F1
Course Rd. Ascot SL5 120 A3
Court Cl. Holy SL6 40 B1
Court Cres. Slough SL1 42 B4
Court Dr. Maid SL6 20 B2
Court Gdns. Camb GU15 151 E3
Court Hill Rd. Farn OX12 7 D4
Court Hill Rd. Let B OX12 7 D4
Court La. Burn SL1 21 E1
Court La. Iver SL0 44 C3
Court La. Slough SL1 41 D2
Court Rd. Maid SL6 20 B2
Courtenay Dr. Caver RG4 59 D4
Courtfield Dr. Maid SL6 39 E3
Courtfield Rd. Ashf TW15 98 A1
Courthouse Rd. Maid SL6 39 E4
Courtlands Ave. Slough SL3 43 E1
Courtlands Hill. Pangb RG8 56 B2
Courtlands. Maid SL6 39 F3
Courtlands Rd. Newb RG14 105 D1
Courtney Rd. Harm TW6 71 D2
Courts Rd. Read RG6 87 D2
Courtyard The. Thea RG7 83 F2
Coventry Rd. Read RG1 86 C4
Coverdale Way. Slough SL2 21 F1
Covert The. Sunn SL5 120 A1
Cow La. East I RG20 30 C4
Cow La. Moul OX10 13 F2
Cow La. Read RG1 58 C1
Cowley Ave. Chert KT16 123 F1
Cowley La. Chert KT16 123 F1
Coworth Cl. Sunn SL5 121 D2
Coworth Rd. Sunn SL5 121 D2

165

Elmsway. Ashf

First St. Newt

Elmsway. Ashf	TW15	98	A2
Elmwood. Maid	SL6	20	A2
Elmwood Rd. Slough	SL2	43	D3
Elsenwood Cres. Camb	GU15	152	A3
Elsenwood Dr. Camb	GU15	152	A4
Elsinore Ave. Stan	TW19	97	F4
Elsley Rd. Read	RG31	57	F2
Elstow Ave. Caver	RG4	59	E3
Elstree Cl. Read	RG31	57	E1
Elsworth Cl. Felt	TW14	98	C4
Eltham Ave. Caver	RG4	59	F3
Elton Dr. Maid	SL6	39	E4
Elvaston Way. Read	RG30	85	D4
Elveden Cl. Winn	RG6	87	F1
Elvendon Rd. Gori	RG8	34	B4
Elwell Cl. Eng G	TW20	96	A1
Ely Ave. Slough	SL1	42	B4
Ely Rd. Harm	TW6	71	F3
Ely Rd. Thea	RG7	83	F2
Embankment The. Wray	TW19	95	E4
Ember Rd. Slough	SL3	44	A2
Emblem Cres. Arbo	RG2	114	C1
Embrook Way. Read	RG31	84	A2
Emerald Cl. Woki	RG41	115	F4
Emerald Ct. Slough	SL1	42	C2
Emery Acres. Upp B	RG8	55	D3
Emery Down Cl. Brac	RG12	119	D3
Emlyns Bldgs. Eton	SL4	67	E4
Emm Cl. Woki	RG41	115	F4
Emma La. Warg	RG10	36	C1
Emmbrook Gate. Woki	RG41	115	F4
Emmbrook Rd. Woki	RG41	115	F4
Emmbrook Vale. Woki	RG41	89	D1
Emmer Green Ct. Caver	RG4	59	E3
Emmets Nest. Binf	RG42	90	B1
Emmets Pk. Binf	RG42	90	B1
Emmview Cl. Woki	RG41	115	F4
Empress Rd. Read	RG31	84	B3
Enborne Cl. Read	RG31	84	B4
Enborne Gr. Newb	RG14	104	C1
Enborne Pl. Newb	RG14	104	C1
Enborne Rd. Ham M	RG14	104	C1
Enborne Rd. Newb	RG14	104	C1
Enborne St. Ham M	RG20	130	A2
Enborne St. Newb	RG14	130	B3
Enborne Way. Brim	RG7	133	F3
Enfield Rd. Harm	TW6	71	F3
Engineers Rd. Newt	RG19	132	A3
Englefield Cl. Eng G	TW20	95	E1
Englefield Cl. Eng G	TW20	95	E1
Englefield Rd. Thea	RG7	83	E2
Engleheart Dr. Felt	TW14	71	F1
Englehurst. Eng G	TW20	95	E1
Englemere Pk. Burl	SL5	119	F3
Englemere Rd. Brac	RG42	90	C1
Englesfield. Camb	GU15	152	B3
English Gdns. Wray	TW19	68	B1
Ennerdale. Brac	RG12	118	A3
Ennerdale Cl. Felt	TW14	98	C4
Ennerdale Cres. Slough	SL1	41	E4
Ennerdale Rd. Read	RG2	86	B2
Ennerdale Way. That	RG19	106	A2
Ensign Cl. Stan	TW19	97	E4
Ensign Way. Stan	TW19	97	E4
Enstone Rd. Wood	RG5	88	A4
Enterprise Way. That	RG19	107	D1
Epping Cl. Read	RG1	85	F4
Epping Way. Brac	RG12	118	C3
Epsom Cl. Camb	GU15	151	E4
Epsom Cres. Newb	RG14	105	D1
Epsom Ct. Read	RG1	85	F3
Epson Sq. Harm	TW6	71	F3
Eric Ave. Caver	RG4	59	D3
Erica Cl. Slough	SL1	41	F3
Erica Cl. West E	GU24	153	F3
Erica Dr. Woki	RG40	116	B3
Eriswell Cl. Winn	RG6	87	F1
Erkenwald Cl. Chert	KT16	123	F1
Erleigh Court Dr. Read	RG6	87	D4
Erleigh Court Gdns. Read	RG6	87	D4
Erleigh Dene. Newb	RG14	104	C1
Erleigh Rd. Read	RG1	86	B3
Ermin Wlk. That	RG19	106	A2
Errington Dr. Wind	SL4	67	D3
Erskine Cl. Silc	RG26	135	F1
Esher Cres. Harm	TW6	71	F3
Esher Rd. Camb	GU15	145	D1
Eskdale Gdns. Holy	SL6	40	A1
Eskdale Rd. Winn	RG41	88	A2
Eskdale Way. Camb	GU15	152	B2
Eskin Cl. Read	RG30	85	D4
Essex Ave. Slough	SL2	42	A4
Essex Pl. Lamb	RG17	25	D2
Essex Rise. New G	RG42	91	F1
Essex St. Newb	RG14	130	B4
Essex St. Read	RG2	86	A3
Ethel Rd. Ashf	TW15	97	F2
Eton Cl. Datch	SL3	68	A4
Eton Ct. Eton	SL4	67	E4
Eton Pl. Mar	SL7	1	B1
Eton Rd. Datch	SL3	68	A4
Eton Rd. Harl	UB7	71	F4
Eton Sq. Eton	SL4	67	E4
Eton Wick Rd. Eton	SL4	42	A1
Eustace Cres. Woki	RG40	116	B4
Evedon. Brac	RG12	118	A1
Evelyn Cres. Shepp	TW16	125	F4
Evelyn Ct. Wood	RG5	87	F3
Evelyn Way. Shepp	TW16	125	F4
Evendons Cl. Woki	RG41	116	A2
Evendons La. Bark	RG41	115	F1
Evenlode. Maid	SL6	39	F4
Evenlode Rd. Bou E	SL8	3	D2
Evenlode Way. Sand	GU17	150	B4
Everard Ave. Slough	SL1	42	C2
Everest Rd. Camb	GU15	151	E4
Everest Rd. Crow	RG45	143	D3
Everest Rd. Stan	TW19	97	F4
Evergreen Dr. Read	RG31	84	C2
Evergreen Rd. Camb	GU16	152	A1
Evergreen Way. Stan	TW19	97	E4
Evergreen Way. Woki	RG41	115	F3
Everington La. Yatt	RG18	53	D1
Everland Rd. Hung	RG17	100	B3
Eversley Rd. Arbo	RG2	114	C1
Eversley Rd. Bark	RG40	140	C3
Eversley St. Finch	RG27	141	D1
Eversley Way. Stai	TW20	123	E4
Evesham Rd. Caver	RG4	59	D3
Evesham Wlk. Crow	GU17	143	E1
Evreham Rd. Iver	SL0	44	C4
Evreux Cl. That	RG19	106	C1
Ewing Way. Newb	RG14	131	D4
Exbourne Rd. Read	RG2	113	E4
Exchange Rd. Ascot	SL5	120	B2
Exeforde Ave. Ashf	TW15	98	A2
Exeter Ct. Read	RG2	113	D4
Exeter Gdns. Yate	GU17	149	D4
Exeter Rd. Stan	TW6	71	F2
Exeter Rd. Thea	RG7	83	F2
Exeter Way. Stan	TW6	71	F3
Exmoor Rd. That	RG19	106	B2
Explorer Ave. Stan	TW19	97	F4
Expressway. Newb	RG14	105	F1
Exwick Sq. Read	RG2	113	E4
Eylham. Pur O T	RG8	57	D3
Eynsford Cl. Caver	RG4	59	F3
Eynsham Rd. Wood	RG5	87	F4
Faggs Rd. Harm	TW14	71	F2
Fair Lawn Gn. Read	RG2	86	C1
Fair Mile. Hen-O-T	RG9	15	E2
Fairacre. Maid	SL6	39	E3
Fairacres Ind Est. Wind	SL4	66	B3
Faircroft. Slough	SL2	22	A1
Faircross. Brac	RG12	118	A3
Faircross Quarters. Herm	RG18	78	C3
Faircross Rd. Read	RG30	85	E3
Fairfax. Brac	RG42	118	A4
Fairfax Pl. Newb	RG14	105	F3
Fairfield App. Wray	TW19	68	B1
Fairfield Ave. Datch	SL3	68	B4
Fairfield Ave. Stai	TW18	96	C2
Fairfield Cl. Datch	SL3	68	B4
Fairfield. Comp	RG20	31	E2
Fairfield Dr. Camb	GU16	151	F2
Fairfield La. Far C	SL2	22	A2
Fairfield Rd. Burn	SL1	21	E1
Fairfield Rd. Gori	RG8	34	B4
Fairfield Rd. Wray	TW19	68	B1
Fairfields. Hung	RG17	100	B3
Fairford Rd. Maid	SL6	39	F4
Fairford Rd. Read	RG31	57	E1
Fairhaven. Eng G	TW20	95	F2
Fairholme. Felt	TW14	98	C4
Fairholme Rd. Ashf	TW15	97	F2
Fairlawn Pk. Wind	SL4	66	C2
Fairlawns Cl. Stai	TW18	97	D1
Fairlea. Maid	SL6	39	D2
Fairlie Rd. Slough	SL1	42	A4
Fairlight Ave. Wind	SL4	67	E3
Fairlop Cl. Bur C	RG31	84	B2
Fairmead Cl. Sand	GU15	150	C4
Fairmead Rd. Shin	RG2	113	F3
Fairoak Way. Tad	RG26	134	B1
Fairsted Cl. Read	RG30	85	D4
Fairview Ave. Read	RG6	87	D3
Fairview Ct. Stai	TW18	97	D1
Fairview Dr. Stai	TW17	124	C2
Fairview Estate. Hen-O-T	RG9	35	F4
Fairview Rd. Burn	SL6	41	D4
Fairview Rd. Hung	RG17	100	B3
Fairview Rd. Slough	SL2	21	F1
Fairview Rd. Woki	RG40	116	B3
Fairwater Dr. Wood	RG5	87	E3
Fairway Ave. Read	RG30	84	B3
Fairway. Chert	KT16	124	A1
Fairway Dr. Char	RG10	61	D3
Fairway Hts. Camb	GU15	152	A3
Fairway The. Burn	SL1	21	E2
Fairway The. Camb	GU15	152	A2
Fairway The. Fla H	HP10	3	E4
Fairway The. Maid	SL6	39	D2
Fairways. Ashf	TW15	98	A1
Fakenham Cl. Read	RG6	114	A4
Fakenham Way. Crow	GU17	143	E1
Falaise. Eng G	TW20	95	F2
Falcon Ave. Read	RG2	86	C1
Falcon Cl. Camb	GU18	152	C4
Falcon Dr. Stan	TW19	70	C1
Falcon Fields. Tad	RG26	135	D1
Falcon House Gdns. Ball H	RG20	129	F1
Falcon Way. Shepp	TW16	125	F4
Falcon Way. Woki	RG41	115	F3
Falcon Way. Yate	GU17	149	D3
Falcons Croft. Woo G	HP10	3	F4
Falconwood. Eng G	TW20	95	F2
Falkland Dr. Newb	RG14	130	C4
Falkland Garth. Newb	RG14	130	B4
Falkland Rd. Caver	RG4	59	D1
Falkland Rd. Newb	RG14	130	B3
Fallowfield Cl. Caver	RG4	59	D2
Fallowfield. Yate	GU17	149	D4
Falmouth Cl. Camb	GU15	152	A2
Falmouth Rd. Read	RG2	113	E4
Falmouth Rd. Slough	SL1	42	A4
Falmouth Way. That	RG19	106	C2
Falstaff Ave. Read	RG6	86	C1
Fane Way. Maid	SL6	39	E3
Fanes Cl. Brac	RG42	117	F4
Faraday Cl. Arbo	RG2	140	C4
Faraday Cl. Slough	SL2	42	A4
Faraday Rd. Newb	RG14	105	D2
Faraday Rd. Slough	SL2	42	A4
Farcrosse Cl. Sand	GU17	150	B4
Fareham Dr. Yate	GU17	149	D4
Faringdon Cl. Sand	GU17	143	E1
Faringdon Dr. Brac	RG12	118	B2
Faringdon Wlk. Read	RG30	85	D2
Farleigh Mews. Caver	RG4	59	F3
Farley Copse. Brac	RG42	117	F4
Farm Cl. Ascot	SL5	120	B2
Farm Cl. Brac	RG42	117	F4
Farm Cl. Brac	RG45	143	E4
Farm Cl. Chert	GU25	123	D2
Farm Cl. Gori	RG8	34	B3
Farm Cl. Holy	SL6	40	B1
Farm Cl. Maid	SL6	39	D4
Farm Cl. Pur O T	RG8	57	E3
Farm Cl. Shepp	TW17	125	D1
Farm Cl. Stai	TW18	96	C2
Farm Cl. Yate	GU17	149	E3
Farm Cres. Slough	SL2	43	E4
Farm Dr. Old W	SL4	68	A1
Farm Dr. Read	RG31	84	A3
Farm Lea. Woo G	HP10	3	F4
Farm Rd. Bou E	SL8	2	C2
Farm Rd. Burn	SL6	41	D3
Farm Rd. Camb	GU16	151	F1
Farm Rd. Hen-O-T	RG9	35	F4
Farm Rd. Maid	SL6	39	D4
Farm Rd. Stai	TW18	97	D1
Farm View. Yate	GU17	149	E3
Farm Way. Stan	TW19	69	F1
Farm Yd. Wind	SL4	67	E4
Farman Cl. Wood	RG5	88	A4
Farmers Cl. Maid	SL6	39	D2
Farmers Cl. Read	RG2	113	E3
Farmers Rd. Stai	TW18	96	C2
Farmers Way. Maid	SL6	39	D2
Farmiloe Cl. Pur O T	RG8	57	E2
Farnburn Ave. Slough	SL1	42	A4
Farnell Rd. Stan	TW18	97	D3
Farnham Cl. Brac	RG12	118	B4
Farnham Dr. Caver	RG4	59	F2
Farnham La. Slough	SL2	22	A2
Farnham Park La. Far C	SL2	22	B2
Farnham Rd. Slough	SL1 & SL2	42	B4
Farningham. Brac	RG12	118	C2
Farnsfield Cl. Read	RG6	114	A4
Farrell Cl. Camb	GU15	151	E2
Farriers Cl. Wood	RG5	87	F4
Farrowdene Rd. Read	RG2	113	E4
Farthing Green La. Sto P	SL2	23	D2
Farthingales The. Maid	SL6	40	A4
Fatherson Rd. Read	RG1	86	B4
Faulkner Pl. Bags	GU19	145	F2
Faversham Rd. Crow	GU17	143	E1
Fawcett Cres. Wood	RG5	87	E3
Fawcett Rd. Wind	SL4	67	D3
Fawler Mead. Brac	RG12	118	C3
Fawley Bottom La. Faw (Bu)	RG9	15	E4
Fawley Cl. Maid	SL6	19	E1
Fawley Rd. Read	RG30	85	E3
Fawns Manor Cl. Felt	TW14	98	B4
Fawns Manor Rd. Felt	TW14	98	B4
Fawsley Cl. Stan	SL3	69	F4
Faygate Way. Read	RG6	87	D1
Feathers La. Wray	TW19	96	A3
Felbridge Cl. Camb	GU16	151	F1
Felix La. Shepp	TW17	125	F2
Felixstowe Cl. Winn	RG6	87	E1
Fellow Gn. West E	GU24	153	F3
Fellow Green Rd. West E	GU24	153	F3
Fells The. Read	RG31	84	A3
Felstead Cl. Read	RG6	86	C2
Feltham Hill Rd. Ashf	TW15	98	A2
Feltham Rd. Ashf	TW15	98	A2
Felthorpe Cl. Read	RG6	114	A4
Felton Way. Read	RG31	84	B4
Fencote. Brac	RG12	118	B2
Fennel Cl. Newb	RG14	105	E3
Fennel Cl. Read	RG6	86	C1
Fenns La. West E	GU24	153	F3
Fenton Ave. Stai	TW18	97	E2
Fern Cl. Camb	GU16	152	B2
Fern Cl. Crow	RG45	143	D3
Fern Cl. Read	RG31	84	B3
Fern Dr. Burn	SL6	41	D4
Fern Glen. Read	RG31	57	E1
Fern La. Lit M	SL7	2	C3
Fern Wlk. Ashf	TW15	97	E2
Fernbank Cres. Burl	SL5	119	E4
Fernbank Pl. Burl	SL5	119	E4
Fernbank Rd. Burl	SL5	119	E4
Fernbank. Woki	RG40	141	E4
Fernbrook Rd. Caver	RG4	58	C3
Ferndale Ave. Read	RG30	85	D2
Ferndale Cl. Read	RG31	57	E2
Ferndale Pk. Holy	SL6	65	F4
Ferndale Rd. Ashf	TW15	97	F2
Ferne Cl. Gori	RG8	34	B4
Fernery The. Stai	TW18	96	C2
Fernhill Cl. Black	GU17	150	C1
Fernhill Cl. Brac	RG42	90	C1
Fernhill La. Black	GU17	150	C1
Fernhill Rd. Black	GU17	150	C1
Fernhill Wlk. Black	GU17	150	C1
Fernhurst Rd. Ashf	TW15	98	B2
Fernhurst Rd. Bur C	RG31	84	B2
Ferniehurst. Camb	GU15	151	F2
Fernley Ct. Maid	SL6	19	E1
Ferrard Cl. Burl	SL5	119	E4
Ferrier Gr. Newb	RG14	131	D4
Ferry Ave. Stai	TW18	96	C1
Ferry La. Bou E	SL8	3	D1
Ferry La. Gori	RG8	34	A3
Ferry La. Hamb	RG9	16	B3
Ferry La. Medm	SL7	17	D3
Ferry La. Shepp	TW17	125	D1
Ferry La. Sou S	RG8	14	A2
Ferry La. Stai	TW18	124	B3
Ferry La. Warg	RG10	36	B1
Ferry La. Wray	TW19	96	A3
Ferry Rd. Maid	SL6	40	B2
Ferry Rd. Sou S	RG8	14	B2
Fettiplace. Gr She	RG17	48	A2
Fetty Pl. Maid	SL6	39	E2
Fidlers La. East I	RG20	30	C4
Fidlers Wlk. Warg	RG10	36	C1
Field Cl. Bur C	RG7	111	D1
Field Cl. Harl	UB7	71	E4
Field End. Warg	RG10	36	C1
Field End. West E	GU24	153	F3
Field House Cl. Brac	SL5	120	A1
Field Hurst. Slough	SL3	43	F1
Field La. Camb	GU16	151	F1
Field Pk. Brac	RG12	118	B4
Field Rd. Black	GU14	150	C1
Field Rd. Pease	RG20	29	E1
Field Rd. Read	RG1	86	A3
Field View. Caver	RG4	59	D2
Field View. Felt	TW13	98	B2
Field View. Stai	TW20	96	B2
Fielden Pl. Brac	RG12	118	B4
Fieldfare Ave. Yate	GU17	149	D3
Fieldhead Gdns. Bou E	SL8	3	D2
Fieldhouse Ind Est. Mar	SL7	1	C1
Fieldhouse La. Mar	SL7	1	C1
Fieldhouse Way. Mar	SL7	1	C1
Fielding Gdns. Crow	RG45	143	D2
Fielding Rd. Maid	SL6	39	D4
Fielding Rd. Sand	GU15	150	C3
Fieldings The. Holy	SL6	65	D4
Fieldridge. Newb	RG14	105	E3
Fields The. Slough	SL1	42	B2
Fieldway. Winn	RG41	88	B1
Fifehead Cl. Ashf	TW15	97	F1
Fifield La. Holy	SL4	65	E2
Fifield Rd. Holy	SL6	65	E4
Fifth Rd. Newb	RG14	104	C1
Fifth St. Gree	RG19	131	F3
Filbert Dr. Read	RG31	84	B4
Filey Rd. Read	RG1	86	C4
Filey Spur. Slough	SL1	42	A2
Filmer Rd. Wind	SL4	66	B3
Finbeck Way. Read	RG6	113	F4
Finch Ct. Maid	SL6	39	E3
Finch Rd. Read	RG6	87	E2
Finch Way. Bur C	RG7	111	D2
Fincham End Dr. Crow	RG45	142	C2
Finchampstead Rd. Finch	RG40	142	A4
Finchampstead Rd. Woki	RG40	142	A4
Findhorn Cl. Sand	GU15	150	B4
Finmere. Brac	RG12	118	B1
Finney Dr. Windl	GU20	146	B2
Finstock Cl. Winn	RG6	87	E1
Finstock Gn. Brac	RG12	118	C3
Fir Cottage Rd. Bark	RG40	141	F4
Fir Cottage Rd. Woki	RG40	141	F4
Fir Dr. Black	GU17	150	B2
Fir Tree Ave. Sto P	SL2	22	C1
Fir Tree Cl. Ascot	SL5	120	A1
Fir Tree Cnr. Tad	RG26	134	C1
Fir Tree La. Newb	RG14	105	F2
Fir Tree Paddock. West I	RG20	10	A1
Firbank Pl. Eng G	TW20	95	D1
Fircroft Cl. Read	RG31	57	E1
Fircroft Cl. Sto P	SL2	23	D3
Fireball Hill. Sunn	SL5	120	B1
Firglen Dr. Yate	GU17	149	E4
Firgrove Rd. Yate	GU17	149	D3
Firlands Ave. Camb	GU15	151	E3
Firlands. Brac	RG12	118	B2
Firmstone Cl. Winn	RG6	87	E1
Firs Ave. Wind	SL4	66	C2
Firs Cl. Woki	RG40	141	F4
Firs Dr. Slough	SL3	43	F3
Firs End. Bur C	RG7	111	D1
Firs La. Maid	SL6	38	C2
Firs La. Read	RG30	85	E3
Firs Rd. Read	RG31	84	B3
Firs The. That	RG18	106	A2
First Ave. Mar	SL7	2	A1
First Cres. Slough	SL1	42	B4
First St. Newt	RG19	132	A3

167
Glebeland Gdns. Shepp
Gwynne Cl. Wind

Glebeland Gdns. Shepp TW17 125 E2
Glebeland Rd. Sand GU15 150 C2
Glebelands Rd. Woki RG40 116 B4
Glebelands. That RG19 106 B2
Glebewood. Brac RG12 118 B2
Glen Ave. Ashf TW15 98 A2
Glen Cl. Stai TW17 125 D3
Glen Innes. Sand GU15 143 F1
Glen The. Silc RG26 135 F1
Glen The. Slough SL3 43 E1
Glenapp Grange. Mort RG7 136 C3
Glenavon Gdns. Slough SL3 43 E2
Glenavon Gdns. Yate GU17 149 E2
Glenbeigh Terr. Read RG1 85 F3
Glendale Ave. Newb RG14 130 B3
Glendale Rd. Tad RG26 135 D1
Glendevon Rd. Wood RG5 87 F4
Gleneagles Cl. Stan TW19 70 B1
Glenfield Rd. Ashf TW15 98 B1
Glenhaven Dr. Stan TW19 70 B1
Glenhurst Cl. Black GU17 150 C2
Glenmore Cl. That RG19 106 B1
Glennon Cl. Read RG30 85 E2
Glenrhondda. Caver RG4 59 D3
Glenrosa Rd. Read RG30 85 D4
Glentworth Pl. Slough SL1 42 B3
Glenwood. Brac RG12 118 B3
Glenwood Dr. Read RG31 84 B4
Globe Farm La. Black GU17 150 A3
Glory Cl. Woo G HP10 3 F4
Glory Mill La. Woo G HP10 3 F4
Gloucester Ave. Slough SL1 42 B4
Gloucester Cres. Stai TW18 97 E1
Gloucester Ct. Read RG30 85 E4
Gloucester Dr. Stai TW18 96 B3
Gloucester Gdns. Bags GU19 145 F2
Gloucester Pl. Wind SL4 67 E3
Gloucester Rd. Bags GU19 145 F2
Gloucester Rd. Maid SL6 19 F1
Gloucester Rd. Newb RG14 104 C1
Gloucester Rd. Read RG30 85 E4
Glyme Wlk. Read RG31 84 C2
Glyncastle. Caver RG4 58 C3
Glynswood. Camb GU15 151 F2
Goaters Rd. Burl SL5 119 E4
Goddard Cl. Shin RG2 113 F3
Goddard Cl. Stai TW17 124 C3
Goddard Ct. Winn RG41 88 A1
Goddards La. Camb GU15 151 D2
Goddington Rd. Bou E SL8 3 D3
Godolphin Rd. Slough SL1 42 B3
Godstow Cl. Wood RG5 87 F4
Goffs Rd. Ashf TW15 98 B2
Gogmore Farm Cl. Chert KT16 123 F1
Gogmore La. Chert KT16 124 A1
Gold Cup La. Burl SL5 119 E4
Goldcrest Cl. Yate GU17 149 D3
Goldcrest Way. Read RG31 84 A3
Golden Ball La. Cook SL6 19 D2
Golden Oak. Far C SL2 22 B3
Golden Orb Wood. Brac RG42 117 E4
Goldfinch La. Newt RG20 131 F2
Golding Cl. That RG19 106 C2
Goldney Rd. Camb GU15 152 B2
Goldsmid Rd. Read RG1 85 F4
Goldsmith Cl. That RG18 106 B3
Goldsmith Cl. Woki RG40 115 F1
Goldsmith Way. Crow RG45 143 D2
Goldsworthy Way. Slough SL1 41 E4
Goldthorpe Gdns. Read RG6 113 F4
Goldwell Dr. Newb RG14 104 C2
Golf Dr. Camb GU15 152 A2
Gooch Cl. Twyf RG10 61 F2
Goodboys La. Bur C RG7 112 A1
Goodboys La. Mort RG7 112 A1
Goodchild Rd. Woki RG40 116 B3
Goodings Gn. Woki RG40 116 C3
Goodliffe Gdns. Pur O T RG31 57 E2
Goodman Pk. Slough SL2 43 E3
Goodman Pl. Stai TW18 96 C2
Goodrich Cl. Caver RG4 59 F3
Goodways Dr. Brac RG12 118 B4
Goodwin Cl. Bur C RG31 84 C2
Goodwin Meadows. Woo G HP10 3 F3
Goodwin Rd. Slough SL2 21 F1
Goodwin Wlk. Newb RG14 130 B3
Goodwood Cl. Bur C RG7 111 D1
Goodwood Cl. Camb GU15 151 E4
Goodwood Rise. Mar B SL7 1 B4
Goodwood Way. Newb RG14 105 E1
Goose Cnr. New G RG42 91 F2
Goose Gn. Far C SL2 22 A2
Goose Gn. Lamb RG17 25 D2
Goose Green Way. That RG19 106 C2
Goose La. Leckh RG20 49 F3
Goose Pool. Chert KT16 123 F1
Gordon Ave. Camb GU15 151 E2
Gordon Cl. Stai TW18 97 D1
Gordon Cres. Camb GU15 151 E2
Gordon Cres. Comp RG20 31 F2
Gordon Dr. Shepp TW17 125 E1
Gordon Pl. Read RG30 85 E4
Gordon Rd. Ashf TW15 97 F3
Gordon Rd. Camb GU15 151 E3
Gordon Rd. Crow RG45 143 E2
Gordon Rd. Maid SL6 39 E4
Gordon Rd. Newb RG14 105 D1
Gordon Rd. Shepp TW17 125 E2
Gordon Rd. Stai TW18 96 B2
Gordon Rd. That RG18 106 A3
Gordon Rd. Wind SL4 66 C3
Gordon Wlk. Yate GU17 149 F3
Gore End Rd. Ball H RG20 129 D2
Gore Rd. Burn SL1 21 D1
Goring La. Bur C RG7 111 D1
Goring Rd. Stai TW18 96 C2
Gorrick Sq. Brac RG41 116 A2
Gorse Bank. Light GU18 153 D4
Gorse Cottage Dr. Cold A RG18 79 E1
Gorse Dr. Wood RG5 88 A4
Gorse Hill La. Vir W GU25 122 B3
Gorse Hill Rd. Vir W GU25 122 B3
Gorse Meade. Slough SL1 42 A3
Gorse Rd. Camb GU16 151 F1
Gorse Rd. Cook SL6 19 F3
Gorse Ride N. Woki RG40 141 F4
Gorse Ride S. Woki RG40 141 F3
Gorselands. Caver RG4 59 D3
Gorselands. Newb RG14 130 B3
Gorselands. Tad RG26 135 E1
Gorselands. Yate GU17 149 E2
Gosbrook Rd. Caver RG4 59 D1
Gosden Rd. West E GU24 153 F3
Gosforth Cl. Read RG6 87 E1
Goslar Way. Wind SL4 67 D3
Gosling Gn. Slough SL3 43 F2
Gosling Rd. Slough SL3 43 F2
Gosnell Cl. Camb GU16 152 B2
Gossmore Cl. Mar SL7 1 C1
Gossmore La. Mar SL7 1 C1
Goswell Hill. Wind SL4 67 E3
Goswells Rd. Wind SL4 67 E3
Gothic Ct. Harl UB7 71 E4
Gothic Ct. Sand GU17 150 A4
Gough's La. New G RG12 91 E1
Goughs Barn La. New G RG42 91 D4
Goughs Meadow. Sand GU17 150 A4
Gould Rd. Felt TW14 98 C4
Govenor's Rd. Sand GU15 150 C3
Govett Ave. Shepp TW17 125 E2
Govett Gr. Windl GU20 146 B3
Gower Pk. Sand GU15 150 C4
Gower St. Read RG1 85 F4
Gower The. Stai TW20 123 D3
Graces La. Chiev RG20 78 A4
Graffham Cl. Read RG6 114 A4
Grafton Cl. Maid SL6 19 F1
Grafton Cl. Slough SL3 43 F4
Grafton Ct. Felt TW14 98 B4
Grafton Rd. Read RG30 84 B4
Graham Cl. Blew OX11 12 A4
Graham Cl. Maid SL6 39 E3
Graham Cl. Read RG31 84 C2
Graham Rd. Cook SL6 19 F3
Graham Rd. Windl GU20 146 B2
Grahame Ave. Pangb RG8 56 B3
Grampian Cl. Harl UB7 71 E4
Grampian Rd. Sand GU17 143 D1
Grampian Way. Slough SL3 44 A1
Gramps Hill. Let B OX12 6 C3
Granby Ct. Read RG1 86 C4
Granby End. Bur C RG7 111 D2
Granby Gdns. Read RG1 86 C4
Grand Ave. Camb GU15 151 E3
Grange Ave. Crow RG45 143 D3
Grange Ave. Read RG6 87 D3
Grange Cl. Gori RG8 34 A3
Grange Cl. Wray TW19 68 C1
Grange Ct. Newb RG14 105 D1
Grange Dr. Bou E HP10 3 E2
Grange Gdns. Far C SL2 22 B4
Grange La. Cook SL6 19 F4
Grange Pl. Stai TW18 124 B4
Grange Rd. Brac RG12 118 B4
Grange Rd. Camb GU15 151 F3
Grange Rd. Cook SL6 19 F4
Grange Rd. Eng G TW20 95 F2
Grange Rd. Hen-O-T RG9 15 F1
Grange The. Burn SL1 21 E1
Grange The. Caver RG4 58 B3
Grange The. Old W SL4 68 A1
Grange Way. Iver SL0 44 C4
Grangely Cl. Bur C RG31 84 B2
Grangewood. Slough SL3 43 E4
Grant Ave. Slough SL1 42 C4
Grant Cl. Shepp TW17 125 D2
Grant Rd. Crow RG45 143 E2
Grant Wlk. Sunn SL5 120 C1
Grantham Cl. Sand GU15 143 F1
Grantham Rd. Read RG30 84 C2
Granthams The. Lamb RG17 25 D2
Granville Ave. Slough SL2 42 B4
Granville Rd. Read RG30 85 D3
Grasmere Ave. Read RG30 57 F1
Grasmere Ave. Slough SL2 43 D3
Grasmere Cl. Felt TW14 98 C4
Grasmere Cl. Stai TW20 96 A1
Grasmere Par. Slough SL2 43 D3
Grasmere Rd. Light GU18 146 A1
Grass Hill. Caver RG4 58 C2
Grassington Pl. That RG19 106 B2
Grassmead. That RG19 106 C1
Grassmere Cl. Winn RG41 88 A1
Grassy La. Maid SL6 39 F4
Grattan Ct. Mar SL7 2 A2
Gratton Dr. Wind SL4 66 C2
Gratton Rd. Read RG2 113 E4
Gratwicke Rd. Read RG30 84 C4
Gravel Hill. Box RG20 103 F3
Gravel Hill. Caver RG4 59 D3
Gravel Hill. Hen-O-T RG9 15 E1
Gravel Rd. Caver RG9 35 D1
Gravelly Cl. Ball H RG20 129 D2
Graveney Dr. Caver RG4 58 C2
Gravett Cl. Hen-O-T RG9 35 E4
Grayling Cl. Mar SL7 18 B4
Grays Cres. Wood RG5 87 E4
Grays La. Ashf TW15 98 A2
Grays Park Rd. Sto P SL2 23 D2
Grays Pl. Slough SL2 42 C3
Grays Rd. Slough SL1 42 C3
Grayshot Dr. Sand GU17 150 B3
Grazeley Rd. Shin RG7 113 D2
Great Auclum Pl. Bur C RG7 111 D1
Great Hill Cres. Maid SL6 39 E3
Great Holland's Rd. Brac RG12 117 F2
Great Hollands Sq. Brac RG12 117 F2
Great Knollys St. Read RG1 85 F4
Great Lea. Shin RG7 113 D3
Great Severals. Kint RG17 102 A1
Great South West Rd. Felt TW14 71 F1
Great South West Rd. Harm TW14 71 F1
Green Acre Mount. Read RG30 84 B4
Green Cl. Burn SL6 41 D4
Green Cl. Maid SL6 19 F1
Green Cres. Fla H HP10 3 E4
Green Croft. Woki RG40 116 C4
Green Dr. Woki RG40 116 B4
Green Dragon La. Fla H HP10 3 D4
Green End Cl. Shin RG7 113 D1
Green End. Yate GU17 149 E4
Green Farm Rd. Bags GU19 145 F2
Green Finch Cl. Brac RG45 142 C3
Green Hill Cl. Camb GU15 152 B3
Green Hill Rd. Camb GU15 152 B3
Green La. Ascot SL5 120 C4
Green La. Ashf TW16 98 C1
Green La. Bags GU19 145 F1
Green La. Black GU17 150 C2
Green La. Bur C RG30 85 D1
Green La. Bur G SL6 38 A3
Green La. Burn SL1 21 E2
Green La. Caver RG9 35 D1
Green La. Eng G TW20 96 A2
Green La. Far C SL2 22 A3
Green La. Hen-O-T RG9 35 E4
Green La. Holy SL6 64 A3
Green La. Hurst RG10 88 C2
Green La. Maid SL6 40 A3
Green La. Maid SL6 40 A3
Green La. Newb RG14 104 C1
Green La. Padw RG7 110 B1
Green La. Pangb RG8 56 B2
Green La. Sand GU17 150 B3
Green La. Sand GU17 150 B4
Green La. Shepp TW17 125 E2
Green La. Slough SL3 68 A3
Green La. Stai TW18 123 F4
Green La. Stai TW18 123 F4
Green La. Stai TW20 96 A2
Green La. That RG19 106 B2
Green La. Wind SL4 67 D3
Green La. Woki RG41 88 B1
Green La. Yate GU17 149 D4
Green Lane Cl. Camb GU15 151 D4
Green Lane Ct. Burn SL1 21 E1
Green Leas. Ashf TW16 98 C1
Green Leas Cl. Ashf TW16 98 C1
Green Pk. Stai TW18 96 C3
Green Rd. Read RG6 87 D3
Green The. Brac RG12 118 A3
Green The. Burn SL1 21 D1
Green The. Chil OX11 10 C4
Green The. Datch SL3 68 A4
Green The. Kint RG17 102 A1
Green The. Slough SL1 42 B2
Green The. Thea RG7 83 E1
Green The. Woki RG41 115 F4
Green The. Woo G HP10 3 F3
Green The. Wray TW19 68 C1
Green Verges. Mar SL7 1 C2
Green Way. Burn SL1 21 D2
Green Wood. Burl SL5 119 E4
Greenacre Ct. Eng G TW20 95 E1
Greenacre. Wind SL4 66 C3
Greenacres Ave. Winn RG41 88 A2
Greenacres. Ball H RG20 129 F1
Greenacres La. Winn RG41 88 A2
Greencroft Gdns. Read RG30 84 C3
Greendale Mews. Slough SL2 43 D3
Greene Fielde End. Stai TW18 97 E1
Greenfern Ave. Slough SL1 41 E4
Greenfield Way. Brac RG45 143 D4
Greenfields. Maid SL6 40 A3
Greenfields Rd. Read RG2 113 D4
Greenfinch Cl. Read RG31 84 A3
Greenham Cl. Gree RG19 131 E4
Greenham Cl. Wood RG5 88 A3
Greenham Mill. Newb RG14 105 D2
Greenham Rd. Newb RG14 105 D1
Greenham Wood. Brac RG12 118 B2
Greenhaven. Yate GU17 149 D3
Greenholme. Camb GU15 152 B3
Greenhow. Brac RG12 118 A3
Greenlands. Ball H RG20 129 F1
Greenlands. Fla H HP10 3 D4
Greenlands Rd. Camb GU15 151 D1
Greenlands Rd. Newb RG14 105 D1
Greenlands Rd. Stai TW18 97 D2
Greenleas Ave. Caver RG4 59 D4
Greenleas. Camb GU16 151 F1
Greenleas Cl. Yate GU17 149 E4
Greeno Cres. Stai TW17 125 D2
Greenock Rd. Slough SL1 42 A4
Greenside. Bou E SL8 3 D3
Greenside. Crow RG45 142 C3
Greenside. Slough SL2 42 A4
Greensward La. Arbo RG2 114 B1
Greenway Dr. Stai TW18 124 A4
Greenway The. Fawl OX12 27 E4
Greenway The. Slough SL1 41 E3
Greenways. Ball H RG20 129 F1
Greenways Dr. Maid SL6 39 D4
Greenways Dr. Sunn SL5 120 C1
Greenways. Eng G TW20 95 F2
Greenways. Lamb RG17 25 D1
Greenways. Sand GU17 143 D1
Greenwood Gr. Winn RG41 88 B2
Greenwood Rd. Crow RG45 143 D3
Greenwood Rd. Read RG30 84 C3
Gregory Cl. Winn RG6 114 B4
Gregory Dr. Old W SL4 68 A1
Grenfell Ave. Maid SL6 39 F3
Grenfell Pl. Maid SL6 39 F3
Grenfell Rd. Maid SL6 39 F3
Grenville Cl. Burn SL1 21 D2
Gresham Rd. Slough SL1 42 A4
Gresham Rd. Stai TW18 96 C2
Gresham Rd. Stai TW18 97 D2
Gresham Way. Read RG30 58 A1
Greyberry Copse Rd. Gree RG19 131 E4
Greyfriars Dr. Ascot SL5 120 A2
Greyfriars Rd. Read RG1 86 A4
Greys Ct. Read RG1 86 B4
Greys Hill. Hen-O-T RG9 15 E1
Greys Rd. Hen-O-T RG9 35 E4
Greystoke Ct. Crow RG45 143 D2
Greystoke Rd. Caver RG4 59 E2
Greystoke Rd. Slough SL2 41 F4
Griffin Cl. Maid SL6 39 F3
Griffin Cl. Slough SL1 42 B2
Griffiths Cl. That RG19 106 C1
Grindle Cl. Cold A RG18 106 B3
Gringer Hill. Maid SL6 39 F4
Groombridge Pl. Newb RG14 104 C3
Grosvenor Ct. Black GU17 150 B2
Grosvenor Dr. Maid SL6 40 B4
Grosvenor Rd. Caver RG4 59 E2
Grosvenor Rd. Stai TW18 97 D1
Grove Cl. Brac RG40 142 C4
Grove Cl. Old W SL4 95 D4
Grove Cl. Slough SL1 43 D2
Grove Cotts. Caver RG4 59 D3
Grove Cross Rd. Camb GU16 151 E1
Grove Ct. Eng G TW20 96 A2
Grove End. Windl GU19 145 F3
Grove Hill. Caver RG4 59 D2
Grove La. Wink RG42 92 A2
Grove Rd. Burn SL1 21 F2
Grove Rd. Camb GU15 151 F3
Grove Rd. Caver RG4 59 D3
Grove Rd. Chert KT16 123 F2
Grove Rd. Hen-O-T RG9 15 F1
Grove Rd. Maid SL6 39 F4
Grove Rd. Newb RG14 104 C3
Grove Rd. Shepp TW17 125 E2
Grove Rd. Wind SL4 67 E3
Grove The. Burl SL5 119 E4
Grove The. Camb GU16 151 E1
Grove The. Eng G TW20 96 A2
Grove The. Read RG1 86 B4
Grove The. Slough SL1 43 D2
Grove The. That RG18 106 B2
Grove The. Twyf RG10 61 E3
Grovefields Ave. Camb GU16 151 E1
Groveland Pl. Read RG30 85 D4
Groveland Rd. Newb RG14 104 C3
Grovelands Ave. Winn RG41 88 B1
Grovelands Cl. Winn RG41 88 B2
Grovelands Rd. Read RG30 85 D4
Grovelands Rd. Shin RG7 113 E1
Groveley Rd. Ashf TW16 98 C2
Groves Lea. Mort RG7 136 C3
Groves Way. Cook SL6 19 F3
Grovestile Waye. Felt TW14 98 B4
Grubwood La. Cook SL6 19 D4
Guards Club Rd. Maid SL6 40 B4
Guards Ct. Went SL5 121 D1
Guards Rd. Oak G SL4 66 B3
Guildford Ave. Felt TW13 98 C3
Guildford Rd. Bags GU19 145 F2
Guildford Rd. Bis GU24 153 F4
Guildford Rd. Light GU18 153 F4
Guildford Rd. West E GU24 153 F4
Guildford St. Chert KT16 124 A1
Guildford St. Stai TW18 97 D1
Gun St. Read RG1 86 A4
Gunthorpe Rd. Mar SL7 2 A2
Gurney Cl. Caver RG4 58 B3
Gurney Dr. Caver RG4 58 B3
Gwendale. Maid SL6 19 E1
Gweneth Ct. Mar SL7 1 B2
Gwent Cl. Maid SL6 39 D2
Gwyn Cl. Newb RG14 130 C4
Gwynne Cl. Read RG31 57 E2
Gwynne Cl. Wind SL4 66 C3

168

Gwyns Piece. Lamb

Hencroft St S. Slough

Gwyns Piece. Lamb	RG17	25	D2
Gypsy La. Mar	SL7	1	C2
Gypsy La. Sto P	SL2	22	C4
Habershon Dr. Camb	GU16	152	B1
Haddon Dr. Wood	RG5	87	F4
Haddon Rd. Maid	SL6	39	E3
Hadfield Rd. Stan	TW19	70	B1
Hadfield Rd. Stan	TW19	97	E4
Hadleigh Rise. Caver	RG4	59	F3
Hadlow Ct. Slough	SL1	42	B3
Hadrian Cl. Stan	TW19	97	F4
Hadrian Way. Stan	TW19	97	F4
Hadrian Wlk E. Read	RG2	86	B2
Hag Hill La. Burn	SL6	41	D4
Hag Hill Rise. Burn	SL6	41	D4
Hagley Rd. Read	RG2	86	A2
Haig Dr. Slough	SL1	42	A2
Haig Rd. Sand	GU15	150	C3
Hailey La. Beed	RG20	29	F1
Hailsham Cl. Crow	GU15	143	E1
Halcyon Terr. Read	RG30	84	C4
Haldane Rd. Caver	RG4	58	C3
Hale End. Brac	RG12	118	C3
Hale St. Stai	TW18	96	C2
Hale Way. Camb	GU16	151	E1
Halewood. Brac	RG12	117	F2
Half Mile Rd. Lamb	RG17	46	A1
Half Moon St. Bags	GU19	145	F2
Halfacre Cl. Shin	RG7	113	D2
Halfpenny La. Chol	OX10	13	F3
Halfpenny La. Went	SL5	121	D1
Halifax Cl. Maid	SL6	39	D4
Halifax Pl. That	RG18	106	B2
Halifax Rd. Maid	SL6	39	D4
Halifax Way. Maid	SL6	39	D4
Halkingcroft. Slough	SL3	43	E2
Hall Cl. Camb	GU15	151	F3
Hall Ct. Datch	SL3	68	A4
Hall Farm Cres. Yate	GU17	149	E3
Hall La. Harl	UB7	71	E4
Hall La. Yate	GU17	149	E3
Hall Meadow. Burn	SL1	21	E2
Hall Place La. Bur G	SL6	38	A4
Hallbrook Gdns. Binf	RG42	90	C1
Halldore Hill. Cook	SL6	19	F4
Halley Dr. Ascot	SL5	119	E4
Hallgrove Bottom. Windl	GU19	145	F3
Halliford Cl. Shepp	TW17	125	F3
Halliford Rd. Shepp	TW17	125	F3
Halls La. Read	RG2	86	C1
Halls La. Read	RG2	113	F4
Halls La. W St L	RG10	63	D3
Halls Rd. Read	RG30	84	B3
Halpin Cl. Read	RG31	84	B2
Halstead Cl. Wood	RG5	87	F4
Halstead House. Tad	RG26	134	C1
Ham La. Eng G	TW20	95	D2
Ham La. Old W	SL4	68	B2
Ham Rd. Ham	SN8	126	A2
Hamble Ave. Black	GU17	150	B3
Hambleden Wlk. Maid	SL6	19	F2
Hambledon Cl. Winn	RG6	87	F1
Hambleton Cl. Camb	GU16	152	A2
Hambridge La. Gree	RG14	105	F1
Hambridge Rd. Newb	RG14	105	E1
Hamilton Ave. Hen-O-T	RG9	15	F1
Hamilton Cl. Chert	KT16	123	F1
Hamilton Cl. Felt	TW13	98	C2
Hamilton Ct. Black	RG14	150	C1
Hamilton Ct. Newb	RG14	131	D4
Hamilton Dr. Sunn	SL5	120	C1
Hamilton Gdns. Burn	SL1	21	D1
Hamilton Rd. Felt	TW13	98	C2
Hamilton Rd. Read	RG1	86	C3
Hamilton Rd. Slough	SL1	42	A4
Hamilton Rd. Warg	RG10	36	C1
Hamlet St. Brac	RG42	118	C4
Hammond Cl. That	RG19	106	C1
Hammond End. Far C	SL2	22	B4
Hammond Way. Light	GU18	146	A1
Hammonds Heath. Mort	RG7	137	D3
Hampden Cl. Sto P	SL2	23	D1
Hampden Rd. Caver	RG4	59	D1
Hampden Rd. Maid	SL6	39	D4
Hampden Rd. Slough	SL3	43	F2
Hampdens The. Newb	RG14	130	B3
Hampshire Ave. Slough	SL1	42	B4
Hampshire Rd. Camb	GU15	151	F4
Hampshire Rise. New G	RG42	91	F1
Hampshire Way. Woki	RG41	115	E3
Hampstead Hill. Caver	RG4	60	B4
Hampstead Norreys Rd. Herm	RG18	79	D4
Hampton Rd. Newb	RG14	104	C1
Hanbury Cl. Burn	SL1	41	D4
Hanbury Dr. Bur C	RG31	84	B2
Hanbury Way. Camb	GU15	151	E2
Hancocks Mount. Ascot	SL5	120	B2
Hancombe Rd. Sand	GU17	143	D1
Handford La. Yate	GU17	149	E3
Hanger Rd. Tad	RG26	134	C1
Hangerfield Cl. Yate	GU17	149	E3
Hangmans Stone La. Chadd	RG20	49	D3
Hanley Cl. Wind	SL4	66	B3
Hannibal Rd. Stan	TW19	97	F4
Hanover Cl. Camb	GU16	151	F1
Hanover Cl. Eng G	TW20	95	D1
Hanover Cl. Slough	SL1	43	D2
Hanover Cl. Wind	SL4	66	C3
Hanover Gdns. Brac	RG12	117	F1
Hanover Way. Wind	SL4	66	C3
Hanwood Cl. Wood	RG5	87	E4
Hanworth Cl. Brac	RG12	118	B2
Hanworth La. Chert	KT16	123	F1
Hanworth Rd. Brac	RG12	118	A1
Harcourt Cl. Dorn	SL6	40	C2
Harcourt Cl. Hen-O-T	RG9	15	E1
Harcourt Cl. Stai	TW20	96	B1
Harcourt Dr. Read	RG6	86	C2
Harcourt Rd. Brac	RG12	118	A2
Harcourt Rd. Camb	GU15	151	D3
Harcourt Rd. Dorn	SL6	40	C2
Harcourt Rd. Wind	SL4	66	C3
Hardell Cl. Eng G	TW20	96	A2
Harding Rd. Wood	RG5	87	E4
Hardwell Way. Brac	RG12	118	C3
Hardwick Cl. Maid	SL6	39	D4
Hardwick La. Chert	KT16	123	E1
Hardwick Rd. Read	RG30	84	C4
Hardwick Rd. Whi-O-T	RG8	56	B4
Hardy Ave. Yate	GU17	149	E2
Hardy Cl. Caver	RG4	59	E1
Hardy Cl. Slough	SL1	42	A3
Hardy Cl. That	RG18	106	B3
Hardy Gn. Crow	RG45	143	D2
Hare Shoots. Maid	SL6	39	F3
Harebell Dr. That	RG18	106	C3
Harefield Cl. Winn	RG41	88	B1
Harefield Rd. Maid	SL6	39	D4
Harewood Dr. Cold A	RG18	106	B4
Harewood Pl. Slough	SL1	43	D2
Hargrave Rd. Maid	SL6	39	E4
Hargreaves Way. Read	RG31	84	C2
Harkness Rd. Burn	SL1	41	D4
Harlech Ave. Caver	RG4	59	E3
Harlech Rd. Black	GU17	150	B2
Harley Rd. Caver	RG4	59	D1
Harlington Cl. Harl	UB7	71	E4
Harlton Cl. Winn	RG6	114	B4
Harmans Water Rd. Brac	RG12	118	B2
Harmar Cl. Woki	RG40	116	C3
Harmondsworth La. Harm	UB7	70	C4
Harness Cl. Read	RG2	113	D3
Harold Rd. Kint	RG17	102	A1
Harpesford Ave. Went	GU25	122	B2
Harpsden Rd. Hen-O-T	RG9	35	F4
Harpsden Way. Hen-O-T	RG9	35	F4
Harpton Cl. Yate	GU17	149	E4
Harrier Cl. Wood	RG5	88	A3
Harrington Cl. Newb	RG14	105	F3
Harrington Cl. Read	RG6	87	E1
Harrington Cl. Wind	SL4	66	C2
Harris Cl. Lamb	RG17	25	D2
Harris Cl. Read	RG5	88	A4
Harris Way. Stai	TW16	125	F4
Harrison Cl. Twyf	RG10	61	F2
Harrison Ct. Stai	TW17	125	D2
Harrison Way. Slough	SL1	41	E3
Harrogate Ct. Slough	SL3	44	A1
Harrogate Rd. Caver	RG4	58	C2
Harrow Bottom Rd. Went	GU25	122	C2
Harrow Cl. Maid	SL6	19	F1
Harrow Ct. Read	RG1	85	F3
Harrow La. Maid	SL6	19	F1
Harrow Rd. Ashf	TW15	98	A3
Harrow Rd. Slough	SL3	43	F2
Harrow Way. Stai	TW17	125	E4
Hart Cl. Brac	RG42	91	D1
Hart Dyke Cl. Brac	RG41	116	A1
Hart St. Hen-O-T	RG9	15	F1
Hart St. Read	RG1	85	F4
Hartford Rise. Camb	GU15	151	E3
Hartigan Pl. Read	RG5	88	A4
Hartland Cl. Slough	SL1	42	B3
Hartland Rd. Read	RG2	86	B1
Hartley Cl. Black	GU17	150	A3
Hartley Cl. Sto P	SL3	23	E2
Hartley Copse. Old W	SL4	68	A1
Hartley Court Rd. Shin	RG7	112	C3
Hartley Way. That	RG18	106	C2
Hartmead Rd. That	RG19	106	C2
Harts Cl. Arbo	RG2	114	C1
Harts Hill Rd. That	RG18	106	C2
Harts La. Sulhd	RG7	110	B3
Harts Leap Cl. Sand	GU17	143	D1
Harts Leap Rd. Sand	GU17	150	A4
Hartsbourne Rd. Read	RG6	87	D2
Hartshill Rd. Tad	RG26	134	C1
Hartslock Ct. Pangb	RG8	56	A3
Hartslock View. Upp B	RG8	34	C1
Hartslock Way. Read	RG31	57	E1
Harvard Cl. Wood	RG5	88	A4
Harvard Rd. Crow	GU15	143	F1
Harvest Cl. Read	RG31	84	A3
Harvest Cl. Yate	GU17	149	D2
Harvest Ct. Stai	TW17	125	D3
Harvest Gn. Newb	RG14	104	C1
Harvest Hill. Bou E	SL8	3	E1
Harvest Hill Rd. Maid	SL6	39	F2
Harvest Rd. Eng G	TW20	95	E1
Harvest Ride. New G	RG42	91	F1
Harvey Rd. Shepp	TW17	125	F1
Harvey Rd. Slough	SL3	44	A2
Harwich Cl. Winn	RG6	87	E1
Harwich Rd. Slough	SL1	42	A4
Harwood Gdns. Old W	SL4	95	D4
Harwood Rd. Mar	SL7	1	B1
Harwood Rise. Ball H	RG20	129	F1
Haslemere Cl. Camb	GU16	152	B2
Haslemere Rd. Wind	SL4	67	D3
Haslett Rd. Shepp	TW17	125	F4
Hasting Cl. Maid	SL6	40	B1
Hatch Cl. Buck	RG7	108	B4
Hatch End. Windl	GU20	146	B2
Hatch Gate La. Know H	RG10	37	D3
Hatch La. Buck	RG7	108	B4
Hatch La. Bur C	RG30	111	E3
Hatch La. Harm	UB7	70	B4
Hatch La. Wind	SL4	67	D3
Hatch Ride. Brac	RG40	142	C4
Hatch Ride. Brac	RG45	143	D4
Hatch The. Oak G	SL4	66	C4
Hatchet La. Ascot	SL5	93	D2
Hatchet La. Old W	SL4	93	D2
Hatchet La. Wink	SL4	93	D2
Hatchets La. Buck	RG18	80	B4
Hatchett Rd. Felt	TW14	98	B4
Hatchgate Cl. Cold A	RG18	106	B4
Hatchgate Copse. Brac	RG12	117	F2
Hatchgate Gdns. Burn	SL1	21	E1
Hatfield Cl. Maid	SL6	39	E3
Hatfield Ct. Bur C	RG31	84	A2
Hatfield Rd. Slough	SL1	43	D2
Hatford Rd. Read	RG30	85	D2
Hatherley Rd. Read	RG1	86	C3
Hatherwood. Yate	GU17	149	F3
Hatton Ave. Far C	SL2	22	B1
Hatton Ct. Wind	SL4	67	E3
Hatton Hill. Asham	RG8	54	A4
Hatton Hill. Windl	GU20	146	B3
Hatton Rd. Felt	TW14	98	B4
Hatton Rd. Harm	TW14	71	F1
Haughurst Hill. Tad	RG26	134	B1
Havelock Cres. Maid	SL6	39	D4
Havelock Rd. Maid	SL6	39	D4
Havelock Rd. Woki	RG41	116	A3
Havelock St. Woki	RG41	116	A3
Haven Rd. Ashf	TW15	98	A3
Haven The. Kint	RG17	102	A1
Haversham Dr. Brac	RG12	118	A2
Haw La. Asham	RG8	53	F4
Hawkchurch Rd. Read	RG2	113	E4
Hawkedon Way. Winn	RG6	87	F1
Hawker Way. Wood	RG5	88	A4
Hawkes Cl. Woki	RG41	116	A4
Hawkes Leap. Windl	GU20	146	A3
Hawkesbury Dr. Bur C	RG31	84	C2
Hawkesworth Dr. Bags	GU19	145	F1
Hawkins Cl. Brac	RG12	119	D4
Hawkins Way. Woki	RG40	116	C3
Hawks Hill. Bou E	SL8	3	E1
Hawkshill Rd. Slough	SL2	22	A1
Hawksway. Stai	TW18	96	C3
Hawkswood Ave. Camb	GU16	151	F1
Hawkswood La. Fulm	SL9	23	F4
Hawksworth Rd. Bur C	RG7	111	D2
Hawley Cl. Bur C	RG31	84	B2
Hawley La. Camb	GU14	151	D1
Hawley Rd. Black	GU17	150	C2
Hawley Way. Ashf	TW15	98	A2
Haws La. Stan	TW19	70	A1
Hawthorn Cl. Brac	RG42	118	A4
Hawthorn Cl. Mar	SL7	1	C2
Hawthorn Gdns. Read	RG2	86	C1
Hawthorn La. Burn	SL2	22	A3
Hawthorn La. New G	RG42	91	F4
Hawthorn Rd. Camb	GU16	151	F1
Hawthorn Rd. Newb	RG14	105	D2
Hawthorn Way. Shepp	TW17	125	E3
Hawthorn Way. Sonn	RG4	60	C1
Hawthorne Cres. Black	GU17	150	C2
Hawthorne Cres. Slough	SL1	42	C4
Hawthorne Rd. Caver	RG4	59	F2
Hawthorne Rd. Stai	TW18	96	B2
Hawthorne Way. Gr She	RG17	48	A2
Hawthorne Way. Stan	TW19	97	E4
Hawthornes. Sulh	RG31	57	D2
Hawthorns The. Char	RG10	61	D2
Hawthorns The. Stan	SL3	69	F3
Hawtrey Cl. Slough	SL1	43	D2
Hawtrey Rd. Wind	SL4	67	E3
Hay La. Fulm	SL3	23	E4
Hay Rd. Read	RG1	85	F3
Hayes La. Bark	RG41	115	E2
Hayes Pl. Mar	SL7	1	B1
Hayfield Cl. Read	RG31	84	B4
Hayley Gn. New G	RG42	91	F2
Haymill Rd. Slough	SL1	21	E1
Haynes Cl. Slough	SL3	43	F1
Hayse Hill. Wind	SL4	66	B3
Haywards Cl. Hen-O-T	RG9	15	E1
Haywards Mead. Eton	SL4	41	F1
Haywards The. That	RG18	106	B2
Haywood. Brac	RG12	118	B1
Haywood Ct. Read	RG1	86	C4
Haywood Way. Read	RG30	84	C3
Hazel Cl. Bur C	RG30	111	D3
Hazel Cl. Eng G	TW20	95	D1
Hazel Cl. Mar B	SL7	1	B3
Hazel Cl. Woki	RG41	115	F3
Hazel Cres. Read	RG2	86	C1
Hazel Dr. Wood	RG5	87	E3
Hazel Gn. Tad	RG26	134	B1
Hazel Gr. Stai	TW18	97	E1
Hazel Gr. That	RG18	106	B3
Hazel Rd. Pur O T	RG8	57	E2
Hazelbank Rd. Chert	KT16	124	B1
Hazelbank. Woki	RG40	141	F3
Hazeldene. Chiev	RG20	51	D1
Hazelhurst Rd. Burn	SL1	21	E2
Hazell Cl. Maid	SL6	39	F4
Hazell Hill. Brac	RG12	118	B3
Hazell Way. Sto P	SL2	22	C3
Hazelmere Cl. Harm	TW14	71	F1
Hazelwood Cl. Read	RG31	57	E1
Hazelwood La. Binf	RG42	90	C2
Hazlemere Rd. Slough	SL2	43	D3
Heacham Cl. Read	RG6	114	A4
Headington Cl. Maid	SL6	39	D4
Headington Cl. Woki	RG40	116	B4
Headington Dr. Woki	RG40	116	B4
Headington Rd. Maid	SL6	39	D4
Headley Cl. Wood	RG5	88	A4
Headley Park Ind Est. Wood	RG5	87	F4
Headley Rd E. Wood	RG5	88	A4
Headley Rd. Wood	RG5	87	F4
Heads La. Ink	RG17	128	A3
Heads La. West W	RG17	128	A3
Heardman Cl. That	RG19	106	C1
Hearmon Cl. Yate	GU17	149	F3
Hearn Rd. Wood	RG5	87	F3
Hearn Wlk. Brac	RG12	118	C4
Hearne Dr. Holy	SL6	40	A1
Hearsey Gdns. Black	GU17	150	A3
Heath Cl. Harl	UB7	71	E4
Heath Cl. Stan	TW19	70	B1
Heath Cl. Vir W	GU25	122	B3
Heath Cl. Woki	RG41	116	A2
Heath Court. Tad	RG26	134	C1
Heath Dr. Caver	RG9	35	D1
Heath End Rd. Tad	RG26	134	C1
Heath Gr. Ashf	TW16	98	C1
Heath Hill Rd N. Crow	RG45	143	D3
Heath Hill Rd S. Crow	RG45	143	D3
Heath La. That	RG18	106	B3
Heath Rd. Bags	GU19	145	F2
Heath Rd. Beac	HP10	3	F4
Heath Rd. Brad	RG7	82	A1
Heath Rd. Read	RG6	87	D3
Heath Rd. Silc	RG26	135	F1
Heath Ride. Finch	RG40	142	B3
Heath Ride. Woki	RG40	142	B3
Heath Rise. Camb	GU15	151	E3
Heath Rise. Vir W	GU25	122	B3
Heathacre. Stan	SL3	69	F3
Heathcote. Maid	SL6	40	A1
Heathcote Rd. Camb	GU15	151	E3
Heathcroft Ave. Ashf	TW16	98	C1
Heather Cl. Woki	RG40	141	F4
Heather Dr. Tad	RG26	134	C1
Heather Dr. Went	SL5	121	D1
Heather Mead. Camb	GU16	151	F1
Heatherdale Rd. Camb	GU15	151	E2
Heatherden Cl. Read	RG2	113	E4
Heatherdene Ave. Finch	RG45	142	C2
Heatherley Cl. Camb	GU15	151	D3
Heatherley Rd. Camb	GU15	151	D3
Heathermount. Brac	RG12	118	C3
Heathermount Dr. Crow	RG45	143	D3
Heathers The. Stan	TW19	97	F4
Heatherside Dr. Vir W	GU25	122	A2
Heatherway. Crow	RG45	143	D3
Heathfield Ave. Ascot	SL5	120	C2
Heathfield Ave. Read	RG30	84	B3
Heathfield Ave. Shipl	RG9	35	D1
Heathfield Cl. Shipl	RG9	35	D1
Heathfield Rd. Bou E	SL1	20	C4
Heathfield Rd. Tapl	SL1	20	C4
Heathlands Dr. Maid	SL6	39	D3
Heathlands Rd. Woki	RG40	116	C1
Heathlands. Tad	RG20	134	C1
Heathmoors. Brac	RG12	118	B2
Heathpark Dr. Windl	GU20	146	C2
Heathrow Cl. Harm	UB7	70	A3
Heathrow Copse. Tad	RG26	134	B1
Heathway. Burl	SL5	119	F4
Heathway. Camb	GU15	151	E3
Heathway Cl. Camb	GU15	151	E3
Heathway. Read	RG31	84	B4
Heathwood Cl. Yate	GU17	149	E4
Heavens Lea. Bou E	SL8	3	E1
Hebden Cl. That	RG19	106	B1
Hedge Lea. Woo G	HP10	3	E4
Hedgeway. Newb	RG14	105	E2
Hedingham Mews. Maid	SL6	39	E4
Hedley Rd. Fla H	HP10	3	D4
Hedsor Hill. Bou E	HP10	3	E1
Hedsor La. Bou E	HP10	3	F1
Hedsor Rd. Bou E	SL8	3	D1
Heelas Rd. Woki	RG41	116	A3
Helena Rd. Wind	SL4	67	E3
Helgiford Gdns. Ashf	TW16	98	C1
Hellyer Way. Bou E	SL8	3	E2
Helmsdale. Brac	RG12	118	C2
Helmsdale Cl. Read	RG30	85	D4
Helston Gdns. Read	RG2	86	A1
Helston La. Wind	SL4	67	D3
Helvellyn Cl. Stai	TW20	96	B1
Hemdean Hill. Caver	RG4	59	D2
Hemdean Rd. Caver	RG4	59	D2
Hemdean Rise. Caver	RG4	59	D2
Hempson Ave. Slough	SL3	43	E2
Hemsdale. Maid	SL6	19	D1
Hemwood Rd. Wind	SL4	66	B2
Hencroft St N. Slough	SL1	42	C2
Hencroft St S. Slough	SL1	42	C2

170

Horton Rd. Datch Kiln La. Sulh

Horton Rd. Datch SL3 68 B3
Horton Rd. Hort SL3 69 D3
Horton Rd. Poyle SL3 69 F2
Horton Rd. Stan TW19 69 F2
Hose Hill. Bur C RG7 & RG30 111 D4
Hosier St. Read RG1 86 A4
Houlton Ct. Bags GU19 145 F1
Houston Way. Finch RG45 142 B3
Howard Ave. Slough SL2 42 C4
Howard Cl. Ashf TW16 98 C1
Howard Rd. Ashf TW15 97 E2
Howard Rd. Newb RG14 105 D1
Howard Rd. Woki RG40 116 B3
Howard St. Read RG1 85 F4
Howarth Rd. Maid SL6 40 A3
Howe La. Holy SL6 63 F1
Howgate Dr. Gori RG8 34 B4
Howth Dr. Wood RG5 87 E4
Hubbard Cl. Twyf RG10 61 F2
Hubberholme. Brac RG12 118 A3
Hubert Rd. Slough SL3 43 E2
Huckleberry Cl. Pur O T RG8 57 E2
Huddington Glade. Yate GU17 149 D3
Hudson Rd. Harl UB7 71 E4
Hudson Rd. Wood RG5 87 F3
Hugh Fraser Dr. Read RG31 84 B3
Hughenden Cl. Maid SL6 39 E3
Hughenden Rd. Slough SL1 42 B4
Hughes Rd. Ashf TW15 98 B1
Hughes Rd. Woki RG40 116 C4
Hull Cl. Slough SL1 42 B2
Humber Cl. That RG18 106 A3
Humber Cl. Woki RG41 115 F4
Humber Way. Sand GU17 150 B4
Humber Way. Slough SL3 44 A1
Hummer Rd. Eng G TW20 96 A2
Humphrey's La. East G RG17 47 E3
Hungerford Ave. Slough SL2 42 C4
Hungerford Cl. Sand GU17 150 B4
Hungerford Dr. Maid SL6 19 F2
Hungerford Dr. Read RG1 85 F3
Hungerford Hill. East G RG17 47 F1
Hungerford Hill. Lamb RG17 25 D1
Hungerford La. Hurst RG10 62 C1
Hungerford La. W St L RG10 62 C1
Hungerford Rd. Kint RG17 101 F2
Huntercombe Cl. Burn SL6 41 E4
Huntercombe Cl. Slough SL6 41 E4
Huntercombe La N. Slough SL1 41 E4
Huntercombe La S. Burn SL6 41 E3
Huntercombe La S. Slough SL6 41 E3
Hunters Chase. Caver RG4 58 C3
Hunters Hill. Bur C RG7 110 C2
Hunters Meadow. Gr She RG17 48 A2
Hunters Mews. Wind SL4 67 E3
Hunters Way. Shin RG7 113 D1
Huntingdonshire Cl. Woki RG41 115 E3
Huntingfield Way. Stai TW20 96 B1
Huntington Cl. Winn RG6 87 F1
Huntley Ct. Read RG1 86 C3
Hunts La. Tapl SL6 20 C2
Huntsmans Meadow. Ascot SL5 119 F4
Huntsmoor Rd. Tad RG26 135 D1
Huntswood La. Burn SL6 20 C2
Huntswood La. Tapl SL6 20 C2
Hurford Dr. That RG19 106 C2
Hurley High St. Hurl SL6 17 F2
Hurley La. Bish SL6 18 A2
Hurley La. Hurl SL6 18 A2
Hurricane Way. Read RG5 88 A4
Hurricane Way. Wood RG5 88 A4
Hursley Cl. Read RG30 84 C4
Hurst Gr. Shepp TW17 125 F1
Hurst La. Vir W TW20 123 D4
Hurst Park Rd. Twyf RG10 61 F1
Hurst Rd. Slough SL1 41 E4
Hurst Rd. Twyf RG10 61 F2
Hurstdene Ave. Stai TW18 97 D1
Hurstfield Dr. Burn SL6 41 D4
Hurstwood. Ascot SL5 120 A2
Huscarle Way. Pur O T RG31 57 E2
Hutsons Cl. Woki RG40 116 B4
Hutton Cl. Newb RG14 105 D2
Hutton Cl. Read RG6 87 D1
Hutton Cl. Windl GU20 146 B2
Hyde End La. Brim RG7 133 E3
Hyde End La. Shin RG7 113 E2
Hyde End Rd. Shin RG7 113 E1
Hyde Gn. Mar SL7 1 C1
Hyde La. Newt RG20 132 A1
Hyde Terr. Ashf TW15 98 C1
Hydes The. Pur O T RG31 57 E2
Hylle Cl. Wind SL4 66 C3
Hyperion Way. Read RG2 86 A2
Hythe Cl. Brac RG12 118 C2
Hythe End Rd. Wray TW19 96 A3
Hythe Field Ave. Stai TW20 96 B1
Hythe Park Rd. Stai TW20 96 B2
Hythe Rd. Stai TW18 96 B2
Hythe The. Stai TW18 96 C2

Ian Mikardo Way. Caver RG4 59 E1
Iberian Way. Camb GU15 152 A3
Ibstock Cl. Read RG30 85 D4
Ibstone Ave. Caver RG4 59 F3
Icknield Pl. Gori RG8 34 B4
Icknield Rd. Gori RG8 34 B4
Ilbury Cl. Shin RG2 113 F3
Ilchester Cl. Maid SL6 39 E3
Ilchester Mews. Caver RG4 59 F3
Ilex Cl. Eng G TW20 95 D1
Ilex Cl. Silc RG26 135 F1
Ilex Cl. Yate GU17 149 D3
Ilfracombe Way. Winn RG6 87 F2
Ilkley Rd. Caver RG4 58 C2
Ilkley Way. That RG19 106 B1
Illingworth Ave. Caver RG4 59 F3
Illingworth Gr. Brac RG12 118 C4
Illingworth. Wind SL4 66 C2
Ilsley Rd. Comp RG20 31 E2
Imperial Rd. Felt TW14 98 C4
Imperial Rd. Wind SL4 67 D3
Imperial Way. Read RG2 113 D4
Impstone Rd. Silc RG26 135 F1
In The Ray. Maid SL6 40 A4
Inchwood. Brac RG12 118 B1
India Rd. Slough SL1 43 D2
Ingle Dell. Camb GU15 151 E2
Ingle Glen. Woki RG40 142 A4
Ingleglen. Far C SL2 22 A4
Ingleside. Stan SL3 69 F3
Ingleton. Brac RG12 118 A3
Inglewood Ave. Camb GU15 152 B3
Inglewood Ct. Read RG30 85 E3
Inglewood Rd. Kint RG17 101 F1
Inhurst La. Tad RG26 134 B1
Inhurst Way. Tad RG26 134 C1
Inkerman Rd. Eton SL4 41 F1
Inkpen Cl. Read RG30 85 D2
Inkpen Rd. Hung RG17 100 C2
Inkpen Rd. Kint RG17 102 A1
Inkpen Rd. Kint RG17 127 D4
Inner Ring E. Harm TW6 71 D2
Inner Ring W. Harm TW6 71 D2
Innings La. Brac RG42 118 C4
Innings La. Whi Wa SL6 63 E4
Institute Rd. Burn SL6 40 C4
Institute Rd. Mar SL7 1 C1
Institute Rd. Tapl SL6 40 C4
Instow Rd. Read RG6 87 D1
Invergordon Cl. Read RG31 84 C2
Inverness Way. Sand GU15 150 B4
Invicta Cl. Felt TW14 98 C4
Inwood Cl. Cook SL6 19 D3
Iona Cres. Slough SL1 41 F4
Ipswich Rd. Slough SL1 42 A4
Irish Hill Rd. Kint RG17 102 A1
Irvine Pl. Vir W GU25 122 C2
Irvine Way. Winn RG6 114 B4
Isaac Newton Rd. Bark RG2 115 D1
Isis Cl. Winn RG41 88 A1
Isis Way. Bou E SL8 3 D2
Isis Way. Sand GU17 150 B4
Island Cl. Stai TW18 96 C2
Island Farm Rd. Bur C RG7 110 B1
Island Farm Rd. Bur C RG7 136 C4
Island Farm Rd. Sulhd RG7 110 B1
Island Rd. Bur C RG2 85 F1
Island Rd. Read RG2 85 F1
Island The. Eng G TW19 96 A3
Islandstone La. Hurst RG10 89 D3
Islet Park Dr. Maid SL6 20 B2
Islet Pk. Maid SL6 20 B2
Islet Rd. Maid SL6 20 B2
Ivanhoe Rd. Bark RG40 141 D3
Iver La. Iver SL0 44 C4
Iverdale Cl. Iver SL0 44 B3
Iverna Gdns. Harm TW14 71 E1
Ives Cl. Yate GU17 149 D4
Ives Rd. Slough SL3 44 A2
Ivy Cl. Holy SL6 65 D4
Ivy Cres. Slough SL1 41 F3
Ivy Dr. Light GU18 153 D4
Ivybank. Read RG31 57 E1
Ivydene Rd. Read RG30 58 B1

Jack St. Newb RG14 105 D2
Jackson Cl. Brac RG12 118 A2
Jacob Cl. Brac RG42 117 E4
Jacob Cl. Wind SL4 66 C3
Jacob Rd. Sand GU15 151 D4
James Butcher Dr. Thea RG7 83 F2
James Cl. Mar SL7 1 C2
James Rd. Camb GU15 151 D1
James St. Read RG1 85 F4
James St. Wind SL4 67 E3
James Watt Rd. Bark RG2 140 C4
James Way. Camb GU15 151 D1
James's La. Bur C RG30 111 F2
Jameston. Brac RG12 118 B1
Jamnagar Cl. Stai TW18 96 C1
Janson Ct. Read RG1 85 F3
Japonica Cl. Woki RG41 115 E2
Jaques's La. Sulhd RG7 110 C3
Jarry Ct. Mar SL7 1 C2
Jarvis Dr. Twyf RG10 61 E3
Jasmine Cl. Woki RG41 115 E4
Jay Cl. Read RG6 87 D1
Jays Nest Cl. Black GU17 150 B2
Jedburgh Cl. That RG19 106 C2
Jefferson Cl. Slough SL3 44 A1
Jeffries Ct. Bou E SL8 3 D1
Jellicoe Cl. Slough SL1 42 A2
Jenkins Hill. Bags GU19 145 E1
Jennery La. Burn SL1 21 E1
Jennetts Cl. Brad RG7 81 F2
Jennings Field. Fla H HP10 3 E4
Jennings Wharf. Wind SL4 67 E4
Jennys Wlk. Yate GU17 149 F3
Jerome Cl. Mar SL7 1 C2
Jerome Rd. Wood RG5 87 F3
Jerrymoor Hill. Woki RG40 141 F4
Jesmond Dene. Newb RG14 104 C2
Jesse Cl. Yate GU17 149 F3
Jesse Terr. Read RG1 85 F4
Jessiman Terr. Stai TW17 125 D2
Jevington. Brac RG12 118 B1
Jig's La N. New G RG42 91 F1
Jig's La S. New G RG42 91 F1
Jigs La S. New G RG42 91 E1
Jobs La. Cook SL6 19 D4
Jocks La. Binf RG42 90 C1
Joel Cl. Read RG6 87 D2
John Childs Cl. Newb RG14 105 D1
John Hunt Cl. That RG19 106 C1
John Nike Way. Binf RG12 117 E4
John Taylor Ct. Slough SL1 42 B3
Johns Cl. Ashf TW15 98 B2
Johnsons La. Cold A RG18 106 B4
Jonathan Hill. Newt RG20 131 D2
Jordan Cl. Caver RG4 59 F3
Jordan Cl. Shin RG7 113 E1
Jordans Cl. Stan TW19 97 E4
Jordans La. Bur C RG7 110 C1
Joseph Ct. New G RG42 91 F1
Josephine Ct. Read RG1 85 F3
Jouldings La. Swal RG7 140 B2
Jourdelays Pas. Eton SL4 67 E4
Journeys End. Slough SL2 42 C4
Jubilee Ave. Burl SL5 119 F4
Jubilee Ave. Woki RG41 116 A4
Jubilee Cl. Burl SL5 119 F4
Jubilee Cl. Silc RG26 135 F1
Jubilee Cl. Stan TW19 97 E4
Jubilee Rd. Bish SL6 38 A3
Jubilee Rd. Finch RG40 141 F2
Jubilee Rd. Newb RG14 105 D1
Jubilee Rd. Read RG6 87 D3
Jubilee Sq. Read RG1 86 A3
Jubilee Way. Felt TW14 98 C4
Judy's Pas. Eton SL4 42 B1
Julius Hill. Brac RG42 118 C4
Julkes La. Arbo RG2 114 C4
Junction Rd. Ashf TW15 98 B2
Junction Rd. Light GU18 146 A1
Junction Rd. Read RG1 86 C3
Juniper. Brac RG12 118 B1
Juniper Dr. Maid SL6 40 A4
Juniper Gdns. Ashf TW16 98 C1
Juniper La. Fla H HP10 3 E4
Juniper La. Woo G HP10 3 E4
Juniper Rd. Mar B SL7 1 B3
Juniper Way. Read RG31 57 E1
Junnipers The. Woki RG41 115 E2
Jupiter Way. Woki RG41 115 F3
Justice Cl. That RG19 106 C1
Jutland Cl. Woki RG41 115 F3
Jutland Pl. Stai TW20 96 B2

Katesgrove La. Read RG1 86 A3
Kathleen Saunders Ct. Thea RG7 83 F2
Kaynes Pk. Burl SL5 119 F4
Kaywood Cl. Slough SL3 43 E2
Keane Cl. Wood RG5 87 F4
Kearsley Rd. Read RG30 85 E3
Keates Gn. Brac RG42 118 A4
Keats Cl. Wood RG5 87 F2
Keats La. Eton SL4 67 E4
Keats Rd. Wood RG5 87 F2
Keats Way. Crow RG45 143 D3
Keats Way. Yate GU17 149 D2
Keble Rd. Maid SL6 39 F4
Keble Way. Crow GU15 143 F1
Keel Dr. Slough SL1 42 B2
Keeler Cl. Wind SL4 66 C2
Keepers Combe. Brac RG12 118 B2
Keepers Farm Cl. Wind SL4 66 C2
Keepers Farm Cl. Wind SL4 66 C3
Keepers Wlk. Vir W GU25 122 B2
Keephatch Rd. Woki RG40 116 C4
Keighley Cl. That RG19 106 B1
Kelburne Cl. Winn RG41 88 B2
Keldholme. Brac RG12 118 A3
Kelly Cl. Shepp TW17 125 F4
Kelmscott Cl. Caver RG4 58 C2
Kelpatrick Rd. Slough SL1 41 E4
Kelsey Ave. Woki RG40 141 F3
Kelsey Cl. Maid SL6 39 E2
Kelsey Gr. Yate GU17 149 F3
Kelso Mews. Caver RG4 59 F3
Kelton Cl. Winn RG6 87 F1
Kelvedon Way. Caver RG4 58 C3
Kelvin Cl. Arbo RG2 140 C4
Kelvin Rd. Newb RG14 105 D2
Kemble Ct. Bur C RG31 84 B2
Kemerton Cl. Bur C RG31 84 B2
Kemp Ct. Bags GU19 145 F1
Kempton Cl. Newb RG14 105 E1
Kenavon Dr. Read RG1 86 B4
Kendal Ave. Caver RG4 59 F3
Kendal Ave. Shin RG2 113 F3
Kendal Cl. Felt TW14 98 C4
Kendal Cl. Slough SL2 43 D3
Kendal Cl. That RG18 106 B2
Kendal Dr. Slough SL2 43 D3
Kendal Gr. Camb GU15 152 B2
Kendrick Cl. Woki RG40 116 B3
Kendrick Rd. Newb RG14 130 B3
Kendrick Rd. Read RG1 86 B3
Kendrick Rd. Slough SL3 43 D2
Kenilworth Ave. Brac RG12 118 B4
Kenilworth Ave. Read RG30 85 E3
Kenilworth Ct. Slough SL1 42 C2
Kenilworth Gdns. Stai TW18 97 E2
Kenilworth Rd. Ashf TW15 97 D3
Kenneally. Oak G SL4 66 B3
Kennedy Cl. Far C SL2 22 B3
Kennedy Cl. Maid SL6 39 E3
Kennedy Cl. Mar SL7 1 C2
Kennedy Cl. Newb RG14 130 B3
Kennedy Dr. Pangb RG8 56 C3
Kennedy Gdns. Read RG6 87 D2
Kennel Ave. Ascot SL5 119 F4
Kennel Cl. Ascot SL5 92 C1
Kennel Gn. Ascot SL5 119 F4
Kennel La. Brac RG42 91 D1
Kennel La. Cook SL6 19 E4
Kennel La. Windl GU20 146 B3
Kennel Ride. Ascot SL5 92 C1
Kennel Wood. Ascot SL5 119 F4
Kennet Centre The. Newb RG14 105 D1
Kennet Cl. That RG19 106 C2
Kennet Ct. Hung RG17 100 C4
Kennet Ct. Woki RG41 115 F3
Kennet Pl. Bur C RG7 111 D2
Kennet Rd. Kint RG17 102 A1
Kennet Rd. Maid SL6 39 F4
Kennet Rd. Newb RG14 104 C2
Kennet Side. Newb RG14 105 E2
Kennet Side. Read RG1 86 B4
Kennet St. Read RG1 86 B4
Kennet Way. Hung RG17 100 C4
Kennett Rd. Bou E SL8 3 D2
Kennett Rd. Slough SL3 44 A2
Kensington Cl. Read RG6 87 D1
Kensington Rd. Read RG30 85 E4
Kent Ave. Slough SL1 42 B4
Kent Cl. Stai TW18 97 E1
Kent Cl. Woki RG41 115 E3
Kent Rd. Read RG30 85 E4
Kent Rd. Windl GU20 146 B3
Kent Way. Maid SL6 19 F1
Kentigern Dr. Brac RG45 143 F3
Kenton Cl. Brac RG12 118 B4
Kenton Cl. Camb GU16 152 A1
Kenton Cl. Mar SL7 1 C1
Kenton Rd. Read RG6 87 E2
Kentons La. Warg RG10 36 B4
Kentons La. Wind SL4 66 C3
Kentwood Cl. Read RG30 57 F1
Kentwood Hill. Read RG31 57 F1
Kenwood Cl. Harm UB7 71 D4
Kenwood Cl. Maid SL6 39 D4
Keppel Spur. Old W SL4 95 D4
Keppel St. Wind SL4 67 E3
Kepple Pl. Bags GU19 145 F2
Kernham Dr. Pur O T RG31 57 E2
Kerria Way. West E GU24 153 F3
Kerris Way. Read RG6 87 D1
Kersey Cres. Newb RG14 104 C3
Kesteven Way. Woki RG41 115 F3
Keston Cl. Caver RG4 59 E1
Kestrel Ave. Stai TW18 96 C3
Kestrel Cl. That RG19 106 A2
Kestrel Path. Slough SL2 21 F1
Kestrel Way. Bur C RG7 111 D1
Kestrel Way. Read RG30 85 D2
Kestrel Way. Woki RG41 115 F3
Keswick Cl. Camb GU15 152 B2
Keswick Cl. Read RG30 84 B4
Keswick Ct. Slough SL2 42 C3
Keswick Dr. Light GU18 153 D4
Keswick Gdns. Wood RG5 87 F3
Keswick Rd. Stai TW20 96 A1
Ketcher Gn. Binf RG42 90 B2
Kettering Cl. Bur C RG31 84 C2
Kevins Dr. Yate GU17 149 F4
Keynsham Way. Crow GU15 143 E1
Keys La. Maid SL6 39 F3
Kibble Gn. Brac RG12 118 B2
Kibblewhite Cres. Twyf RG10 61 E3
Kidderminster Rd. Slough SL2 22 A1
Kidmore End Rd. Caver RG4 59 D4
Kidmore End Rd. Maple RG4 59 D4
Kidmore Rd. Caver RG4 58 C3
Kidwells Cl. Maid SL6 39 F4
Kidwells Park Dr. Maid SL6 39 F4
Kier Pk. Ascot SL5 120 B3
Kilburn Cl. Bur C RG31 84 B2
Kildare Gdns. Caver RG4 59 E2
Killarney Dr. Maid SL6 39 F4
Kilmartin Gdns. Camb GU16 151 F1
Kilmington Cl. Brac RG12 118 C1
Kilmiston Ave. Shepp TW17 125 E2
Kilmore Dr. Camb GU15 152 A2
Kilmuir Cl. Sand GU15 150 B4
Kiln Cl. Harl UB7 71 E4
Kiln Cl. Herm RG18 79 E4
Kiln Dr. Herm RG18 78 C3
Kiln La. Ascot SL5 93 D1
Kiln La. Bou E SL8 3 E2
Kiln La. Brac RG12 118 A4
Kiln La. Mort RG7 137 E3
Kiln La. Shipl RG9 35 E1
Kiln La. Sulh RG31 84 A4

171

Kiln La. Sunn

Lewisham Way. Crow

Kiln La. Sunn	SL5	121	D2
Kiln Pl. Maid	SL6	19	D2
Kiln Rd. Caver	RG4	59	E4
Kiln Rd. Newb	RG14	105	E3
Kiln Ride Extension. Woki	RG40	142	A3
Kiln Ride. Upp B	RG8	54	C3
Kiln Ride. Woki	RG40	142	A4
Kiln View Rd. Read	RG2	86	B1
Kilnsea Dr. Read	RG6	87	E1
Kilnsea Dr. Winn	RG6	87	E1
Kilowna Cl. Char	RG10	61	D2
Kilross Rd. Felt	TW14	98	C4
Kimber Cl. Wind	SL4	67	D2
Kimberley. Brac	RG12	118	B1
Kimberley Cl. Read	RG1	85	F3
Kimberley Cl. Slough	SL3	43	F1
Kimbers Cl. Newb	RG14	104	C2
Kimbers Dr. Burn	SL1	21	E1
Kimbers Dr. Newb	RG14	104	B3
Kimbers La. Maid	SL6	39	F2
Kimmeridge. Brac	RG12	118	C2
Kimpton Cl. Read	RG6	113	F4
King Edward St. Slough	SL1	42	B2
King Edward VII Ave. Wind	SL4	67	F4
King Edwards Rd. Burl	SL5	119	F4
King Edwards Rise. Burl	SL5	92	C1
King Edwards Rise. Burl	SL5	119	F4
King George Cl. Ashf	TW16	98	C2
King James Way. Hen-O-T	RG9	35	E4
King Johns Cl. Wray	TW19	68	B1
King St. Chert	KT16	124	A1
King St. Maid	SL6	39	F3
King St. Mort	RG7	137	D3
King St. Read	RG1	86	A4
King Stable St. Eton	SL4	67	E4
King Street La. Winn	RG41	88	B1
King's Wlk. Sand	GU15	150	C3
Kingfisher Court Ind Est. Newb	RG14	105	E2
Kingfisher Ct. Slough	SL2	22	A1
Kingfisher Ct. Twyf	RG10	61	F2
Kingfisher Dr. Stai	TW18	96	C2
Kingfisher Dr. Wood	RG5	87	E3
Kingfisher Dr. Yate	GU17	149	D3
Kingfisher Pl. Read	RG1	86	A4
Kinghorn La. Maid	SL6	19	E2
Kinghorn Pk. Maid	SL6	19	E2
Kings Ave. Ashf	TW16	98	C1
Kings Cl. Hen-O-T	RG9	15	E1
Kings Cl. Stai	TW18	97	E1
Kings Cres. Camb	GU15	151	E4
Kings Gr. Maid	SL6	39	F3
Kings Keep. Sand	GU17	143	D1
Kings La. Cook	SL6	19	D4
Kings La. Eng G	TW20	95	D2
Kings La. Windl	GU20	146	C3
Kings Mead. Newb	RG14	130	B3
Kings Meadow Rd. Read	RG1	86	A4
Kings Rd. Ascot	SL5	120	B2
Kings Rd. Caver	RG4	59	E1
Kings Rd. Crow	RG45	143	E3
Kings Rd. Eng G	TW20	96	A2
Kings Rd. Hen-O-T	RG9	15	E1
Kings Rd. Newb	RG14	105	D1
Kings Rd. Read	RG1	86	B4
Kings Rd. Silc	RG7	136	A1
Kings Rd. Slough	SL1	42	C2
Kings Rd W. Newb	RG14	105	D1
Kings Rd. West E	GU24	153	F3
Kings Rd. Wind	SL4	67	E2
Kings Ride. Ascot	SL5	119	E3
Kings Ride. Brac	SL5	119	E3
Kings Ride. Camb	GU15	151	E4
Kings Ride Pk.Brac	SL5	119	E2
Kings Wlk. Read	RG1	86	A4
Kings Wood. Medm	SL7	17	E4
Kingsbridge Cotts. Brac	RG40	142	C4
Kingsbridge Hill. Swal	RG7	139	D3
Kingsbridge Rd. Newb	RG14	104	C1
Kingsbridge Rd. Read	RG2	86	B1
Kingsbury Cres. Stai	TW18	96	B2
Kingsbury Dr. Old W	SL4	68	A1
Kingsclear Pk. Camb	GU15	151	E2
Kingsdown Cl. Read	RG6	87	D1
Kingsfield. Wind	SL4	66	B3
Kingsford Cl. Wood	RG5	88	A3
Kingsgate St. Read	RG1	86	B4
Kingsland Grange. Newb	RG14	130	C4
Kingsley Ave. Camb	GU15	151	E2
Kingsley Ave. Eng G	TW20	95	D1
Kingsley Cl. Char	RG10	61	D3
Kingsley Cl. Crow	RG45	143	D2
Kingsley Cl. Newb	RG14	105	D3
Kingsley Cl. Read	RG2	113	D4
Kingsley Dr. Mar B	SL7	1	B3
Kingsmere Rd. Brac	RG42	117	F4
Kingston Ave. Felt	TW14	71	F1
Kingston Cres. Stai	TW15	97	E2
Kingston Gdns. Read	RG2	86	B1
Kingston La. Sulhd	RG7	110	B3
Kingston Rd. Camb	GU15	152	A4
Kingston Rd. Stai	TW18	97	E1
Kingsway. Black	GU17	150	C3
Kingsway. Caver	RG4	59	F3
Kingsway. Far C	SL2	22	B3
Kingsway. Iver	SL0	44	C4
Kingsway. Stan	TW19	97	E4
Kingsway. That	RG19	106	C1
Kingswick Cl. Ascot	SL5	120	B3
Kingswick Dr. Ascot	SL5	120	B3
Kingswood Cl. Eng G	TW20	95	E2
Kingswood Creek. Wray	TW19	68	B1
Kingswood Ct. Maid	SL6	39	F3
Kingswood Rise. Eng G	TW20	95	E2
Kinross Ave. Ascot	SL5	119	F2
Kinross Cl. Ashf	TW16	98	C2
Kinross Ct. Ascot	SL5	119	F2
Kinross Dr. Ashf	TW16	98	C2
Kinson Rd. Read	RG30	58	A1
Kintbury Rd. Kint	RG17	127	F3
Kipling Cl. That	RG18	106	B3
Kipling Cl. Yate	GU17	149	E2
Kirkfell Cl. Read	RG31	57	E1
Kirkham Cl. Caver	RG4	59	F3
Kirkham Cl. Crow	GU15	143	E1
Kirkstall Ct. Bur C	RG31	84	B2
Kirkstone Cl. Camb	GU15	152	B2
Kirkwall Spur. Slough	SL1	42	C4
Kirkwood Cres. Bur C	RG7	110	C2
Kirton Cl. Read	RG30	85	D4
Kirtons Farm Rd. Bur C	RG2 & RG30	85	E1
Kitsmead La. Went	GU25	122	B1
Kittiwake Cl. Wood	RG5	88	A4
Kitwood Dr. Winn	RG6	87	F1
Klondyke. Mar	SL7	1	B1
Knapp Rd. Ashf	TW15	97	F2
Knapp The. Read	RG6	87	D2
Knappe Cl. Hen-O-T	RG9	35	E4
Knighton Cl. Caver	RG4	59	D2
Knights Cl. Stai	TW20	96	B1
Knights Cl. Wind	SL4	66	B3
Knights La. Ball H	RG20	129	E2
Knights Way. Caver	RG4	59	D3
Knightsbridge Cres. Stai	TW18	97	D1
Knightsbridge Dr. Head	RG19	132	A2
Knightsbridge Rd. Camb	GU15	151	F4
Knightswood. Brac	RG12	118	A1
Knoll Cl. Let B	OX12	6	C4
Knoll Rd. Camb	GU15	151	E3
Knoll The. Pur O T	RG31	57	D1
Knoll Wlk. Camb	GU15	151	E3
Knollmead. Bur C	RG31	84	B2
Knollys Rd. Silc	RG26	135	F1
Knolton Way. Slough	SL2	43	E4
Knossington Cl. Read	RG6	87	E1
Knott La. Been	RG7	109	D2
Knowle Cl. Caver	RG4	58	B2
Knowle Gn. Stai	TW18	97	D2
Knowle Gr. Went	GU25	122	B1
Knowle Grove Cl. Went	GU25	122	B1
Knowle Hill. Went	GU25	122	B1
Knowle Park Ave. Stai	TW18	97	D2
Knowle Rd. Wood	RG5	87	F2
Knowles Ave. Finch	RG45	142	C3
Knowles Ave. Finch	RG45	142	C3
Knowsley Cl. Maid	SL6	19	D1
Knowsley Rd. Sulh	RG31	57	E2
Knox Gn. Binf	RG42	90	B2
Korda Cl. Stai	TW17	124	C3
Krooner Rd. Camb	GU15	151	D2
Kybes La. Shin	RG7	112	B3
Kyle Cl. Brac	RG12	118	A3
La Roche Cl. Slough	SL3	43	E2
Laburnam Pl. Eng G	TW20	95	D1
Laburnham Rd. Maid	SL6	39	F3
Laburnum Cl. Mar	SL7	1	C2
Laburnum Gdns. Read	RG2	86	C1
Laburnum Gr. Newb	RG14	105	D2
Laburnum Gr. Slough	SL3	69	D4
Laburnum Rd. Chert	KT16	124	A1
Laburnum Way. Stan	TW19	97	F4
Laburnums The. Black	GU17	150	A3
Lacewood Gdns. Read	RG2	86	C1
Lacey Cl. Stai	TW20	96	B1
Ladbroke Cl. Wood	RG5	87	F3
Ladbrooke Rd. Slough	SL1	42	B2
Ladwell Cl. Newb	RG14	130	B3
Lady Jane Ct. Caver	RG4	59	E2
Lady Margaret Rd. Sunn	SL5	120	C1
Ladybank. Brac	RG12	118	A1
Ladymask Cl. Read	RG31	84	C2
Laffords The. Brad	RG7	82	A1
Laggan Rd. Maid	SL6	19	F1
Laggan Sq. Maid	SL6	19	F1
Laird Ct. Bags	GU19	145	F1
Lake Ave. Slough	SL1	42	B3
Lake End Rd. Burn	SL6	41	D3
Lake End Rd. Dorn	SL4	41	D2
Lake End Way. Crow	RG45	143	D2
Lake Rd. Vir W	GU25	122	A3
Lake Side The. Black	GU17	150	B2
Lakeland Dr. Camb	GU16	151	F1
Lakeside. Brac	RG42	91	E1
Lakeside Dr. Sto P	SL2	22	C2
Lakeside. Maid	SL6	20	A1
Lakeside Rd. Iver	SL3	69	F4
Lakeside. Read	RG6	87	D2
Lalande Cl. Woki	RG41	115	F3
Laleham Rd. Shepp	TW17	125	D2
Laleham Rd. Stai	TW17	125	D2
Laleham Rd. Stai	TW18	96	C1
Laleys Gn. Herm	RG18	78	C2
Lamb Cl. That	RG18	106	B3
Lambert Ave. Slough	SL3	43	F2
Lambert Cres. Black	GU17	150	B2
Lambeth Ct. Read	RG30	84	C4
Lambfields. Thea	RG7	83	E2
Lambly Hill. Vir W	GU25	122	B2
Lambourn Pl. Lamb	RG17	25	D2
Lambourn Rd. Newb	RG20	104	B3
Lambourne Cl. Read	RG31	84	B4
Lambourne Dr. Bags	GU19	145	E1
Lambourne Dr. Maid	SL6	39	E2
Lambourne Gdns. Read	RG6	87	E2
Lambourne Gr. Brac	RG12	118	C4
Lambridge La. Hen-O-T	RG9	15	E2
Lambridge La. Shipl	RG9	15	E2
Lambridge Wood Rd. Hen-O-T	RG9	15	D2
Lambs La. Shin	RG7	139	D4
Lambwood Hill. Shin	RG7	112	B1
Lamerton Rd. Read	RG2	86	B1
Lammas Ave. Wind	SL4	67	E3
Lammas Ct. Wind	SL4	67	E3
Lammas Dr. Wray	TW18	96	B2
Lammas Mead. Binf	RG42	90	C1
Lammas Rd. Slough	SL1	41	E4
Lamorna Cres. Read	RG31	57	E1
Lamp Acres. Newb	RG14	105	D3
Lamplighters Wlk. Read	RG31	84	C2
Lamsden Way. Bur C	RG7	111	D2
Lanark Cl. Camb	GU16	151	F1
Lanark Cl. Wood	RG5	88	A3
Lancashire Hill. New G	RG42	91	F1
Lancaster Ave. Slough	SL2	22	B1
Lancaster Cl. Eng G	TW20	95	E2
Lancaster Cl. Hung	RG17	100	B2
Lancaster Cl. Read	RG1	86	B3
Lancaster Cl. That	RG18	106	B2
Lancaster Gdns. Read	RG6	87	D2
Lancaster Rd. Maid	SL6	39	D4
Lancaster Sq. Hung	RG17	100	B2
Lancastria Mews. Maid	SL6	39	E4
Lancelot Cl. Slough	SL1	42	A2
Lancing Cl. Read	RG30	85	E4
Lancing Rd. Felt	TW13	98	C3
Landen Ct. Woki	RG40	116	A2
Landon Way. Ashf	TW15	98	A1
Landrake Cres. Read	RG2	86	B1
Landseer Cl. Sand	GU15	150	C3
Landsend La. Char	RG10	61	D1
Lane End Cl. Shin	RG2	113	F3
Lane The. Chert	KT16	124	A3
Lane The. Chil	OX11	10	C4
Lane The. Vir W	GU25	122	C3
Laneswood. Mort	RG7	136	C3
Langborough Rd. Woki	RG40	116	B3
Langdale Cl. Maid	SL6	40	A3
Langdale Dr. Ascot	SL5	119	F4
Langdale Gdns. Read	RG6	86	C1
Langdon Cl. Camb	GU15	152	B2
Langford Cl. Caver	RG4	59	E3
Langham Pl. Eng G	TW20	95	F2
Langhams Way. Warg	RG10	36	C1
Langley Broom. Slough	SL3	43	F1
Langley Bsns Centre. Slough	SL3	44	A2
Langley Common Rd. Arbo	RG2	114	C1
Langley Common Rd. Bark	RG40	114	C1
Langley Cres. Harl	UB7	71	F4
Langley Dr. Camb	GU15	151	E3
Langley Hill Cl. Read	RG31	84	B3
Langley Hill. Read	RG31	84	B3
Langley Park Rd. Iver	SL0	44	B3
Langley Park Rd. Slough	SL3	44	B3
Langley Rd. Slough	SL3	43	E2
Langley Rd. Stai	TW18	96	C1
Langley Way. Mar	SL7	1	B1
Langton Cl. Maid	SL6	39	E4
Langton Cl. Slough	SL1	41	E3
Langton Way. Stai	TW20	96	B1
Langtons Meadow. Far C	SL2	22	B3
Langworthy End. Holy	SL6	65	D4
Langworthy La. Holy	SL6	65	D4
Laniver Cl. Read	RG6	87	D1
Lansdowne Ave. Slough	SL1	42	C3
Lansdowne Ct. Slough	SL1	42	C3
Lansdowne Rd. Read	RG30	84	B4
Lansdowne Rd. Stai	TW18	97	D1
Lapwing Cl. Read	RG31	84	B3
Larch Ave. Ascot	SL5	120	C2
Larch Ave. Sunn	SL5	120	C2
Larch Ave. Woki	RG41	116	A4
Larch Cl. Bur C	RG30	111	D2
Larch Cl. Camb	GU15	151	F4
Larch Cl. Slough	SL2	42	A4
Larch Dr. Wood	RG5	87	F3
Larches Way. Black	GU17	150	A3
Larchfield Rd. Maid	SL6	39	F3
Larchside Cl. Shin	RG7	113	D1
Larchwood Dr. Eng G	TW20	95	D1
Larchwood Glade. Camb	GU15	152	A4
Larges Bridge Dr. Brac	RG12	118	B3
Larges La. Brac	RG12	118	B4
Larissa Cl. Read	RG31	57	F1
Lark Ave. Stai	TW18	96	C3
Larkham Cl. Felt	TW13	98	C3
Larkings La. Sto P	SL2	23	D2
Larks-Meade. Read	RG6	87	D1
Larksfield. Eng G	TW20	95	E1
Larkspur Cl. Woki	RG41	115	E4
Larkspur Gdns. That	RG18	106	C2
Larkswood Cl. Read	RG31	57	E2
Larkswood Cl. Sand	GU17	143	D1
Larkswood Dr. Crow	RG45	143	D3
Lascelles Rd. Slough	SL3	43	D2
Lashbrook Mead. Shipl	RG9	36	A2
Lashbrook Rd. Shipl	RG9	36	A2
Lassell Gdns. Maid	SL6	40	A4
Lasswade Rd. Chert	KT16	123	F1
Latham Ave. Camb	GU16	151	F1
Latimer. Brac	RG12	118	A1
Latimer Dr. Bur C	RG31	84	B2
Latimer Rd. Woki	RG41	116	A3
Latton Cl. Chil	OX11	10	C4
Laud Way. Woki	RG40	116	C3
Lauder Cl. Camb	GU16	151	F1
Lauds Cl. Hen-O-T	RG9	15	E1
Launceston Ave. Caver	RG4	59	F3
Launcestone Cl. Read	RG6	87	D1
Laundry La. Sand	GU15	150	C3
Lauradale. Brac	RG12	118	A3
Laurel Ave. Eng G	TW20	95	D2
Laurel Ave. Slough	SL3	43	F2
Laurel Cl. Camb	GU15	151	E2
Laurel Cl. Stan	SL3	69	F4
Laurel Cl. Woki	RG41	115	F3
Laurel Dr. Read	RG31	57	D3
Laurence Cres. Windl	GU20	146	B2
Lauser Rd. Stan	TW19	97	E4
Lavenham Dr. Wood	RG5	87	F4
Lawford Cres. Yate	GU17	149	E3
Lawkland. Far C	SL2	22	A1
Lawn Cl. Datch	SL3	68	B4
Lawrence Cl. Woki	RG40	116	B3
Lawrence Ct. Wind	SL4	67	E3
Lawrence Gr. Binf	RG42	117	E4
Lawrence Mead. Kint	RG17	102	A1
Lawrence Rd. Read	RG30	85	D4
Lawrence Way. Sand	GU15	150	C2
Lawrence Way. Slough	SL1	41	E4
Lawrences La. Cold A	RG18	106	B3
Lawson La. Chil	OX11	10	B4
Lawson Way. Windl	SL5	121	D2
Laxton Gn. Maid	SL6	39	E2
Layburn Cres. Slough	SL3	69	D4
Laylands Gn. Kint	RG17	102	A1
Layton Rise. Sulh	RG31	57	E2
Laytons La. Shepp	TW16	125	F4
Le Marchant Hts. Camb	GU16	151	F2
Le Marchant Rd. Camb	GU15 & GU16	151	F2
Lea Cl. Mar B	SL7	1	B3
Lea Cl. Read	RG30	85	D2
Lea Croft. Crow	RG45	143	D3
Lea Rd. Camb	GU15	151	D1
Lea The. Stai	TW20	96	B1
Lea The. Woki	RG40	141	F4
Leacroft Cl. Stai	TW18	97	D2
Leacroft Rd. Iver	SL0	44	C4
Leacroft. Stai	TW18	97	D2
Leacroft. Sunn	SL5	121	D2
Leafield Copse. Brac	RG12	118	C3
Leaholme Gdns. Slough	SL1	41	E4
Leander Pl. Read	RG31	84	B2
Leas Dr. Iver	SL0	44	C4
Leaver Rd. Hen-O-T	RG9	15	E1
Leaves Gn. Brac	RG12	118	B2
Ledbury Cl. Read	RG30	58	A1
Ledbury Dr. Bur C	RG31	84	B2
Ledger La. Holy	SL6	65	E3
Ledgers Rd. Slough	SL1	42	B2
Ledran Cl. Winn	RG6	87	E1
Lee La. Bish	SL6	18	C1
Lee La. Maid	SL6	18	C1
Leeds Rd. Slough	SL1	42	C3
Lees Cl. Maid	SL6	39	D3
Lees Gdns. Maid	SL6	39	D3
Lees Wlk. Mar	SL7	1	B1
Leeson Gdns. Eton	SL4	41	F1
Leicester. Brac	RG12	118	C1
Leicester Cl. Hen-O-T	RG9	15	E2
Leigh Field. Mort	RG7	136	C3
Leigh Pk. Datch	SL3	68	B4
Leigh Rd. Slough	SL1	42	A3
Leigh Sq. Wind	SL4	66	B3
Leighton Gdns. Maid	SL6	20	A1
Leiston Cl. Winn	RG6	87	E1
Leiston Spur. Slough	SL1	42	C4
Leith Cl. Brac	RG45	143	D4
Lemart Cl. Read	RG30	84	C4
Lemington Gr. Brac	RG12	118	A2
Leney Cl. Woki	RG40	116	B4
Lenham Cl. Woki	RG41	88	C1
Lennox Cl. Bur C	RG31	84	A2
Lennox Rd. Read	RG6	87	D3
Lent Green La. Burn	SL1	21	D1
Lent Rise Rd. Burn	SL1 & SL6	41	D4
Leopold Wlk. Read	RG1	86	B4
Leppington. Brac	RG12	118	A1
Lerwick Dr. Slough	SL1	42	C4
Lesford Rd. Read	RG1	85	F3
Leslie Southern Ct. Newb	RG14	105	D2
Lesters Rd. Cook	SL6	19	D3
Letchworth Ave. Felt	TW14	98	C4
Letcombe Sq. Brac	RG12	118	C3
Letcombe St. Read	RG1	86	A4
Leverkusen Rd. Brac	RG12	118	A3
Leverton La. Hung	RG17	73	D1
Lewendon Rd. Newb	RG14	104	C3
Lewington Mews. Hung	RG17	100	B2
Lewins Way. Slough	SL1	41	F3
Lewis Wlk. Newb	RG14	130	B3
Lewisham Way. Crow	GU15	143	E1

172

Lexington Ave. Maid

Macphail Cl. Woki

Lexington Ave. Maid	SL6	39	E3
Lexington Gr. Read	RG2	113	E3
Leyburn Cl. Wood	RG5	88	A4
Leycester Cl. Windl	GU20	146	A3
Leyland Gdns. Shin	RG2	113	F3
Leylands La. Stan	TW19	69	F2
Leys Gdns. Newb	RG14	104	C2
Leyside. Crow	RG45	143	D3
Lichfield Cl. Wood	RG6	87	E1
Lichfields. Brac	RG12	118	C4
Liddell Cl. Finch	RG40	141	F2
Liddell. Oak G	SL4	66	B2
Liddell Sq. Oak G	SL4	66	B3
Liddell Way. Ascot	SL5	119	F2
Lido Rd. Chil	OX11	9	F4
Lidstone Cl. Winn	RG6	114	B4
Liebenrood Rd. Read	RG30	85	E3
Lightlands La. Cook	SL6	19	F3
Lightwater Meadow. Light	GU18	153	D4
Lightwater Rd. Light	GU18	153	E4
Lightwood. Brac	RG12	118	B2
Lilac Cl. Pur O T	RG8	57	E3
Lilacs The. Woki	RG41	115	E2
Lillibrooke Cres. Maid	SL6	39	D2
Lily Hill Dr. Brac	RG12	118	C4
Lily Hill Rd. Brac	RG12	118	C4
Lima Ct. Read	RG1	85	F3
Lime Ave. Camb	GU15	152	A3
Lime Cl. Newb	RG14	105	E2
Lime Cl. Woki	RG41	115	F3
Lime Tree Rd. Gori	RG8	34	A3
Lime Wlk. Brac	RG12	118	B3
Lime Wlk. Maid	SL6	39	D4
Limecroft. Yate	GU17	149	E3
Limefield Cl. Winn	RG6	87	F2
Limerick Cl. Brac	RG42	118	A4
Limes Cl. Ashf	TW15	98	A2
Limes Rd. Eng G	TW20	95	F2
Limmer Cl. Woki	RG41	115	E2
Limmerhill Rd. Woki	RG41	115	F3
Linchfield Rd. Datch	SL3	68	B3
Lincoln Cl. Camb	GU15	152	A2
Lincoln Cl. Winn	RG41	88	A2
Lincoln Gdns. Twyf	RG10	61	E3
Lincoln Hatch La. Burn	SL1	21	E1
Lincoln Rd. Maid	SL6	39	D4
Lincoln Rd. Read	RG2	86	B2
Lincoln Way. Slough	SL1	41	E3
Lincoln Way. Stai	TW16	125	F4
Lincolnshire Gdns. New G	RG42	91	F1
Lind Cl. Read	RG6	87	D1
Lindale Cl. Went	GU25	121	F3
Lindberg Way. Wood	RG5	61	D1
Linden Ave. Maid	SL6	19	E1
Linden Cl. Holy	SL6	65	D4
Linden Cl. Newb	RG14	104	C2
Linden Cl. Woki	RG41	115	F2
Linden Ct. Camb	GU15	151	F4
Linden Ct. Eng G	TW20	95	D1
Linden Dr. Far C	SL2	22	B2
Linden Rd. Newt	RG20	131	F2
Linden Rd. Read	RG2	86	C1
Linden Rd. Wood	RG5	87	E2
Linden Way. Shepp	TW17	125	E2
Lindenhill Rd. Brac	RG42	117	F4
Lindores Rd. Holy	SL6	65	D4
Lindsay Cl. Stan	TW19	70	B1
Lindsay Dr. Shepp	TW17	125	E2
Lindsey Cl. Woki	RG41	115	F3
Lindsey Gdns. Felt	TW14	98	B4
Lines Rd. Hurst	RG10	88	C3
Ling Dr. Light	GU18	152	C4
Lingfield Rd. Newb	RG14	131	E4
Lingholm Cl. Maid	SL6	39	E3
Lingholm Cl. Read	RG30	84	C3
Lingwood. Brac	RG12	118	B2
Link Rd. Datch	SL3	68	B3
Link Rd. Felt	TW14	98	C4
Link Rd. Newb	RG14	105	D1
Link The. Slough	SL2	43	D4
Link The. Yate	GU17	149	E4
Link Way. Arbo	RG2	114	C1
Link Way. Stai	TW18	97	D1
Link Way. That	RG18	106	A2
Links App. Fla H	HP10	3	D4
Links Dr. Read	RG30	85	D4
Links Rd. Ashf	TW15	97	F2
Links Rd. Fla H	HP10	3	E4
Links The. Burl	SL5	119	F4
Links Way. Fla H	HP10	3	D4
Linkscroft Ave. Ashf	TW15	98	A1
Linkswood Rd. Burn	SL1	21	E2
Linkway. Camb	GU15	151	E2
Linkway. Crow	RG45	142	C3
Linnet Ave. Newt	RG20	131	F2
Linnet Cl. Read	RG31	84	A3
Lintott Ct. Stan	TW19	70	B1
Lion Cl. Stai	TW17	124	C3
Lip La. Wick	RG20	75	F2
Lipscomb Cl. Herm	RG18	79	D3
Lipscombe Cl. Newb	RG14	104	C2
Liscombe. Brac	RG12	118	A1
Lisle Cl. Newb	RG14	104	C3
Lismore Cl. Wood	RG5	87	F2
Lismore Pk. Slough	SL2	42	C4
Lisset Rd. Maid	SL6	40	A3
Lister Cl. Pur O T	RG8	57	E3
Liston Rd. Mar	SL7	1	B1
Litcham Spur. Slough	SL1	42	B4
Lithgows Rd. Harm	TW6	71	F2
Littington Cl. Winn	RG6	114	B4
Little Aldershot La. Tad	RG26	134	A1
Little Bowden La. Pangb	RG8	55	F2
Little Buntings. Wind	SL4	66	C2
Little Cl. Fla H	HP10	3	D3
Little Croft Rd. Gori	RG8	34	B3
Little Croft. Yate	GU17	149	E3
Little Elms. Harl	UB7	71	E4
Little Fryth. Woki	RG40	142	B3
Little Glebe. Sonn	RG4	60	C2
Little Heath Rd. Read	RG31	84	A4
Little Hill Rd. Hurst	RG10	88	B2
Little Johns La. Read	RG30	85	E4
Little La. Buck	RG7	107	E3
Little London Rd. Silc	RG7	136	A1
Little Marlow Rd. Mar	SL7	1	C2
Little Moor. Sand	GU17	143	E1
Little Oak Dr. Read	RG31	84	B4
Little Paddock. Camb	GU15	152	A4
Little Ringdale. Brac	RG12	118	C3
Little St. Read	RG1	85	F4
Little Sutton La. Iver	SL3	44	B1
Little Sutton La. Slough	SL3	69	D4
Little Vigo. Yate	GU17	149	D2
Little Woodlands. Wind	SL4	66	C2
Littlebrook Ave. Slough	SL2	21	F1
Littlebrook Ave. Slough	SL2	41	F4
Littlecote Dr. Read	RG1	85	F3
Littlecote Rd. Frox	SN8	99	D3
Littlecroft Rd. Eng G	TW20	95	F2
Littledale Cl. Brac	RG12	118	C3
Littledown Rd. Slough	SL1	42	C3
Littlefield Gn. Whi Wa	SL6	63	F3
Littlejohns La. Read	RG30	58	B1
Littleport Spur. Slough	SL1	42	C4
Littlestead Cl. Caver	RG4	59	F3
Littleton La. Stai	TW17	124	C2
Littleton Rd. Stai	TW15	98	B1
Liverpool Rd. Read	RG1	86	C4
Liverpool Rd. Slough	SL1	42	A4
Livery Cl. Read	RG1	86	A4
Livingstone Gdns. Wood	RG5	87	F3
Livingstone Rd. Newb	RG14	105	D1
Llangar Gr. Crow	RG45	143	D3
Llanvair Cl. Ascot	SL5	120	A2
Llanvair Dr. Ascot	SL5	119	F2
Lochbridge Ct. Maid	SL6	40	B4
Lochinvar Cl. Slough	SL1	42	A2
Lochinver. Brac	RG12	118	A1
Lock Ave. Maid	SL6	20	B1
Lock La. Maid	SL6	39	E2
Lock Mead. Maid	SL6	20	B1
Lock Path. Dorn	SL4	66	B4
Lock Pl. Read	RG1	86	B4
Lock Rd. Mar	SL7	1	C1
Lockbridge Rd. Bou E	SL8	3	D2
Locke Gdns. Slough	SL3	43	E2
Lockets Cl. Wind	SL4	66	B3
Lockram Rd. Bur C	RG7	111	E1
Lockram Rd. Mort	RG7	111	E1
Locks Ride. Burl	SL5	92	B1
Lockstile Mead. Gori	RG8	34	B3
Lockstile Way. Gori	RG8	34	B3
Lockton Chase. Ascot	SL5	119	E3
Loddon Bridge Rd. Winn	RG5	87	F3
Loddon Bridge Rd. Wood	RG5	87	F3
Loddon Cl. Camb	GU15	152	A3
Loddon Dr. Char	RG10	61	D4
Loddon Dr. Maid	SL6	39	E4
Loddon Hall Rd. Twyf	RG10	61	F3
Loddon Rd. Bou E	SL8	3	D2
Loddon Spur. Slough	SL1	42	C4
Lodge Cl. Eng G	TW20	95	E2
Lodge Cl. Mar	SL7	1	C1
Lodge Gr. Yate	GU17	149	F3
Lodge Rd. Hurst	RG10	88	C4
Lodge Way. Ashf	TW15	97	F3
Lodge Way. Stai	TW17	125	E4
Lodge Way. Wind	SL4	66	C2
Logan Cl. Read	RG30	84	C4
Lois Dr. Shepp	TW17	125	D2
Lomond Ave. Caver	RG4	59	F3
London Rd. Ascot	SL5	119	F3
London Rd. Ashf	TW15	97	E3
London Rd. Bags	GU19	145	F2
London Rd. Binf	RG42	117	E4
London Rd. Black	GU17	150	B2
London Rd. Blew	OX11	11	F4
London Rd. Brac	RG12	118	C3
London Rd. Camb	GU15	151	E3
London Rd. Datch	SL3	68	B4
London Rd. Eng G	TW20	95	E1
London Rd. Newb	RG14	105	E2
London Rd. Read	RG1	86	B4
London Rd. Read	RG6	87	D4
London Rd. Slough	SL3	43	F1
London Rd. Stan	TW19	97	E3
London Rd. Sunn	SL5	121	E3
London Rd. That	RG18	105	E2
London Rd. That	RG18	106	C2
London Rd. Twyf	RG10	61	F3
London Rd. Went	SL5	121	E2
London Rd. Windl	GU20	146	B4
London St. Chert	KT16	124	A1
London St. Read	RG1	86	A4
Lone Acre. Windl	GU20	146	C2
Long Barn La. Read	RG2	86	B2
Long Cl. Far C	SL2	22	A3
Long Cl. Kint	RG17	102	A1
Long Dr. Burn	SL1	21	E1
Long Furlong Dr. Slough	SL2	21	F1
Long Gr. Tad	RG26	134	B1
Long Grove. Buck	RG7	107	E3
Long Half Acre. Bish	SL6	38	A2
Long Hedge. Lamb	RG17	25	E1
Long Hill Rd. Burl	SL5	119	D4
Long La. Brig	RG20	28	C2
Long La. Cold A	RG18	78	C1
Long La. Cook	SL6	19	E3
Long La. Herm	RG18	78	C1
Long La. Holy	SL6	64	B2
Long La. Holy	SL6	64	C3
Long La. Pur O T	RG31	57	D2
Long La. Stan	TW19	97	F4
Long La. Sulh	RG31	57	D2
Long La. Wint	RG18	78	C1
Long Mickle. Sand	GU17	143	D1
Long Readings La. Slough	SL2	22	A1
Longacre. Newb	RG14	130	B4
Longbourne Way. Chert	KT16	123	F2
Longbridge Rd. That	RG19	106	C1
Longcroft Rd. That	RG19	106	C1
Longdon Rd. Winn	RG41	88	B1
Longdown Rd. Sand	GU17	143	D1
Longfield Rd. Twyf	RG10	61	E3
Longford Ave. Felt	TW14	71	F1
Longford Ave. Stan	TW19	97	F4
Longford Cl. Camb	GU15	151	E2
Longford Way. Stan	TW19	97	F4
Longhurst Cl. Caver	RG4	59	E2
Longlands Way. Camb	GU15	152	B3
Longleat Dr. Sulh	RG31	57	D2
Longleat Gdns. Maid	SL6	39	E3
Longleat Way. Felt	TW14	98	B4
Longmead. Ball H	RG20	129	F1
Longmead La. Burn	SL1	21	E3
Longmead. Wind	SL4	66	C3
Longmeadow. Camb	GU16	151	F2
Longmoor La. Mort	RG7	137	D4
Longmoors. Brac	RG42	117	F4
Longmore Rd. Read	RG2	113	E3
Longridge Cl. Read	RG30	85	D4
Longs Way. Woki	RG40	116	C4
Longshot Ind Est. Brac	RG12	117	F4
Longshot La. Brac	RG12	117	E4
Longside Cl. Stai	TW20	123	E4
Longview. Beac	HP10	3	F4
Longwater La. Finch	RG27	141	F2
Longwater Rd. Brac	RG12	118	B2
Longwater Rd. Finch	RG40	141	F1
Longworth Ave. Read	RG31	84	A4
Longworth Dr. Maid	SL6	20	B1
Lonsdale Cl. Maid	SL6	20	A1
Lonsdale Way. Holy	SL6	40	B1
Loosen Dr. Maid	SL6	39	D2
Lord Knyvett Cl. Stan	TW19	70	B1
Loring Rd. Wind	SL4	66	C3
Lorne Cl. Slough	SL1	42	A2
Lorne Pl. Read	RG1	85	F4
Lorne St. Read	RG1	85	F4
Lorraine Rd. Camb	GU15	151	F4
Lory Hill La. Beac	HP10	3	F4
Losfield Rd. Wind	SL4	66	C3
Lossie Dr. Iver	SL0	44	A3
Loughborough. Brac	RG12	118	C2
Loundyes Cl. That	RG18	106	A2
Lovatt Cl. Read	RG31	84	A4
Love Green La. Iver	SL0	44	C4
Love Hill La. Slough	SL3	44	A3
Love La. Iver	SL0	44	B4
Love La. Newb	RG14	105	D3
Lovedean Ct. Brac	RG12	118	C2
Lovejoy La. Wind	SL4	66	B3
Lovel La. Wink	SL4	93	D2
Lovel Rd. Wink	SL4	93	D2
Lovelace Cl. Hurl	SL6	17	F2
Lovelace Rd. Brac	RG12	117	F3
Lovell Cl. Hen-O-T	RG9	35	E4
Lovells Cl. Light	GU18	146	A1
Loverock Rd. Read	RG30	58	B1
Loverock Rd. Read	RG30	58	B1
Loves Cl. Bur C	RG7	111	D2
Loves Wood. Mort	RG7	136	C3
Lovett Gdns. Maid	SL6	20	B2
Lovett Rd. Stai	TW18	96	B2
Lowbrook Dr. Maid	SL6	39	D2
Lowbury. Brac	RG12	118	C3
Lower Armour Rd. Read	RG31	57	E1
Lower Boyndon Rd. Maid	SL6	39	F3
Lower Britwell Rd. Slough	SL2	21	E1
Lower Broadmoor Rd. Crow	RG45	143	E2
Lower Brook St. Read	RG1	86	A3
Lower Bungalows. Gori	RG8	34	B4
Lower Canes. Yate	GU17	149	D3
Lower Charles St. Camb	GU15	151	E3
Lower Church Rd. Sand	GU17	149	F4
Lower Cippenham La. Slough	SL1	41	F3
Lower Common. Finch	RG27	140	C1
Lower Cookham Rd. Maid	SL6	20	B1
Lower Earley Way (N). Winn	RG6	87	F1
Lower Earley Way. Read	RG6	114	B4
Lower Earley Way (W). Read	RG6	113	F4
Lower Earley Way. Winn	RG6	114	B4
Lower Elmstone Dr. Read	RG31	57	E1
Lower Farm Way. Newb	RG19	105	F1
Lower Field Rd. Read	RG1	86	A3
Lower Henley Rd. Caver	RG4	59	E2
Lower Lees Rd. Slough	SL2	22	A1
Lower Meadow Rd. Read	RG2	86	B1
Lower Mill Field. Bags	GU19	145	E1
Lower Nursery. Sunn	SL5	121	D2
Lower Pound La. Mar	SL7	18	B4
Lower Rd. Chil	OX11	10	B4
Lower Rd. Cook	SL6	19	F4
Lower Ridge. Bou E	SL8	3	D2
Lower Sandhurst Rd. Finch	RG40	142	B1
Lower Sandhurst Rd. Sand	RG40 &		
	RG45	142	B1
Lower Village Rd. Ascot	SL5	120	B2
Lower Way. That	RG19	105	F2
Lower Way. That	RG19	106	A2
Lower Wokingham Rd. Brac	RG40	142	B3
Lower Wokingham Rd. Finch	RG40	142	B3
Lowes Cl. Shipl	RG9	36	A2
Lowestoft Cl. Winn	RG6	87	E1
Lowestoft Dr. Slough	SL1	41	E4
Lowfield Cl. Light	GU18	153	D4
Lowfield Gn. Caver	RG4	59	F2
Lowfield Rd. Caver	RG4	59	E3
Lowlands Rd. Black	GU17	150	B2
Lowlands Rd. Stan	TW19	70	B1
Lowry Cl. Sand	GU15	150	B3
Lowther Cl. Woki	RG41	115	F4
Lowther Rd. Woki	RG41	115	F4
Loxwood Cl. Felt	TW14	98	B4
Loxwood. Read	RG6	87	E1
Lucan Dr. Stai	TW18	97	E1
Lucas Cl. Yate	GU17	149	E3
Lucas Green Rd. West E	GU24	153	F2
Lucey Cl. Sulh	RG31	57	D2
Lucie Ave. Ashf	TW15	98	A1
Luckley Rd. Brac	RG41	116	A2
Luckley Wood. Brac	RG41	116	A2
Luckmore Dr. Read	RG6	87	D2
Luddington Ave. Vir W	GU25	122	C4
Ludlow. Brac	RG12	118	A1
Ludlow Cl. Newb	RG14	105	F3
Ludlow Rd. Felt	TW13	98	C3
Ludlow Rd. Maid	SL6	39	F3
Luff Cl. Wind	SL4	66	C2
Luker Ave. Hen-O-T	RG9	15	E2
Lulworth Rd. Read	RG2	113	E4
Lunds Farm Rd. Wood	RG5	88	A4
Lundy La. Read	RG30	85	E4
Lupin Cl. Bags	GU19	145	E1
Lupin Ride. Brac	RG45	143	D4
Lupin Ride. Crow	RG45	143	D3
Luscombe Cl. Caver	RG4	59	E2
Lutmans Haven. Know H	RG10	37	F3
Lutterworth Cl. Brac	RG42	91	E1
Lutton Cl. Read	RG6	113	F4
Lych Gate Cl. Sand	GU17	149	F4
Lycroft Cl. Gori	RG8	34	B4
Lydbury. Brac	RG12	118	C3
Lydford Ave. Slough	SL2	42	B4
Lydford Rd. Read	RG1	86	C3
Lydney. Brac	RG12	118	A1
Lydsey Cl. Slough	SL2	22	A1
Lyefield Ct. Caver	RG4	59	D3
Lyell Rd. Oak G	SL4	66	B2
Lyme Gr. Read	RG31	57	E1
Lymington Ave. Yate	GU17	149	E3
Lymington Gate. Caver	RG4	58	C3
Lynch Hill La. Slough	SL2	21	F1
Lynch La. Lamb	RG17	25	D1
Lynden Mews. Read	RG2	86	A2
Lyndhurst Ave. Black	GU17	150	B3
Lyndhurst Ave. Cook	SL6	19	F3
Lyndhurst Cl. Brac	RG12	119	D3
Lyndhurst Rd. Ascot	SL5	120	A3
Lyndhurst Rd. Gori	RG8	34	B3
Lyndhurst Rd. Read	RG30	58	A1
Lyndwood Dr. Old W	SL4	68	A1
Lyne Cl. Went	GU25	122	C2
Lyne Crossing Rd. Chert	GU25	123	D2
Lyne La. Chert	GU25	123	D1
Lyne Rd. Went	GU25	122	C2
Lynegrove Ave. Ashf	TW15	98	B2
Lyneham Gdns. Maid	SL6	19	D1
Lyneham Rd. Crow	RG45	143	D3
Lynmouth Rd. Read	RG1	59	D1
Lynn Cl. Ashf	TW15	98	B2
Lynton Cl. Wood	RG5	87	E3
Lynton Ct. Newb	RG14	105	D2
Lynton Gn. Maid	SL6	39	F4
Lynwood Ave. Eng G	TW20	95	F1
Lynwood Ave. Slough	SL3	43	E2
Lynwood Chase. Brac	RG12	91	E1
Lynwood Cres. Sunn	SL5	120	C2
Lyon Cl. That	RG19	106	C1
Lyon Rd. Crow	RG45	143	E3
Lyon Sq. Read	RG30	85	D4
Lyon Way. Camb	GU16	151	E1
Lysander Cl. Wood	RG5	88	A4
Lytham. Brac	RG12	117	F2
Lytham Cl. Read	RG30	85	E2
Lytham End. Sulh	RG31	57	D2
Lytham Rd. Wood	RG5	87	F4
Macbeth Ct. Brac	RG42	118	C4
Macdonald Rd. Light	GU18	153	D4
Mace Cl. Read	RG6	87	D1
Mackay Cl. Read	RG31	84	C2
Mackenzie St. Slough	SL1	42	C2
Macklin Cl. Hung	RG17	100	B3
Macphail Cl. Woki	RG40	116	C4

173

Macrae Rd. Yate — Mews The. Read

Street	Postcode	Page	Grid
Macrae Rd. Yate	GU17	149	E3
Maddle Rd. Lamb	RG17	24	B4
Madeira Wlk. Wind	SL4	67	E3
Madingley. Brac	RG12	118	A1
Mafeking Rd. Wray	TW19	96	A3
Magdalen Rd. Stai	TW17	124	C3
Magdalene Rd. Crow	GU15	143	F1
Magill Cl. Shin	RG7	113	D1
Magna Carta La. Wray	TW19	95	F4
Magna Rd. Eng G	TW20	95	D1
Magnolia Cl. Sand	GU15	143	E1
Magnolia Gdns. Slough	SL3	43	E2
Magnolia Way. Woki	RG41	115	F3
Magpie Cl. That	RG19	106	A2
Magpie Way. Read	RG31	84	A3
Magpie Way. Slough	SL2	21	F1
Maguire Dr. Camb	GU16	152	B2
Mahonia Cl. West E	GU24	153	F3
Maiden Erlegh Dr. Read	RG6	87	D2
Maiden Lane Centre. Read	RG6	87	E1
Maiden Pl. Read	RG6	87	E1
Maidenhead Bsns Campus The. Whi Wa	SL6	38	C1
Maidenhead Court Pk. Maid	SL6	20	A2
Maidenhead Rd. Binf	RG40	89	E2
Maidenhead Rd. Cook	SL6	19	F3
Maidenhead Rd. New G	RG42	91	D3
Maidenhead Rd. Oak G	SL4	66	C4
Maidenhead Rd. Wind	SL4	66	C4
Maidens Gn. Burl	SL4	92	A3
Maidensfield. Winn	RG41	88	B1
Main Dr. Burl	RG42	119	D4
Main St. Chil	OX11	10	B4
Main St. Gree	RG19	131	F3
Main St. Newt	RG19	132	A3
Main St. Yate	GU17	149	E4
Mainprize Rd. Brac	RG12	118	C4
Mainstone Rd. Bis	GU24	153	F2
Maise Webster Cl. Stan	TW19	97	E4
Maitland Rd. Read	RG1	85	F4
Maize La. New G	RG42	91	F1
Majendie Cl. Newb	RG14	104	B3
Majors Farm Rd. Datch	SL3	68	C4
Makepiece Rd. Brac	RG42	91	D1
Maker Cl. Read	RG30	85	D2
Makins Rd. Hen-O-T	RG9	35	E4
Malders La. Cook	SL6	19	E2
Malders La. Maid	SL6	19	E2
Maldon Cl. Read	RG30	85	E3
Malet Cl. Stai	TW20	96	B1
Malham Fell. Brac	RG12	118	A3
Malham Rd. That	RG19	106	B2
Mallard Cl. Read	RG6	87	D2
Mallard Cl. Twyf	RG10	61	F2
Mallard Dr. Slough	SL1	41	F3
Mallard Row. Read	RG1	86	A4
Mallard Way. Yate	GU17	149	D3
Mallards The. Gr She	RG17	48	A2
Mallards The. Stai	TW18	124	A4
Mallards Way. Camb	GU18	152	C4
Mallards Way.Light	GU18	153	D4
Mallory Ave. Caver	RG4	59	E3
Mallow Pk. Maid	SL6	19	E1
Mallowdale Rd. Brac	RG12	118	C1
Malone Rd. Wood	RG5	87	E3
Malpas Rd. Slough	SL2	43	D3
Malt Hill. Eng G	TW20	95	F2
Malt Hill. New G	RG42	91	F3
Malt House. Old W	SL4	95	D4
Malt Shovel La. Lamb	RG17	24	C2
Maltby Way. Read	RG6	114	A4
Malthouse Cl. That	RG19	106	C1
Malthouse La. Read	RG1	85	F4
Malthouse La. West E	GU24	153	F4
Maltings Pl. Read	RG1	86	A4
Maltings The. West I	RG20	10	A1
Malton Ave. Slough	SL1	42	A3
Malvern Cl. Wood	RG5	87	F3
Malvern Ct. Newb	RG14	104	C1
Malvern Rd. Harl	UB7	71	F4
Malvern Rd. Maid	SL6	19	E1
Malvern Way. Twyf	RG10	61	E4
Malyons The. Shepp	TW17	125	E2
Man's Hill. Bur C	RG7	111	E1
Manchester Rd. Read	RG1	86	C4
Mandarin Ct. Newb	RG14	105	E1
Mandarin Ct. Newb	RG14	105	E1
Mandeville Cl. Read	RG30	84	C3
Mandeville Ct. Eng G	TW20	96	A2
Mandeville Rd. Stai	TW17	125	D2
Manea Cl. Winn	RG6	114	B4
Manfield Cl. Slough	SL2	22	A1
Manners Rd. Wood	RG5	87	E4
Mannock Way. Read	RG5	88	A4
Manor Cl. Brac	RG42	91	D1
Manor Cres. Comp	RG20	31	E2
Manor Ct. Mar	SL7	1	B2
Manor Farm Ave. Shepp	TW17	125	D2
Manor Farm Cl. Wind	SL4	66	C2
Manor Farm Cotts. Old W	SL4	68	A1
Manor Farm La. Eng G	TW20	96	A2
Manor Farm La. Tidm	RG8	56	B1
Manor Farm Rd. Read	RG2	86	A1
Manor Gr. Holy	SL6	65	E3
Manor House Ct. Shepp	TW17	125	D1
Manor House Dr. Ascot	SL5	93	D1
Manor House La. Slough	SL3	68	A3
Manor La. Chiev	RG20	51	D1
Manor La. Harl	UB7	71	E4
Manor La. Herm	RG18	79	D4
Manor La. Leckh	RG20	49	F3
Manor La. Maid	SL6	39	F2
Manor La. Newb	RG14	105	F3
Manor La. That	RG18	105	F3
Manor Leaze. Stai	TW20	96	A2
Manor Park Cl. Read	RG30	84	B3
Manor Park Dr. Woki	RG40	141	F3
Manor Park Dr. Yate	GU17	149	E3
Manor Pk. Frox	SN8	99	D2
Manor Pl. Newb	RG14	104	B3
Manor Pl. Stai	TW18	97	D2
Manor Rd. Ashf	TW15	98	A2
Manor Rd. Farn	OX12	7	D4
Manor Rd. Gori	RG8	34	A3
Manor Rd. Hen-O-T	RG9	35	E4
Manor Rd. Maid	SL6	39	F2
Manor Rd. Shepp	TW17	125	F1
Manor Rd. Whi-O-T	RG8	56	B4
Manor Rd. Wind	SL4	66	C3
Manor Rd. Woki	RG41	116	A1
Manor Way. Bags	GU19	145	F2
Manor Way. Eng G	TW20	95	F1
Manor Way. Holy	SL6	65	D4
Manor Wood Gate. Shipl	RG9	36	A2
Manorcrofts Rd. Eng G	TW20	96	A1
Manse Cl. Harl	UB7	71	E4
Mansel Cl. Slough	SL2	43	D4
Mansell Cl. Wind	SL4	66	C3
Mansell Dr. Newb	RG14	130	B3
Mansfield Cl. Burl	SL5	119	E4
Mansfield Cres. Brac	RG12	118	A2
Mansfield Pl. Burl	SL5	119	E4
Mansfield Rd. Read	RG1	85	F3
Mansfield Rd. Woki	RG41	115	F3
Mansion House St. Newb	RG14	105	D2
Mansion La. Iver	SL0	44	B3
Manston Dr. Brac	RG12	118	B2
Mant Cl. Wick	RG20	75	E3
Manygate La. Shepp	TW17	125	E2
Maple Cl. Maid	SL6	39	E3
Maple Cl. Sand	GU17	142	C1
Maple Cl. Sand	GU17	150	B3
Maple Cl. Winn	RG41	88	B2
Maple Cres. Newb	RG14	105	D2
Maple Cres. Slough	SL2	43	D3
Maple Ct. Eng G	TW20	95	D1
Maple Ct. Gori	RG8	34	A3
Maple Dr. Brac	RG45	143	E4
Maple Dr. Camb	GU18	152	C4
Maple Gdns. Read	RG2	86	C1
Maple Gdns. Stan	TW15	97	F3
Maple Gdns. Yate	GU17	149	E3
Maple La. Upp B	RG8	55	D3
Maple Rise. Mar	SL7	1	C2
Mapledene. Caver	RG4	58	C2
Mapledurham Dr. Pur O T	RG8	57	E3
Mapledurham View. Read	RG31	57	E1
Mapledurham Wlk. Maid	SL6	19	F2
Maplin Pk. Slough	SL3	44	B2
Marathon Cl. Read	RG5	88	A4
Marbeck Cl. Wind	SL4	66	B3
Marchant Ct. Mar	SL7	2	A2
Marchwood Ave. Caver	RG4	59	E4
Marconi Rd. Newb	RG14	105	D2
Marcus Cl. Read	RG30	85	D4
Mardale. Camb	GU15	152	B2
Mare La. Whi Wa	SL6	63	F2
Marefield Rd. Mar	SL7	1	B1
Marefield. Read	RG6	87	E1
Marescroft Rd. Slough	SL2	41	F4
Marfleet Cl. Winn	RG6	87	F1
Margaret Cl. Read	RG2	113	E4
Margaret Cl. Stai	TW18	97	E1
Marigold Cl. Brac	RG45	142	C3
Marina Way. Iver	SL0	44	C3
Marina Way. Slough	SL1	41	E3
Mariners La. Brad	RG7	82	A2
Marion Ave. Shepp	TW17	125	D2
Marish Wharf. Slough	SL3	43	F2
Markby Way. Winn	RG6	87	F1
Market La. Slough	SL3	44	B2
Market Pl. Brac	RG12	118	A4
Market Pl. Hen-O-T	RG9	15	E1
Market Pl. Newb	RG14	105	D2
Market Pl. Read	RG1	86	A4
Market Pl. Woki	RG40	116	B3
Market Sa. Mar	SL7	1	B1
Market Sq. Stai	TW18	96	C2
Market St. Brac	RG12	118	A4
Market St. Maid	SL6	39	F4
Market St. Newb	RG14	105	D1
Market St. Wind	SL4	67	E3
Markham Centre Trading Est The. Thea	RG7	83	F1
Marks Rd. Woki	RG41	116	A4
Marlborough Ave. Read	RG1	86	B3
Marlborough Cl. Maid	SL6	39	D3
Marlborough Ct. Read	RG1	85	F3
Marlborough Rd. Ashf	TW15	97	F2
Marlborough Rd. Maid	SL6	39	D3
Marlborough Rd. Slough	SL3	43	F1
Marlborough Rise. Camb	GU15	151	F3
Marlborough Way. Read	RG31	84	A2
Marlin Ct. Mar	SL7	1	B1
Marling Cl. Read	RG31	57	E1
Marlow Bridge La. Bish	SL7	18	C4
Marlow Mill. Mar	SL7	1	C1
Marlow Rd. Bish	SL6	18	C2
Marlow Rd. Bou E	SL8	2	B3
Marlow Rd. Hen-O-T	RG9	15	F2
Marlow Rd. Lit M	SL7	2	B3
Marlow Rd. Maid	SL6	39	F4
Marlow Rd. Mar B	SL7	1	A3
Marlowes The. Newb	RG14	130	C4
Marlston Rd. Herm	RG18	79	E3
Marmion Rd. Hen-O-T	RG9	35	F4
Marriott Cl. Harm	TW14	71	E1
Mars Cl. Woki	RG41	115	F3
Marsack St. Caver	RG4	59	E1
Marsh La. Herm	RG18	78	B2
Marsh La. Hung	RG17	100	A3
Marsh La. Newb	RG14	105	D2
Marsh La. Tapl	SL6	40	C3
Marsh Rd. That	RG18	106	C2
Marshall Cl. Camb	GU16	152	B2
Marshall Cl. Read	RG8	57	E2
Marshall Rd. Sand	GU15	150	B3
Marshalls Ct. Newb	RG14	104	B3
Marshfield. Old W	SL3	68	B3
Marshland Sq. Caver	RG4	59	D3
Marshwood Rd. Light	GU18	153	E4
Marston Dr. Newb	RG14	105	E3
Marston Way. Ascot	SL5	119	F4
Marten Pl. Sulh	RG31	57	D2
Martin Cl. Wind	SL4	66	B3
Martin Cl. Wood	RG5	87	F3
Martin Rd. Maid	SL6	39	F4
Martin Rd. Slough	SL1	42	C2
Martin Way. Camb	GU16	151	F1
Martindale Ave. Camb	GU15	152	B2
Martineau La. Hurst	RG10	88	C4
Martins Cl. Black	GU17	150	B2
Martins Dr. Woki	RG41	116	A4
Martins La. Brac	RG12	118	C3
Martins Plain. Sto P	SL2	22	C2
Martins The. That	RG19	106	C1
Marunden Gn. Slough	SL2	21	F1
Mary Mead. New G	RG42	91	F1
Maryland. Woki	RG40	141	F4
Maryside. Slough	SL3	43	F2
Mascoll Path. Slough	SL2	21	F1
Masefield Rd. That	RG18	106	B2
Masefield Way. Stan	TW19	97	F4
Mason Cl. Yate	GU17	149	F3
Mason Pl. Sand	GU17	149	F4
Mason St. Read	RG1	85	F4
Masonic Hall Rd. Chert	KT16	123	F2
Masons Rd. Slough	SL1	41	F3
Master Cl. Read	RG5	88	A4
Mathisen Way. Stan	SL3	69	F3
Matlock Rd. Caver	RG4	58	C2
Matson Dr. Rem H	RG9	15	F1
Matthews Chase. Binf	RG42	90	C1
Matthews Cl. That	RG19	106	A2
Matthews La. Stai	TW18	96	C2
Matthews Rd. Camb	GU15	144	B1
Matthewsgreen Rd. Woki	RG41	116	A4
Maultway Cl. Camb	GU15	152	A4
Maultway Cres. Camb	GU15	152	A4
Maultway N. Camb	GU15	145	D1
Maultway The. Camb	GU15	152	B3
Mawbray Cl. Read	RG6	87	E1
Maxine Cl. Sand	GU17	143	D1
Maxwell Cl. Wood	RG5	87	F4
Maxwell Rd. Ashf	TW15	98	B1
May Cl. Sand	GU15	143	E1
May Fields. Woki	RG41	115	D4
May Tree Cl. Mar B	SL7	1	B3
May's La. Padw	RG7	136	A4
Maybrick Cl. Sand	GU17	142	C1
Maybury Cl. Slough	SL1	41	E4
Mayfair Dr. Newb	RG14	104	C1
Mayfair. Read	RG30	84	B4
Mayfield Ave. Read	RG31	84	A2
Mayfield Cl. Ashf	TW15	98	A1
Mayfield Dr. Caver	RG4	59	E2
Mayfield Gdns. Stai	TW18	96	C1
Mayfield Rd. Camb	GU15	151	D1
Mayfield Rd. Woo G	HP10	3	F3
Mayflower Dr. Yate	GU17	149	D4
Mayflower Way. Far C	SL2	22	B4
Maying The. Read	RG2	113	F4
Maynard Cl. Cold A	RG18	106	B3
Mayo Rd. Shepp	TW17	125	F1
Mayors La. Newb	RG14	105	D1
Mayow Cl. That	RG19	106	C1
Maypole Rd. Burn	SL6	41	D4
Mays Cl. Read	RG6	87	D3
Mays La. Read	RG6	87	D3
Mays Rd. Woki	RG40	116	C3
Mc Carthy Way. Woki	RG40	141	F4
McCraes Wlk. Warg	RG10	36	B1
McNair Cl. Read	RG6	87	D1
Mead Ave. Slough	SL3	44	A2
Mead Cl. Eng G	TW19	95	F4
Mead Cl. Mar	SL7	1	C2
Mead Cl. Pease	RG20	50	B4
Mead Cl. Read	RG31	84	A3
Mead Cl. Slough	SL3	44	A2
Mead Cl. Stai	TW20	96	A1
Mead La. Chert	KT16	124	B1
Mead La. Upp B	RG8	55	E3
Mead The. Gr She	RG17	48	A2
Mead Way. Slough	SL1	41	E4
Mead Wlk. Slough	SL3	44	A2
Meadfield Ave. Slough	SL3	44	A2
Meadfield Rd. Slough	SL3	44	A2
Meadhurst Rd. Chert	KT16	124	A1
Meadow Cl. Black	GU17	150	B2
Meadow Cl. Comp	RG20	31	F3
Meadow Cl. Gori	RG8	34	B3
Meadow Cl. Mar	SL7	1	C1
Meadow Cl. Moul	OX10	13	F2
Meadow Cl. Old W	SL4	68	A1
Meadow Cl. That	RG19	106	B2
Meadow Ct. Stai	TW18	96	C3
Meadow Gdns. Stai	TW18	96	B2
Meadow La. Eton	SL4	67	E4
Meadow Rd. Ashf	TW15	98	B2
Meadow Rd. Hen-O-T	RG9	15	F1
Meadow Rd. Newb	RG14	130	C4
Meadow Rd. Read	RG1	58	C1
Meadow Rd. Read	RG6	87	E2
Meadow Rd. Slough	SL3	43	F2
Meadow Rd. Went	GU25	121	F2
Meadow Rd. Woki	RG41	116	A3
Meadow View La. Holy	SL6	64	C4
Meadow View. Mar B	SL7	1	C3
Meadow View. Winn	RG41	88	B2
Meadow Walk. Woki	RG41	116	A3
Meadow Way. Bou E	SL8	3	D3
Meadow Way. Brac	RG42	91	D1
Meadow Way. Dorn	SL6	40	C2
Meadow Way. Holy	SL6	65	E3
Meadow Way. Old W	SL4	68	A1
Meadow Way. Sand	GU17	150	B3
Meadow Way. Thea	RG7	83	F2
Meadow Way. West E	GU24	153	F3
Meadow Way. Woki	RG41	116	A3
Meadowbank Rd. Light	GU18	146	B1
Meadowbrook Cl. Stan	SL3	69	F3
Meadowcroft Rd. Read	RG2	113	E4
Meadowlea Cl. Harm	UB7	70	B4
Meadows The. Fla H	HP10	3	D4
Meadowside Rd. Pangb	RG8	56	B3
Meadowside. Sulh	RG31	57	D1
Meadowsweet Cl. That	RG18	106	C2
Meadowview. Stan	TW19	69	F1
Meadway. Ashf	TW15	98	A2
Meadway. Camb	GU16	151	F1
Meadway Cl. Stai	TW18	97	D1
Meadway. Stai	TW18	97	D1
Meadway The. Read	RG30	84	C4
Meare Estate. Woo G	HP10	3	F4
Mearings The. Bur C	RG30	111	F3
Measham Way. Read	RG6	87	E1
Meashill Way. Chil	OX11	9	F4
Meavy Gdns. Read	RG2	86	A1
Medallion Pl. Maid	SL6	40	A4
Medina Cl. Woki	RG41	115	F4
Medlake Rd. Stai	TW20	96	B1
Medlar Dr. Black	GU17	150	C2
Medway Cl. That	RG18	106	A3
Medway Cl. Woki	RG41	115	F4
Melbourne Ave. Slough	SL1	42	B4
Melbourne Ave. Winn	RG41	88	B1
Melbury Cl. Chert	KT16	124	A1
Meldreth Way. Winn	RG6	87	E1
Meldrum Cl. Newb	RG14	130	B3
Melford Gn. Caver	RG4	59	F3
Melksham Cl. Read	RG6	113	F4
Melling Cl. Winn	RG6	87	F2
Melody Cl. Winn	RG41	88	B2
Melrose Ave. Read	RG6	87	D3
Melrose. Brac	RG12	118	A1
Melrose Gdns. Arbo	RG2	114	C1
Melton Ct. Maid	SL6	39	F3
Melville Ave. Camb	GU16	151	F1
Membury Wlk. Brac	RG12	118	C3
Memorial Ave. Shipl	RG9	35	F1
Mendip Cl. Char	RG10	61	D2
Mendip Cl. Harl	UB7	71	E4
Mendip Cl. Slough	SL3	44	A1
Mendip Rd. Brac	RG12	118	C2
Menpes Rd. Pur O T	RG31	57	E2
Meon Cl. Tad	RG26	135	D1
Merchants Pl. Read	RG1	86	A4
Mercia Rd. Maid	SL6	39	E2
Mercian Way. Slough	SL1	41	E3
Mercury Ave. Woki	RG41	115	F3
Mere Cl. Mar	SL7	1	C1
Mere Rd. Shepp	TW17	125	D2
Mere Rd. Slough	SL1	42	C2
Mereoak La. Shin	RG7	112	C2
Merlewood. Brac	RG12	118	B2
Merlin Cl. Brac	RG42	92	A1
Merlin Cl. Slough	SL3	69	D4
Merrifield Cl. Winn	RG6	114	B4
Merrivale Gdns. Read	RG2	86	A1
Merron Cl. Yate	GU17	149	E3
Merryhill Green Hill. Winn	RG41	88	B2
Merryhill Rd. Brac	RG42	118	A4
Merryman Dr. Brac	RG45	143	D3
Merryweather Cl. Woki	RG40	115	F1
Merrywood Pk. Camb	GU15	151	F2
Mersey Way. That	RG18	106	A3
Merton Cl. Crow	GU15	143	F1
Merton Cl. Maid	SL6	39	E2
Merton Rd. Read	RG2	86	A1
Merton Rd. Slough	SL1	43	D2
Merton Rd. Slough	SL1	43	D2
Mervyn Rd. Shepp	TW17	125	E1
Merwin Way. Wind	SL4	66	B2
Metcalf Rd. Ashf	TW15	98	A2
Meteor Cl. Wood	RG5	88	A4
Mews The. Read	RG1	86	C3

174
Mews The. Swal — New Rd. Hurl

Mews The. Swal RG7 140 B4
Mey Cl. Read RG31 84 B3
Meyrick Dr. Newb RG14 130 B3
Michael Cl. Maid SL6 39 E3
Michaelmas Cl. Yate GU17 149 E2
Micheldever Way. Brac RG12 118 C2
Michelet Cl. Light GU18 146 A1
Micklands Rd. Caver RG4 59 F2
Mickle Hill. Sand GU17 143 D1
Midcroft. Slough SL2 22 A1
Middle Cl. Camb GU15 152 B3
Middle Cl. Newb RG14 130 B4
Middle Gn. Slough SL3 43 F3
Middle Gordon Rd. Camb GU15 151 E3
Middle Hill. Eng G TW20 95 E2
Middle Wlk. Burn SL1 21 E1
Middlefields. Twyf RG10 61 F3
Middlegreen Rd. Slough SL3 43 E3
Middlemoor Rd. Camb GU16 151 F1
Middleton Ct. Newb RG14 105 F3
Middleton Rd. Camb GU15 151 F4
Midsummer Meadow. Caver RG4 58 C3
Midway Ave. Chert KT16 124 A3
Midway Ave. Stai TW20 123 D3
Midwinter Cl. Read RG30 84 C4
Milbanke Ct. Brac RG12 117 F4
Milbanke Way. Brac RG12 117 F4
Mildenhall Cl. Winn RG6 87 E1
Mildenhall Rd. Slough SL1 42 C4
Mile Elm. Mar SL7 2 A2
Miles Pl. Camb GU18 152 C4
Miles Way. Wood RG5 88 A4
Milestone Ave. Char RG10 61 D3
Milestone Cres. Char RG10 61 D2
Milestone Way. Caver RG4 59 E3
Milford Rd. Read RG1 58 C1
Milkhouse Rd. Box RG20 103 E2
Mill Bank. Kint RG17 102 A2
Mill Cl. Woki RG41 115 F4
Mill Farm Ave. Stai TW16 98 C1
Mill Field. Bags GU19 145 E2
Mill Gn. Binf RG42 90 C1
Mill Gn. Caver RG4 59 E1
Mill House La. Stai TW20 123 D3
Mill La. Ascot SL5 121 D4
Mill La. Brac RG12 117 F3
Mill La. Bur C RG31 84 C2
Mill La. Cook SL6 20 B4
Mill La. Hen-O-T RG9 35 F4
Mill La. Hort SL3 69 D2
Mill La. Hurl SL6 17 F2
Mill La. Lamb RG17 25 E2
Mill La. Newb RG14 105 D2
Mill La. Padw RG7 109 E1
Mill La. Read RG1 86 A4
Mill La. Read RG6 87 F2
Mill La. Sand GU17 149 E4
Mill La. Shipl RG9 36 A1
Mill La. Stai TW20 123 E3
Mill La. Tapl SL6 40 B4
Mill La. Wind SL4 67 D4
Mill La. Winn RG6 87 F1
Mill La. Yate GU17 149 E4
Mill Mead. Stai TW18 96 C2
Mill Pl. Datch SL3 68 B3
Mill Pond Rd. Windl GU20 146 A3
Mill Rd. Bur C RG30 84 C1
Mill Rd. Caver RG4 59 E1
Mill Rd. Gori RG8 34 B4
Mill Rd. Mar SL7 1 C1
Mill Rd. Shipl RG9 36 A2
Mill Reef Cl. That RG19 105 F2
Mill Ride. Burl SL5 119 E4
Mill St. Iver SL3 69 E4
Mill St. Slough SL2 42 C3
Millbank Cres. Wood RG5 87 F3
Millbank. Mar SL7 1 C1
Millboard Rd. Bou E SL8 3 D2
Millbridge Rd. Yate GU17 149 D4
Millbrook Way. Stan SL3 69 F3
Milldown Ave. Gori RG8 34 B4
Milldown Rd. Gori RG8 34 B4
Millers Cl. Gori RG8 34 A4
Millers Cl. Stai TW18 97 D2
Millers Field. Gr She RG17 48 A2
Millers Gr. Read RG31 84 C2
Millers La. Old W SL4 68 A1
Milley La. Warg RG10 62 A4
Milley Rd. W St L RG10 62 C3
Millfield. Lamb RG17 25 D1
Millfield. Stai TW17 125 F4
Millgreen La. Head RG19 132 C2
Millins Cl. Sand GU15 143 F1
Millmead. Woki RG41 116 A4
Millmere. Yate GU17 149 E4
Mills Spur. Old W SL4 95 D4
Millside. Bou E SL8 3 E2
Millstream La. Slough SL1 41 F3
Millstream Way. Woo G HP10 3 F4
Millworth La. Shin RG2 113 F2
Milman Cl. Brac RG12 119 D4
Milman Rd. Read RG2 86 A3
Milner Rd. Burn SL1 41 D4
Milsom Cl. Shin RG2 113 F3
Milton Cl. Brac RG12 118 A2
Milton Cl. Hen-O-T RG9 15 E1
Milton Cl. Hort SL3 69 D2
Milton Dr. Stai TW17 124 C3
Milton Dr. Woki RG40 116 A3
Milton Gdns. Stan TW19 97 F4
Milton Gdns. Woki RG40 116 A3
Milton Rd. Eng G TW20 95 F2
Milton Rd. Far C SL2 22 B1
Milton Rd. Read RG6 87 D4
Milton Rd. Woki RG40 116 A4
Milton Way. Twyf RG10 61 F3
Milverton Cl. Maid SL6 39 D2
Milward Gdns. Brac RG12 117 E4
Mina Ave. Slough SL3 43 E2
Minchin Gn. Binf RG42 90 B2
Minden Cl. Woki RG41 115 F3
Minerva Cl. Stan TW19 70 A1
Ministry Rd. Newt RG19 132 A3
Minley Rd. Yate GU17 149 F1
Minniecroft Rd. Burn SL1 21 D1
Minorca Ave. Camb GU16 152 C1
Minorca Rd. Camb GU16 152 C1
Minstead Cl. Brac RG12 118 C3
Minstead Dr. Yate GU17 149 E3
Minster St. Read RG1 86 A4
Minster Way. Slough SL3 43 F2
Minsterley Ave. Shepp TW17 125 F3
Mint Cl. Read RG6 86 C1
Minton Cl. Read RG30 84 C4
Minton Rise. Burn SL6 41 D4
Mirador Cres. Slough SL2 43 E3
Mire La. W St L RG10 62 B2
Misbourne Ct. Slough SL3 44 A1
Missenden Cl. Felt TW14 98 C4
Missenden Gdns. Slough SL1 41 D4
Mistletoe Rd. Yate GU17 149 E2
Mitcham Cl. Read RG2 86 A3
Mitcham Rd. Camb GU15 145 D1
Mitcham Rd. Camb GU15 145 D1
Mitchell Cl. Slough SL1 42 A2
Mitchell Way. Wood RG5 88 A4
Mitford Cl. Read RG2 113 E4
Mitre Cl. Shepp TW17 125 E2
Mixnams La. Chert KT16 124 A3
Moat Dr. Slough SL2 43 E4
Modbury Gdns. Read RG2 86 B1
Moffatts Cl. Sand GU17 150 A4
Moffy Hill. Maid SL6 19 F1
Mohawk Way. Wood RG5 88 A4
Mole Rd. Arbo RG41 114 C3
Moles Cl. Woki RG40 116 B3
Mollison Cl. Wood RG5 88 A4
Molly Millar Bridge. Woki RG41 116 A2
Molly Millars Cl. Woki RG41 116 A2
Molly Millars La. Woki RG41 116 A2
Molyneux Rd. Windl GU20 146 B2
Monarch Cl. Felt TW14 98 C4
Mondial Way. Stan UB7 71 E4
Moneyrow Gn. Holy SL6 65 D4
Monkey Island La. Holy SL6 40 C1
Monks Cl. Ascot SL5 120 A2
Monks Dr. Ascot SL5 120 A2
Monks Hollow. Mar B SL7 1 C3
Monks La. Newb RG14 130 C4
Monks Rd. Vir W GU25 122 B3
Monks Rd. Wind SL4 66 B3
Monks Way. Harm UB7 70 C4
Monks Way. Read RG30 85 E3
Monks Way. Stai TW18 97 E1
Monks Wlk. Ascot SL5 120 A2
Monksfield Way. Slough SL2 22 A1
Monkshood Cl. Woki RG40 116 C4
Monkswood Cl. Newb RG14 130 C4
Monktons La. Mort RG7 137 E3
Mons Cl. Woki RG41 115 F3
Mons Wlk. Stai TW20 96 B2
Monsell Gdns. Stai TW18 96 C2
Montacute Dr. That RG19 106 C1
Montagu Rd. Slough SL3 68 A3
Montague Cl. Camb GU15 151 D3
Montague Cl. Light GU18 146 A1
Montague Rd. Slough SL1 42 C3
Montague St. Caver RG4 59 E1
Montague St. Read RG1 86 B4
Montague Terr. Newb RG14 131 D4
Monteagle La. Yate GU17 149 D3
Monteagle La. Yate GU17 149 E3
Montem La. Slough SL1 42 B2
Montgomery Cl. Sand GU17 150 A4
Montgomery Dr. Shin RG7 113 D1
Montgomery Pl. Slough SL2 43 E4
Montgomery Rd. Newb RG14 130 C4
Montpelier Ct. Wind SL4 67 E3
Montpelier Dr. Caver RG4 59 E3
Montrose Ave. Datch SL3 68 B4
Montrose Ave. Slough SL1 42 A4
Montrose Cl. Ashf TW15 98 B2
Montrose Cl. Camb GU16 151 F1
Montrose Dr. Maid SL6 39 D3
Montrose Rd. Felt TW14 71 E1
Montrose Way. Datch SL3 68 B4
Montrose Wlk. Read RG31 84 C3
Monument Cl. Newb RG14 130 B4
Monycrower Dr. Maid SL6 39 F4
Moor Cl. Sand GU15 143 F1
Moor Cl. Woki RG40 141 F4
Moor Copse Cl. Read RG6 87 D2
Moor End. Holy SL6 40 B1
Moor La. Harm UB7 70 B4
Moor La. Maid SL6 19 F1
Moor La. Newb RG14 104 C2
Moor La. Stan TW19 &
TW18 96 B3
Moor Pl. Windl GU20 146 A3
Moorbridge Rd. Maid SL6 40 A4
Moordale Ave. Brac RG42 90 C1
Moore Cl. Slough SL1 42 A2
Moore Grove Cres. Eng G TW20 95 F1
Moores Gn. Woki RG40 116 C4
Moores La. Eton SL4 41 F1
Moores Pl. Hung RG17 100 B3
Moorfield Terr. Maid SL6 40 A4
Moorfields Cl. Stai TW18 123 F4
Moorhayes Dr. Stai TW18 124 B3
Moorhen Dr. Read RG6 87 D1
Moorland Rd. Harm UB7 70 B4
Moorlands Dr. Maid SL6 38 C4
Moorlands Pl. Camb GU15 151 D2
Moorlands Rd. Camb GU15 151 D2
Moormede Cres. Stai TW18 96 C2
Moors The. Pangb RG8 56 B3
Moors The. That RG19 106 B1
Moorside Cl. Camb GU14 151 D1
Moorside Cl. Maid SL6 19 F1
Moorside. Woo G HP10 3 F4
Moorstown Ct. Slough SL1 42 C2
Moray Ave. Sand GU15 150 B4
Mordaunt Dr. Crow RG45 143 D2
Morden Cl. Brac RG12 118 C3
Moreau Wlk. Slough SL3 43 F4
Morecambe Ave. Caver RG4 58 C3
Moreland Ave. Iver SL3 69 E4
Moreleigh Cl. Read RG2 113 E4
Morella Cl. Vir W GU25 122 B3
Morello Dr. Slough SL3 43 F3
Moretaine Rd. Ashf TW15 97 E3
Moreton Way. Slough SL1 41 E3
Morgan Rd. Read RG1 86 B3
Moriston Cl. Read RG30 85 D4
Morlais. Caver RG4 59 D3
Morlands Ave. Read RG30 85 D3
Morley Cl. Slough SL3 43 F2
Morley Cl. Yate GU17 149 D3
Morley Pl. Hung RG17 100 B3
Mornington Ave. Woki RG40 141 F4
Mornington Cl. Tad RG26 134 C1
Mornington Rd. Ashf TW15 98 B2
Morpeth Cl. Read RG2 86 B2
Morrice Cl. Slough SL3 44 A1
Mortimer Cl. Read RG2 113 E4
Mortimer La. Mort RG7 137 E3
Mortimer Rd. Slough SL3 43 E2
Morton Pl. Thea RG7 83 F2
Morton Rd. Hort SL3 69 D3
Moss Cl. Caver RG4 59 E2
Mossy Vale. Maid SL6 19 E1
Moulsham Copse La. Yate GU17 149 D4
Moulsham La. Yate GU17 149 D4
Mount Cl. Far C SL2 22 B4
Mount Cl. Newb RG14 105 D1
Mount Cl The. Went GU25 122 B2
Mount Felix. Shepp TW17 125 F1
Mount La. Brac RG12 118 B4
Mount La. Chadd RG20 49 D4
Mount Lee. Eng G TW20 95 F2
Mount Pleasant. Brac RG12 118 B3
Mount Pleasant Cl. Light GU18 146 A1
Mount Pleasant Gr. Read RG1 86 A3
Mount Pleasant. Read RG1 86 A3
Mount Pleasant. Sand GU17 143 D1
Mount Pleasant. Tad RG26 135 D1
Mount Pleasant. Woki RG41 116 A3
Mount Rd. That RG18 106 C2
Mount St. Read RG2 86 A3
Mount The. Caver RG4 58 C2
Mount The. Caver RG4 59 D2
Mount The. Read RG1 86 B3
Mount The. Went GU25 122 B2
Mount View. Hen-O-T RG9 15 E1
Mountain Ash. Mar B SL7 1 B3
Mountbatten Cl. Newb RG14 105 E3
Mountbatten Cl. Slough SL1 43 D2
Mountbatten Rise. Sand GU17 142 C1
Mountfield. Gori RG8 34 B4
Mounts Hill. Old W SL4 93 E3
Mounts Hill. Wink SL4 93 E3
Mountsfield Cl. Stan TW19 70 A1
Mowbray Cres. Eng G TW20 96 A2
Mowbray Dr. Read RG30 85 D4
Mower Cl. Woki RG40 116 C4
Moyleen Rise. Mar SL7 1 B1
Muckhatch La. Stai TW20 123 D4
Mud La. Finch RG27 140 C1
Mud La. Pease RG20 50 B3
Muirfield Cl. Read RG1 86 B4
Mulberry Ave. Stan TW19 97 F4
Mulberry Bsns Pk. Woki RG41 116 A2
Mulberry Cl. Crow RG45 143 E2
Mulberry Cl. Sand GU15 143 E1
Mulberry Cl. Wood RG5 87 F3
Mulberry Dr. Slough SL3 43 F1
Mulberry Trees. Shepp TW17 125 E1
Mulberry Way. Thea RG7 83 F2
Mulfords Hill. Tad RG26 135 D1
Mulgrave Rd. Camb GU16 151 F1
Mullens Rd. Stai TW20 96 B2
Mulroy Dr. Camb GU15 152 A3
Mumbery Hill. Warg RG10 36 C1
Muncaster Cl. Ashf TW15 98 A2
Muncaster Rd. Ashf TW15 98 A2
Munces Rd. Mar B SL7 1 B3
Munday Ct. Binf RG42 90 C1
Mundaydean La. Mar SL7 1 A2
Mundesley Spur. Slough SL1 42 C4
Mundesley St. Read RG1 86 A3
Munkle Marsh. That RG19 107 D2
Munnings Dr. Sand GU15 150 C3
Munro Ave. Wood RG5 87 F2
Murdoch Cl. Stai TW18 97 D2
Murdoch Rd. Woki RG40 116 B3
Murray Ct. Ascot SL5 120 B2
Murray Rd. Woki RG41 116 A3
Murrellhill La. Binf RG42 117 E4
Murrells La. Camb GU15 151 D2
Murrin Rd. Maid SL6 39 E4
Mushroom Castle La. Burl RG42 92 A1
Mustard La. Sonn RG4 60 C1
Mustard Mill Rd. Stai TW18 96 C2
Muswell Cl. Thea RG7 83 F2
Mutton Oaks. Brac RG12 117 E4
Myers Way. Camb GU16 152 B1
Myline Sq. Woki RG40 116 B3
Myrke The. Datch SL3 42 C1
Myrke The. Slough SL3 42 C1
Myrtle Ave. Harm TW14 71 F1
Myrtle Cl. Bur C RG7 111 D2
Myrtle Cl. Light GU18 153 D4
Myrtle Cl. Stan SL3 69 F3
Myrtle Cl. Sulh RG31 57 E2
Myrtle Cres. Slough SL2 42 C3
Myrtle Dr. Black GU17 150 B3
Myton Wlk. Thea RG7 83 F2

Nabbs Hill Cl. Read RG31 84 B3
Nairn Cl. Camb GU16 151 F1
Nalderhill Rd. Box RG20 103 D3
Napier Cl. Crow RG45 143 E3
Napier Dr. Camb GU15 152 A4
Napier Rd. Ashf TW15 98 B1
Napier Rd. Crow RG45 143 E2
Napier Rd. Harm TW6 70 B3
Napier Rd. Maid SL6 39 D3
Napier Rd. Read RG1 86 B4
Napier Wlk. Ashf TW15 98 B1
Napper Cl. Burl SL5 119 E4
Narromine Dr. Read RG31 84 C2
Naseby. Brac RG12 118 A1
Naseby Rise. Newb RG14 105 E3
Nash Cl. Read RG6 87 D2
Nash Gdns. Ascot SL5 119 F4
Nash Grove La. Woki RG40 115 F1
Nash Pk. Binf RG42 90 A1
Nash Rd. Slough SL3 44 A1
Nashdom La. Burn SL1 21 D3
Natalie Cl. Felt TW14 98 B4
Neath Gdns. Read RG30 84 C4
Needham Cl. Wind SL4 66 C3
Neil Cl. Ashf TW15 98 B2
Nell Gwynn Ave. Shepp TW17 125 E2
Nell Gwynne Ave. Ascot SL5 120 B3
Nell Gwynne Cl. Ascot SL5 120 B3
Nelson Cl. Brac RG12 118 C4
Nelson Cl. Felt TW14 98 C4
Nelson Cl. Slough SL3 43 E1
Nelson Rd. Ashf TW15 97 F2
Nelson Rd. Caver RG4 59 E1
Nelson Rd. Harm TW6 70 C3
Nelson Rd. Wind SL4 66 C2
Nelson Way. Sand GU15 150 C2
Nelsons La. Hurst RG10 89 D3
Nene Rd. Harm TW6 71 D3
Neptune Cl. Woki RG41 115 F3
Neptune Rd. Harm TW6 71 E3
Netherton. Brac RG12 118 A3
Netley Cl. Caver RG4 59 F3
Netley Rd (N). Harm TW6 71 E3
Netley Rd. Stan TW6 71 E3
Nettlecombe. Brac RG12 118 C2
Nettleton Rd. Harm TW6 71 D3
Nevelle Cl. Brac RG42 117 E4
Neville Cl. Sto P SL2 22 C3
Neville Cl. W St L RG10 62 C3
Neville Dr. That RG19 106 C2
Nevis Rd. Read RG31 57 E2
New Bath Rd. Char RG10 61 E3
New Bath Rd. Twyf RG10 61 E3
New Bath Rd. Warg RG10 61 E3
New Bright St. Read RG1 86 A3
New Ct. Mar SL7 1 B1
New Forest Ride. Brac RG12 118 C2
New Forest Ride. Burl RG12 119 D3
New Ham Rd. Harm TW6 71 E3
New Hill. Pur O T RG8 57 E3
New Lane Hill. Read RG30 84 C3
New Meadow. Burl SL5 119 E4
New Mile Rd. Ascot SL5 120 B4
New Mill La. Finch RG27 140 C1
New Mill Rd. Bark RG27 140 C2
New Park Rd. Ashf TW15 98 B2
New Rd. Black GU17 150 C2
New Rd. Bou E SL8 3 D2
New Rd. Brac RG12 118 B4
New Rd. Bur C RG7 111 F1
New Rd. Burl SL5 92 C1
New Rd. Cook SL6 19 F4
New Rd. Crow RG45 143 E3
New Rd. Datch SL3 68 B3
New Rd. Felt TW14 71 E1
New Rd. Harl UB7 71 E4
New Rd. Holy SL6 65 D4
New Rd. Hurl SL6 17 F2

175

New Rd. Mar B

Orchard Cl. Ashf

New Rd. Mar B SL7 1 B3
New Rd. Mort RG7 111 F1
New Rd. Newb RG14 105 E1
New Rd. Read RG1 86 B3
New Rd. Sand GU17 150 A4
New Rd. Shipl RG9 36 A2
New Rd. Slough SL3 44 A2
New Rd. Stai TW17 125 D3
New Rd. Stai TW18 96 B2
New Rd. Twyf RG10 61 E4
New Rd. Twyf RG10 61 F3
New Rd. Windl GU20 146 A2
New Rd. Woki RG41 115 D4
New Sq. Felt TW14 98 B4
New St. Bee H RG7 138 A1
New St. Hen-O-T RG9 15 F1
New St. Stai TW18 97 D2
New Way. Brad RG7 82 A1
New Wickham La. Eng G TW20 96 A1
New Wickham La. Stai TW20 96 A1
New Wokingham Rd. Crow RG45 143 D3
New Zealand Ave. Shepp TW17 125 F1
Newall Rd. Harm TW6 71 E3
Newalls Rise. Warg RG10 36 C1
Newark Rd. Windl GU20 146 A3
Newark St. Read RG1 86 A3
Newber Way. Slough SL1 42 B2
Newbery Cl. Read RG31 57 E1
Newbery Way. Slough SL1 42 B2
Newbewrry Cres. Wind SL4 66 B3
Newbold Rd. Newb RG14 104 B3
Newbolt Cl. That RG18 106 B3
Newbury Dr. Maid SL6 40 A3
Newbury Hill. Hamp N RG18 52 C3
Newbury La. Comp RG20 31 E2
Newbury Rd. Gr She RG17 48 A1
Newbury Rd. Harm TW6 70 C3
Newbury Rd. Herm RG18 79 D3
Newbury Rd. Lamb RG17 25 E1
Newbury St. Kint RG17 102 A1
Newbury St. Lamb RG17 25 D1
Newcastle Rd. Read RG2 86 B2
Newchurch Rd. Slough SL2 41 F4
Newchurch Rd. Tad RG26 135 D1
Newfield Gdns. Mar SL7 1 C2
Newfield Rd. Mar SL7 1 C2
Newfield Way. Mar SL7 1 C1
Newhaven Cres. Ashf TW15 98 B2
Newhaven Spur. Slough SL2 22 A1
Newhurst Gdns. New G RG42 91 E2
Newlands Ave. Caver RG4 59 D2
Newlands Cl. Yate GU17 149 E3
Newlands Dr. Maid SL6 39 D4
Newlands Dr. Stan SL3 69 F2
Newlyn Gdns. Read RG2 86 A1
Newlyn Rd. Harm TW6 71 D3
Newmarket Cl. Winn RG6 87 E1
Newport Cl. Newb RG14 105 D2
Newport Rd. Harm TW6 71 D3
Newport Rd. Newb RG14 105 D2
Newport Rd. Read RG1 59 D1
Newport Rd. Slough SL2 21 F1
Newquay Dr. Read RG6 87 D1
Newton Ave. Caver RG4 59 E3
Newton Cl. Slough SL3 43 F2
Newton Ct. Old W SL4 68 A1
Newton La. Old W SL4 68 A1
Newton Rd. Harm TW6 70 C3
Newton Rd. Mar SL7 1 C2
Newtonside Orch. Old W SL4 68 A1
Newtown Gdns. Hen-O-T RG9 35 F4
Newtown Rd. Hen-O-T RG9 35 F4
Newtown Rd. Hen-O-T RG9 35 F4
Newtown Rd. Newb RG14 & RG20 131 D4
Newtown Rd. Sand GU17 150 A4
Newtown. Tad RG26 135 D1
Niagara Rd. Hen-O-T RG9 35 F4
Nicholas Rd. Hen-O-T RG9 35 D4
Nicholls. Oak G SL4 66 B2
Nicholson Wlk. Eng G TW20 96 A2
Nicholsons La. Maid SL6 39 F4
Nideggen Cl. That RG19 106 B2
Nightingale Cres. Brac RG12 118 B2
Nightingale Gdns. Sand GU17 150 A4
Nightingale La. Mort RG7 137 E3
Nightingale Pk. Burn SL2 21 F3
Nightingale Rd. Wood RG5 87 E2
Nightingales The. Newb RG14 131 D4
Nightingales The. Stan TW19 97 F4
Nimrod Cl. Wood RG5 88 A4
Nimrod Rd. Harm TW6 71 D3
Nimrod Way. Harm TW6 71 D3
Nimrod Way. Read RG2 86 A3
Nine Elms Cl. Felt TW14 98 C4
Nine Mile Ride. Bark RG40 142 B4
Nine Mile Ride. Brac RG40 142 B4
Nine Mile Ride. Woki RG40 142 B4
Nixey Cl. Slough SL1 43 D2
Noakes Hill. Asham RG8 54 A4
Nobel Dr. Stan UB7 71 F4
Nobles Way. Eng G TW20 95 F1
Norcot Rd. Read RG30 84 C4
Norden Cl. Maid SL6 39 E2
Norden Meadows. Maid SL6 39 E3
Norden Rd. Maid SL6 39 E3
Norelands Dr. Burn SL1 21 E2
Nores Rd. Read RG2 113 E4
Norfolk Ave. Slough SL1 42 B4
Norfolk Chase. New G RG42 91 F1
Norfolk Cl. Woki RG41 115 F3
Norfolk Park Cotts. Maid SL6 39 F4
Norfolk Rd. Maid SL6 39 F4
Norlands La. Stai TW18 123 F4
Norlands. That RG18 106 B3
Norman Ave. Hen-O-T RG9 15 F1
Norman Rd. Ashf TW15 98 B1
Norman Rd. Caver RG4 59 E2
Normandy Wlk. Stai TW20 96 B2
Normanhurst. Ashf TW15 98 A2
Normans The. Slough SL2 43 D4
Normanstead Rd. Read RG31 84 B4
Normay Rise. Newb RG14 130 B3
Normoor Rd. Bur C RG7 110 C1
Norreys Ave. Woki RG40 116 B4
Norreys Dr. Maid SL6 39 E2
Norris Field. Chadd RG20 49 D4
Norris La. Chadd RG20 49 D4
Norris Rd. Read RG6 87 D3
Norris Rd. Stai TW18 96 C2
North Burnham Cl. Burn SL1 21 D2
North Cl. Felt TW14 71 E1
North Cl. Medm SL7 17 E4
North Cl. Wind SL4 66 C3
North Croft. Woo G HP10 3 F3
North Dr. Sulhd RG7 110 B4
North Dr. Went GU25 121 F2
North End La. Went SL5 121 D1
North Fryerne. Yate GU17 149 E4
North Gn. Brac RG12 118 B4
North Gn. Maid SL6 19 F1
North Gn. Slough SL1 42 C3
North Gr. Chert KT16 123 F2
North Hatton Rd. Harm TW6 71 E3
North Links Rd. Fla H HP10 3 D4
North Lodge Dr. Burl SL5 119 E4
North Lodge Mews. Read RG30 85 E2
North Pk. Iver SL0 44 B2
North Rd. Burl SL5 119 D4
North Rd. Felt TW14 71 E1
North Rd. Maid SL6 39 F4
North Rd. Moul OX10 13 F2
North St. Caver RG4 59 D1
North St. Eng G TW20 95 F1
North St. Read RG1 85 F4
North St. Wink SL4 93 D3
North Standen Rd. Hung RG17 100 A2
North Star La. Maid SL6 39 E3
North Town Cl. Maid SL6 19 F1
North Town Mead. Maid SL6 19 F1
North Town Moor. Maid SL6 19 F1
North Town Rd. Maid SL6 19 F1
North Wlk. Thea RG7 83 F2
Northam Cl. Winn RG6 87 F2
Northampton Ave. Slough SL1 42 B4
Northampton Cl. Brac RG12 118 C3
Northborough Rd. Slough SL2 22 A1
Northbourne Cl. Read RG6 87 D1
Northbrook Copse. Brac RG12 118 C2
Northbrook Rd. Caver RG4 59 E3
Northbrook St. Newb RG14 105 D2
Northbury Ave. Twyf RG10 61 F3
Northbury La. Twyf RG10 61 F3
Northcott. Brac RG12 118 A1
Northcourt Ave. Read RG2 86 B2
Northcroft Cl. Eng G TW20 95 D2
Northcroft Gdns. Eng G TW20 95 D2
Northcroft La. Newb RG14 104 C2
Northcroft Rd. Eng G TW20 95 D2
Northcroft. Slough SL2 22 A1
Northcroft Villas. Eng G TW20 95 D2
Northdean. Maid SL6 19 F1
Northend Cl. Fla H HP10 3 E4
Northern Ave. Newb RG14 105 D3
Northern Hts. Bou E SL8 3 D3
Northern Perimeter Rd. Harm TW6 71 E3
Northern Perimeter Rd (W). Harm TW6 70 C3
Northern Rd. Slough SL2 22 B1
Northern Woods. Fla H HP10 3 E4
Northfield Ave. Shipl RG9 36 A2
Northfield Ct. Chert TW18 124 A4
Northfield Ct. Hen-O-T RG9 15 E2
Northfield End. Hen-O-T RG9 15 E2
Northfield. Light GU18 153 D4
Northfield Rd. Eton SL4 41 F1
Northfield Rd. Maid SL6 19 F1
Northfield Rd. Read RG1 59 D1
Northfield Rd. Shipl RG9 36 A2
Northfield Rd. Stai TW18 124 A4
Northfield Rd. That RG18 106 A2
Northfields. Chiev RG20 51 D2
Northfields. Lamb RG17 25 D2
Northgate Dr. Camb GU15 152 A4
Northington Cl. Brac RG12 118 C2
Northmead Rd. Slough SL2 41 F4
Northolt Rd. Harm TW6 70 C3
Northrop Rd. Harm TW6 71 F3
Northumberland Ave. Read RG2 86 B2
Northumberland Cl. New G RG42 91 F1
Northumberland Cl. Stan TW19 70 C1
Northumberland Cres. Felt TW14 71 F1
Northumbria Rd. Maid SL6 39 D2
Northview. Hung RG17 100 B3
Northway. Newb RG14 105 D1
Northway. That RG18 106 B3
Northway. Woki RG41 115 F4
Northwood Dr. Newb RG14 105 E2
Northwood Rd. Harm TW6 70 B3
Norton Cl. Newb RG14 130 B3
Norton Pk. Ascot SL5 120 B2
Norton Rd. Camb GU15 152 B3
Norton Rd. Read RG1 86 C4
Norton Rd. Swal RG7 139 E2
Norton Rd. Woki RG40 116 B3
Norton Rd. Wood RG5 87 F3
Norway Dr. Slough SL2 43 D4
Norwich Ave. Camb GU15 151 F2
Norwich Dr. Wood RG5 87 E4
Norwood Cres. Harm TW6 71 E3
Norwood Rd. Read RG1 86 C4
Notley End. Eng G TW20 95 E1
Notton Way. Read RG6 113 F4
Nuffield Dr. Crow GU15 143 F1
Nuffield Rd. Bark RG2 140 C4
Nugee Ct. Crow RG45 143 D3
Nugent Ct. Mar SL7 1 C2
Nuneaton. Brac RG12 118 C2
Nunhide La. Sulh RG8 83 F3
Nuns Acre. Gori RG8 34 A4
Nuns Wlk. Vir W GU25 122 B2
Nuptown La. Burl RG42 91 F4
Nursery Cl. Hurst RG10 88 C4
Nursery Gdns. Pur O T RG8 57 D3
Nursery Gdns. Shepp TW16 125 F4
Nursery Gdns. Stai TW18 97 D1
Nursery La. Burl SL5 119 F4
Nursery La. Slough SL3 43 E3
Nursery Rd. Burn SL6 41 D4
Nursery Rd. Shepp TW16 125 F4
Nursery Way. Wray TW19 68 B1
Nursery Wlk. Mar SL7 1 A1
Nut La. W St L RG10 62 C3
Nutbean La. Swal RG7 139 F3
Nuthatch Dr. Read RG6 87 D2
Nuthurst. Brac RG12 118 C2
Nutley. Brac RG12 118 A1
Nutley Cl. Yate GU17 149 E3
Nutmatch Cl. Stan TW19 97 F4
Nutmeg Cl. Read RG6 86 C1
Nutter's Hill. Swal RG2 140 A4
Nutty La. Stai TW17 125 E3
Oak Ave. Sand GU15 143 E1
Oak Ave. Stai TW20 96 B1
Oak Dr. Bur C RG7 110 C1
Oak Dr. Wood RG5 88 A3
Oak End Way. Padw RG7 109 E2
Oak Farm Cl. Sand GU17 150 B3
Oak Grove Cres. Sand GU15 150 C3
Oak Hill. Frox SN8 99 E2
Oak La. Eng G TW20 95 E3
Oak La. Wind SL4 67 D3
Oak Stubbs La. Dorn SL6 40 C2
Oak Tree Ave. Mar SL7 1 C2
Oak Tree Cl. Mar SL7 1 B2
Oak Tree Cl. Tad RG26 135 D1
Oak Tree Cl. Went GU25 122 B2
Oak Tree Copse. Read RG31 57 F2
Oak Tree Dr. Eng G TW20 95 E2
Oak Tree Mews. Brac RG12 118 B3
Oak Tree Rd. Mar SL7 1 B2
Oak Tree Rd. Read RG31 57 E1
Oak Tree Rd. That RG19 106 C1
Oak Tree Wlk. Pur O T RG8 57 E3
Oak View. Read RG31 84 B4
Oak Way. Felt TW14 98 C4
Oak Way. Wood RG5 87 E2
Oakdale. Brac RG12 118 B2
Oakdale Cl. Read RG31 84 B4
Oakdale Wlk. Wood RG5 88 A4
Oakdene. Bur C RG7 111 D1
Oakdene. Sunn SL5 120 C2
Oaken Gr. Maid SL6 19 E1
Oaken Gr. Newb RG14 130 B4
Oakengates. Brac RG12 118 A1
Oakfield Ave. Slough SL1 42 A3
Oakfield Rd. Ashf TW15 98 A2
Oakfield Rd. Black GU17 150 C2
Oakfield Rd. Bou E SL8 3 D2
Oakfield Rd. Silc RG26 135 F1
Oakhall Dr. Ashf TW16 98 C2
Oakham Cl. Read RG31 57 E1
Oakhurst. Maid SL6 20 A2
Oaklands Cl. Ascot SL5 92 C1
Oaklands Dr. Ascot SL5 92 C1
Oaklands Dr. Woki RG41 116 A3
Oaklands La. Crow RG45 143 D4
Oaklands Pk. Woki RG41 116 A2
Oaklands. Yate GU17 149 E3
Oaklea Dr. Finch RG27 140 C1
Oakley Cres. Slough SL1 42 C3
Oakley Green Rd. Holy SL4 66 A3
Oakley Green Rd. Oak G SL4 66 A3
Oakley Rd. Camb GU15 151 D2
Oakley Rd. Caver RG4 58 C2
Oakley Rd. Newb RG14 105 E2
Oakridge. West E GU24 153 F3
Oaks Rd. Shipl RG9 36 A2
Oaks Rd. Stan TW19 70 B1
Oaks The. Brac RG12 118 B4
Oaks The. Yate GU17 149 E3
Oakside Way. Read RG2 113 F4
Oaktree Way. Sand GU17 143 D1
Oakway Dr. Camb GU16 151 F1
Oakwood Rd. Brac RG12 118 C4
Oakwood Rd. Vir W GU25 122 B2
Oakwood Rd. Windl GU20 146 C2
Oareborough. Brac RG12 118 C3
Oast House Cl. Wray TW19 95 F4
Oatlands Dr. Shepp TW17 125 F1
Oatlands Dr. Slough SL1 42 B4
Oatlands Rd. Shin RG2 113 F3
Oban Ct. Slough SL1 42 B2
Oban Gdns. Wood RG5 87 F2
Obelisk Way. Camb GU15 151 E3
Oberon Way. Stai TW17 124 C3
Ockwells Rd. Maid SL6 39 E2
Octavia. Brac RG12 118 A1
Octavia Way. Stai TW18 97 D1
Oddfellows Rd. Newb RG14 104 C1
Odell Cl. Read RG6 114 A4
Odencroft Rd. Slough SL2 22 A1
Odiham Ave. Caver RG4 59 F3
Odiham Rd. Swal RG7 139 E1
Odney La. Cook SL6 20 A4
Ogmore Cl. Read RG30 84 C4
Okingham Cl. Sand GU15 143 E1
Old Acre La. Char RG10 61 D3
Old Barn Cl. Caver RG4 59 D3
Old Bath Rd. Char RG10 61 D3
Old Bath Rd. Newb RG14 104 C2
Old Bath Rd. Sonn RG4 60 B1
Old Bisley Rd. Camb GU16 152 B2
Old Bracknell Cl. Brac RG12 118 A3
Old Bracknell La E. Brac RG12 118 A3
Old Bracknell La W. Brac RG12 118 A3
Old Charlton Rd. Shepp TW17 125 E2
Old Court Cl. Maid SL6 39 D2
Old Dean Rd. Camb GU15 151 E4
Old Elm Dr. Read RG30 84 B4
Old Farm Cres. Read RG31 57 E1
Old Farm Dr. Brac RG12 91 E1
Old Ferry Dr. Wray TW19 68 B1
Old Fives Ct. Burn SL1 21 D1
Old Forest Rd. Read RG41 88 C1
Old Forge Cl. Maid SL6 40 A2
Old Forge Cres. Shepp TW17 125 D2
Old Green La. Camb GU15 151 E4
Old Hayward La. Hung RG17 73 E2
Old Kiln Rd. Fla H HP10 3 D4
Old La. Ham M RG20 102 C1
Old La. Head RG19 133 F1
Old La The. Read RG1 85 F3
Old Lands Hill. Brac RG12 118 B4
Old Marsh La. Dorn SL6 40 C2
Old Mill Ct. Twyf RG10 61 E3
Old Mill La. Maid SL6 40 B2
Old Newtown Rd. Newb RG14 104 C1
Old Nursery Pl. Ashf TW15 98 A2
Old Orchard The. Bur C RG31 84 C2
Old Pasture Rd. Camb GU16 151 F2
Old Pond Cl. Camb GU15 151 E1
Old Portsmouth Rd. Camb GU15 152 A3
Old Post Office La. Maid SL6 39 F4
Old Sawmill La. Crow RG45 143 E3
Old School Ct. Wray TW19 95 F4
Old School La. Yate GU17 149 E3
Old School Yd The. Lamb RG17 25 D1
Old Slade La. Iver SL0 44 C1
Old St. Chiev RG20 51 E3
Old St. Chiev RG20 51 F1
Old St. Herm RG18 78 C4
Old Station La. Wray TW19 69 D1
Old Station Way. Bou E HP10 3 F3
Old Station Yd The. Lamb RG17 25 D1
Old Vicarage Way. Bou E HP10 3 E2
Old Watery La. Woo G HP10 3 F4
Old Welmore. Yate GU17 149 F3
Old Whitley Wood. Read RG2 113 E3
Old Wokingham Rd. Brac RG45 143 E4
Oldacre. West E GU24 153 F4
Oldacres. Maid SL6 40 A4
Oldbury. Brac RG12 117 F3
Oldbury Rd. Chert KT16 123 F1
Oldcorne Hollow. Yate GU17 149 D3
Olde Farm Dr. Black GU17 150 A3
Oldershaw Mews. Maid SL6 39 D4
Oldfield Cl. Read RG6 87 D4
Oldfield Rd. Maid SL6 40 A4
Oldhouse La. Light GU20 146 B1
Oldmoor La. Woo G HP10 3 F4
Oldstead. Brac RG12 118 B2
Oldway La. Slough SL1 41 E3
Oleander Cl. Brac RG45 143 D4
Oliver Dr. Read RG31 84 B3
Oliver Rd. Ascot SL5 120 A3
Olivers Paddock. Mar B SL7 1 B3
Ollerton. Brac RG12 118 A1
Omega Way. Stai TW20 123 E4
Omers Rise. Bur C RG7 110 C2
One Pin La. Far C SL2 22 B4
Onslow Dr. Ascot SL5 93 D1
Onslow Gdns. Caver RG4 59 E2
Onslow Mews. Chert KT16 124 A2
Onslow Rd. Went SL5 121 D1
Opal Way. Woki RG41 115 F4
Opendale Rd. Burn SL1 41 D4
Opladen Way. Brac RG12 118 C2
Orbit Cl. Woki RG40 141 F3
Orchard Ave. Ashf TW15 98 B1
Orchard Ave. Harm TW14 71 E1
Orchard Ave. Slough SL1 41 E4
Orchard Ave. Wind SL4 67 D3
Orchard Chase. Hurst RG10 88 C4
Orchard Cl. Ashf TW15 98 B1

176
Orchard Cl. Black
Pinchington La. Gree

Orchard Cl. Black GU17 150 C1
Orchard Cl. Hen-O-T RG9 15 F1
Orchard Cl. Herm RG18 79 E4
Orchard Cl. Maid SL6 40 A2
Orchard Cl. Newb RG14 105 E3
Orchard Cl. Pur O T RG31 57 E2
Orchard Cl. Shin RG7 113 D1
Orchard Cl. Shipl RG9 35 F1
Orchard Cl. West E GU24 153 E3
Orchard Cl. Woki RG40 116 B3
Orchard Cl. Wool RG7 108 B1
Orchard Ct. Harm UB7 70 B4
Orchard Ct. Read RG2 113 E4
Orchard Dr. Bou E HP10 3 E2
Orchard Estate. Twyf RG10 61 F3
Orchard Gate. Far C SL2 22 B4
Orchard Gate. Sand GU17 150 A4
Orchard Gr. Caver RG4 59 F2
Orchard Gr. Fla H HP10 3 D4
Orchard Gr. Maid SL6 39 E4
Orchard Hill. Windl GU20 146 B2
Orchard Park Cl. Hung RG17 100 B2
Orchard Pl. Woki RG40 116 B3
Orchard Rd. Hurst RG10 88 C4
Orchard Rd. Mort RG7 137 D3
Orchard Rd. Old W SL4 68 A1
Orchard St. Read RG1 86 A3
Orchard The. Eng G TW20 96 A2
Orchard The. Fla H HP10 3 D4
Orchard The. Light GU18 153 D4
Orchard The. Mar SL7 1 C2
Orchard The. Thea RG7 83 F2
Orchard The. Vir W GU25 122 C2
Orchard Way. Ashf TW15 97 F3
Orchard Way. Camb GU15 151 D1
Orchard Way. Slough SL3 43 F3
Orchardene. Newb RG14 105 D2
Orchards The. Ashf TW15 98 B2
Orchardville. Burn SL1 21 D1
Orchids The. Chil OX11 10 B4
Oregon Ave. Read RG31 57 E2
Oregon Wlk. Woki RG40 141 F4
Oriel Hill. Camb GU15 151 E2
Oriental Rd. Ascot SL5 120 B3
Orion. Brac RG12 118 A1
Orkney Cl. Bur C RG31 84 C2
Ormathwaites Cnr. New G RG42 91 F1
Ormonde Rd. Woki RG41 116 A3
Ormsby St. Read RG1 85 F4
Orrin Cl. Read RG30 85 D4
Orts Rd. Newb RG14 105 D1
Orts Rd. Read RG1 86 B4
Orville Cl. Wood RG5 88 A4
Orwell Cl. Caver RG4 58 C2
Orwell Cl. Wind SL4 67 E2
Osborne Ave. Stan TW19 97 F4
Osborne Dr. Light GU18 153 D4
Osborne La. New G RG42 91 E2
Osborne Mews. Wind SL4 67 E3
Osborne Rd. Eng G TW20 95 F1
Osborne Rd. Read RG30 85 D4
Osborne Rd. Wind SL4 67 E2
Osborne Rd. Woki RG40 116 B3
Osborne St. Slough SL1 42 C2
Osbourne Ct. Wind SL4 67 E3
Osmans Cl. Burl RG42 92 A1
Osnaburgh Hill. Camb GU15 151 D3
Osney Rd. Maid SL6 19 F1
Osterley Cl. Woki RG40 116 C3
Osterley Dr. Caver RG4 59 F3
Ostler Gate. Maid SL6 19 E1
Oswald Cl. New G RG42 91 F1
Othello Gr. Brac RG42 118 C4
Otter Cl. Brac RG45 143 D4
Ouseley Rd. Old W SL4 95 E4
Overbridge Sq. Newb RG14 105 F2
Overbury Ave. Woki RG41 88 C1
Overdale Rise. Camb GU16 151 F2
Overdown Rd. Read RG31 57 E1
Overlanders End. Read RG31 57 F2
Overlord Cl. Camb GU15 151 E4
Owen Rd. Newb RG14 105 D3
Owen Rd. Windl GU20 146 B3
Owl Cl. Woki RG41 115 F3
Owlsmoor Rd. Sand GU15 143 E1
Owston. Read RG6 87 E1
Oxenhope. Brac RG12 118 A3
Oxford Ave. Burn SL1 21 D2
Oxford Ave. Harl UB7 71 F4
Oxford Ave. Slough SL1 41 F4
Oxford Cl. Stai TW15 98 B1
Oxford Rd E. Wind SL4 67 E3
Oxford Rd. Mar SL7 1 B1
Oxford Rd. Newb RG14 104 B3
Oxford Rd. Read RG1 & RG30 & RG31 58 A1
Oxford Rd. Sand GU15 143 F1
Oxford Rd. Wind SL4 67 D3
Oxford Rd. Woki RG41 116 A3
Oxford St. Caver RG4 59 D1
Oxford St. Hung RG17 100 C4
Oxford St. Lamb RG17 25 D2
Oxford St. Newb RG14 104 C2

Pacific Cl. Felt TW14 98 C4
Pack and Prime La. Hen-O-T RG9 15 E1
Padbury Cl. Felt TW14 98 C4
Paddick Cl. Sonn RG4 60 C2
Paddock Cl. Camb GU15 152 A3
Paddock Cl. Whi Wa SL6 39 D1
Paddock Hts. Twyf RG10 61 F2
Paddock Rd. Caver RG4 59 E1
Paddock Rd. Newb RG14 130 C4
Paddock The. Crow RG45 143 D3
Paddock The. Maid SL6 19 E1
Paddock The. Newb RG14 105 E1
Paddock The. Slough SL3 68 A3
Paddocks The. Fla H HP10 3 D4
Paddocks Way. Chert KT16 124 A1
Padstow Cl. Slough SL3 43 F2
Padstow. Felt TW14 98 C4
Padstow Gdns. Read RG2 86 A1
Padworth Rd. Mort RG7 136 B4
Padworth Rd. Silc RG7 136 B4
Page Rd. Felt TW14 98 B4
Pages Croft. Woki RG40 116 B3
Paget Cl. Mar SL7 1 C2
Paget Dr. Maid SL6 39 D2
Paget Rd. Slough SL3 43 F1
Pagoda The. Maid SL6 20 A1
Paice Gn. Woki RG40 116 B4
Paices Hill. Alde RG7 135 D3
Paley St. Holy SL6 64 A3
Palmer Cl. Brac RG40 143 D4
Palmer Park Ave. Read RG6 87 D3
Palmer School Rd. Woki RG40 116 B3
Palmera Ave. Bur C RG31 84 B2
Palmers Cl. Maid SL6 39 D2
Palmers Hill. Asham RG8 54 B3
Palmers La. Bur C RG7 111 D1
Palmers La. Bur C RG7 112 A2
Palmerston Ave. Slough SL3 43 D2
Palmerstone Rd. Read RG6 87 D3
Pamber Heath Rd. Silc RG26 135 F1
Pamber Rd. Silc RG7 136 A1
Pamela Row. Holy SL6 65 D4
Panbourne Hill. Pangb RG8 56 B3
Pangbourne Rd. Upp B RG8 55 E2
Pangbourne St. Read RG30 58 A1
Pankhurst Dr. Brac RG12 118 B2
Pans Gdns. Camb GU15 151 F2
Pantile Row. Slough SL3 44 A1
Papist Way. Chol OX10 14 A4
Paprika Cl. Read RG6 87 D1
Parade The. Ashf TW16 98 C1
Parade The. Bou E SL8 3 D2
Parade The. Tad RG26 135 D1
Parade The. Wood RG5 87 F4
Paradise Rd. Hen-O-T RG9 15 E1
Paradise Way. Buck RG7 108 B4
Park Ave. Camb GU15 151 E2
Park Ave. Stai TW18 97 D1
Park Ave. Stai TW20 96 B1
Park Ave. That RG18 106 B2
Park Ave. Woki RG40 116 A3
Park Ave. Wray TW19 68 B2
Park Cl. Wind SL4 67 E3
Park Cres. Read RG30 85 D3
Park Cres. Sunn SL5 120 C2
Park Cnr. Wind SL4 66 C2
Park Dr. Sunn SL5 120 C2
Park End. Newb RG14 105 D2
Park Gr. Read RG30 85 D3
Park La. Bark RG40 141 D3
Park La. Bee H RG7 137 E1
Park La. Binf RG42 90 C1
Park La. Box RG20 103 D1
Park La. Burn SL1 21 F4
Park La. Camb GU15 151 E3
Park La. Char RG10 61 D2
Park La. Hort SL3 69 D2
Park La. Newb RG14 105 D2
Park La. Read RG31 84 B4
Park La. Slough SL3 43 D2
Park La. That RG18 106 B2
Park Mews. Stan TW19 97 F4
Park Rd. Ashf TW15 98 A2
Park Rd. Brac RG12 118 B4
Park Rd. Camb GU15 151 E2
Park Rd. Eng G TW20 96 A2
Park Rd. Far C SL2 22 B2
Park Rd. Hen-O-T RG9 15 F1
Park Rd. Sand GU17 150 B4
Park Rd. Shepp TW17 125 D1
Park Rd. Stan TW19 70 B1
Park Rd. Sto P SL2 22 B2
Park Rd. Woki RG40 116 A3
Park St. Bags GU19 145 F2
Park St. Camb GU15 151 E3
Park St. Hung RG17 100 B3
Park St. Maid SL6 39 F4
Park St. Newb RG14 105 D2
Park St. Slough SL1 42 C2
Park St. Stan SL3 69 E3
Park St. Wind SL4 67 E3
Park The. Lamb RG17 25 D2
Park View. Bags GU19 145 F2
Park View Dr N. Char RG10 61 D3
Park View Dr S. Char RG10 61 D2
Park Wall La. Upp B RG8 34 B1
Park Way. Hung RG17 100 C2
Park Way. Newb RG14 105 D2
Park Wlk. Pur O T RG8 57 E3
Parkcorner La. Arbo RG41 114 C3
Parkgate. Burn SL1 21 E1
Parkhill Cl. Black GU17 150 B2
Parkhill Dr. Read RG31 57 E1
Parkhill Rd. Black GU17 150 B2
Parkhouse La. Read RG30 85 E3
Parkland Ave. Slough SL3 43 E1
Parkland Dr. Brac RG12 118 C4
Parkland Gr. Ashf TW15 98 A2
Parkland Rd. Ashf TW15 98 A2
Parkside. Hen-O-T RG9 15 E1
Parkside. Maid SL6 19 E1
Parkside Rd. Read RG30 85 E3
Parkside Rd. Sunn SL5 121 D2
Parkside Rd. That RG18 106 B3
Parkside Wlk. Slough SL1 43 D2
Parkstone Dr. Camb GU15 151 E2
Parkview Chase. Slough SL1 41 F4
Parkview. Fla H HP10 3 D4
Parkway. Camb GU15 151 E2
Parkway. Crow RG45 143 D3
Parkway Dr. Sonn RG4 60 C2
Parkway. Mar SL7 2 A2
Parlaunt Rd. Slough SL3 44 A1
Parliament La. Burn SL1 20 C3
Parnham Ave. Light GU18 153 E4
Parry Green N. Slough SL3 43 F1
Parry Green S. Slough SL3 44 A1
Parsley Cl. Read RG6 86 C1
Parsonage Gdns. Mar SL7 1 C1
Parsonage La. Far C SL2 22 B2
Parsonage La. Hung RG17 100 B3
Parsonage La. Lamb RG17 25 D1
Parsonage La. Wind SL4 67 D3
Parsonage Pl. Lamb RG17 25 D2
Parsonage Rd. Eng G TW20 95 E2
Parsons Cl. Bark RG2 141 D4
Parsons Cl. Newb RG14 104 C1
Parsons Field. Sand GU17 150 A4
Parsons Wood La. Far C SL2 22 B3
Part La. Swal RG7 139 F2
Parthia Cl. Read RG1 86 A3
Partridge Ave. Yate GU17 149 D3
Partridge Dr. Read RG31 84 B3
Partridge Mead. Maid SL6 19 F1
Paschal Rd. Camb GU15 151 F4
Pasture Cl. Read RG6 114 A4
Patches Field. Mar B SL7 1 C3
Paterson Cl. Camb GU16 152 B2
Paterson Rd. Ashf TW15 97 E2
Pates Manor Dr. Felt TW14 98 B4
Patricia Cl. Slough SL1 41 F3
Patrick Gdns. New G RG42 91 F1
Patrick Rd. Caver RG4 59 D1
Patriot Pl. Read RG1 86 B4
Patten Ash Dr. Woki RG40 116 C4
Patten Ave. Yate GU17 149 E3
Pavenham Cl. Read RG6 114 A4
Pavilion Gdns. Stai TW18 97 D1
Pavy Cl. That RG19 106 C1
Paxton Ave. Slough SL1 42 B2
Payley Dr. Woki RG40 116 C4
Paynesdown Rd. That RG19 106 B3
Peace La. Cook SL6 19 F3
Peach St. Woki RG40 116 B3
Peachy Dr. That RG19 106 C1
Peacock Ave. Felt TW14 98 B4
Peacock La. Brac RG12 117 E3
Peacock Rd. Mar SL7 2 A2
Pear Tree La. Newb RG14 105 E3
Pear Tree Rd. Ashf TW15 98 B2
Pearce Cl. Maid SL6 19 F1
Pearce Rd. Maid SL6 19 F1
Pearces Orch. Hen-O-T RG9 15 E2
Pearl Gdns. Slough SL1 42 A3
Pearmain Cl. Shepp TW17 125 D2
Pearmans Glade. Read RG2 113 F4
Pearson Rd. Sonn RG4 60 B2
Pearson Way. Wood RG5 87 F3
Peascod Pl. Wind SL4 67 E3
Peascod St. Wind SL4 67 E3
Pease Hill. Buck RG7 107 F4
Peasemore Hill. Pease RG20 50 A4
Pebble Hill. Kint RG17 128 A3
Peddlars Gr. Yate GU17 149 F3
Peel Cl. Caver RG4 59 E1
Peel Cl. Wind SL4 67 D2
Peel Cl. Wood RG5 88 A4
Peel Ct. Slough SL1 42 A4
Pegasus Cl. That RG19 106 A2
Pegasus Ct. Read RG31 84 B4
Peggotty Pl. Crow GU15 143 F1
Pegs Green Cl. Read RG30 85 D3
Peket Cl. Stai TW18 123 F4
Pelican La. Newb RG14 105 D2
Pelican Rd. Alde RG26 135 F1
Pell St. Read RG1 86 A3
Pelling Hill. Old W SL4 95 D4
Pemberton Gdns. Bur C RG31 84 B2
Pemberton Rd. Slough SL2 21 F1
Pembroke. Brac RG12 118 A1
Pembroke Broadway. Camb GU15 151 E3
Pembroke Cl. Ascot SL5 120 B2
Pembroke Cl. Bur C RG7 111 E2
Pembroke Pl. Caver RG4 59 E2
Pembroke Rd. Newb RG14 105 D2
Pembury Ct. Harl UB7 71 E4
Pendals Cl. Hamp N RG18 52 C3
Pendell Ave. Harl UB7 71 F4
Pendennis Ave. Caver RG4 59 F3
Pendine Pl. Brac RG12 118 A2
Pendlebury. Brac RG12 118 A1
Pendragon Way. Camb GU15 152 B2
Pendred Rd. Read RG2 113 E3
Peninsular Cl. Felt TW14 71 F1
Penling Cl. Cook SL6 19 F3
Penn Cl. Caver RG4 59 D3
Penn Meadow. Sto P SL2 22 C2
Penn Rd. Datch SL3 68 B3
Penn Rd. Farc SL2 22 B1
Penn Rd. Newb RG14 104 B3
Pennfields. Twyf RG10 61 F3
Pennine Cl. Read RG31 84 A3
Pennine Rd. Slough SL2 42 A4
Pennine Way. Char RG10 61 D2
Pennine Way. Harl UB7 71 E4
Pennylets Gn. Sto P SL2 23 D3
Pennypiece. Gori RG8 34 B4
Pennyroyal Ct. Read RG1 86 A3
Penroath Ave. Read RG30 85 E3
Penrose Ave. Wood RG5 87 F3
Penrose Cl. Newb RG14 104 C3
Penry La. Shepp TW17 125 F1
Pensford Cl. Crow RG45 143 D4
Penshurst Rd. Maid SL6 39 E3
Pentland Ave. Stai TW17 125 D2
Pentland Cl. Read RG30 84 C3
Pentland Pl. That RG19 106 B1
Pentland Rd. Slough SL2 42 A4
Pentlands The. Kint RG17 102 B1
Penton Ave. Stai TW18 123 F4
Penton Hall Dr. Stai TW18 124 A4
Penton Hook Rd. Stai TW18 124 A4
Penton Rd. Stai TW18 96 C1
Penwood Ct. Maid SL6 39 D4
Penwood Gdns. Brac RG12 117 E2
Penwood La. Mar SL7 1 B1
Penwood Rd. Ball H RG20 130 B2
Penyston Rd. Maid SL6 39 E4
Penzance Spur. Slough SL2 22 A1
Peppard La. Hen-O-T RG9 35 F4
Peppard Rd. Caver RG4 59 E3
Pepper La. Read RG6 86 C2
Pepys Cl. Slough SL3 69 D4
Perch Cl. Mar SL7 18 B4
Percival Rd. Felt TW13 98 C3
Percy Ave. Ashf TW15 98 A2
Percy Bryant Rd. Stai TW16 98 C1
Percy Pl. Slough SL3 68 A3
Peregrine Cl. Brac RG12 118 A2
Peregrine Cl. Woki RG41 115 F3
Peregrine Rd. Shepp TW16 125 F4
Periam Cl. Hen-O-T RG9 35 E4
Perkins Way. Woki RG41 116 A3
Perrin Cl. Ashf TW15 97 F2
Perry Oaks. Brac RG12 118 C4
Perry Oaks Dr. Harm TW6 70 B3
Perry Way. Brac RG12 118 C4
Perry Way. Camb GU18 152 C4
Perrycroft. Wind SL4 66 C2
Perryfields Way. Burn SL1 21 D1
Perryhill Dr. Sand GU17 142 C1
Perryman Way. Slough SL2 21 F1
Perserverance Hill. Hen-O-T RG9 35 D3
Perth Ave. Slough SL1 42 A4
Perth Cl. Wood RG5 61 D1
Perth Trad Est. Slough SL1 42 A4
Peterhouse Cl. Crow GU15 143 F1
Petersfield Ave. Slough SL2 43 D3
Petersfield Ave. Stai TW18 97 E1
Petersfield Rd. Stai TW18 97 E2
Petrel Cl. Woki RG41 115 F3
Petts La. Stai TW17 125 D3
Petworth Ave. Read RG30 84 C2
Petworth Ct. Wind SL4 67 D3
Pevensey Ave. Caver RG4 59 F3
Pevensey Rd. Slough SL2 42 A4
Pewsey Vale. Brac RG12 118 C2
Pheasant Cl. Winn RG41 88 B1
Pheasants Croft. Maid SL6 39 D3
Philip Dr. Fla H HP10 3 E4
Philip Rd. Stai TW18 97 E1
Phillimore Rd. Caver RG4 59 E4
Phillips Cl. Wood RG5 61 D1
Phipps Cl. Whi Wa SL6 39 D1
Phipps Rd. Burn SL1 41 F4
Phoebe Ct. Read RG1 86 A3
Phoenix Cl. Woki RG41 115 F3
Phoenix Wlk. Newb RG14 130 B3
Phyllis Court Dr. Faw (Bu) RG9 15 F2
Pickering. Brac RG12 118 A3
Picket Post Cl. Brac RG12 118 C3
Picketts La. Pangb RG8 55 F2
Pickford Dr. Slough SL3 43 F3
Pickins Piece. Hort SL3 69 D3
Pickwell Cl. Wood RG6 87 E1
Picton Way. Caver RG4 59 D2
Piercefield. Bur C RG31 84 B2
Pierces Hill. Read RG31 57 E1
Pierson Rd. Wind SL4 66 B3
Pigeonhouse La. Wink SL4 92 C2
Pigeons Farm Rd. Gree RG20 131 E4
Piggotts Rd. Caver RG4 59 E1
Pigott Rd. Woki RG40 116 C4
Pike Cl. Mar SL7 18 B4
Pike St. Newb RG14 105 D2
Pikeshaw Way. Read RG31 57 E1
Pimento Dr. Read RG6 86 C1
Pimpernel Pl. That RG18 106 C2
Pincents La. Sulh RG31 84 A3
Pinchcut. Bur C RG7 111 D2
Pinchington La. Gree RG14 & RG19 131 D4

177

Pindar Pl. Newb — Ravens Field. Slough

Pindar Pl. Newb RG14 105 F3
Pine Ave. Camb GU15 151 E2
Pine Cl. Maid SL6 39 D4
Pine Cl. Sand GU15 150 C4
Pine Croft Rd. Woki RG41 116 A1
Pine Dr. Black GU17 150 C2
Pine Dr. Mort RG7 136 C3
Pine Dr. Woki RG40 142 A4
Pine Gr. Twyf RG10 61 E3
Pine Gr. Windl GU20 146 B2
Pine Mount Rd. Camb GU15 151 E2
Pine Ridge. Newb RG14 105 E3
Pine Ridge Rd. Bur C RG7 111 D2
Pine Trees Bsns Pk. Stai TW18 96 C2
Pine Way. Eng G TW20 95 D1
Pinecote Dr. Sunn SL5 120 C1
Pinecroft. Mar SL7 1 B2
Pinefields Cl. Crow RG45 143 D2
Pinehill Rd. Crow RG45 143 E2
Pinehill Rise. Sand GU17 150 B4
Pinehurst. Ascot SL5 120 B2
Pines The. Twyf RG10 61 F4
Pinetree Ct. Caver RG4 59 D3
Pinewood Ave. Crow RG45 143 E3
Pinewood Cl. Tad RG26 134 B1
Pinewood Dr. Stai TW18 97 D2
Pinewood Gdns. Bags GU19 145 E2
Pinewood Rd. Vir W GU25 122 A3
Pinewood Rd. Went GU25 122 A3
Pingewood Rd. Bur C RG30 85 D1
Pingewood Rd S. Bur C RG30 112 B4
Pingewood Rd S. Shin RG30 112 B4
Pinglestone Cl. Harm UB7 70 C4
Pink La. Burn SL1 21 D2
Pinkneys Dr. Maid SL6 38 C4
Pinkneys Rd. Maid SL6 39 D4
Pinks La. Tad RG26 134 C1
Pipers Cl. Burn SL1 21 E1
Pipers Ct. That RG19 107 D1
Pipers End. Vir W GU25 122 B3
Pipers Way. That RG19 107 D1
Pipit Cl. That RG19 106 A2
Pippins Ct. Ashf TW15 98 A1
Pippins The. Slough SL3 43 F3
Pipsons Cl. Yate GU17 149 E3
Pitch Pl. Binf RG42 90 B2
Pitcroft Ave. Read RG6 87 D3
Pitfield La. Mort RG7 137 E2
Pitfield La. Silc RG7 137 E2
Pitford Rd. Wood RG5 88 A4
Pitts Cl. Binf RG42 90 B1
Pitts La. Read RG6 87 D4
Pitts Rd. Slough SL1 42 B3
Plackett Way. Slough SL1 41 E3
Plaitinson Rd. Read RG2 113 E3
Planes The. Chert KT16 124 B1
Plantation Cl. Herm RG18 78 C3
Plantation Rd. Chil OX11 9 F4
Plantation Rd. Tad RG26 134 C1
Plantation Row. Camb GU15 151 D3
Platt La. Lamb RG17 45 E3
Play Platt. Thea RG7 83 F2
Players Gn. Wood RG5 87 F3
Playhatch Rd. Caver RG4 60 A3
Plough La. Sto P SL2 23 D2
Plough La. Woki RG40 116 C3
Plough Rd. Yate GU17 149 F4
Ploughlands. Brac RG42 117 F4
Ploughlands. Brac RG42 117 F4
Ploughlees La. Slough SL1 42 C3
Plover Cl. Stai TW18 96 C3
Plover Cl. Woki RG41 115 F3
Plover La. Finch RG27 140 C1
Plowden Way. Shipl RG9 35 F1
Plumpton Rd. Newb RG14 105 E1
Plumtrees. Read RG6 87 D1
Pluto Rd. Chil OX11 9 F4
Plymouth Ave. Wood RG5 87 E3
Plymouth Rd. Slough SL1 41 F4
Plympton Cl. Winn RG6 87 F2
Pococks La. Eton SL4 42 C1
Poffley Pl. That RG19 107 D2
Pointers Cl. Chiev RG20 51 D1
Points The. Maid SL6 39 D2
Polehampton Cl. Twyf RG10 61 E2
Pollard Cl. Old W SL4 68 A1
Pollard Gr. Camb GU15 152 B2
Pollardrow Ave. Brac RG42 117 F4
Pollards Way. Read RG31 84 B2
Polsted Rd. Read RG31 57 E1
Polyanthus Way. Brac RG45 143 D4
Pond Cl. Newb RG14 130 B4
Pond Croft. Yate GU17 149 F3
Pond Head La. Read RG6 87 E2
Pond La. Herm RG18 79 E4
Pond La. Maple RG4 57 F4
Pond Moor Rd. Brac RG12 118 A2
Pond Rd. Stai TW20 96 B1
Pondside Cl. Harl UB7 71 E4
Pool End Cl. Stai TW17 125 D2
Pool La. Slough SL1 42 C3
Pool La. W St L RG10 63 D3
Poole Cl. Read RG30 85 D4
Pooley Ave. Stai TW20 96 A2
Pooley Green Cl. Stai TW20 96 B2
Pooley Green Rd. Stai TW20 96 B2
Poolmans Rd. Wind SL4 66 B2
Pope Cl. Felt TW14 98 C4
Popes Cl. Iver SL3 69 E4
Popes La. Cook SL6 19 E4
Popeswood Rd. Binf RG42 117 E4
Popham Cl. Brac RG12 118 C2
Poplar Ave. Read RG30 84 C3
Poplar Ave. Windl GU20 146 A3
Poplar Cl. Stan SL3 69 F3
Poplar Gdns. Read RG2 86 C1
Poplar La. Hurst RG10 62 A1
Poplar La. Winn RG41 88 B2
Poplar Rd. Ashf TW15 98 B2
Poplars Gr. Maid SL6 20 A1
Poplars The. Ascot SL5 120 A2
Poppy Dr. That RG18 106 C2
Poppy Pl. Woki RG40 116 A3
Poppy Way. Read RG31 84 B3
Poppyhills Rd. Camb GU15 151 F4
Porchester. Ascot SL5 120 A3
Porchester Rd. Newb RG14 105 D1
Porchfield Cl. Read RG6 87 D1
Porlock Cl. That RG19 106 B1
Porlock Pl. Bur C RG31 84 B2
Port Down. Hung RG17 100 C3
Porter Cl. Winn RG6 114 B4
Porter End. Newb RG14 131 D4
Portesbery Hill Dr. Camb GU15 151 F3
Portesbery Rd. Camb GU15 151 F3
Portland Cl. Slough SL2 21 E1
Portland Cres. Felt TW13 98 B2
Portland Gdns. Read RG30 84 B4
Portland Rd. Ashf TW15 97 F3
Portlands. Mar SL7 1 B1
Portlock Rd. Maid SL6 39 E4
Portman Cl. Brac RG42 118 A4
Portman Rd. Read RG30 58 B1
Portnall Dr. Went GU25 121 F2
Portnall Rd. Went GU25 121 F2
Portnall Rise. Went GU25 121 F2
Portrush Rd. Wood RG5 87 E3
Portsmouth Rd. Camb GU15 & GU16 152 A4
Portway Cl. Read RG1 85 F3
Portway. Swal RG7 139 E1
Portway. Tad RG26 134 C1
Post Horn Pl. Read RG31 84 C2
Post Office La. Bur C RG30 111 E3
Post Office La. Slough SL3 43 E4
Post Office Rd. Ink RG17 127 F3
Posting House Mews. Newb RG14 104 C2
Potley Hill Rd. Yate GU17 149 F3
Pottery La. Ink RG17 127 F3
Pottery Rd. Read RG30 57 F1
Potts Pl. Mar SL7 1 B1
Poulcott. Wray TW19 68 C1
Pound Cres. Mar SL7 1 B1
Pound La. Hurst RG10 89 D3
Pound La. Lit M SL7 2 B2
Pound La. Mar SL7 1 B1
Pound La. Newb RG20 104 B2
Pound La. Sonn RG4 60 C1
Pound La. That RG19 106 A2
Pound La. Windl GU20 146 B2
Pound Piece. Hung RG17 100 B3
Pound Rd. Chert KT16 124 A1
Pound St. Newb RG14 104 C1
Pound The. Cook SL6 19 F4
Poundfield La. Cook SL6 19 F4
Poundfield Way. Twyf RG10 61 F2
Powis Cl. Maid SL6 39 D2
Powney Rd. Maid SL6 39 E4
Poyle Gdns. Brac RG12 118 B4
Poyle La. Burn SL1 21 D2
Poyle Rd. Stan SL3 69 F3
Poynings. Iver SL0 44 C1
Precincts The. Burn SL1 21 E1
Prescott. Brac RG12 117 F1
Prescott Rd. Stan SL3 69 F3
Preston Pl. Newb RG14 105 E3
Preston Rd. Read RG2 86 A3
Preston Rd. Slough SL2 43 E3
Preston Rd. Stai TW17 125 D2
Prestwood. Slough SL2 43 D4
Pretoria Rd. Chert KT16 123 F1
Priest Ave. Woki RG40 116 C3
Priest Hill. Caver RG4 59 D2
Priest Hill. Eng G SL4 95 E3
Priest La. West E GU24 153 E3
Priestwood Ave. Brac RG42 117 F4
Priestwood Court Rd. Brac RG42 118 A4
Primrose Cl. Pur O T RG8 57 E3
Primrose La. Winn RG41 88 B2
Primrose Lea. Mar SL7 1 B1
Primrose Way. Sand GU17 143 D1
Primrose Wlk. Brac RG12 118 B2
Prince Albert Dr. Brac SL5 119 E2
Prince Andrew Cl. Maid SL6 20 A1
Prince Andrew Rd. Maid SL6 20 A1
Prince Andrew Way. Burl SL5 119 E4
Prince Consort Cotts. Wind SL4 67 E3
Prince Consort Dr. Brac SL5 119 E3
Prince Dr. Sand GU17 143 D1
Prince Hold Rd. That RG19 106 A2
Prince of Wales Ave. Read RG30 85 E4
Prince William Dr. Read RG31 57 E1
Princes Cl. Eton SL4 41 F1
Princes La. Pease RG20 50 B3
Princes Rd. Ashf TW15 97 F2
Princes Rd. Bou E SL8 3 E2
Princes Rd. Eng G TW20 95 F1
Princes Rd. Felt TW13 98 C3
Princes St. Read RG1 86 B4
Princes St. Slough SL1 43 D2
Princes Way. Bags GU19 145 F1
Princess Ave. Wind SL4 67 D2
Princess Marina Dr. Bark RG2 115 D1
Princess Marina Dr. Bark RG2 140 C4
Princess St. Maid SL6 39 F3
Princess Way. Camb GU15 151 E3
Prior Croft Cl. Camb GU15 152 A2
Prior End. Camb GU15 152 A3
Prior Rd. Camb GU15 152 A3
Priors Cl. Maid SL6 40 A1
Priors Cl. Slough SL1 43 D2
Priors Court Rd. Chiev RG18 78 C4
Priors La. Black GU17 150 A3
Priors Rd. Tad RG26 135 D1
Priors Rd. Wind SL4 66 B2
Priors Way. Maid SL6 40 A1
Priors Wood. Woki RG45 142 B2
Priory Ave. Caver RG4 59 D1
Priory Ave. Hung RG17 100 B2
Priory Cl. Hung RG17 100 B2
Priory Cl. Went SL5 121 D1
Priory Ct. Winn RG41 88 B2
Priory Gn. Stai TW18 97 D2
Priory La. New G RG42 91 E1
Priory Mews. Stai TW18 97 D2
Priory Rd. Burl SL5 119 D4
Priory Rd. Hung RG17 100 B2
Priory Rd. Newb RG14 105 D1
Priory Rd. Slough SL1 41 E4
Priory Rd. Went SL5 121 D1
Priory The. Winn RG41 88 B2
Priory Way. Datch SL3 68 A4
Priory Way. Harm UB7 70 C4
Priory Wlk. Brac RG12 118 C3
Proctors Rd. Woki RG40 116 C3
Promenade Rd. Caver RG4 59 D1
Promenade. Wind SL4 67 E4
Prospect Ct. Read RG30 85 D3
Prospect La. Eng G TW20 95 D2
Prospect Pl. Hurl SL6 17 F2
Prospect Pl. Newb RG14 105 D1
Prospect Pl. Stai TW18 96 C2
Prospect Rd. Hung RG17 100 B3
Prospect Rd. Mar SL7 1 B1
Prospect St. Caver RG4 59 D1
Prospect St. Read RG1 85 F4
Providence La. Harl UB7 71 E4
Providence Pl. Maid SL6 39 F4
Prune Hill. Eng G TW20 95 E1
Prunus Cl. West E GU24 153 F3
Pudding Hill. Know H RG10 37 E3
Pudding La. Brig RG20 28 C1
Puffers Way. Newb RG14 104 C1
Pump La N. Lit M SL7 1 C3
Pump La s. Lit M SL7 2 A2
Pump La. Shin RG7 112 B1
Pump La. Wink SL5 120 C4
Pumpkin Hill. Burn SL1 21 F3
Pundles La. Whi Wa SL6 63 E3
Purbrook Ct. Brac RG12 118 C2
Purcell Rd. Crow RG45 143 D4
Purfield Dr. Warg RG10 36 C1
Purley La. Pur O T RG8 57 E3
Purley Rise. Pur O T RG8 56 C3
Purley Village. Pur O T RG8 57 E3
Purley Way. Pangb RG8 56 C3
Purslane. Woki RG40 116 B3
Purssell Cl. Maid SL6 39 D2
Purton Ct. Far C SL2 22 B3
Purton La. Far C SL2 22 B3
Putman Pl. Hen-O-T RG9 15 F1
Pyegrove Chase. Brac RG12 118 C1
Pykes Hill. Asham RG8 54 B2
Pyle Hill. Newb RG14 105 D1
Pyrcroft Rd. Chert KT16 123 F1

Quadrant Ct. Brac RG12 118 C3
Quadrant The. Maid SL6 40 A3
Qualitas. Brac RG12 117 F1
Quantock Ave. Caver RG4 59 E3
Quantock Cl. Char RG10 61 D2
Quantock Cl. Harl UB7 71 E4
Quantock Cl. Slough SL3 44 A1
Quantocks The. That RG19 106 B1
Quarrington Cl. That RG19 106 C1
Quarry Bank. Light GU18 153 D4
Quarry La. Yate GU17 149 F3
Quarrydale Dr. Mar SL7 1 C1
Quartz Cl. Woki RG41 115 E4
Quaves Rd. Slough SL3 43 E2
Quebec Gdns. Black GU17 150 B2
Quebec Rd. Hen-O-T RG9 35 F4
Queen Annes Cl. Old W SL4 94 A3
Queen Annes Gate. Caver RG4 59 E2
Queen Annes Rd. Wind SL4 67 E2
Queen Charlotte St. Wind SL4 67 E3
Queen Cl. Hen-O-T RG9 15 F1
Queen Elizabeth Rd. Camb GU15 144 B1
Queen Mary Ave. Camb GU15 151 D3
Queen Mary Rd. Stai TW17 125 E4
Queen St. Caver RG4 59 D2
Queen St. Chert KT16 124 A1
Queen St. Hen-O-T RG9 15 F1
Queen St. Maid SL6 39 F4
Queen Victoria St. Read RG1 86 A4
Queen's Rd. Newb RG14 105 D1
Queens Acre. Wind SL4 67 E2
Queens Cl. Burl SL5 119 F4
Queens Cl. Old W SL4 68 A1
Queens Cotts. Read RG1 86 A4
Queens Ct. Slough SL1 42 C3
Queens Dr The. Read RG6 86 C2
Queens Gate. Wind SL4 67 E2
Queens Hill Rise. Ascot SL5 120 B3
Queens La. Maid SL6 39 F4
Queens Mead. Datch SL3 68 A3
Queens Park Gdns. Felt TW13 98 C3
Queens Pine. Brac RG12 118 C2
Queens Pl. Ascot SL5 120 A3
Queens Rd. Ascot SL5 120 B2
Queens Rd. Bis GU24 153 F1
Queens Rd. Camb GU15 151 D2
Queens Rd. Caver RG4 59 E1
Queens Rd. Datch SL3 68 A4
Queens Rd. Eng G TW20 95 F1
Queens Rd. Eton SL4 41 F1
Queens Rd. Mar SL7 1 B1
Queens Rd. Read RG1 86 B4
Queens Rd. Slough SL1 42 C3
Queens Rd. Wind SL4 67 E3
Queens Way. Kint RG17 102 A1
Queens Wlk. Ashf TW15 97 E2
Queensborough Dr. Caver RG4 58 C3
Queensbury Pl. Black GU17 150 B2
Queenshill Lodge. Ascot SL5 120 A3
Queensmere Rd. Slough SL1 43 D2
Queensway. Caver RG4 59 E3
Queensway. Maid SL6 19 F1
Quentin Rd. Wood RG5 87 E3
Quentin Way. Vir W GU25 122 A3
Quinbrookes. Slough SL2 43 E4
Quince Cl. Ascot SL5 120 B3
Quincy Rd. Eng G TW20 96 A2
Quintilis. Brac RG12 117 F1
Quoiting Sq. Mar SL7 1 B1
Quoitings Dr. Mar SL7 1 B1

Race Course Rd. Newb RG14 105 D1
Raceview Bsns Centre. Newb RG14 105 D1
Rachaels Lake View. New G RG42 91 F1
Rackstraw Rd. Crow GU15 143 E1
Radbourne Rd. Bur C RG31 84 B2
Radcliffe Way. Brac RG42 117 F4
Radcot Ave. Slough SL3 44 A2
Radcot Cl. Maid SL6 19 F2
Radcot Cl. Wood RG5 87 F4
Radical Ride. Woki RG40 141 F4
Radley Bottom. Wick RG17 101 E4
Radley Cl. Felt TW14 98 C4
Radnor Cl. Hen-O-T RG9 15 F1
Radnor Rd. Brac RG12 118 C3
Radnor Rd. Read RG6 87 E2
Radnor Way. Slough SL3 43 F1
Radstock La. Read RG6 87 D1
Radstock Rd. Read RG1 86 C4
Raeburn Way. Sand GU15 150 B3
Raeburn Way. Sand GU15 150 B4
Ragdale. Bur C RG7 111 D2
Raggleswood Cl. Read RG6 87 E2
Raghill. Alde RG7 135 E3
Raglan Gdns. Caver RG4 59 E2
Ragley Mews. Caver RG4 59 E3
Ragmans Cl. Mar B SL7 1 B4
Ragstone Rd. Slough SL1 42 C2
Railside. Wool RG7 108 C1
Railton Cl. Read RG2 113 E4
Railway App. Chert KT16 123 F1
Railway Rd. Newb RG14 105 D1
Railway Terr. Slough SL2 42 C3
Railway Terr. Stai TW18 96 B2
Railways Cotts. Gori RG8 34 B3
Rainsborough Chase. Maid SL6 39 D2
Rainworth Cl. Read RG6 114 A4
Raleigh Cl. Slough SL1 42 A3
Raleigh Cl. Wood RG5 87 F3
Raleigh Ct. Stai TW18 97 D2
Raleigh Rd. Felt TW13 98 C3
Ralphs Ride. Brac RG12 118 C3
Rambler Cl. Burn SL6 41 D4
Rambler La. Slough SL3 43 E2
Rambury Cl. Brac RG12 117 F2
Ramptons La. Silc RG7 136 A3
Ramsay Rd. Windl GU20 146 C3
Ramsbury Dr. Read RG6 87 D2
Ramsey Cl. Winn RG6 87 F1
Rances La. Woki RG40 116 C3
Randall Cl. Slough SL3 43 F1
Randall Mead. Binf RG42 90 A1
Randell Cl. Black GU17 150 C1
Randolph Rd. Read RG1 59 D1
Randolph Rd. Slough SL3 43 F2
Ranelagh Cres. Burl SL5 119 E4
Ranelagh Dr. Brac RG12 118 B3
Range Rd. Brac RG40 142 A4
Range Ride. Sand GU15 150 C4
Range View. Sand GU15 150 C4
Range Way. Shepp TW17 125 D1
Rangewood Ave. Read RG30 84 C2
Rapley Cl. Camb GU15 151 F4
Rapley Gn. Brac RG12 118 B2
Ratby Cl. Read RG6 87 E1
Raven Cl. Yate GU17 149 D3
Ravendale Mews. Stai TW18 97 D1
Ravendale Rd. Shepp TW16 125 F4
Ravenglass Cl. Read RG6 87 E2
Ravens Field. Slough SL3 43 E2

Ravensbourne Ave. Stan TW19 97 F4
Ravensbourne Dr. Wood RG5 87 F4
Ravenscourt. Shepp TW16 125 F4
Ravenscroft Rd. Hen-O-T RG9 15 E1
Ravensdale Rd. Ascot SL5 120 A2
Ravensfield. Eng G TW20 95 E1
Ravenshoe Cl. Bou E SL8 3 D2
Ravenstone Rd. Camb GU15 152 B3
Ravenswood Ave. Crow RG45 142 C3
Ravenswood Ave. Finch RG45 142 C3
Ravenswood Dr. Camb GU15 152 A3
Ravensworth Rd. Silc RG7 136 C3
Ravensworth Rd. Slough SL2 22 A1
Rawlinson Rd. Camb GU15 151 D3
Ray Dr. Maid SL6 40 A4
Ray Lea Cl. Maid SL6 40 A4
Ray Lea Rd. Maid SL6 40 A4
Ray Lodge Mews. Maid SL6 40 A4
Ray Mead Ct. Maid SL6 20 B1
Ray Mead Rd. Maid SL6 40 A4
Ray Mill Rd E. Maid SL6 20 A1
Ray Mill Rd W. Maid SL6 40 A4
Ray Park Ave. Maid SL6 40 A4
Ray Park La. Maid SL6 40 A4
Ray Park Rd. Maid SL6 40 A4
Ray St. Maid SL6 40 A4
Raymond Cl. Stan SL3 69 F3
Raymond Rd. Maid SL6 39 E4
Raymond Rd. Slough SL3 44 A2
Rayners Cl. Iver SL3 69 E4
Rays Ave. Wind SL4 66 C4
Raywood Cl. Harl UB7 71 E4
Reading Bridge. Read RG1 86 A4
Reading Link Retail Pk. Read RG2 86 A3
Reading Rd. Aldw RG8 33 D1
Reading Rd. Arbo RG2 114 B2
Reading Rd. Bark RG40 140 C2
Reading Rd. Black GU17 150 A2
Reading Rd. Bur C RG7 111 E2
Reading Rd. Chol OX10 14 A4
Reading Rd. Finch RG27 140 C2
Reading Rd. Gori RG8 34 C3
Reading Rd. Hen-O-T RG9 15 F1
Reading Rd. Moul OX10 14 A4
Reading Rd. Pangb RG8 56 B3
Reading Rd. Stre RG8 34 A3
Reading Rd. Woki RG41 115 F4
Reading Rd. Wood RG5 87 E4
Recreation La. Shin RG7 113 D1
Recreation Rd. Bou E SL8 3 D2
Recreation Rd. Bur C RG7 111 D1
Recreation Rd. Read RG30 84 C4
Recreation Rd. Warg RG10 36 C1
Rectory Cl. Brac RG12 118 B3
Rectory Cl. Far C SL2 22 A1
Rectory Cl. Newb RG14 104 C1
Rectory Cl. Sand GU17 149 F4
Rectory Cl. Stai TW17 125 D3
Rectory Cl. Wind SL4 67 D3
Rectory Cl. Woki RG40 116 B3
Rectory La. Blew OX11 12 C4
Rectory La. Brac RG12 118 A3
Rectory La. Windl GU20 146 B2
Rectory Rd. Caver RG4 59 D1
Rectory Rd. Padw RG7 135 F4
Rectory Rd. Stre RG8 33 E4
Rectory Rd. Tapl SL6 20 C1
Rectory Rd. Woki RG40 116 B3
Red Cottage Dr. Bur C RG31 84 B2
Red Cottage Mews. Slough SL3 43 E2
Red Cross Rd. Gori RG8 34 B3
Red Ct. Slough SL1 42 C3
Red Hill. Shipl RG9 35 D3
Red House Cl. Read RG6 114 A4
Red La. Alde RG7 135 E3
Red Leaf Cl. Slough SL3 43 F3
Red Lion Way. Woo G HP10 3 F3
Red Rd. West E GU18 152 C4
Red Rose. Binf RG42 90 B2
Red Shute Hill. Herm RG18 79 D2
Red Shute Ind Est. Herm RG18 79 D2
Redberry Cl. Caver RG4 59 E3
Redcrest Gdns. Camb GU15 151 F3
Reddington Dr. Slough SL3 43 F1
Redditch. Brac RG12 118 B1
Redfield Ct. Newb RG14 105 E2
Redford Cl. Felt TW13 98 C3
Redford Rd. Wind SL4 66 B3
Redhatch Dr. Read RG6 87 D1
Redlands Rd. Read RG1 86 B3
Redlane Hill. Alde RG7 135 E3
Redleaves Ave. Ashf TW15 98 A1
Redmayne. Camb GU15 152 B2
Redriff Cl. Maid SL6 39 E3
Redruth Gdns. Read RG2 86 A1
Redshots Cl. Mar SL7 1 C2
Redvers Rd. Brac RG12 118 A2
Redwood Ave. Wood RG5 88 A3
Redwood. Burn SL1 21 D2
Redwood Dr. Camb GU15 152 B2
Redwood Dr. Windl SL5 121 D2
Redwood Gdns. Slough SL1 42 B3
Redwood. Stai TW18 123 F4
Redwood Way. Read RG31 57 E2
Redwoods The. Wind SL4 67 E2
Reed Cl. Iver SL0 44 C4
Reed Wlk. Newb RG14 105 E2
Reeds Ave. Read RG6 86 C2
Reeds Hill. Brac RG12 118 A2

Reedsfield Cl. Ashf TW15 98 A3
Reedsfield Rd. Ashf TW15 98 A2
Reeve Rd. Holy SL6 65 D4
Reeves Way. Woki RG41 116 A2
Reform Rd. Maid SL6 40 A4
Regency Hts. Caver RG4 58 C2
Regent Cl. Hung RG17 100 B3
Regent Cl. Read RG6 87 E1
Regent Cl. Wood RG6 87 E1
Regent Ct. Bags GU19 145 F1
Regent Ct. Maid SL6 39 F4
Regent Ct. Read RG1 86 A4
Regent Ct. Wind SL4 67 E3
Regent St. Read RG1 86 C4
Regent Way. Camb GU16 152 A1
Regents Pl. Sand GU17 150 B4
Regents Wlk. Ascot SL5 120 B1
Regis Cl. Read RG2 113 E4
Regnum Dr. Newb RG14 105 D3
Reid Ave. Maid SL6 39 F3
Rembrandt Cl. Woki RG41 115 E3
Rembrandt Way. Read RG1 85 F3
Remembrance Rd. Newb RG14 104 C1
Remenham Church La.
Rem H RG9 16 A2
Remenham La. RemH RG9 15 F2
Renault Rd. Wood RG5 88 A3
Renfree Way. Shepp TW17 125 D1
Rennie Cl. Ashf TW15 97 E3
Repton Cl. Maid SL6 39 E2
Repton Rd. Read RG6 87 E2
Restwold Cl. Read RG30 85 E2
Retford Cl. Wood RG5 60 C1
Retreat The. Eng G TW20 95 F2
Retreat The. Holy SL6 65 E4
Revel Rd. Woo G HP10 3 E4
Revesby Cl. Maid SL6 39 E2
Revesby Cl. West E GU24 153 E3
Rex Ave. Ashf TW15 98 A2
Reynards Cl. Winn RG41 88 B1
Reynolds Gn. Sand GU15 150 B3
Rhodes Cl. Stai TW20 96 B2
Rhodes Cl. Winn RG6 87 F2
Rhododendron Cl. Burl SL5 92 C1
Rhododendron Wlk. Burl SL5 92 C1
Ribbleton Cl. Winn RG6 87 F2
Ribstone Rd. Maid SL6 39 D2
Ricard Rd. Old W SL4 68 A1
Richards Cl. Harl UB7 71 E4
Richborough Cl. Read RG6 87 D1
Richfield Ave. Read RG1 58 C1
Richings Way. Iver SL0 44 C2
Richmond Ave. Felt TW14 71 F1
Richmond Ave. Felt TW14 98 C4
Richmond Cl. Camb GU16 151 F1
Richmond Cres. Slough SL1 43 D3
Richmond Cres. Stai TW18 96 C2
Richmond Dr. Shepp TW17 125 E2
Richmond Rd. Caver RG4 58 C2
Richmond Rd. Read RG30 85 E4
Richmond Rd. Sand GU15 150 C4
Richmond Rd. Stai TW18 96 C2
Richmond Rise. Woki RG41 115 F4
Richmondwood. Went SL5 121 D1
Rickman Cl. Arbo RG2 114 C1
Rickman Cl. Brac RG12 118 B2
Rickman Cl. Wood RG5 87 E3
Rickmans La. Sto P SL2 22 C3
Riddings La. Head RG19 133 E1
Riders La. Bur C RG7 112 A2
Rideway Cl. Camb GU15 151 D2
Ridge Hall Cl. Caver RG4 58 C2
Ridge Mount Rd. Windl SL5 121 D1
Ridge The. Cold A RG18 106 B4
Ridge The. Upp B RG8 55 F4
Ridge Way. Iver SL0 44 C3
Ridgebank. Slough SL1 41 F3
Ridgemead Rd. Eng G TW20 95 D3
Ridgemount Cl. Sulh RG31 57 D1
Ridgeway Cl. Light GU18 153 D4
Ridgeway Cl. Mar SL7 1 C2
Ridgeway. Iver SL0 44 C3
Ridgeway. Shepp TW17 125 F1
Ridgeway The. Brac RG12 118 B3
Ridgeway The. Caver RG4 59 D2
Ridgeway The. Light GU18 146 A1
Ridgeway The. Mar SL7 1 C2
Ridgeway The. Wood RG5 87 F3
Ridgeway. Warg RG10 36 C1
Riding Court Rd. Datch SL3 68 C4
Riding Way. Woki RG41 115 F3
Ridings The. Camb GU16 152 A2
Ridings The. Caver RG4 59 E4
Ridings The. Iver SL0 44 C1
Ridings The. Maid SL6 39 D3
Ridlington Cl. Winn RG6 87 F1
Riley Rd. Mar SL7 1 B1
Riley Rd. Read RG30 84 C4
Ring The. Brac RG12 118 B4
Ringmead. Brac RG12 117 F2
Ringwood. Brac RG12 117 F1
Ringwood Cl. Ascot SL5 120 A3
Ringwood Rd. Black GU17 150 B3
Ringwood Rd. Read RG30 58 A1
Ripley Ave. Eng G TW20 95 F1
Ripley Cl. Slough SL3 43 F1
Ripley Rd. Read RG30 58 A1
Ripon Cl. Camb GU15 152 B2
Ripplesmere. Brac RG12 118 B3

Ripplesmore Cl. Sand GU17 150 A4
Ripston Rd. Ashf TW15 98 B2
Risborough Rd. Maid SL6 39 F4
Rise Rd. Sunn SL5 120 C2
Rise The. Caver RG4 59 D2
Rise The. Cold A RG18 106 B4
Rise The. Crow RG45 142 C3
Rise The. Crow RG45 143 D3
Rise The. Finch RG40 141 D1
Rise The. Woki RG41 116 A4
Riseley Rd. Maid SL6 39 E4
Rissington Cl. Read RG31 57 F2
River Gdns. Maid SL6 40 B2
River Gdns. Pur O T RG8 57 E3
River Mount. Shepp TW17 125 F1
River Park Ave. Stai TW18 96 B2
River Pk. Newb RG14 105 E2
River Rd. Caver RG4 58 B2
River Rd. Read RG1 86 A3
River Rd. Stai TW18 123 F4
River Rd. Tapl SL6 40 B4
River Rd. Yate GU17 149 D4
River St. Wind SL4 67 E4
River View. Fla H HP10 3 D4
River Wlk. Newb RG14 105 E2
Riverbank. Stai TW18 96 C1
Riverdene Dr. Winn RG41 88 A2
Riverfield Rd. Stai TW18 96 C1
Rivermead Ct. Bish SL7 18 C4
Rivermead Rd. Camb GU15 151 D1
Rivermead Rd. Wood RG5 87 F3
Riverpark Dr. Mar SL7 1 C1
Riversdale Ct. Read RG1 86 C4
Riversdell Cl. Chert KT16 123 F1
Riverside Ave. Light GU18 153 E4
Riverside. Bou E SL8 3 E2
Riverside. Brad RG7 82 B3
Riverside Cl. Stai TW18 123 F4
Riverside Dr. Stai TW18 96 C2
Riverside Dr. Stai TW18 123 F4
Riverside. Eng G TW19 96 A3
Riverside Pl. Stan TW19 70 C1
Riverside Rd. Stai TW18 &
TW19 96 C1
Riverside Rd. Stan TW19 70 B1
Riverside Rd. Stan TW19 70 C1
Riverside. Shepp TW17 125 F1
Riverside Way. Camb GU15 151 D2
Riverside. Wray TW19 95 E4
Riverview Rd. Pangb RG8 56 B3
Riverway. Gr She RG17 48 A2
Riverway. Stai TW18 124 A4
Riverwoods Ave. Mar SL7 2 A1
Riverwoods Dr. Mar SL7 2 A1
Rixman Cl. Maid SL6 39 E3
Rixon Cl. Slough SL3 43 F4
Road Hill. Box RG20 76 B2
Roberts Cl. Stan TW19 70 B1
Roberts Gr. Woki RG41 115 F2
Roberts Rd. Camb GU15 151 D3
Roberts Rd. Sand GU15 151 D3
Roberts Way. Eng G TW20 95 E1
Robertsfield. That RG19 105 F2
Robertson Cl. Newb RG14 131 D4
Robin Cl. Bur C RG7 111 D2
Robin Cl. Bur C RG7 111 D2
Robin Hill Dr. Camb GU15 152 A2
Robin Hood Cl. Slough SL1 41 F3
Robin Hood Way. Winn RG41 88 B2
Robin La. Sand GU17 143 E1
Robin Way. Read RG31 84 A3
Robin Way. Stai TW18 96 C3
Robin Willis Way. Old W SL4 68 A1
Robindale Ave. Read RG6 87 E2
Robinhood La. Winn RG41 88 B2
Robins Bow. Camb GU15 151 D2
Robins Cl. Newb RG14 130 C4
Robins Grove Cres. Yate GU17 149 D3
Robins Hill. Ink RG17 127 F3
Robinson Ct. Read RG6 87 D1
Rochester Ave. Felt TW13 98 C3
Rochester Ave. Wood RG5 60 C1
Rochford Way. Burn SL6 41 D4
Rochfords Gdns. Slough SL2 43 E3
Rockbourne Gdns. Read RG30 58 A1
Rockfield. Lamb RG17 25 D1
Rockfield Way. Sand GU15 150 B4
Rockingham Rd. Newb RG14 104 C1
Rockmoor La. Link SP11 147 D1
Rodney Way. Stan SL3 69 F3
Rodway Rd. Read RG30 57 F1
Roebuck Estate. Binf RG42 90 B1
Roebuck Gn. Slough SL1 41 F3
Roebuts Cl. Newb RG14 130 C4
Rogers La. Sto P SL2 22 C2
Rogers's La. East G RG17 47 E3
Rogosa Rd. West E GU24 153 F3
Rokeby Cl. Brac RG12 118 B4
Rokeby Cl. Newb RG14 131 D4
Rokeby Dr. Maple RG4 58 B4
Rokes Pl. Yate GU17 149 D3
Rokesby Rd. Slough SL2 21 F1
Rolls La. Holy SL6 64 C4
Roman Fields. Silc RG7 136 A1
Roman Lea. Cook SL6 19 F4
Roman Ride. Finch RG45 142 B3
Roman Way. Bou E SL8 3 D2
Roman Way. Read RG6 87 E2
Roman Way. That RG18 106 A3

Romans Gate. Silc RG26 135 F1
Romany Cl. Read RG30 58 A1
Romany La. Read RG30 58 A1
Romeo Hill. Brac RG42 118 C4
Romney Cl. Ashf TW15 98 B2
Romney Ct. Mar SL7 1 C2
Romsey Cl. Black GU17 150 B3
Romsey Cl. Slough SL3 43 F2
Romsey Rd. Read RG30 58 A1
Rona Ct. Read RG30 85 D4
Ronaldsay Spur. Slough SL1 42 C4
Rood Hill. Wick RG20 76 B2
Rook Cl. Woki RG41 115 F3
Rook Rd. Bou E HP10 3 E2
Rookery Ct. Mar SL7 1 B1
Rookery Rd. Stai TW18 97 D2
Rooksfield. Newt RG20 132 A1
Rooksmead Rd. Shepp TW16 125 F4
Rooksnest La. Kint RG17 128 A3
Rookswood. Brac RG42 91 D1
Rookwood Ave. Sand GU15 143 F1
Rope Wlk. That RG19 106 B2
Rosa Ave. Ashf TW15 98 A2
Rosary Gdns. Ashf TW15 98 A2
Rosary Gdns. Yate GU17 149 E3
Rose Cl. Wood RG5 88 A4
Rose Gdns. Stan TW19 97 E4
Rose Hill. Binf RG42 90 B2
Rose Hill. Burn SL1 21 D3
Rose Ind Est. Mar B SL7 1 B3
Rose Kiln La. Bur C RG1 &
RG2 86 A2
Rose Kiln La. Read RG1 &
RG2 86 A2
Rose La. Know H RG10 37 D4
Rose St. Woki RG40 116 B3
Rose Wlk. Read RG1 86 A4
Rose Wlk. Slough SL2 42 A4
Roseacre Cl. Stai TW17 125 D2
Rosebank Cl. Cook SL6 19 F4
Rosebay. Woki RG40 116 C4
Rosebery Rd. Maple RG4 58 B4
Rosecroft Way. Shin RG2 113 F3
Rosedale. Binf RG42 90 B2
Rosedale Cres. Read RG6 87 D4
Rosedale Gdns. Brac RG12 118 A2
Rosedale Gdns. That RG19 106 B1
Rosedene La. Sand GU15 150 B3
Rosefield Rd. Stai TW18 97 D2
Rosehill Pk. Caver RG4 59 E4
Roseleigh Cl. Maid SL6 39 D4
Rosemary Ave. Read RG6 86 C1
Rosemary Gdns. Black GU17 150 B3
Rosemary La. Sand GU17 150 B3
Rosemary La. Stai TW20 123 D3
Rosemead Ave. Felt TW13 98 C3
Rosemead Ave. Sulh RG31 57 D2
Rosemead. Chert KT16 124 A1
Rosery The. Bou E SL8 3 D2
Roses La. Wind SL4 66 B3
Rosewood Dr. Stai TW17 124 C2
Rosewood Way. Far C SL2 22 B4
Rosewood Way. West E GU24 153 F3
Rosewood. Wood RG5 87 E2
Rosier Cl. That RG19 106 C1
Rosken Gr. Far C SL2 22 A2
Roslyn Rd. Wood RG5 87 E3
Ross Rd. Maid SL6 39 F2
Ross Rd. Read RG1 58 C1
Ross Rd. Read RG1 59 D1
Rossendale Rd. Caver RG4 59 E2
Rossett Cl. Brac RG12 118 A3
Rossey Pl. Eton SL4 42 B1
Rossington Pl. Read RG2 113 E4
Rossiter Cl. Slough SL3 43 F1
Rosslyn Cl. Ashf TW16 98 C1
Rother Cl. Sand GU17 150 B4
Rotherfield Ave. Woki RG41 116 A4
Rotherfield Cl. Thea RG7 83 F2
Rotherfield Rd. Hen-O-T RG9 35 F4
Rotherfield Way. Caver RG4 59 D2
Rothwell Gdns. Wood RG5 61 D1
Rothwell Wlk. Caver RG4 59 E1
Rotton Row Hill. Brad RG7 81 F2
Roughgrove Copse. Binf RG42 90 A1
Rounce La. West E GU24 153 E3
Round Cl. Yate GU17 149 F3
Round End. Newb RG14 130 B3
Roundabout La. Woki RG41 115 E4
Roundfield. Buck RG7 107 D3
Roundhead Rd. Thea RG7 83 E2
Roundway. Camb GU15 152 B3
Roundway Cl. Camb GU15 152 B3
Roundway. Stai TW20 96 B2
Routh Ct. Felt TW14 98 B4
Routh La. Read RG30 84 C3
Row La. Caver RG4 59 F4
Rowallan Cl. Caver RG4 59 E3
Rowan Ave. Stai TW20 96 B2
Rowan Cl. Camb GU15 151 F4
Rowan Cl. Woki RG41 115 F3
Rowan Dr. Brac RG45 143 E4
Rowan Dr. Crow RG45 143 E3
Rowan Dr. Newb RG14 105 D3
Rowan Dr. Wood RG5 87 F4
Rowan Way. Bur C RG30 111 D3
Rowan Way. Slough SL2 42 A4
Rowanhurst Dr. Far C SL2 22 B4
Rowans Cl. Black GU14 150 C1

179

Rowans The. Ashf

School Rd. Read

Rowans The. Ashf TW16 98 C2
Rowcroft Rd. Arbo RG2 140 C4
Rowdell Dr. Read RG2 86 B1
Rowe Ct. Read RG30 85 D4
Rowland Cl. Wind SL4 66 B2
Rowland Way. Read RG6 86 C1
Rowland Way. Stai TW15 98 B1
Rowley Cl. Brac RG12 118 C3
Rowley La. Sto P SL3 23 E2
Rowley Rd. Read RG2 86 A2
Roxborough Way SL6 38 C2
Roxburgh Cl. Camb GU15 152 B2
Roxford Cl. Shepp TW17 125 F2
Roxwell Cl. Slough SL1 41 F3
Roy Cl. Herm RG18 78 C3
Royal Ave. Read RG31 84 B3
Royal Free Ct. Wind SL4 67 E3
Royal Victoria Gdns. Ascot SL5 120 A2
Roycroft La. Woki RG40 141 F4
Royston Cl. Read RG30 84 C4
Royston Way. Slough SL1 41 E4
Rubus Cl. West E GU24 153 F3
Ruby Cl. Slough SL1 42 A2
Ruby Cl. Woki RG41 115 F4
Rudd Hall Rise. Camb GU15 151 F2
Ruddlesway. Wind SL4 66 B3
Rudland Cl. That RG19 106 B1
Rudsworth Cl. Iver SL3 69 E4
Rugby Cl. Sand GU15 143 F1
Ruggles-Brise Rd. Ashf TW15 97 E2
Rumseys La. Blew OX11 12 A4
Runnemede Rd. Eng G TW20 96 A2
Runnymede Ct. Eng G TW20 96 A2
Rupert Cl. Hen-O-T RG9 15 F2
Rupert Rd. Newb RG14 130 C4
Rupert St. Read RG1 86 B4
Ruperts La. Hen-O-T RG9 15 F2
Ruscombe Gdns. Datch SL3 68 A4
Ruscombe La. Twyf RG10 61 F3
Ruscombe Pk. Twyf RG10 61 F3
Ruscombe Rd. Twyf RG10 61 F3
Ruscombe Way. Felt TW14 98 C4
Rushall Cl. Read RG6 113 F4
Rusham Park Ave. Eng G TW20 95 F1
Rusham Rd. Eng G TW20 95 F1
Rushbrook Rd. Wood RG5 87 E4
Rushburn. Woo G HP10 3 F3
Rushden Dr. Read RG2 86 C1
Rushes The. Maid SL6 40 A3
Rushes The. Mar SL7 18 B4
Rushey Way. Read RG6 87 E1
Rushington Ave. Maid SL6 39 F3
Rushmoor Gdns. Bur C RG31 84 A2
Ruskin Ave. Felt TW14 71 F1
Ruskin Rd. Stai TW18 96 C1
Ruskin Way. Woki RG41 115 E3
Russell Ct. Maid SL6 39 F4
Russell Dr. Stan TW19 70 B1
Russell Rd. Maple RG4 58 B4
Russell Rd. Newb RG14 104 C1
Russell Rd. Shepp TW17 125 E1
Russell St. Read RG1 85 F4
Russell St. Wind SL4 67 E3
Russell Way. Winn RG41 88 A1
Russet Cl. Stan TW19 69 F1
Russet Gdns. Camb GU15 151 E2
Russet Glade. Bur C RG7 111 D1
Russet Glade. Caver RG4 59 E4
Russet Rd. Maid SL6 39 E2
Russington Rd. Shepp TW17 125 E2
Russley Gn. Woki RG40 116 A1
Rustington Cl. Read RG6 87 D1
Ruston Way. Ascot SL5 119 F4
Rutherford Wlk. Read RG31 84 A4
Rutherwyk Rd. Chert KT16 123 F1
Rutland Pl. Maid SL6 39 E3
Rutland Rd. Maid SL6 39 E3
Rutland Rd. Read RG30 85 E4
Ruxbury Rd. Chert KT16 123 E2
Ryan Mount. Sand GU17 150 A4
Ryans Mount. Mar SL7 1 B1
Rycroft. Wind SL4 66 C2
Rydal Ave. Read RG30 57 F1
Rydal Cl. Camb GU15 152 B3
Rydal Dr. That RG19 106 A2
Rydal Pl. Light GU18 153 D4
Rydal Way. Stai TW20 96 A1
Ryde The. Stai TW18 124 A4
Rydings. Wind SL4 66 C2
Rye Cl. Brac RG12 118 B4
Rye Cl. Maid SL6 39 D2
Rye Cl. New G RG12 91 E1
Rye Ct. Slough SL1 43 D2
Rye Gr. Light GU18 146 C1
Ryecroft Cl. Warg RG10 36 C1
Ryecroft Cl. Wood RG5 60 C1
Ryecroft Gdns. Black GU17 150 C2
Ryehurst La. Binf RG42 90 C3
Ryeish La. Shin RG7 113 E2
Ryemead La. Wink SL4 92 B3
Ryhill Way. Read RG6 113 F4
Ryland Cl. Felt TW13 98 C2
Rylstone Cl. Maid SL6 39 E2
Rylstone Rd. Read RG30 85 E4
Ryvers Rd. Slough SL3 43 F2
Ryves Ave. Yate GU17 149 D3

Sackville St. Read RG1 86 A4
Saddleback Rd. Camb GU15 151 F4
Saddlewood. Camb GU15 151 E2
Sadlers Ct. Woki RG41 88 B1
Sadlers End. Woki RG41 115 E4
Sadlers La. Woki RG41 115 E4
Sadlers Rd. Ink RG17 127 D3
Saffron Cl. Datch SL3 68 A3
Saffron Cl. Newb RG14 104 C2
Saffron Cl. Read RG6 87 E2
Saffron Rd. Brac RG12 118 A3
Sage Cl. Read RG6 87 D1
Sage Rd. Sulh RG31 57 E2
Sagecroft Rd. That RG18 106 B3
St Adrian's Cl. Maid SL6 39 D2
St Agnes Terr. Lamb RG17 25 D1
St Albans St. Wind SL4 67 E3
St Andrews Ave. Wind SL4 66 C3
St Andrews. Brac RG12 117 F2
St Andrews Cl. Old W SL4 68 A1
St Andrews Cl. Shepp TW17 125 E3
St Andrews Cl. Woki RG45 142 C3
St Andrews Cl. Wray TW19 68 C1
St Andrews Cres. Wind SL4 66 C3
St Andrews Rd. Caver RG4 58 C2
St Andrews Rd. Hen-O-T RG9 35 E4
St Andrews Way. Slough SL1 41 E3
St Annes Ave. Stan TW19 97 E4
St Annes Cl. Hen-O-T RG9 15 E1
St Annes Glade. Bags GU19 145 E2
St Annes Rd. Caver RG4 59 D1
St Anns Cl. Chert KT16 123 F2
St Anns Hill Rd. Chert KT16 123 E2
St Anns Rd. Chert KT16 123 F2
St Anthonys Cl. Brac RG42 118 A4
St Anthonys Way. Harm TW14 71 F2
St Barnabas Rd. Caver RG4 59 D3
St Barnabas Rd. Read RG2 86 C1
St Bartholomews Rd. Read RG1 86 C4
St Bernards Rd. Slough SL3 43 E2
St Birinus Rd. Read RG31 84 B3
St Catherines Cl. Woki RG41 88 A1
St Catherines Hill. Silc RG7 136 C3
St Catherines Rd. Camb GU16 151 F1
St Chads Rd. Maid SL6 39 D2
St Christophers Gdns. Burl SL5 119 E4
St Clements Cl. Wood RG6 87 E1
Saint-Cloud Way. Maid SL6 40 A4
St Columba's Cl. Maid SL6 39 D2
St Cuthberts Cl. Eng G TW20 95 E1
St David's Cl. Maid SL6 39 D2
St David's Rd. Newb RG14 104 C1
St Davids Cl. Caver RG4 58 C3
St Donats Pl. Newb RG14 105 D1
St Dunstans Rd. Felt TW13 98 C3
St Edwards Rd. Read RG6 87 D3
St Elizabeth Cl. Read RG2 113 D4
St Elmo Cres. Far C SL2 22 B1
St Georges Ave. Newb RG14 104 C1
St Georges Cl. Wind SL4 66 C3
St Georges Cres. Slough SL1 41 E3
St Georges La. Ascot SL5 120 A3
St Georges La. Ascot SL5 120 A3
St Georges Rd. Camb GU15 151 E3
St Georges Rd. Read RG30 85 E4
St Georges Terr. Read RG30 85 D4
St Giles Cl. Read RG1 86 A3
St Helens Cres. Sand GU17 150 A4
St Helier Cl. Woki RG41 116 A2
St Hildas Ave. Ashf TW15 97 F2
St Ives Cl. Thea RG7 83 E1
St Ives Rd. Maid SL6 40 A4
St James Cl. Pangb RG8 56 B3
St James Cl. Twyf RG10 61 F3
St James Pl. Slough SL1 41 E4
St James Rd. Woki RG40 141 F4
St James Wlk. Iver SL0 44 C2
St Johns Cl. Wood RG5 87 F4
St Johns Ct. Eng G TW20 96 A2
St Johns Dr. Wind SL4 67 D3
St Johns Hill. Read RG1 86 B4
St Johns Rd. Ascot SL5 92 C1
St Johns Rd. Caver RG4 59 E1
St Johns Rd. Mort RG7 137 D3
St Johns Rd. Newb RG14 105 D1
St Johns Rd. Read RG1 86 B4
St Johns Rd. Sand GU17 150 B4
St Johns Rd. Slough SL2 43 D3
St Johns Rd. That RG19 106 B2
St Johns Rd. Wind SL4 67 D3
St Johns St. Read GU7 86 B4
St Joseph's Ct. Newb RG14 105 D2
St Judes Cl. Eng G TW20 95 E2
St Judes Rd. Eng G TW20 95 E2
St Katherines Rd. Hen-O-T RG9 35 E4
St Laurence Way. Slough SL1 43 D2
St Leonards Ave. Wind SL4 67 E3
St Leonards Hill. Wind SL4 66 C2
St Leonards Rd. Wind SL4 66 B1
St Leonards Rd. Wind SL4 67 E2
St Leonards Wlk. Iver SL0 44 C2
St Lukes Rd. Maid SL6 39 F4
St Lukes Rd. Old W SL4 68 A1
St Lukes Way. Caver RG4 59 D2
St Margarets Ave. Ashf TW15 98 A2
St Margarets Rd. Maid SL6 39 D4
St Marks Cl. Brad RG7 83 D3
St Marks Cl. That RG19 106 B2
St Marks Cres. Maid SL6 39 D4
St Marks Pl. Wind SL4 67 E3
St Marks Rd. Binf RG42 90 B1
St Marks Rd. Binf RG42 117 E4
St Marks Rd. Hen-O-T RG9 35 E4
St Marks Rd. Maid SL6 39 E4
St Marks Rd. Wind SL4 67 E3
St Martins Cl. Wood RG6 87 E1
St Martins Ct. Stai TW18 97 E2
St Mary's Rd. Camb GU15 151 E3
St Marys Ave. Pur O T RG8 57 E3
St Marys Ave. Stan TW19 97 E4
St Marys Butts. Read RG1 86 A4
St Marys Cl. Hen-O-T RG9 35 D4
St Marys Cl. Maid SL6 40 A4
St Marys Cl. Sand GU17 150 B4
St Marys Cl. Stan TW19 97 E4
St Marys Cres. Stan TW19 97 E4
St Marys Dr. Felt TW14 98 B4
St Marys Gdns. Bags GU19 145 F2
St Marys Gdns. Bags GU19 145 F2
St Marys Hill. Ascot SL5 120 B2
St Marys La. Wink SL4 92 B3
St Marys Rd. Ascot SL5 120 A2
St Marys Rd. Mort RG7 137 D3
St Marys Rd. Newb RG14 105 D2
St Marys Rd. Slough SL3 43 E2
St Marys Rd. Woki RG41 88 A1
St Marys Way. Bur C RG7 111 D2
St Marys Wlk. Maid SL6 39 F4
St Michael's Rd. Newb RG14 104 C1
St Michaels Cl. Lamb RG17 25 D1
St Michaels Ct. Slough SL1 21 E1
St Michaels Ct. Twyf RG10 61 F3
St Michaels Rd. Camb GU15 151 D3
St Michaels Rd. Read RG30 84 B4
St Michaels Rd. Sand GU17 149 F4
St Micheals Rd. Ashf TW15 98 A2
St Nazaire Cl. Stai TW20 96 B2
St Nicholas Dr. Shepp TW17 125 D1
St Nicholas Rd. Newb RG14 104 C1
St Olaves Cl. Stai TW18 96 C1
St Patricks Ave. Char RG10 61 D3
St Patricks Cl. Maid SL6 39 D2
St Pauls Ave. Slough SL2 43 D3
St Pauls Cl. Ashf TW15 98 B2
St Pauls Ct. Read RG1 86 A3
St Pauls Gate. Woki RG41 116 A3
St Pauls Rd. Stai TW18 96 B1
St Peter St. Mar SL7 1 C1
St Peters Ave. Caver RG4 58 C2
St Peters Cl. Burn SL1 21 D1
St Peters Cl. Old W SL4 68 A1
St Peters Cl. Stai TW18 96 C1
St Peters Gdns. Yate GU17 149 E3
St Peters Hill. Caver RG4 58 C2
St Peters Rd. Maid SL6 19 E1
St Peters Rd. Read RG6 87 D3
St Pinnock Ave. Stai TW18 124 A4
St Richards Rd. Newb RG14 105 D2
St Ronans Rd. Read RG30 85 D4
St Saviours Rd. Read RG1 85 F3
St Sebastian Cl. Woki RG40 142 C4
St Stephens Cl. Caver RG4 59 D1
St Swithins Cl. Wick RG20 75 E2
St Swithuns Ct. Twyf RG10 61 E2
St Theresas Rd. Harm TW14 71 F2
St Thomas Ct. That RG18 106 C2
St Thomas Wlk. Iver SL3 69 E4
Salamanca. Finch RG45 142 C3
Salcombe Dr. Read RG6 87 D2
Salcombe Rd. Ashf TW15 97 F3
Salcombe Rd. Newb RG14 104 C1
Salcombe Rd. Read RG2 86 B2
Sale Garden Cotts. Woki RG40 116 B3
Saleby Cl. Winn RG6 87 F1
Salford Cl. Read RG2 113 E4
Salisbury Ave. Slough SL2 42 B4
Salisbury Cl. Woki RG41 116 A1
Salisbury Rd. Harm TW6 71 E1
Salisbury Rd. Hung RG17 100 B2
Salisbury Rd. Read RG30 85 F4
Salisbury Rd. Sand GU17 150 B3
Salmon Cl. Shin RG7 113 D1
Salmond Rd. Read RG2 113 E3
Salt Hill Ave. Slough SL1 42 B3
Salt Hill Dr. Slough SL1 42 B3
Salt Hill Way. Slough SL1 42 B3
Salters Rd. Maid SL6 40 A4
Saltersgate Cl. Winn RG6 87 E1
Salwey Cl. Brac RG12 118 A2
Samarkand Cl. Camb GU15 152 A2
Samian Pl. Binf RG42 90 C1
Sampage Cl. Read RG2 113 E3
Sampson Pk. Brac RG42 117 E4
Sampsons Gn. Slough SL2 21 F1
Sanctuary Cl. Read RG30 84 C4
Sanctuary Rd. Stan TW6 71 D1
Sandcroft Rd. Caver RG4 58 C3
Sandells Ave. Ashf TW15 98 B2
Sanden Cl. Hung RG17 100 B3
Sandford Down. Brac RG12 118 C2
Sandford Dr. Wood RG5 60 C1
Sandford La. Hurst RG10 88 B3
Sandgate Ave. Read RG30 57 F1
Sandhills Ct. Vir W GU25 122 C2
Sandhills La. Vir W GU25 122 C2
Sandhills Way. Read RG31 84 C2
Sandhurst La. Black GU17 150 A3
Sandhurst Rd. Brac RG40 142 A4
Sandhurst Rd. Crow RG45 143 D2
Sandhurst Rd. Yate GU17 149 F4
Sandisplatt Rd. Maid SL6 39 D3
Sandleford Cl. Read RG2 113 E3
Sandleford Rise. Newb RG14 131 D4
Sandlers End. Slough SL2 22 A1
Sandown Ave. Read RG31 84 A2
Sandown Cl. Black GU17 150 B3
Sandown Dr. Camb GU16 151 F1
Sandown Rd. Slough SL2 41 F4
Sandown Way. Newb RG14 105 E1
Sandpit Hill. Newb RG14 &
RG20 130 B2
Sandpit La. Swal RG7 140 A3
Sandringham Ct. Slough SL1 41 E4
Sandringham Dr. Ashf TW15 97 E2
Sandringham Rd. Maid SL6 19 F1
Sandringham Rd. Stan TW6 70 C1
Sandringham Way. Read RG31 84 A2
Sands Farm Dr. Burn SL1 21 E1
Sandstone Cl. Winn RG41 88 B1
Sandy Cl. Herm RG18 79 D2
Sandy Dr. Felt TW14 98 C4
Sandy La. Brac RG12 118 B4
Sandy La. Camb GU15 151 F3
Sandy La. Herm RG18 78 C2
Sandy La. Sand GU17 143 D1
Sandy La. Sunn SL5 121 D2
Sandy La. Vir W GU25 122 C3
Sandy La. Woki RG41 115 E2
Sandy Mead. Holy SL6 40 B1
Sandy Way. Shepp TW17 125 F1
Sandygate Cl. Mar SL7 1 B2
Sandygate Rd. Mar SL7 1 B2
Sapgood Cl. That RG19 106 C1
Sapphire Cl. Woki RG41 115 F4
Sarsby Dr. Wray TW19 96 A3
Sarum. Brac RG12 117 F1
Sarum Cres. Woki RG40 116 B4
Sarum Rd. Tad RG26 135 D1
Sarum Way. Hung RG17 100 B2
Saturn Cl. Woki RG41 115 F3
Saunders Cl. Twyf RG10 61 F2
Saunders Ct. Purl RG8 57 D3
Saunton Ave. Harl UB7 71 F4
Savernake Cl. Read RG30 84 C4
Savernake Way. Brac RG12 118 C2
Savill Way. Mar SL7 1 C1
Saville Cres. Ashf TW15 98 B1
Saville Gdns. Camb GU15 152 A3
Savory Wlk. Binf RG42 90 B1
Savoy Gr. Black GU17 150 B2
Sawmill Rd. Herm RG18 79 D2
Sawpit Rd. Hurst RG10 88 C4
Sawtry Cl. Winn RG6 87 F1
Sawyers Cl. Whi Wa SL6 39 D1
Sawyers Cl. Wind SL4 66 C4
Sawyers Cres. Whi Wa SL6 39 D1
Saxe Cl. Bur C RG7 111 D2
Saxon Cl. Slough SL3 43 F2
Saxon Gdns. Tapl SL6 20 B1
Saxon Rd. Ashf TW15 98 B1
Saxon Way. Harm UB7 70 B4
Saxon Way. Old W SL4 68 A1
Sayers Cl. Gree RG14 131 D4
Scafell Cl. Read RG31 57 E1
Scafell Rd. Slough SL2 41 F4
Scampton Rd. Stan TW6 70 C1
Scania Wlk. Burl RG42 92 A1
Scarborough Rd. Stan TW6 71 E1
Scarborough Way. Slough SL1 42 A2
Scarletts La. Warg RG10 37 E1
Scholars Cl. Caver RG4 58 C2
Scholars Cl. Gr She RG17 48 A2
Scholars Cl. Gr She RG17 48 A2
School Gn. Shin RG2 113 F2
School Hill. Crow RG45 143 E2
School Hill. Sand GU17 143 D1
School Hill. Warg RG10 36 B1
School La. Bags GU19 145 F1
School La. Bish SL6 38 A2
School La. Box RG20 76 C2
School La. Bur C RG7 111 D1
School La. Caver RG4 59 D1
School La. Caver RG4 59 D3
School La. Cook SL6 19 D4
School La. Cook SL6 20 A4
School La. East G RG17 47 E3
School La. Eng G TW20 96 A2
School La. Frox SN8 99 D1
School La. Lit M SL7 2 B3
School La. Maid SL6 19 F1
School La. Medm SL7 17 D3
School La. Shepp TW17 125 D2
School La. Sto P SL2 23 D2
School La. W St L RG10 62 C2
School La. Warg RG10 36 B1
School La. Windl GU20 146 B2
School La. Yate GU17 149 D3
School Rd. Ascot SL5 120 B2
School Rd. Ashf TW15 98 A1
School Rd. Bark RG41 114 C1
School Rd. Bis GU24 153 F2
School Rd. Bur C RG30 111 E3
School Rd. Chiev RG20 78 A4
School Rd. Comp RG20 31 F2
School Rd. Harm UB7 70 B4
School Rd. Hurst RG10 88 C4
School Rd. Padw RG7 109 F1
School Rd. Read RG2 114 C1
School Rd. Read RG31 84 B4

180

School Rd. Swal

Sparvell Way. Camb

School Rd. Swal	RG7	139	F2
School Rd. Windl	GU20	146	A3
School Rd. Woki	RG40	116	B3
School Rd. Woo G	HP10	3	F3
School Terr. Read	RG1	86	C4
Schroder Ct. Eng G	TW20	95	D2
Scotland Hill. Sand	GU17	143	D1
Scotlands Dr. Far C	SL2	22	A3
Scots Cl. Stan	TW19	97	E4
Scots Dr. Woki	RG41	115	F4
Scott Cl. Caver	RG4	59	D3
Scott Cl. Far C	SL2	22	B4
Scott Cl. Wood	RG5	88	A4
Scott Terr. Brac	RG12	118	C4
Scottalls La. Hamp N	RG18	52	C3
Scotts Ave. Ashf	TW16	98	C1
Scotts Way. Ashf	TW16	98	C1
Scours La. Read	RG30	58	A1
Scratchface La. Brad	RG7	81	F3
Scrivens Mead. That	RG19	106	C2
Scylla Cres. Felt	TW14	98	A4
Scylla Rd. Felt	TW6	71	D1
Seacourt Rd. Slough	SL3	44	A1
Seaford Gdns. Wood	RG5	87	F3
Seaford Rd. Stan	TW19	70	B1
Seaford Rd. Woki	RG40	116	B3
Sealand Rd. Stan	TW6	71	D1
Searles Farm La. Bur C	RG30	85	D1
Seaton Dr. Ashf	TW15	97	F3
Seaton Gdns. Read	RG2	86	B1
Seaton Rd. Camb	GU15	151	D3
Second Cres. Slough	SL1	42	B4
Second St E. Newt	RG19	132	A3
Second St W. Gree	RG19	131	F3
Second St W. Newt	RG19	132	A2
Sedgefield Rd. Newb	RG14	131	E4
Sedgmoor Gdns. Fla H	HP10	3	D4
Sedgmoor La. Fla H	HP10	3	D4
Sedgmoor Rd. Fla H	HP10	3	D4
Seebys Oak. Sand	GU15	150	B3
Sefton Cl. Sto P	SL2	22	C2
Sefton Cl. West E	GU24	153	F3
Sefton Paddock. Sto P	SL2	23	D3
Segsbury Gr. Brac	RG12	118	C3
Selborne Gdns. Read	RG30	58	A1
Selbourne Cl. Black	GU17	150	B3
Selby Rd. Ashf	TW15	98	B1
Selcourt Cl. Wood	RG5	87	E4
Sellafield Way. Read	RG6	87	E1
Selsdon Ave. Wood	RG5	87	F4
Selsey Way. Read	RG6	114	A4
Selwood Cl. Stan	TW19	70	B1
Selwood Gdns. Stan	TW19	70	B1
Selwyn Dr. Yate	GU17	149	D3
Send Rd. Caver	RG4	59	E1
Setley Way. Brac	RG12	119	D3
Seton Dr. Read	RG31	84	C3
Sett The. Yate	GU17	149	D3
Sevenoaks Rd. Read	RG6	87	D2
Seventh St. Gree	RG19	131	F3
Severn Cl. Sand	GU17	150	B4
Severn Cl. That	RG18	106	A3
Severn Cres. Slough	SL3	69	D4
Severn Way. Read	RG30	84	C3
Sewell Ave. Woki	RG41	116	A4
Sewell Cl. Cold A	RG18	79	D1
Seymour Ave. Shin	RG2	113	F3
Seymour Cl. Maid	SL6	39	D2
Seymour Court Rd. Mar	SL7	1	B2
Seymour Court Rd. Mar B	SL7	1	B2
Seymour Ct La. Mar B	SL7	1	A3
Seymour Park Rd. Mar	SL7	1	B2
Seymour Plain. Mar	SL7	1	B3
Seymour Plain. Mar B	SL7	1	B3
Seymour Rd. Slough	SL1	42	B2
Seymour Way. Ashf	TW16	98	C1
Shackleton Rd. Slough	SL1	42	C3
Shackleton Way. Wood	RG5	88	A4
Shaftesbury Cres. Stai	TW18	97	E1
Shaftesbury Mount. Black	GU17	150	B2
Shaftesbury Rd. Bis	GU24	153	F2
Shaftesbury Rd. Read	RG30	85	D4
Shaftsbury Cl. Brac	RG12	118	B2
Shaggy Calf La. Slough	SL2	43	D3
Shakespeare Cl. Caver	RG4	59	E3
Shakespeare Rd. That	RG18	106	B2
Shakespeare Way. Brac	RG42	118	C4
Shalbourne Cl. Hung	RG17	100	A3
Shalbourne Rise. Camb	GU15	151	E3
Sharney Ave. Slough	SL3	44	A2
Sharnwood Dr. Read	RG31	84	C3
Sharpethorpe Cl. Read	RG6	87	D1
Shaw Farm Rd. Newb	RG14	105	D3
Shaw Hill. Newb	RG14	105	D3
Shaw Pk. Crow	RG45	143	D2
Shaw Rd. Newb	RG14	105	D2
Shaw Rd. Read	RG1	85	F3
Shaw The. Cook	SL6	19	F3
Sheehy Way. Slough	SL2	43	D3
Sheep Leaze La. Pease	RG20	29	E1
Sheep Wlk. Caver	RG4	59	D2
Sheepcote La. Bou E	HP10	3	F1
Sheepcote La. Holy	SL6	64	B2
Sheepcote Rd. Eton	SL4	42	A1
Sheepcote Rd. Wind	SL4	66	C3
Sheepdrove Rd. Lamb	RG17	25	E2
Sheephouse Rd. Maid	SL6	20	A1
Sheephouse Way. Chadd	RG20	49	D3
Sheepridge La. Bou E	SL7	2	C4
Sheepridge La. Fla H	SL7	2	C4
Sheepwalk. Shepp	TW17	124	C2
Sheepwalk. Stai	TW17	124	C2
Sheepwash. Newt	RG20	131	D1
Sheepways La. Maple	RG4	58	A4
Sheerlands Rd. Arbo	RG2	140	C4
Sheerlands Rd. Bark	RG2	140	C4
Sheet St. Wind	SL4	67	E3
Sheet Street Rd. Old W	SL4	94	A4
Sheet Street Rd. Wind	SL4	67	E1
Sheffield Rd. Harm	TW6	71	E1
Sheffield Way. Harm	TW6	71	E1
Shefford Cres. Woki	RG40	116	B4
Sheldon Gdns. Read	RG2	86	B1
Shelgate Wlk. Wood	RG5	87	E4
Shelley Ave. Brac	RG12	118	C4
Shelley Cl. Medm	SL7	17	E4
Shelley Cl. Slough	SL3	43	F1
Shelley Cl. Wood	RG5	87	F2
Shelley Ct. Camb	GU15	151	E3
Shelley Rd. Mar	SL7	1	C2
Shelley Rd. That	RG18	106	B2
Shelley Walk. Yate	GU17	149	D3
Shelson Ave. Felt	TW13	98	C2
Shelton Ct. Slough	SL3	43	E2
Shenstone Cl. Woki	RG40	142	A4
Shenstone Dr. Burn	SL1	21	E1
Shenstone Pk. Ascot	SL5	120	C3
Shenstone Rd. Read	RG2	86	A2
Shephards La. Brac	RG42	91	D1
Shepherds Ave. Read	RG6	87	D4
Shepherds Chase. Bags	GU19	145	F1
Shepherds Cl. Hurl	SL6	17	F2
Shepherds Cl. Shepp	TW17	125	D2
Shepherds Hill. Brac	RG12	118	B4
Shepherds Hill. Comp	RG20	31	F2
Shepherds Hill. Wood	RG6	87	E4
Shepherds House La. Read	RG6	87	D4
Shepherds La. Caver	RG4	58	B3
Shepherds La. Hurl	SL6	17	F2
Shepherds Mount. Comp	RG20	31	F2
Shepherds Rise. Comp	RG20	31	F2
Shepherds Way. Crow	RG45	142	C2
Shepherds Wlk. Wood	RG6	87	E4
Shepley Dr. Read	RG30	85	E2
Shepley Dr. Went	SL5	121	E2
Shepley End. Went	SL5	121	E2
Shepperton Court Dr. Shepp	TW17	125	D2
Shepperton Rd. Stai	TW18	124	B3
Sheraton Cl. Black	GU17	150	C2
Sheraton Dr. Read	RG31	57	E1
Sherborne Cl. Stan	SL3	69	F3
Sherborne Rd. Felt	TW14	98	B4
Sherbourne Dr. Went	SL5	121	E2
Sherbourne Dr. Wind	SL4	66	C2
Sherbourne Dr. Wood	RG5	87	F4
Sherbourne Wlk. Far C	SL2	22	B4
Sherfield Cl. Read	RG2	86	B2
Sherfield Dr. Read	RG2	86	B2
Shergold Way. Cook	SL6	19	F3
Sheridan Ave. Caver	RG4	59	D2
Sheridan Cres. Tad	RG26	134	C1
Sheridan Way. Woki	RG41	115	F3
Sherman Rd. Read	RG1	86	A3
Sherman Rd. Slough	SL1	42	C4
Sherrardmead. Newb	RG14	105	D3
Sherring Cl. Brac	RG42	91	E1
Sherwood Cl. Brac	RG12	119	D4
Sherwood Cl. Slough	SL3	43	F2
Sherwood Dr. Maid	SL6	39	D3
Sherwood Gdns. Hen-O-T	RG9	35	E4
Sherwood Pl. Purl	RG8	57	D2
Sherwood Rd. Winn	RG41	88	B1
Sherwood Rise. Pur O T	RG8	57	D3
Sherwood St. Read	RG30	85	E4
Shield Rd. Felt	TW15	98	B2
Shifford Cres. Maid	SL6	19	F2
Shildon Cl. Camb	GU15	152	B2
Shinfield Rd. Read	RG2	86	C2
Shinfield Rise. Read	RG2	86	C1
Shipley Cl. Wood	RG5	61	D1
Shipton Cl. Read	RG31	57	E1
Shire Cl. Bags	GU19	145	F1
Shire's Head Cl. Read	RG30	85	E3
Shires The. Woki	RG41	115	F2
Shires Way. Yate	GU17	149	E4
Shirley Ave. Read	RG2	113	E4
Shirley Ave. Wind	SL4	66	C3
Shirley Rd. Maid	SL6	39	E3
Shooters Hill. Pangb	RG8	56	A3
Shop La. Leckh	RG20	49	F3
Shop La. Newb	RG20	104	C3
Shoppenhangers Rd. Maid	SL6	39	F2
Shoreham Rd (E). Stan	TW6	70	C1
Shoreham Rd (W). Stan	TW6	70	C1
Shoreham Rise. Burn	SL2	21	E1
Short La. Stan	TW19	97	F4
Short Rd. Stan	TW6	70	C1
Short St. Caver	RG4	59	D1
Short St. Pangb	RG8	56	B3
Short St. Read	RG1	86	A3
Short The. Pur O T	RG8	57	E3
Shortfern. Slough	SL2	43	E4
Shortheath La. Sulhd	RG7	110	C2
Shortland. Harl	UB7	71	E4
Shortlands Hill. Moul	OX10	13	E2
Shortwood Ave. Ashf	TW18	97	D2
Shrewsbury Rd. Harm	TW6	71	E1
Shrivenham Cl. Sand	GU15	150	B4
Shrubbs Hill La. Went	SL5	121	E2
Shrubland Dr. Read	RG30	85	D2
Shrublands Dr. Light	GU18	153	D4
Shute End. Woki	RG40	116	A3
Shyshack La. Tad	RG26	134	C1
Sibley Park Rd. Read	RG6	87	D1
Sibson. Read	RG6	87	E1
Sidbury Cl. Sunn	SL5	121	D2
Sidestrand Rd. Newb	RG14	130	C4
Sidmouth Grange Cl. Read	RG6	87	D4
Sidmouth Grange Rd. Read	RG6	87	D4
Sidmouth St. Read	RG1	86	B4
Sidney Rd. Stai	TW18	97	D2
Sidney Rd. Wind	SL4	66	B2
Silbury Cl. Bur C	RG31	84	A2
Silchester Rd. Read	RG30	85	E2
Silchester Rd. Tad	RG26	135	E1
Silco Dr. Maid	SL6	39	F3
Silver Birches. Woki	RG41	115	E2
Silver Cl. Maid	SL6	39	D3
Silver Dr. Camb	GU16	152	B2
Silver Fox Cres. Wood	RG5	87	E3
Silver Hill. Sand	GU15	150	C4
Silver La. Padw	RG7	136	A4
Silver St. Read	RG1	86	A3
Silverdale Rd. Read	RG6	87	E2
Silverdale Rd. Tad	RG26	135	D1
Silverdale Rd. Warg	RG10	36	C1
Silverglades. Yate	GU17	149	E2
Silverthorne Dr. Caver	RG4	58	C3
Silvertrees Dr. Maid	SL6	39	D3
Silverwood Dr. Camb	GU15	152	A4
Silwood. Brac	RG12	117	F1
Silwood Cl. Ascot	SL5	120	B4
Silwood Rd. Sunn	SL5	120	C3
Simkins Cl. Burl	RG42	92	A1
Simmonds Cl. Brac	RG42	117	F4
Simmonds St. Read	RG1	86	A4
Simmons Cl. Slough	SL3	44	A1
Simmons Field. That	RG18	106	C2
Simmons Pl. Stai	TW18	96	C2
Simmons Rd. Hen-O-T	RG9	15	E2
Simms Farm La. Silc	RG7	136	C2
Simons Cl. Pur O T	RG31	57	E2
Simons La. Woki	RG41	115	E4
Simons Wlk. Eng G	TW20	95	E1
Simpson Cl. Maid	SL6	40	A4
Sindlesham Rd. Arbo	RG2	114	C2
Singer La. Hen-O-T	RG9	15	F1
Singers Cl. Hen-O-T	RG9	35	F4
Sinhurst Rd. Camb	GU15	151	D2
Sipson Cl. Harm	UB7	71	D4
Sipson La. Harl	UB7	71	D4
Sipson Rd. Harm	UB7	71	D4
Sipson Way. Harm	UB7	71	D4
Sirius Cl. Woki	RG41	115	F3
Six Acre La. Ham	RG17	126	A3
Sixth St. Gree	RG19	131	F3
Skeffling Cl. Winn	RG6	87	F1
Skelmerdale Way. Winn	RG6	87	F2
Skerrit Way. Read	RG8	57	E2
Skillman Dr. That	RG19	106	C2
Skilton Rd. Read	RG31	57	E2
Skimpedhill La. Brac	RG12	118	A4
Skinners Green La. Ham M	RG14	130	A4
Skippons Cl. Newb	RG14	130	B3
Skydmore Path. Slough	SL2	21	F1
Skye Cl. Read	RG31	84	C2
Skyes Dr. Stai	TW18	97	D2
Skylings. Newb	RG14	105	E2
Skyport Dr. Harm	UB7	70	B4
Slade Hill Gdns. Ball H	RG20	129	F1
Slaidburn Gn. Brac	RG12	118	C1
Slanting Hill. Herm	RG18	79	D3
Sledmere Ct. Felt	TW14	98	C4
Slim Rd. Camb	GU15	151	D3
Sloan Ct. Gori	RG8	34	B3
Slopes The. Caver	RG4	59	E1
Slough Rd. Datch	SL3	68	A4
Slough Rd. Eton	SL4	42	C1
Slough Rd. Slough	SL3	42	C1
Smallmead Rd. Bur C	RG2	85	E1
Smallmead Rd. Read	RG2	86	A1
Smallridge. Newb	RG14	130	B2
Smith Sq. Brac	RG12	118	B4
Smitham Bridge Rd. Hung	RG17	100	B3
Smithfield Cl. Whi Wa	SL6	39	D2
Smithfield Rd. Maid	SL6	39	D2
Smiths Hill. Let B	OX12	6	C3
Smiths La. Wind	SL4	66	C3
Smithys Gn. Windl	GU20	146	B2
Snape Spur. Slough	SL1	42	C4
Snipe La. Newt	RG20	131	F1
Snowball Hill. Whi Wa	SL6	64	A4
Snowberry Cl. Woki	RG41	115	F3
Snowden Cl. Wind	SL4	66	B2
Snowden Dr. Read	RG31	84	A3
Snowdon Cl. That	RG19	106	B1
Snowdon Rd. Harm	TW6	71	E1
Snowdon Rd W. Harm	TW6	71	E1
Snowdrop Copse. That	RG18	106	C2
Snowdrop Gr. Winn	RG41	88	B2
Snows Paddock. Windl	GU20	146	A4
Snows Ride. Windl	GU20	146	A3
Soham Cl. Winn	RG6	114	B4
Soho Cres. Bou E	HP10	3	E2
Soke Rd. Alde	RG7	135	F2
Soke Rd. Silc	RG7	135	F2
Soldiers Rise. Brac	RG40	142	B4
Solent Rd. Stan	TW6	70	C1
Somerford Cl. Maid	SL6	40	A4
Somersby Cres. Maid	SL6	39	F2
Somerset Cl. Hung	RG17	100	B3
Somerset Cl. Woki	RG41	115	E3
Somerset Way. Iver	SL0	44	C2
Somerset Wlk. Read	RG31	84	A3
Somerton Gdns. Read	RG6	87	D1
Somerton Gr. That	RG19	106	B1
Somerville Cres. Yate	GU17	149	F3
Somerville Gr. Woki	RG41	115	E2
Somerville Rd. Eton	SL4	42	B1
Sonning La. Sonn	RG4	60	B1
Sonning Meadows. Sonn	RG4	60	B1
Sonninge Cl. Sand	GU15	150	B4
Sopwith Cl. Wood	RG5	88	A4
Sorrel Cl. Bur C	RG7	111	D2
Sorrel Cl. Newb	RG14	105	E3
Sorrel Cl. Woki	RG40	116	C4
Sorrel Dr. Light	GU18	152	C4
Sospel Ct. Far C	SL2	22	B2
South Ave. Hen-O-T	RG9	35	F4
South Ave. Stai	TW20	96	B1
South Cl. Medm	SL7	17	E4
South Cl. Slough	SL1	41	E3
South Cl. Woki	RG40	116	B2
South Dr. Read	RG2	86	C1
South Dr. Sonn	RG4	60	B1
South Dr. Sulhd	RG7	110	B4
South Dr. Went	GU25	122	A1
South Dr. Woki	RG40	116	B3
South End Rd. Brad	RG7	82	A1
South Field Cl. Dorn	SL4	41	E2
South Gate Ave. Felt	TW13	98	B2
South Gn. Slough	SL1	42	C3
South Gr. Chert	KT16	123	F2
South Hill Rd. Brac	RG12	118	A2
South Lake Cres. Wood	RG5	87	F3
South Lynn Cres. Brac	RG12	118	A2
South Meadow. Crow	RG45	143	E2
South Meadow La. Eton	SL4	67	E4
South Path. Wind	SL4	67	E3
South Pl. Mar	SL7	1	C1
South Rd. Bis	GU24	153	F2
South Rd. Crow	RG45	143	F2
South Rd. Eng G	TW20	95	E1
South Rd. Maid	SL6	39	F3
South Row. Chil	OX11	10	B4
South St. Blew	OX11	12	A4
South St. Caver	RG4	59	D1
South St. Read	RG1	86	B4
South St. Stai	TW18	96	C2
South View Ave. Caver	RG4	59	E1
South View. Hung	RG17	100	B3
South View Pk. Caver	RG4	59	E1
Southampton Cl. Black	GU17	150	B3
Southampton Rd. Stan	TW6	70	C1
Southampton St. Read	RG1	86	A3
Southampton Way. Stan	TW6	70	C1
Southbourne Dr. Bou E	SL8	3	D2
Southbury La. Twyf	RG10	61	F3
Southcote Ave. Felt	TW13	98	C3
Southcote Dr. Camb	GU15	152	A3
Southcote Farm La. Read	RG30	85	E2
Southcote La. Read	RG30	85	E2
Southcote Rd. Read	RG30	85	E3
Southcroft. Eng G	TW20	95	D2
Southcroft. Slough	SL2	22	A1
Southdown Rd. Caver	RG4	59	D3
Southdown Rd. Tad	RG26	135	D1
Southdown Rd. That	RG19	105	F2
Southend. That	RG18	106	B3
Southern Hill. Read	RG1	86	B3
Southern Perimeter Rd. Harm	TW6	71	E1
Southern Perimeter Rd. Stan	TW6	70	B1
Southern Rd. Camb	GU15	151	E3
Southerndene Cl. Read	RG31	57	E1
Southfield Gdns. Burn	SL1	41	D4
Southfields Ave. Ashf	TW15	98	A1
Southlands Cl. Woki	RG40	116	B3
Southlands Rd. Woki	RG40	116	B2
Southlea Rd. Datch	SL3	68	A3
Southside. Chert	KT16	124	A3
Southview Cl. Twyf	RG10	61	F3
Southview Rd. Mar	SL7	1	C2
Southville Cl. Felt	TW14	98	C4
Southville Cres. Felt	TW14	98	C4
Southville Rd. Felt	TW14	98	C4
Southwark Cl. Yate	GU17	149	E3
Southway. Camb	GU15	151	D2
Southwell Park Rd. Camb	GU15	151	E3
Southwick. Bags	GU19	145	F1
Southwick Ct. Brac	RG12	118	C2
Southwold. Brac	RG12	117	F1
Southwold Cl. Winn	RG6	87	E1
Southwold Spur. Slough	SL3	44	B2
Southwood Gdns. Bur C	RG7	111	D2
Southwood Gdns. Cook	SL6	19	F3
Southwood Rd. Cook	SL6	19	F3
Southwood. Woki	RG40	116	B2
Sovereign Way. Read	RG31	84	B3
Sovreign Dr. Camb	GU15	152	B4
Spackman Cl. That	RG19	106	B1
Spackmans Way. Slough	SL1	42	B2
Spade Oak Meadows. Bou E	SL8	2	C2
Span Hill. Caver	RG4	60	B4
Sparrow Cl. Woki	RG41	115	F3
Sparrowbill. Brig	RG20	28	C1
Sparvell Way. Camb	GU15	151	E3

181

Speedwell Way. That

Sunley Cl. Newb

Speedwell Way. That RG18 106 C2
Speen Hill Cl. Newb RG14 104 C2
Speen La. Newb RG14 104 B2
Speen Lodge Ct. Newb RG14 104 C2
Speen Pl. Newb RG14 104 C2
Spelthorne Gr. Stai TW16 98 C1
Spelthorne La. Stai TW17 125 E4
Spencer Cl. Silc RG26 135 F1
Spencer Cl. Woki RG41 115 E3
Spencer Gdns. Eng G TW20 95 E2
Spencer Rd. Brac RG42 117 F4
Spencer Rd. Newb RG14 130 B3
Spencer Rd. Read RG2 113 D4
Spencer Rd. Slough SL3 43 F2
Spencers Cl. Maid SL6 39 E4
Spencers La. Cook SL6 19 F3
Spencers Rd. Maid SL6 39 E4
Spenwood Cl. Shin RG7 113 D1
Sperling Rd. Maid SL6 19 F1
Spey Rd. Read RG30 85 D4
Spinfield La. Mar SL7 1 A1
Spinfield La W. Mar SL7 1 B1
Spinfield Mount. Mar SL7 1 A1
Spinfield Pk. Mar SL7 1 B1
Spinis. Brac RG12 117 F1
Spinner Gn. Brac RG12 118 A2
Spinners Wlk. Mar SL7 1 B1
Spinners Wlk. Wind SL4 67 E3
Spinney Cl. Caver RG4 59 D4
Spinney Dr. Felt TW14 98 B4
Spinney. Slough SL1 42 A3
Spinney The. Camb GU15 152 B3
Spinney The. Read RG31 84 C2
Spinney The. Sunn SL5 120 C2
Spinney The. Woki RG40 141 F4
Spinney The. Yate GU17 149 E4
Spinningwheel La. Binf RG42 90 B4
Spitfire Way. Wood RG5 88 A4
Spittal St. Mar SL7 1 B1
Spode Cl. Read RG30 84 C4
Spout La N. Stan TW19 70 A2
Spout La. Stan TW19 70 A2
Spray La. Brig RG20 28 B1
Spray Rd. Ham SN8 126 C2
Spray Rd. Ink RG17 127 D2
Spriggs Cl. That RG19 106 B1
Spring Ave. Eng G TW20 95 F1
Spring Cl. Maid SL6 19 F1
Spring Cl. Pangb RG8 55 E3
Spring Gdns. Ascot SL5 120 A3
Spring Gdns. Bou E SL8 3 D2
Spring Gdns. Burl SL5 92 C1
Spring Gdns. Camb GU15 152 A3
Spring Gdns. Mar SL7 1 C2
Spring Gdns. Shin RG7 113 D1
Spring Gdns. Woo G HP10 3 F4
Spring Gr. Read RG1 86 A3
Spring Hill. Maid SL6 39 F2
Spring La. Alde RG7 135 E4
Spring La. Ast T OX11 12 C4
Spring La. Caver RG4 60 A3
Spring La. Cold A RG18 106 B4
Spring La. Cook SL6 19 E3
Spring La. Far C SL2 22 B3
Spring La. Mort RG7 137 D3
Spring La. Slough SL1 41 F3
Spring La. Swal RG7 139 D2
Spring Meadow. Brac RG12 118 B4
Spring Meadows. Gr She RG17 48 A2
Spring Rd. Felt TW13 98 C3
Spring Rise. Eng G TW20 95 F1
Spring Wlk. Warg RG10 36 B1
Spring Wood La. Bur C RG7 111 D1
Spring Woods. Sand GU17 143 E1
Spring Woods. Vir W GU25 122 A3
Springate Field. Slough SL3 43 F2
Springcross Ave. Black GU17 150 B2
Springdale. Read RG6 87 D1
Springdale. Woki RG40 141 F4
Springfield Cl. Chert KT16 124 A1
Springfield Cl. Wind SL4 67 D3
Springfield End. Gori RG8 34 B4
Springfield Gr. Shepp TW16 125 F4
Springfield La. Newb RG14 131 D4
Springfield. Light GU18 153 E4
Springfield Pk. Holy SL6 40 B1
Springfield Pk. Twyf RG10 61 F2
Springfield Rd. Ashf TW15 97 F2
Springfield Rd. Binf RG12 117 E4
Springfield Rd. Camb GU15 152 A3
Springfield Rd. Silc RG26 135 F1
Springfield Rd. Slough SL3 69 D4
Springfield Rd. Wind SL4 67 D3
Springhill Rd. Gori RG8 34 B4
Spruce Dr. Light GU18 153 D4
Spruce Rd. Wood RG5 88 A3
Spur The. Slough SL1 41 E4
Spur The. Warg RG10 36 C2
Spurcroft Rd. That RG19 106 C1
Square The. Bags GU19 145 F2
Square The. Harm UB7 70 A3
Square The. Pangb RG8 56 B3
Square The. Shin RG7 113 D1
Squires Bridge Rd. Stai TW17 124 C3
Squires Rd. Stai TW17 125 D3
Squires Wlk. Ashf TW15 98 B1
Squirrel Cl. Sand GU17 150 A4
Squirrel Rise. Mar B SL7 1 B3
Squirrels Drey. Crow RG45 142 C3
Squirrels Way. Read RG6 87 D1
Stable Cl. Bur C RG7 111 D2
Stable Croft. Bags GU19 145 E1
Stable Ct. Newb RG14 105 D3
Stable View. Yate GU17 149 E4
Stables Ct. Mar SL7 1 A1
Stacey's Ind Est. Tad RG26 135 E1
Staddlestone Cl. Read RG31 57 E1
Stadium Way. Read RG30 58 A1
Staff College Rd. Camb GU15 151 D3
Staff College Rd. Sand GU15 151 D3
Stafferton Way. Maid SL6 40 A3
Stafford Ave. Slough SL2 22 B1
Stafford Cl. Burn SL6 41 D4
Stafford Cl. Wood RG5 87 F4
Stafford Lake. Bis GU24 153 F1
Staffordshire Cl. Read RG30 84 C4
Staffordshire Croft. New G RG42 91 F1
Stag Hill. Chil F RG17 73 D1
Stainash Cres. Stai TW18 97 D2
Staines By-Pass. Stai TW18 97 E2
Staines La. Chert KT16 124 A2
Staines Lane Cl. Chert KT16 123 F2
Staines Rd. Felt TW14 98 B4
Staines Rd. Stai TW18 & KT16 123 F2
Staines Rd W. Ashf TW15 98 B1
Staines Rd. Wray TW19 95 F4
Stainford Cl. Ashf TW15 98 B2
Stamford Ave. Camb GU16 151 F1
Stamford Rd. Maid SL6 39 E3
Stanbrook Cl. Brad RG7 82 A1
Stanfield. Tad RG26 135 D1
Stanham Rd. Read RG30 84 C4
Stanhope Heath. Stan TW19 70 B1
Stanhope Rd. Read RG2 86 B2
Stanhope Rd. Sand GU15 150 C2
Stanhope Rd. Slough SL1 41 E4
Stanhope Way. Stan TW19 70 B1
Stanlake La. Twyf RG10 61 F2
Stanley Cl. Mar SL7 1 C2
Stanley Cotts. Slough SL2 42 C3
Stanley Gr. Read RG1 85 F4
Stanley Green E. Slough SL3 43 F1
Stanley Green W. Slough SL3 43 F1
Stanley Rd. Ashf TW15 97 F2
Stanley Rd. Newb RG14 105 D1
Stanley Rd. Woki RG40 116 C3
Stanley St. Read RG1 85 F4
Stanmore Cl. Ascot SL5 120 A3
Stanmore Gdns. Mort RG7 136 C3
Stanmore Rd. Beed RG20 30 B1
Stanmore Rd. East I RG20 30 C4
Stanshawe Rd. Read RG1 86 A4
Stanstead Rd. Stan TW6 70 C1
Stanton Cl. Read RG6 87 E2
Stanton Way. Slough SL3 43 F1
Stanwell Cl. Stan TW19 70 B1
Stanwell Gdns. Stan TW19 70 B1
Stanwell Moor Rd. Harm TW19 70 A2
Stanwell Moor Rd. Stan TW19 70 A2
Stanwell New Rd. Stai TW18 97 D3
Stanwell Rd. Ashf TW15 97 F2
Stanwell Rd. Felt TW14 98 A4
Stanwell Rd. Hort SL3 69 E2
Stanwell Rd. Stan SL3 69 E2
Stapleford Rd. Read RG30 85 E2
Staplehurst. Brac RG12 117 F1
Stapleton Cl. Mar SL7 1 C2
Stapleton Cl. Newb RG14 130 B3
Star La. Know H RG10 37 F2
Star La. Read RG1 86 A4
Star Post Rd. Camb GU15 151 F4
Star Rd. Caver RG4 59 E1
Starling Cl. Woki RG41 115 F3
Starlings Dr. Read RG31 84 A3
Starmead Dr. Woki RG40 116 C3
Starting Gates. Newb RG14 105 E1
Startins La. Cook SL6 19 E4
Starwood Ct. Slough SL3 43 E2
Statham Ct. Brac RG42 117 F4
Station App. Ashf TW15 97 F2
Station App. Mar SL7 1 C1
Station App. Read RG1 86 A4
Station App. Shepp TW17 125 E2
Station App. Stai TW18 97 D2
Station App. Vir W GU25 122 B3
Station Cres. Ashf TW15 97 F2
Station Hill. Ascot SL5 120 A3
Station Hill. Cook SL6 19 F4
Station Hill. Hamp N RG18 52 C3
Station Hill. Read RG1 86 A4
Station Par. Vir W GU25 122 B3
Station Rd. Ashf TW15 97 F2
Station Rd. Bags GU19 145 F2
Station Rd. Ball H RG20 130 A2
Station Rd. Bou E SL8 3 D2
Station Rd. Brac RG12 118 A4
Station Rd. Camb GU16 151 E1
Station Rd. Chert KT16 124 A1
Station Rd. Cook SL6 19 F4
Station Rd. East G RG17 47 E3
Station Rd. Eng G TW20 96 A2
Station Rd. Gori RG8 34 B3
Station Rd. Gr She RG17 48 A2
Station Rd. Hen-O-T RG9 15 F1
Station Rd. Hung RG17 100 B3
Station Rd. Kint RG17 102 A1
Station Rd. Lamb RG17 25 D1
Station Rd. Mar SL7 1 C1
Station Rd. Newb RG14 104 B3
Station Rd. Newb RG14 105 D1
Station Rd. Pangb RG8 56 B3
Station Rd. Read RG1 86 A4
Station Rd. Read RG6 87 E2
Station Rd. Shepp TW17 125 E2
Station Rd. Shipl RG9 36 A2
Station Rd. Slough SL1 41 F4
Station Rd. Slough SL3 44 A2
Station Rd. Sunn SL5 121 D2
Station Rd. Tapl SL6 40 C4
Station Rd. That RG19 106 C1
Station Rd. Thea RG7 83 F2
Station Rd. Twyf RG10 61 E2
Station Rd. Warg RG10 36 B1
Station Rd. Woki RG40 116 A3
Station Rd. Wool RG7 108 B1
Station Rd. Wray TW19 69 D1
Station Rise. Mar SL7 1 C1
Staunton Rd. Slough SL2 42 B4
Staveley Rd. Ashf TW15 98 B1
Staverton Cl. Brac RG42 91 D1
Staverton Cl. Woki RG40 116 C3
Staverton Rd. Read RG2 86 B2
Stayne End. Went GU25 122 A3
Steam Farm La. Harm TW14 71 F2
Steeple Wlk. Read RG6 113 F4
Steerforth Copse. Crow GU15 143 F1
Stepgates. Chert KT16 124 A1
Stephen Cl. Stai TW20 96 B1
Stephen Cl. Twyf RG10 61 F2
Stephen's Rd. Mort RG7 136 C3
Stephens Cl. Mort RG7 136 C3
Stephens Firs. Mort RG7 136 C3
Stephenson Cl. That RG18 106 B2
Stephenson Rd. Bark RG2 141 D4
Stephenson Rd. Wind SL4 67 D4
Sterling Way. Read RG30 58 A1
Stevens Hill. Yate GU17 149 F3
Stevenson Dr. Binf RG42 90 B2
Stewart Ave. Slough SL1 42 C4
Stewart Ave. Stai TW17 125 D3
Stewart Cl. Holy SL6 65 E3
Stewarts Dr. Far C SL2 22 A4
Stewarts Way. Mar B SL7 1 B4
Stile Rd. Slough SL3 43 E2
Stilton Cl. Winn RG6 87 F1
Stilwell Cl. Yate GU17 149 F3
Stirling Cl. Camb GU16 151 F1
Stirling Cl. Caver RG4 59 E3
Stirling Cl. Wind SL4 66 B3
Stirling Rd. Slough SL1 42 A4
Stirling Rd. Stan TW6 70 C1
Stirling Way. That RG18 106 B2
Stockbridge Way. Yate GU17 149 E2
Stockbury Cl. Read RG6 87 D1
Stockdales Rd. Eton SL4 41 F1
Stockton Rd. Read RG2 86 B1
Stockwells. Tapl SL6 20 B1
Stockwood Rise. Camb GU15 151 F3
Stoke Common Rd. Fulm SL3 23 D4
Stoke Common Rd. Sto P SL3 23 D4
Stoke Court Dr. Sto P SL2 22 C2
Stoke Gdns. Slough SL1 42 C3
Stoke Gn. Sto P SL2 23 D1
Stoke Park Ave. Far C SL2 22 A1
Stoke Poges La. Slough SL1 & SL2 42 C4
Stoke Rd. Slough SL2 42 C4
Stoke Wood. Sto P SL2 22 C4
Stokeford Cl. Brac RG12 118 C2
Stokes View. Pangb RG8 56 B3
Stokesay. Slough SL2 42 C3
Stokesley Rise. Woo G HP10 3 F4
Stomp Rd. Burn SL1 21 E1
Stomp Rd. Burn SL1 41 D4
Stomp Rd. Slough SL1 41 D4
Stompits Rd. Holy SL6 65 E4
Stone Cres. Felt TW14 98 C4
Stone House La. Cook SL6 2 B1
Stone St. Read RG30 58 A1
Stonea Cl. Winn RG6 114 B4
Stonebridge Field. Eton SL4 42 A1
Stonecroft Ave. Iver SL0 44 C4
Stonefield Pk. Maid SL6 39 E4
Stonegate. Camb GU15 152 B3
Stoneham Cl. Read RG30 85 D3
Stonehaven Dr. Wood RG5 88 A3
Stonehill Rd. Light GU18 146 A1
Stonehouse Rise. Camb GU16 151 F1
Stoneleigh Ct. Camb GU16 151 F1
Stoney Cl. Yate GU17 149 E2
Stoney La. Burn SL2 22 A2
Stoney La. Cold A RG18 105 E3
Stoney La. Newb RG14 105 E3
Stoney La. That RG19 106 C2
Stoney Meade. Slough SL1 42 A3
Stoney Rd. Brac RG42 118 A4
Stoney Ware. Bish SL7 18 C4
Stoney Ware Cl. Bish SL7 18 C4
Stoneyfield. Been RG7 109 D3
Stoneyland Ct. Eng G TW20 95 F2
Stoneylands Rd. Eng G TW20 95 F2
Stookes Way. Yate GU17 149 D2
Stour Cl. Read RG30 85 D4
Stour Cl. Slough SL1 42 A2
Stovell Rd. Wind SL4 67 D4
Stowe Rd. Slough SL1 41 F3
Strachey Cl. Tidm RG8 56 B1
Straight Bit. Fla H HP10 3 D4
Straight La. Lamb RG17 46 C3
Straight Mile The. Hurst RG10 & RG40 89 E3
Straight Mile The. W St L RG10 62 C1
Straight Rd. Old W SL4 68 A1
Strand La. Cook SL6 19 F3
Strand View Wlk. Cook SL6 19 F3
Strand Way. Wood RG6 87 E1
Stranraer Gdns. Slough SL1 42 C3
Stranraer Rd. Stan TW6 70 C1
Stratfield. Brac RG12 117 F1
Stratfield Rd. Slough SL1 43 D2
Stratford Cl. Slough SL2 21 E1
Stratford Dr. Bou E HP10 3 E2
Stratford Gdns. Maid SL6 39 E2
Stratford Rd. Harm TW6 71 E1
Stratford Way. Read RG31 84 A3
Strathcona Cl. Fla H HP10 3 E4
Strathcona Way. Fla H HP10 3 E4
Strathearn Ave. Harl UB7 71 F4
Stratheden Pl. Read RG1 85 F4
Strathmore Dr. Char RG10 61 D2
Strathy Cl. Read RG30 85 D4
Stratton Gdns. Read RG2 86 B1
Stratton Rd. Shepp TW16 125 F4
Strawberry Hill. New G RG42 91 F1
Strawberry Hill. Newb RG14 104 C2
Streatley and Goring Bridge. Gori RG8 34 A3
Streatley Hill. Stre RG8 33 F3
Street The. Alde RG7 135 D4
Street The. Brad RG7 83 D3
Street The. Mort RG7 137 E3
Street The. Moul OX10 14 A3
Street The. Sou S RG8 14 A2
Street The. Swal RG7 139 E4
Street The. Tidm RG8 56 B1
Street The. W St L RG10 63 D3
Streets Heath. West E GU24 153 F4
Stretton Cl. Brad RG7 82 A1
Strode St. Eng G TW20 96 A2
Strodes Cres. Stai TW18 97 E2
Stroller Cl. That RG19 105 F2
Stroma Ct. Slough SL1 41 E3
Strongrove Hill. Hung RG17 100 B3
Stroud Cl. Wind SL4 66 B2
Stroud Farm Rd. Holy SL6 65 D4
Stroud Way. Ashf TW15 98 A1
Stroude Rd. Vir W GU25 122 C3
Strouds Meadow. Cold A RG18 106 B4
Strouds The. Been RG7 108 C3
Stuart Cl. Caver RG4 59 D3
Stuart Cl. Wind SL4 66 C3
Stuart Rd. Newb RG14 130 B3
Stuart Way. Stai TW18 97 D1
Stuart Way. Vir W GU25 122 A3
Stuart Way. Wind SL4 66 C3
Stubbles La. Cook SL6 19 D3
Stubbs Folly. Sand GU15 150 B4
Studios Rd. Stai TW17 124 C3
Studland Cl. Read RG2 113 E4
Sturbridge Cl. Wood RG6 87 E1
Sturdee Cl. Camb GU16 151 F1
Sturges Rd. Woki RG40 116 B3
Sturt Gn. Holy SL6 64 C4
Styventon Pl. Chert KT16 123 F1
Sucks La. Asham RG8 54 B2
Suffolk Cl. Slough SL1 41 F4
Suffolk Cl. Woki RG41 115 E3
Suffolk Rd. Maid SL6 39 E2
Suffolk Rd. Read RG30 85 E4
Suffork Cl. Bags GU19 145 F1
Sulham La. Pangb RG8 56 C2
Sulham La. Pur O T RG8 56 C2
Sulham La. Sulh RG8 56 C2
Sulham Wlk. Read RG30 85 D2
Sulhamstead Hill. Sulhd RG7 110 B3
Sulhamstead La. Sulhd RG7 110 B2
Sulhamstead Rd. Bur RG7 & RG30 111 D3
Sulhamstead Rd. Sulhd RG7 111 D3
Sullivan Rd. Camb GU15 151 D3
Sumburgh Way. Slough SL1 42 C4
Summer Gdns. Camb GU15 152 B3
Summerfield Cl. Woki RG41 88 C1
Summerfield Rise. Gori RG8 34 B4
Summerhouse La. Harm UB7 70 B4
Summerlea. Slough SL1 42 A3
Summerleaze Rd. Maid SL6 20 A1
Summers Rd. Burn SL1 21 E1
Summit Cl. Woki RG40 141 F4
Sun Gdns. Bur C RG7 111 D1
Sun La. Maid SL6 39 F4
Sun La. Swal RG7 139 D1
Sun Pas. Wind SL4 67 E3
Sun Ray Estate. Sand GU17 150 A4
Sun St. Read RG1 86 B4
Sunbury Cres. Felt TW13 98 C3
Sunbury Rd. Eton SL4 67 E4
Sunbury Rd. Felt TW13 98 C3
Sunderland Cl. Wood RG5 88 A4
Sunderland Pl. That RG18 106 B2
Sunderland Rd. Maid SL6 39 D4
Sundew Cl. Camb GU18 153 E4
Sundew Cl. Woki RG40 116 C4
Sundon Cres. Went GU25 122 B2
Sundown Rd. Ashf TW15 98 B2
Sunley Cl. Newb RG14 130 B3

182
Sunmead Rd. Shepp
Tozer Wlk. Wind

Sunmead Rd. Shepp TW16 125 F3
Sunning Ave. Sunn SL5 120 C1
Sunninghill Cl. Ascot SL5 120 B3
Sunninghill Rd. Ascot SL5 120 B3
Sunninghill Rd. Windl GU20 146 A4
Sunninghill Rd. Wink SL4 & SL5 93 E1
Sunnybank. Mar SL7 1 B2
Sunnyside. Newb RG14 104 C3
Surbiton Rd. Camb GU15 145 D1
Surley Row. Caver RG4 59 D3
Surly Hall Wlk. Wind SL4 66 C3
Surrey Ave. Camb GU15 151 D2
Surrey Ave. Slough SL2 22 B1
Surrey Ct. New G RG42 91 F1
Surrey Rd. Read RG2 86 A2
Surridge Ct. Bags GU19 145 F1
Sussex Cl. Slough SL1 43 D2
Sussex Gdns. Wood RG5 87 F4
Sussex La. Shin RG7 113 E1
Sussex Pl. Slough SL1 43 D2
Sutcliffe Ave. Read RG6 87 E2
Sutherland Ave. Shepp TW16 125 F4
Sutherland Chase. Ascot SL5 119 F4
Sutherland Gdns. Shepp TW16 125 F4
Sutherland Gr. Read RG31 84 C2
Sutherlands Ave. Read RG1 86 B3
Sutherlands. Newb RG14 130 C4
Sutton Ave. Slough SL3 43 E2
Sutton Cl. Cook SL6 20 A4
Sutton Cl. Maid SL6 39 E3
Sutton La. Slough SL3 44 B1
Sutton Pl. Slough SL3 69 D4
Sutton Rd. Camb GU15 145 D1
Sutton Rd. Cook SL6 20 A3
Sutton Rd. Newb RG14 104 B3
Sutton Wlk. Read RG1 86 B3
Suttons Park Ave. Read RG6 86 C4
Swabey Rd. Slough SL3 44 A1
Swainstone Rd. Read RG2 86 A3
Swaledale. Brac RG12 118 A2
Swallow Cl. Read RG31 84 B3
Swallow Cl. Stai TW18 96 C2
Swallow Cl. Yate GU17 149 D3
Swallow St. Iver SL0 44 B4
Swallow Way. Woki RG41 115 F3
Swallowfield Dr. Read RG2 113 E3
Swallowfield. Eng G TW20 95 D1
Swallowfield Gdns. Thea RG7 83 F2
Swallowfield Rd. Arbo RG2 114 B1
Swan La. Sand GU17 150 A4
Swan Pl. Read RG1 86 A4
Swan Rd. Iver SL0 44 C4
Swancote Gn. Brac RG12 118 A2
Swangate. Hung RG17 100 B4
Swanholm Gdns. Read RG31 84 C2
Swanmore Cl. Winn RG6 87 F1
Swanscourt. Twyf RG10 61 F2
Swansdown Wlk. That RG19 106 A2
Swansea Rd. Harm TW6 71 E1
Swansea Rd. Read RG1 59 D1
Swansea Terr. Read RG31 57 E1
Swanston Field. Whi-O-T RG8 56 B4
Sweeps La. Eng G TW20 95 F2
Sweet Briar Dr. Bur C RG31 84 B2
Sweetbriar. Brac RG45 143 D4
Sweetzers Piece. Silc RG7 136 C3
Swepstone Cl. Read RG6 87 E1
Swift Cl. Woki RG41 115 F3
Swift La. Windl GU19 145 F2
Swinbrook Cl. Read RG31 57 E2
Swindon Rd. Harm TW6 71 E1
Swinley Rd. Brac SL5 119 E2
Swiss Cottage Cl. Read RG31 84 B4
Switchback Cl. Maid SL6 19 E1
Switchback Rd N. Cook SL6 19 F2
Switchback Rd N. Maid SL6 19 F2
Switchback Rd S. Maid SL6 19 E1
Switchback The. Maid SL6 19 E1
Sycamore Cl. Bur C RG30 111 D2
Sycamore Cl. Camb GU16 151 F1
Sycamore Cl. Maid SL6 39 E2
Sycamore Cl. Sand GU17 150 A4
Sycamore Cl. Wood RG5 87 E3
Sycamore Ct. Wind SL4 67 E2
Sycamore Dr. Camb GU16 151 F1
Sycamore Dr. Mar B SL7 1 B3
Sycamore Dr. Twyf RG10 61 E3
Sycamore Rd. Read RG2 86 C1
Sycamore Rise. Brac RG12 118 B3
Sycamore Rise. Newb RG14 105 E3
Sycamore Wlk. Eng G TW20 95 D1
Sycamore Wlk. Slough SL3 43 F4
Sycamores The. Black GU17 150 A3
Sydings The. Newb RG14 104 B3
Sydney Cl. Brac RG45 143 E4
Sydney Cres. Ashf TW15 98 A1
Sydney Gr. Slough SL1 42 B4
Syke Cluan. Iver SL0 44 C2
Syke Ings. Iver SL0 44 C2
Sykes Rd. Slough SL1 42 A4
Sylvan Ridge. Sand GU17 143 D1
Sylvan Wlk. Read RG30 85 E2
Sylvanus. Brac RG12 117 F1
Sylverns Ct. New G RG42 91 E1
Sylvester Cl. Newb RG14 104 C3
Sylvester Rd. Maid SL6 19 F1
Symondson Mews. Binf RG42 90 B2
Sympson Rd. Tad RG26 135 E1
Tachbrook Rd. Felt TW14 98 C4
Tadcroft Wlk. Read RG31 84 C2
Tadham Pl. That RG19 106 B1
Tadley Common Rd. Tad RG26 135 E1
Tadmor Cl. Shepp TW17 125 F3
Taff Way. Read RG30 85 D4
Tag La. Warg RG10 37 D1
Talbot Ave. Slough SL3 43 F2
Talbot Cl. Caver RG4 59 E1
Talbot Cl. Newb RG14 104 C3
Talbot Ct. Read RG1 86 A4
Talbot Pl. Bags GU19 145 F2
Talbot Pl. Datch SL3 68 B3
Talbot Rd. Ashf TW15 97 F2
Talbot Way. Sulh RG31 57 E2
Talbots Dr. Maid SL6 39 D3
Talfourd Ave. Read RG6 87 D3
Talisman Cl. Woki RG45 142 B3
Tall Trees. Stan SL3 69 F3
Tallis La. Read RG30 85 E2
Tamar Gdns. Read RG2 86 B2
Tamar Way. Slough SL3 44 A1
Tamar Way. Woki RG41 115 F4
Tamarind Way. Read RG6 86 C1
Tamarisk Ave. Read RG2 86 C1
Tamarisk Rise. Woki RG40 116 B4
Tamarisk Way. Slough SL1 42 A2
Tamerisk Ct. That RG18 106 C2
Tamworth. Brac RG12 118 B1
Tamworth Cl. Wood RG6 87 E1
Tandem. Brac RG12 117 F4
Tangier La. Eton SL4 67 E4
Tanglewood Ride. West E GU24 153 F4
Tanglewood. Woki RG40 142 A4
Tangley Dr. Brac RG41 116 A2
Tanglyn Ave. Stai TW17 125 D2
Tanhouse La. Woki RG41 116 A3
Tank Rd. Sand GU15 150 C3
Tanner Ct. Newb RG14 105 D2
Tanners Cl. Bur C RG7 110 C1
Tanners La. Maple RG4 58 C4
Tanners Yd. Bags GU19 145 F2
Tape La. Hurst RG10 88 C4
Taplow Common Rd. Burn SL1 21 D2
Taplow Common Rd. Tapl SL1 21 D2
Taplow Rd. Burn SL6 41 D4
Tarbat Ct. Sand GU15 150 B4
Tarbay La. Oak G SL4 66 B2
Target Cl. Felt TW14 71 F1
Target Hill. New G RG42 91 E1
Targett Ct. Winn RG41 88 A1
Tarlton Ct. Read RG30 84 C3
Tarmac Way. Harm UB7 70 A4
Tarn La. Newb RG14 130 C4
Tarnbrook Way. Brac RG12 118 C1
Tarragon Cl. New G RG42 91 E1
Tarragon Cl. Read RG6 86 C1
Tarragon Way. Bur C RG7 111 D2
Tarrants Hill. Hung RG17 100 B3
Tasker Cl. Harl UB7 71 E4
Tatchbrook Cl. Maid SL6 40 A4
Tattersall Cl. Woki RG40 116 C3
Tavistock Cl. Maid SL6 39 D4
Tavistock Cl. Stai TW18 97 E1
Tavistock Rd. Read RG2 86 A2
Tawfield. Brac RG12 117 F1
Tay Rd. Read RG30 85 D4
Taylors Cl. Mar SL7 1 C1
Tazewell Ct. Read RG1 85 F3
Tebbit Cl. Brac RG12 118 B4
Teesdale Rd. Slough SL2 41 F4
Tekels Ave. Camb GU15 151 E2
Tekels Way. Camb GU15 151 F2
Telford Cres. Wood RG5 60 C1
Telford Dr. Slough SL1 42 A2
Telston Cl. Bou E SL8 3 D3
Tempest Rd. Stai TW20 96 B1
Templar Cl. Sand GU17 150 A4
Templars Pl. Mar SL7 1 C1
Temple Gdns. Stai TW18 123 F4
Temple La. Bish SL7 18 B3
Temple Mill Island. Bish SL7 18 B3
Temple Pk. Hurl SL6 17 F2
Temple Pl. Read RG1 86 A3
Temple Rd. Wind SL4 67 E3
Temple Way. Binf RG42 90 C1
Temple Way. Brac RG42 117 F4
Temple Way. Far C SL2 22 B4
Templecroft. Ashf TW15 98 B1
Templedene Ave. Stai TW18 97 E1
Templeton Gdns. Read RG2 86 B1
Templewood La. Far C SL2 22 B4
Ten Acre La. Stai TW20 123 E4
Tenaplas Dr. Upp B RG8 54 C3
Tenby Ave. Caver RG4 59 E3
Tenby Dr. Ascot SL5 120 B2
Tennyson Rd. Ashf TW15 97 F2
Tennyson Rd. That RG18 106 B2
Tennyson Rd. Wood RG5 87 F2
Tennyson Way. Slough SL2 21 F1
Teresa Vale. New G RG42 91 F1
Tern Cl. Read RG30 85 D3
Terrace Rd N. Binf RG42 90 B2
Terrace Rd S. Binf RG42 90 B1
Terrace The. Ascot SL5 120 B2
Terrace The. Camb GU15 151 D3
Terrace The. Crow RG45 143 E3
Terrace The. Maid SL6 40 B2
Terrace The. Woki RG40 116 A3
Terrington Hill. Mar SL7 1 B1
Terrys La. Cook SL6 19 F4
Tesimond Dr. Yate GU17 149 D3
Tessa Rd. Read RG1 58 C1
Test Cl. Read RG30 85 D4
Testwood Rd. Wind SL4 66 B3
Teviot Rd. Read RG30 84 C4
Thakerays The. That RG19 106 B1
Thames Ave. Chert KT16 124 A3
Thames Ave. Pangb RG8 56 B3
Thames Ave. Read RG1 59 D1
Thames Ave. Wind SL4 67 E4
Thames Cl. Bou E SL8 3 D2
Thames Cl. Chert KT16 124 B1
Thames Cres. Maid SL6 20 A1
Thames Dr. Char RG10 60 C4
Thames Ind Est. Mar SL7 1 C1
Thames Mead. Wind SL4 66 C3
Thames Meadow. Shepp TW17 125 F1
Thames Rd. Gori RG8 34 A3
Thames Rd. Slough SL3 44 A2
Thames Rd. That RG18 106 A3
Thames Reach. Medm SL7 17 E4
Thames Reach. Pur O T RG8 55 E3
Thames Side. Chert KT16 & TW18 124 B1
Thames Side. Hen-O-T RG9 15 F1
Thames Side Prom. Read RG1 59 D1
Thames Side. Read RG1 59 D1
Thames Side. Stai TW18 96 C1
Thames Side. Stai TW18 96 C1
Thames Side. Wind SL4 67 E4
Thames St. Shepp TW17 125 F1
Thames St. Sonn RG4 60 B2
Thames St. Stai TW18 96 C2
Thames St. Wind SL4 67 E4
Thamesfield Ct. Shepp TW17 125 E1
Thamesfield Gdns. Mar SL7 1 C1
Thanington Way. Read RG6 87 D1
Thatchers Dr. Maid SL6 39 D3
Theal Cl. Sand GU15 150 B4
Theale Rd. Bur C RG30 111 E3
Theobald Dr. Read RG31 57 E2
Theobalds Way. Camb GU16 152 B2
Thetford Mews. Caver RG4 59 E3
Thetford Rd. Ashf TW15 97 F3
Thibet Rd. Sand GU17 150 B4
Thicket Gr. Maid SL6 38 C4
Thicket Rd. Read RG30 84 C4
Thickthorne La. Stai TW18 97 E1
Third Ave. Mar SL7 1 C1
Third Cres. Slough SL1 42 B4
Third St. Gree RG19 131 F3
Third St. Newt RG19 132 A3
Thirkleby Cl. Slough SL1 42 B3
Thirlmere Ave. Read RG30 57 F1
Thirlmere Ave. Slough SL1 41 E4
Thirlmere Cl. Stai TW20 96 A1
Thirtover. Cold A RG18 79 D1
Thistledown. Read RG31 57 E1
Thistleton Way. Winn RG6 87 F1
Thomas Dr. New G RG42 91 F1
Thomas La. Woki RG40 141 F4
Thomas Rd. Bou E HP10 3 E2
Thompkins La. Burn SL2 22 A3
Thompson Cl. Herm RG18 78 C3
Thompson Cl. Slough SL3 44 A1
Thompson Dr. That RG19 106 C1
Thomson Wlk. Bur C RG31 84 C2
Thorburn Chase. Sand GU15 150 B3
Thorn Cl. Woki RG41 115 E2
Thorn Dr. Slough SL3 43 F4
Thorn La. Read RG1 86 A4
Thorn St. Read RG1 86 A4
Thornaby Pl. Woo G HP10 3 F4
Thornbank Cl. Stan TW19 70 A1
Thornbers Way. Char RG10 61 D3
Thornbridge Rd. Read RG2 113 D4
Thornbury Cl. Crow RG45 143 D3
Thornbury Gn. Twyf RG10 61 E3
Thorncroft. Eng G TW20 95 E1
Thorndike. Slough SL2 42 A4
Thorndown La. Windl GU20 146 B2
Thorndown La. Windl GU20 146 B2
Thorne Cl. Brac RG45 143 D4
Thorne Cl. Stai TW15 98 B1
Thorney Cl. Winn RG6 87 F1
Thorney La N. Iver SL0 44 C3
Thorney La S. Iver SL0 44 C3
Thornfield Gn. Black GU17 150 C2
Thornfield. Head RG19 132 B2
Thornford Rd. Gree RG19 132 B2
Thornford Rd. Head RG19 132 C2
Thornford Rd. That RG19 132 B2
Thornhill. Brac RG12 118 C3
Thornhill Way. Stai TW17 125 D2
Thorningdown. Chil OX11 10 B4
Thornton Mews. Read RG30 85 E4
Thornton Rd. Read RG30 85 E4
Thorp Cl. Binf RG42 90 B2
Thorpe By Pass. Stai TW20 123 D3
Thorpe Cl. Woki RG41 116 A2
Thorpe Lea Rd. Stai TW20 96 A1
Thorpe Rd. Chert KT16 123 E2
Thorpe Rd. Stai TW18 96 B2
Thorpe Rd. Stai TW20 123 E2
Thrale Mews. Read RG30 85 D4
Three Acre Rd. Newb RG14 130 C4
Three Firs Way. Bur C RG7 110 C1
Three Gables La. Stre RG8 34 A4
Three Post La. Lamb RG17 25 D1
Threshfield. Brac RG12 118 A2
Thrift La. Holy SL6 64 B4
Throgmorton Rd. Yate GU17 149 D3
Thrush Cl. Bur C RG7 111 D2
Thurlby Way. Maid SL6 39 E2
Thurlestone Cl. Shepp TW17 125 E2
Thurlestone Gdns. Read RG2 86 B1
Thurnscoe Cl. Read RG6 113 F4
Thurso Cl. Read RG30 85 D4
Thurston Rd. Slough SL1 42 C4
Thyme Cl. Read RG6 87 D1
Tichborne Cl. Black GU17 150 B3
Tichbourne Cl. Camb GU16 151 F2
Tickenor Dr. Woki RG40 141 F4
Tickhill Cl. Read RG6 113 F4
Tidmarsh La. Pangb RG8 56 A1
Tidmarsh La. Tidm RG8 56 A1
Tidmarsh Rd. Pangb RG8 56 B2
Tidmarsh Rd. Tidm RG8 56 B2
Tidmarsh St. Read RG30 58 A1
Tiffany Cl. Woki RG41 115 E3
Tiger Cl. Wood RG5 88 A4
Tigerseye Cl. Woki RG41 115 E4
Tilbury Cl. Caver RG4 59 E2
Tile Barn Row. Ball H RG20 129 F1
Tilecotes Cl. Mar SL7 1 B1
Tilehurst La. Binf RG42 90 B2
Tilehurst Rd. Read RG1 & RG30 85 E4
Tilling Cl. Read RG31 57 D1
Tillys La. Stai TW18 96 C2
Tilney Way. Read RG6 113 F4
Tilstone Ave. Eton SL4 41 F1
Tilstone Cl. Eton SL4 41 F1
Timbers Wlk. Maid SL6 39 D3
Timline Gn. Brac RG12 118 C4
Timsway. Stai TW18 96 C2
Tindal Cl. Yate GU17 149 E3
Tinkers La. Wind SL4 66 B3
Tinkers La. Windl SL5 121 D2
Tinsey Cl. Stai TW20 96 A2
Tinsley Cl. Read RG6 113 F4
Tintagel Dr. Camb GU16 151 F1
Tintagel Rd. Brac RG40 142 A4
Tintern Cl. Slough SL1 42 B2
Tintern Cres. Read RG1 85 F3
Tinwell Cl. Winn RG6 87 F1
Tippett Rise. Read RG2 86 A3
Tippings La. Wood RG5 88 A4
Tippits Mead. Brac RG42 117 E4
Tiptree Cl. Read RG6 113 F4
Titcombe Way. Kint RG17 102 A1
Tite Hill. Eng G TW20 95 E2
Tithe Barn Dr. Holy SL6 40 B1
Tithe Cl. Holy SL6 40 B1
Tithe Ct. Slough SL3 44 A1
Tithe La. Wray TW19 69 D1
Tithe Meadows. Went GU25 122 B2
Tithebarn Gr. Read RG31 84 C2
Titlarks Hill Rd. Went SL5 121 D1
Tiverton Cl. Wood RG5 60 C1
Toad La. Black GU17 150 C2
Tockley Rd. Burn SL1 21 D1
Tofrek Terr. Read RG30 85 E4
Tokers Green Rd. Maple RG4 58 C4
Tokersgreen La. Caver RG4 58 B3
Tokersgreen La. Maple RG4 58 B3
Toll Gdns. Brac RG12 118 C3
Tollgate. Maid SL6 39 D3
Tolpuddle Way. Yate GU17 149 F3
Tomlin Cl. That RG19 106 C1
Tomlin Rd. Slough SL2 21 F1
Tomlins Ave. Camb GU16 151 F1
Tomlinson Dr. Brac RG40 142 A4
Top Common. New G RG42 91 E1
Topaz Cl. Slough SL1 42 A3
Topaz Cl. Woki RG41 115 F4
Tope Cres. Bark RG2 140 C4
Tope Rd. Bark RG2 140 C4
Torcross Gr. Bur C RG31 84 A2
Torin Ct. Eng G TW20 95 E2
Torquay Spur. Slough SL2 22 A1
Torridge Rd. Slough SL3 69 D4
Torrington Rd. Read RG2 86 B1
Toseland Way. Winn RG6 87 F2
Totnes Rd. Read RG2 86 B1
Tottenham Wlk. Crow GU15 143 E1
Totterdown. Bur C RG7 110 C1
Toutley Cl. Woki RG41 88 C1
Toutley Rd. Woki RG41 89 D1
Tower Cl. Caver RG4 59 E4
Tower Cl. Fla H HP10 3 E4
Tower Hill. Chadd RG20 49 D4
Towers Dr. Crow RG45 143 D2
Town Farm Way. Stan TW19 97 E4
Town La. Bou E HP10 3 E2
Town La. Stan TW19 70 B1
Town La. Stan TW19 97 E4
Town Sq. Brac RG12 118 B4
Town Sq. Camb GU15 151 E3
Town Tree Rd. Ashf TW15 98 A2
Townsend Cl. Brac RG12 118 C2
Townsend Rd. Aldw RG8 32 C2
Townsend Rd. Ashf TW15 97 F2
Townsend Rd. Stre RG8 34 A4
Towpath. Shepp TW17 124 C1
Tozer Wlk. Wind SL4 66 B2

183

Trafalgar Cl. Woki

Ward Stone Pk. Brac

Trafalgar Cl. Woki	RG41	115	F3
Trafalgar Ct. Read	RG1	85	E3
Trafalgar Way. Sand	GU15	150	C2
Trafford Rd. Read	RG1	58	C1
Travic Rd. Slough	SL2	21	F1
Travis Ct. Slough	SL2	22	A1
Travis La. Sand	GU17	150	B4
Tredegar Rd. Caver	RG4	59	D3
Tree Cl. Read	RG30	84	B4
Tree Tops Ave. Camb	GU15	152	A4
Trees Rd. Bou E	SL8	3	D2
Treesmill Dr. Maid	SL6	39	E2
Treeton Cl. Read	RG6	113	F4
Trefoil Cl. Woki	RG40	116	C4
Trefoil Dro. That	RG18	106	C2
Treforgan. Caver	RG4	58	C3
Trelawney Ave. Slough	SL3	43	F2
Trelawney Dr. Read	RG31	57	E1
Trelleck Rd. Read	RG1	85	F3
Tremayne Wlk. Camb	GU15	152	B2
Trenchard Rd. Holy	SL6	65	D4
Trenches La. Slough	SL3	44	A3
Trent Cl. Woki	RG41	115	F4
Trent Cres. That	RG18	106	A3
Trent Rd. Slough	SL3	69	D4
Trenthams Cl. Pur O T	RG8	57	D3
Trenton Cl. Camb	GU16	152	A1
Tresham Cres. Yate	GU17	149	D3
Trevelyan. Brac	RG12	117	F1
Trevithick Cl. Felt	TW14	98	C4
Triangle The. Read	RG30	84	B4
Trindledown. Brac	RG42	91	D1
Tring Rd. Read	RG31	57	E1
Trinity Ave. Mar	SL7	1	B2
Trinity Cl. Stan	TW19	70	B1
Trinity Cl. Sunn	SL5	121	D2
Trinity. Crow	GU15	143	F1
Trinity Pl. Read	RG1	85	F4
Trinity Pl. Wind	SL4	67	E3
Trinity Rd. Mar	SL7	1	B1
Triumph Cl. Harl	UB7	71	E3
Trotsworth Ave. Vir W	GU25	122	C3
Trotwood Cl. Crow	GU15	143	F1
Trout Cl. Mar	SL7	18	B4
Trout Wlk. Newb	RG14	105	E2
Troutbeck Cl. Twyf	RG10	61	E3
Trowes La. Bee H	RG7	138	B2
Trowes La. Swal	RG7	139	E3
Trumbull Rd. Brac	RG42	91	D1
Trumps Green Cl. Vir W	GU25	122	C2
Trumps Mill La. Went	GU25	122	C2
Trumpsgreen Ave. Went	GU25	122	B2
Trumpsgreen Rd. Went	GU25	122	B2
Truro Cl. Maid	SL6	39	D4
Truss Hill Rd. Ascot	SL5	120	B2
Trust Cnr. Hen-O-T	RG9	35	F4
Trusthorpe Cl. Winn	RG6	87	F1
Tubbs Farm Cl. Lamb	RG17	25	D1
Tubwell Rd. Sto P	SL2	23	D2
Tudor Cl. Ashf	TW15	97	F2
Tudor Cl. Woki	RG40	116	C3
Tudor Dr. Woo G	HP10	3	E4
Tudor Dr. Yate	GU17	149	E2
Tudor Gdns. Slough	SL1	41	E4
Tudor La. Old W	SL4	95	E4
Tudor Rd. Ashf	TW15	98	B1
Tudor Rd. Newb	RG14	105	D1
Tudor Rd. Read	RG1	86	A4
Tudor Way. Wind	SL4	66	C3
Tunnel Link Rd. Stan	TW6	71	D1
Tunnel Rd E. Harm	TW6	71	D3
Tunnel Rd W. Harm	TW6	71	D3
Tuns Hill Cotts. Read	RG6	87	D3
Tuns La. Hen-O-T	RG9	15	F1
Tuns La. Slough	SL1	42	B2
Tupsley Rd. Read	RG1	85	F3
Turf Hill Rd. Camb	GU15	151	F4
Turks La. Silc	RG7	137	D2
Turmeric Cl. Read	RG6	86	C1
Turnberry. Brac	RG12	117	F1
Turnbridge Cl. Read	RG6	114	A4
Turner Pl. Sand	GU15	150	B3
Turner Rd. Slough	SL3	43	E2
Turners Cl. Stai	TW18	97	D2
Turners Dr. That	RG19	106	C1
Turnery The. That	RG19	106	B2
Turnfields. That	RG19	106	B2
Turnoak Pk. Wind	SL4	66	C2
Turnpike Rd. Brac	RG42	117	F4
Turnpike Rd. Newb	RG14	105	F2
Turnpike Rd. That	RG19	105	F2
Turnstone Cl. Winn	RG41	88	A2
Turnstone End. Yate	GU17	149	D3
Turnville Cl. Light	GU18	146	A1
Turpin Rd. Felt	TW14	71	F1
Turpins Gr. Maid	SL6	39	D3
Turpins Rise. Windl	GU20	146	A3
Turton Way. Slough	SL1	42	B2
Tuscam Way. Sand	GU15	150	C2
Tuscan Cl. Read	RG30	57	F1
Tuxford Mews. Read	RG30	85	D4
Tweed Ct. Read	RG30	85	D4
Tweed Rd. Slough	SL3	69	D4
Twin Oaks. Caver	RG4	59	D3
Twinches La. Slough	SL1	42	A3
Two Tree Hill. Hen-O-T	RG9	35	D4
Twyford Rd. Binf	RG10 & RG42	90	B4
Twyford Rd. W St L	RG10	62	C3
Twyford Rd. Woki	RG40	89	D1
Twynham Rd. Maid	SL6	39	D4
Tyberton Pl. Read	RG1	85	F3
Tydehams. Newb	RG14	130	C4
Tyle Pl. Old W	SL4	68	A1
Tyle Rd. Read	RG30	84	B4
Tyler Cl. Caver	RG4	58	C3
Tylers La. Buck	RG7	80	A1
Tylers Pl. Read	RG30	84	C4
Tyne Way. That	RG18	106	A3
Tyrell Gdns. Wind	SL4	66	C2
Tytherton. Brac	RG12	118	B4
Uffington Cl. Read	RG31	84	B4
Uffington Dr. Brac	RG12	118	C3
Uffoott Cl. Read	RG6	113	F4
Ullswater. Brac	RG12	117	F1
Ullswater Cl. Light	GU18	146	A1
Ullswater Cl. Slough	SL1	41	E4
Ullswater Cl. That	RG19	106	A2
Ullswater Dr. Read	RG31	57	E2
Ullswater Rd. Light	GU18	146	A1
Ulster Cl. Caver	RG4	59	E3
Umberville Way. Slough	SL2	21	F1
Underhill Cl. Maid	SL6	39	F3
Underhill. Moul	OX10	14	A2
Underwood. Brac	RG12	117	F2
Underwood Rd. Read	RG30	85	D2
Union Cl. Sand	GU15	143	F1
Union Rd. Brad	RG7	82	B2
Union St. Read	RG1	86	A4
Unity Cl. Caver	RG4	59	D3
Unwin Ave. Harm	TW14	71	E1
Upavon Dr. Read	RG1	85	F3
Upavon Gdns. Brac	RG12	118	C2
Upcroft. Wind	SL4	67	D2
Updown Hill. Windl	GU20	146	B2
Upland Rd. Camb	GU15	151	E4
Uplands Cl. Sand	GU17	150	A4
Uplands. Hung	RG17	100	B3
Uplands. Mar B	SL7	1	B3
Uplands Rd. Caver	RG4	58	C3
Upper Bray Rd. Maid	SL6	40	B2
Upper Broadmoor Rd. Crow	RG45	143	E3
Upper Charles St. Camb	GU15	151	E3
Upper Chobham Rd. Camb	GU15	152	A2
Upper College Ride. Camb	GU15	151	F4
Upper Crown St. Read	RG1	86	A3
Upper Eddington. Hung	RG17	100	C4
Upper End. Chadd	RG20	49	D4
Upper Gordon Rd. Camb	GU15	151	E3
Upper Halliford Rd. Shepp	TW17	125	F3
Upper Lambourn Rd. Lamb	RG17	25	D2
Upper Lees Rd. Slough	SL2	22	A1
Upper Meadow Rd. Read	RG2	86	B1
Upper Nursery. Sunn	SL5	121	D2
Upper Park Rd. Camb	GU15	151	F3
Upper Red Cross Rd. Gori	RG8	34	B3
Upper Redlands Rd. Read	RG1	86	C3
Upper Village Rd. Ascot	SL5	120	B2
Upper Warren Ave. Caver	RG4	58	B2
Upper Woodcote Rd. Caver	RG4	58	B3
Uppingham Dr. Wood	RG5	60	C1
Uppingham Gdns. Caver	RG4	59	E3
Upshire Gdns. Brac	RG12	118	C3
Upton Cl. Hen-O-T	RG9	15	F1
Upton Cl. Slough	SL1	42	C2
Upton Court Rd. Slough	SL3	43	D1
Upton Lea Par. Slough	SL2	43	D3
Upton Pk. Slough	SL1	42	C2
Upton Rd. Read	RG30	85	D4
Upton Rd. Slough	SL1	43	D2
Urquhart Rd. That	RG19	106	C1
Usk Rd. Read	RG30	84	C3
Uxbridge Rd. Slough	SL2 & SL3	43	E3
Vachel Rd. Read	RG1	86	A4
Vale Cres. Read	RG30	57	F1
Vale Gr. Slough	SL1	42	C2
Vale Rd. Camb	GU15	151	D2
Vale Rd. Wind	SL4	66	C3
Valentia Cl. Read	RG30	85	E4
Valentia Rd. Read	RG30	85	E4
Valentine Cl. Read	RG2	113	F4
Valentine Cres. Caver	RG4	59	E2
Valentine Wood Ind Est. Alde	RG7	135	F2
Valeview Dr. Bee H	RG7	138	B3
Valley Cl. Caver	RG4	59	D2
Valley Cl. Gori	RG8	34	B3
Valley Cres. Woki	RG41	116	A4
Valley End. Iver H	SL3	23	E1
Valley Rd. Bur C	RG7	111	D2
Valley Rd. Hen-O-T	RG9	35	D4
Valley Rd. Newb	RG14	130	C4
Valley Way. Silc	RG26	135	F1
Valon Rd. Arbo	RG2	140	C4
Valpy St. Read	RG1	86	A4
Valroy Cl. Camb	GU15	151	E3
Vanbrugh Ct. Read	RG1	86	B4
Vandyke. Brac	RG12	117	F2
Vanlore Way. Read	RG31	84	B3
Vanners La. Ham M	RG20	129	E3
Vansittart Rd. Bish	SL7	18	C4
Vansittart Rd. Wind	SL4	67	D3
Vantage Rd. Slough	SL1	42	A3
Vanwall Bsns Pk. Maid	SL6	39	E3
Vanwall Rd. Maid	SL6	39	E2
Vastern Rd. Caver	RG1	59	D1
Vaughan Copse. Eton	SL4	42	B1
Vaughan Way. Slough	SL2	21	F1
Vauxhall Dr. Wood	RG5	88	A3
Vegal Cres. Eng G	TW20	95	E2
Venetia Cl. Caver	RG4	59	E4
Venning Rd. Bark	RG2	140	C4
Ventnor Rd. Read	RG31	57	E1
Venus Cl. Woki	RG41	115	F3
Verbena Cl. Winn	RG41	88	A2
Verey Cl. Twyf	RG10	61	F2
Vermont Rd. Slough	SL2	21	F1
Vermont Woods. Woki	RG40	141	F4
Verney Cl. Mar	SL7	1	B1
Verney Mews. Read	RG30	85	E4
Verney Rd. Slough	SL3	44	A1
Vernon Cres. Read	RG2	113	D4
Vernon Dr. Ascot	SL5	119	F4
Vernon Rd. Felt	TW13	98	C3
Verran Rd. Camb	GU15	151	E2
Viburnum Ct. West E	GU24	153	F3
Vicarage Ave. Stai	TW20	96	A2
Vicarage Cl. Cook	SL6	20	A4
Vicarage Cl. Woki	RG40	141	F3
Vicarage Cres. Stai	TW20	96	A2
Vicarage Ct. Felt	TW20	98	B4
Vicarage Ct. Stai	TW20	96	A1
Vicarage Dr. Maid	SL6	40	B2
Vicarage Gdns. Ascot	SL5	120	A2
Vicarage Gdns.Bur G	SL6	63	F4
Vicarage Gdns. Whi Wa	SL6	63	F4
Vicarage La. Cold A	RG18	106	B4
Vicarage La. Stai	TW18	124	B3
Vicarage La. Wray	TW19	95	F4
Vicarage La. Yate	GU17	149	E4
Vicarage Rd. Ashf	TW16	98	C1
Vicarage Rd. Bags	GU19	145	E2
Vicarage Rd. Black	GU17	150	C2
Vicarage Rd. Hen-O-T	RG9	35	F4
Vicarage Rd. Maid	SL6	39	F4
Vicarage Rd. Read	RG2	86	B3
Vicarage Rd. Stai	TW18	96	C3
Vicarage Rd. Stai	TW20	96	A1
Vicarage Rd. Yate	GU17	149	E4
Vicarage Way. Iver	SL3	69	E4
Vicarage Wlk. Maid	SL6	40	B2
Vicarage Wood Way. Read	RG31	57	D1
Vickers Cl. Shin	RG2	113	F2
Vickers Cl. Wood	RG5	88	A4
Victor Rd. That	RG19	106	C2
Victor Rd. Wind	SL4	67	E2
Victor Way. Wood	RG5	88	A4
Victoria Ave. Camb	GU15	151	D3
Victoria Cres. Iver	SL0	44	C3
Victoria Ct. Bags	GU19	145	F1
Victoria Dr. Black	GU17	150	B2
Victoria Gdns. Newb	RG14	105	D2
Victoria La. Harl	UB7	71	E4
Victoria Rd. Ascot	SL5	120	A2
Victoria Rd. Caver	RG4	59	D2
Victoria Rd. Eton	SL4	41	F1
Victoria Rd. Far C	SL2	22	B3
Victoria Rd. Mar	SL7	1	C1
Victoria Rd. Mort	RG7	136	C3
Victoria Rd. Read	RG31	84	B4
Victoria Rd. Sand	GU15	143	F1
Victoria Rd. Slough	SL2	43	D3
Victoria Rd. Stai	TW18	96	C3
Victoria Rd. Warg	RG10	36	C1
Victoria St. Eng G	TW20	95	E1
Victoria St. Read	RG1	86	B4
Victoria St. Slough	SL1	42	C2
Victoria St. Wind	SL4	67	E3
Victory Rd. Chert	KT16	124	A1
Vigo La. Yate	GU17	149	E2
Viking. Brac	RG12	117	F2
Village Cl. Read	RG2	113	D3
Village Rd. Dorn	SL4	41	E2
Village Rd. Stai	TW20	123	E3
Village The. Finch	RG40	141	F2
Village Way. Ashf	TW15	98	A2
Village Way. Yate	GU17	149	E4
Villiers Mead. Woki	RG41	116	A3
Villiers Rd. Slough	SL2	42	B4
Villiers Way. Newb	RG14	130	B3
Villiers Wlk. Newb	RG14	130	B3
Vincent Cl. Chert	KT16	123	F1
Vincent Cl. Harm	UB7	71	D4
Vincent Cl. Wood	RG5	87	F3
Vincent Dr. Shepp	TW17	125	F3
Vincent Rd. Chert	KT16	123	F1
Vincent Rd. That	RG18	106	C2
Vincent Rise. Brac	RG12	118	C3
Vine Cl. Stan	TW19	70	A1
Vine Cres. Read	RG30	85	D2
Vine Rd. Sto P	SL2	22	C3
Vineries Cl. Harm	UB7	71	D4
Vinery The. Warg	RG10	36	B1
Vines The. Woki	RG41	115	E2
Vineyard Dr. Bou E	SL8	3	D3
Viola Ave. Stan	TW19	97	F4
Viola Croft. Brac	RG42	118	C4
Virginia Ave. Vir W	GU25	122	B2
Virginia Beeches. Vir W	GU25	122	A1
Virginia Cl. Stai	TW18	124	B3
Virginia Dr. Vir W	GU25	122	B3
Virginia Way. Read	RG30	85	D3
Viscount Rd. Stan	TW19	97	F4
Viscount Way. Harm	TW6	71	F2
Viscount Way. Wood	RG5	88	A4
Vivien Cl. Cook	SL6	19	F3
Voller Dr. Read	RG31	84	B3
Volunteer Rd. Thea	RG7	83	E1
Vulcan Cl. Sand	GU17	150	A4
Vulcan Cl. Wood	RG5	61	D1
Vulcan Way. Sand	GU17	150	A4
Wabone Rd. Bou E	SL8	3	D2
Wade Dr. Slough	SL1	42	A3
Wadham Cl. Shepp	TW17	125	E1
Wadham. Crow	GU15	143	F1
Wagbullock Rise. Brac	RG12	118	B2
Waggoners Hollow. Bags	GU19	145	F1
Wagtail Cl. Twyf	RG10	61	F2
Waingels Rd. Char	RG10	61	D1
Waingels Rd. Wood	RG10	61	D1
Wakefield Cres. Sto P	SL2	22	C3
Wakeford Cl. Silc	RG26	135	F1
Wakeford Ct. Alde	RG26	135	F1
Wakelins End. Cook	SL6	19	F4
Wakeman Rd. Bou E	SL8	3	D2
Wakemans. Pangb	RG8	55	E2
Walbury. Brac	RG12	118	C3
Waldeck Rd. Maid	SL6	40	A4
Waldeck St. Read	RG1	86	A3
Waldegrave Pl. Newb	RG14	105	D2
Walden Ave. Arbo	RG2	114	B2
Waldens Cl. Bou E	SL8	3	D2
Waldorf Hts. Black	GU17	150	B2
Waldron Hill. Brac	RG12	118	C4
Walgrove Gdns. Whi Wa	SL6	63	F4
Walk The. Ashf	TW16	98	C1
Walk The. Eton	SL4	42	A1
Walker Cl. Felt	TW14	98	C4
Walker Rd. Maid	SL6	40	A2
Walkers La. Lamb	RG17	25	D2
Walkers Pl. Read	RG30	85	E4
Walkers Ridge. Camb	GU15	151	F3
Wall La. Silc	RG7	136	B1
Wallace Cl. Mar	SL7	1	C2
Wallace Cl. Shepp	TW17	125	E3
Wallace Cl. Wood	RG5	87	E3
Wallcroft Cl. Binf	RG42	90	C1
Walled Gdn The. Warg	RG10	36	B1
Wallingford Cl. Brac	RG12	118	C3
Wallingford Rd. Comp	RG20	31	F3
Wallingford Rd. Gori	RG8 & OX10	14	B3
Wallingford Rd. Sou S	RG8 & OX10	14	B3
Wallingford Rd. Stre	RG8	34	A4
Wallington Rd. Camb	GU15	145	D1
Wallington's Rd. Kint	RG17	101	F1
Wallis Ct. Slough	SL1	43	D2
Wallis Dr. Newb	RG14	105	F3
Wallner Way. Woki	RG40	116	C3
Walmer Cl. Crow	RG45	143	E3
Walmer Cl. Read	RG30	85	D3
Walmer Rd. Wood	RG5	60	C1
Walnut Cl. Woki	RG41	115	F3
Walnut Cl. Yate	GU17	149	E2
Walnut Tree Cl. Bou E	SL8	3	D1
Walnut Tree Cl. Twyf	RG10	61	F3
Walnut Tree Ct. Gori	RG8	34	B3
Walnut Tree Rd. Stai	TW17	125	E4
Walnut Tree Rd. Stai	TW17	125	E4
Walnut Way. Bou E	SL8	3	D1
Walnut Way. Read	RG30	84	B4
Walpole Rd. Old W	SL4	95	D4
Walpole Rd. Slough	SL1	41	E4
Walrus Cl. Wood	RG5	88	A4
Walsh Ave. New G	RG42	91	F1
Walter Rd. Woki	RG41	115	F4
Walters Cl. Cold A	RG18	106	B4
Waltham Cl. Crow	GU15	143	E1
Waltham Cl. Whi Wa	SL6	38	C1
Waltham Rd. Twyf	RG10	61	F2
Waltham Rd. Twyf	RG10	62	A3
Waltham Rd. Whi Wa	SL6	38	C1
Walton Ave. Hen-O-T	RG9	35	F4
Walton Bridge Rd. Shepp	TW17	125	F1
Walton Cl. Wood	RG5	87	E4
Walton Dr. Ascot	SL5	119	F4
Walton Gdns. Felt	TW13	98	C2
Walton La. Burn	SL2	21	F2
Walton La. Shepp	TW17	125	F1
Walton Way. Newb	RG14	105	E2
Wandhope Way. Read	RG31	57	E1
Wanstraw Gr. Brac	RG12	118	C1
Wantage Cl. Brac	RG12	118	C2
Wantage Rd. Gr She	RG17	48	B3
Wantage Rd. Lamb	RG17	25	E3
Wantage Rd. Read	RG30	85	E4
Wantage Rd. Sand	GU15	150	B4
Wantage Rd. Stre	RG8	33	F4
Wapshott Rd. Stai	TW18	96	C2
War Memorial Pl. Hen-O-T	RG9	35	F4
Waram Cl. Hung	RG17	100	C4
Warbler Cl. Read	RG31	84	A3
Warbler Dr. Read	RG6	87	D1
Warborough Ave. Read	RG31	84	A4
Warborough Rd. Let B	OX12	7	D4
Warbreck Dr. Sulh	RG31	57	D2
Warbrook La. Finch	RG27	141	D1
Ward Cl. Iver	SL0	44	C3
Ward Cl. Woki	RG40	116	B4
Ward Gdns. Slough	SL1	41	F3
Ward Royal. Wind	SL4	67	D3
Ward Stone Pk. Brac	RG12	118	C1

184

Wardle Ave. Read

Whitelands Dr. Burl

Wardle Ave. Read	RG31	57	E1
Wardle Cl. Bags	GU19	145	F2
Wareham Rd. Brac	RG12	118	C2
Warehouse Rd. Gree	RG19	131	F3
Warfield Rd. Brac	RG12 & RG42	91	E1
Warfield Rd. Felt	TW14	98	C4
Warfield St. New G	RG42	91	E2
Wargrave Hill. Warg	RG10	36	B1
Wargrave Rd. Rem H	RG9	36	A4
Wargrave Rd. Twyf	RG10	61	E3
Wargrove Dr. Sand	GU15	150	B4
Waring Cl. Winn	RG6	114	B4
Warley Rise. Sulh	RG31	57	E2
Warner Cl. Harl	UB7	71	E4
Warner Cl. Slough	SL1	41	F3
Warners Hill. Cook	SL6	19	E4
Warnford Rd. Read	RG30	84	C4
Warnsham Cl. Read	RG6	87	D1
Warren Cl. Bur C	RG7	111	D2
Warren Cl. Sand	GU17	150	A4
Warren Cl. Slough	SL3	43	F2
Warren Down. Brac	RG42	117	F4
Warren House Rd. Bint	RG40	89	E1
Warren House Rd. Woki	RG40	116	B4
Warren La. Woki	RG40	141	F3
Warren Rd. Ashf	TW15	98	C1
Warren Rd. Newb	RG14	130	B3
Warren Rd. Wood	RG5	60	B1
Warren Rise. Camb	GU16	151	F2
Warren Row. Burl	SL5	119	E4
Warren Row Rd. Know H	RG10	37	E3
Warren The. Caver	RG4	58	C2
Warrington Ave. Slough	SL1	42	B4
Warrington Spur. Old W	SL4	95	D4
Warwick Ave. Slough	SL2	22	B1
Warwick Ave. Stai	TW18	97	E1
Warwick Ave. Stai	TW18	123	E4
Warwick. Brac	RG12	118	C2
Warwick Cl. Camb	GU15	152	A2
Warwick Cl. Maid	SL6	39	D2
Warwick Dr. Newb	RG14	105	D1
Warwick Rd. Ashf	TW15	97	F2
Warwick Rd. Read	RG2	86	B2
Wasdale Cl. Crow	GU15	143	E1
Wash Hill. Bou E	HP10	3	F2
Wash Hill Lea. Bou E	HP10	3	E2
Wash Water. Ham M	RG20	130	A2
Wash Water. Newb	RG20	130	A2
Washington Ct. Mar	SL7	2	A2
Washington Dr. Slough	SL1	41	E3
Washington Dr. Wind	SL4	66	C2
Washington Gdns. Woki	RG40	142	A4
Washington Rd. Caver	RG4	59	D1
Wasing La. Brim	RG7	134	B3
Watchetts Dr. Camb	GU15	151	E1
Watchetts Lake Cl. Camb	GU15	151	E2
Watchetts Rd. Camb	GU15	151	D2
Watchmoor Rd. Camb	GU15	151	D2
Water La. Gree	RG19	131	E4
Water Rd. Read	RG30	85	D4
Water St. Hamp N	RG18	52	C3
Waterbeach Rd. Slough	SL1	42	B4
Waterfall Cl. Vir W	GU25	122	A3
Waterford Way. Woki	RG40	116	B3
Waterham Rd. Brac	RG12	118	A2
Waterhouse Mead. Sand	GU15	150	C4
Waterloo Cl. Felt	TW14	98	C4
Waterloo Cres. Woki	RG40	116	C3
Waterloo Rd. Crow	RG45	143	D2
Waterloo Rd. Read	RG2	86	A3
Waterloo Rd. Woki	RG40	116	C3
Waterloo Rise. Read	RG2	86	A2
Waterman Pl. Read	RG1	59	D1
Watermans Rd. Hen-O-T	RG9	35	F4
Watermans Way. Warg	RG10	36	B1
Watermead. Felt	TW14	98	C4
Watermill Ct. Wool	RG7	108	B1
Waters Dr. Stai	TW18	96	C2
Watersfield Cl. Read	RG6	87	D1
Waterside Ct. Newb	RG14	105	E2
Waterside Dr. Pur O T	RG8	57	E3
Waterside Dr. Slough	SL3	44	A2
Waterside Gdns. Read	RG1	86	A4
Waterside Park Ind Est. Brac	RG12	117	F4
Waterside. Woo G	HP10	3	F4
Watersplash La. Ascot	SL5	120	C4
Watersplash La. Wink	SL5	120	C4
Watersplash Rd. Stai	TW17	125	D3
Watery La. Chert	KT16	123	E1
Watery La. Kint	RG20	128	C3
Watery La. Woo G	HP10	3	F4
Watkins Cl. Woki	RG40	141	F4
Watlington St. Read	RG1	86	B4
Watmore La. Winn	RG41	88	B1
Watreside Dr. Thea	RG7	83	F2
Watson Cl. Woki	RG40	115	F1
Watts La. Blew	OX11	12	A4
Wavell Cl. Read	RG2	86	C1
Wavell Gdns. Slough	SL2	21	F1
Wavell Rd. Maid	SL6	39	D3
Wavendene Ave. Stai	TW20	96	B1
Waverley. Brac	RG12	117	F2
Waverley Cl. Camb	GU15	151	F2
Waverley Dr. Camb	GU15	151	F3
Waverley Dr. Vir W	GU25	122	A3
Waverley Rd. Bags	GU19	145	F2
Waverley Rd. Read	RG30	85	E4
Waverley Rd. Slough	SL1	42	B4
Waverley Way. Woki	RG40	115	F1
Waverley Way. Woki	RG40	141	F4
Waverleys The. That	RG18	106	B2
Waybrook Cres. Read	RG1	86	C3
Wayland Cl. Brac	RG12	118	C3
Waylen St. Read	RG1	85	F4
Ways End. Camb	GU15	151	F2
Wayside Mews. Maid	SL6	39	F4
Weald Rise. Read	RG30	57	F1
Wealden Way. Read	RG30	57	F1
Wealden Way. Read	RG30	84	C4
Weavers La. Ink	RG17	127	E3
Weavers Wlk. Newb	RG14	105	D2
Webb Cl. Bags	GU19	145	F1
Webb Cl. Binf	RG42	90	C1
Webb Cl. Slough	SL3	43	E1
Webb Ct. Woki	RG40	116	C4
Webbs Acre. That	RG19	106	C1
Webbs La. Been	RG7	109	D4
Webster Cl. Maid	SL6	39	D3
Wedderburn Cl. Winn	RG41	88	B1
Wedgewood Way. Read	RG30	57	F1
Weekes Dr. Slough	SL1	42	A2
Weighbridge Row. Read	RG1	58	C1
Weir Cl. Read	RG31	84	C2
Weir Pl. Stai	TW18	123	F4
Weir Rd. Chert	KT16	124	A1
Welbeck. Brac	RG12	117	F2
Welbeck Rd. Maid	SL6	39	E3
Welby Cl. Maid	SL6	39	D2
Welby Cres. Winn	RG41	88	A1
Weldale St. Read	RG1	85	F4
Welford Rd. Wood	RG5	88	A4
Well Cl. Camb	GU15	151	D2
Well House La. Swal	RG27	140	A2
Well Meadow. Newb	RG14	105	D3
Welland Cl. Read	RG31	57	E1
Welland Cl. Slough	SL3	69	D4
Wellbank. Tapl	SL6	20	C1
Wellcroft Rd. Slough	SL1	42	A3
Weller Dr. Bark	RG40	141	D3
Weller Dr. Camb	GU15	151	E2
Wellers La. New G	RG42	91	E4
Wellesley Ave. Iver	SL0	44	C2
Wellesley Cl. Bags	GU19	145	E2
Wellesley Dr. Brac	RG45	142	C3
Wellesley Dr. Finch	RG45	142	C3
Wellesley Rd. Slough	SL1	43	D2
Welley Ave. Wray	TW19	68	C2
Welley Rd. Hort	SL3 & TW19	68	C1
Welley Rd. Wray	TW19 & SL3	68	C1
Wellfield Cl. Read	RG31	84	B4
Wellhill Rd. Fawl	OX12	27	E3
Wellhouse La. Buck	RG18	79	F3
Wellhouse La. Herm	RG18	79	F3
Wellhouse Rd. Maid	SL6	19	F1
Wellington Ave. Read	RG2	86	B2
Wellington Ave. Vir W	GU25	122	A2
Wellington Ave. Went	GU25	122	A2
Wellington Bsns Pk. Woki	RG45	142	C2
Wellington Cl. Newb	RG14	105	E3
Wellington Cl. Sand	GU17	150	B4
Wellington Cl. Shepp	TW17	125	F1
Wellington Cres. Tad	RG26	134	B1
Wellington Dr. Brac	RG12	118	C2
Wellington Rd. Ashf	TW15	97	F2
Wellington Rd. Crow	RG45	143	E3
Wellington Rd. Harm	TW14	71	F1
Wellington Rd. Maid	SL6	39	E4
Wellington Rd. Sand	GU17	150	B4
Wellington Rd. Woki	RG40	116	A3
Wellington St. Slough	SL1	43	D2
Wellingtonia Ave. Finch	RG45	142	B2
Wells Cl. Wind	SL4	67	D4
Wells La. Ascot	SL5	120	A3
Welsh La. Swal	RG7	139	D1
Welshmans Rd. Silc	RG7	136	A3
Welwick Cl. Winn	RG6	87	F1
Welwyn Ave. Felt	TW14	71	F1
Wendan Rd. Newb	RG14	130	C4
Wendover Dr. Camb	GU16	152	B2
Wendover Pl. Stai	TW18	96	B2
Wendover Rd. Bou E	SL8	3	D3
Wendover Rd. Burn	SL1	41	D4
Wendover Rd. Slough	SL1	41	D4
Wendover Rd. Stai	TW18	96	B2
Wendover Way. Read	RG30	84	B4
Wenlock Edge. Char	RG10	61	D2
Wenlock Way. That	RG19	106	B1
Wensley Cl. Twyf	RG10	61	E3
Wensley Rd. Read	RG1	85	F3
Wensleydale Dr. Camb	GU15	152	B3
Wentworth Ave. Burl	SL5	119	E4
Wentworth Ave. Read	RG2	113	E4
Wentworth Ave. Slough	SL2	22	A1
Wentworth Cl. Ashf	TW15	98	A2
Wentworth Cl.Brac	RG45	142	C3
Wentworth Cl. Yate	GU17	149	E3
Wentworth Cres. Maid	SL6	39	E3
Wentworth Ct. Newb	RG14	105	D1
Wentworth Dr. Vir W	GU25	122	A2
Wentworth Way. Burl	SL5	119	E4
Wescott Rd. Woki	RG40	116	B3
Wesley Dr. Eng G	TW20	96	A1
Wessex Cl. Hung	RG17	100	B3
Wessex Gdns. Twyf	RG10	61	F2
Wessex Rd. Bou E	SL8	3	D1
Wessex Rd. Harn	TW6	70	C2
Wessex Way. Maid	SL6	39	D2
Wessons Hill. Cook	SL6	19	E4
West Cl. Ashf	TW15	97	F2
West Cl. Medm	SL7	17	E4
West Cres. Wind	SL4	66	C3
West Dean. Maid	SL6	39	F4
West Dr. Read	RG31	84	C3
West Dr. Sonn	RG4	60	C1
West Dr. Went	GU25	121	F1
West Dr. Went	GU25	122	A1
West End Cl. Sto P	SL2	22	C2
West End La. Harl	UB7	71	E4
West End La. Sto P	SL2	22	C2
West End Rd. Silc	RG7	136	C3
West Fryerne. Yate	GU17	149	E4
West Gn. Yate	GU17	149	D4
West Green Ct. Read	RG1	85	F3
West Hill. Read	RG1	86	A3
West Mead. Maid	SL6	19	F1
West Mills. Newb	RG14	104	C2
West Mills Yard. Newb	RG14	104	C2
West Point. Slough	SL1	41	E3
West Ramp. Harm	TW6	71	D3
West Rd. Camb	GU15	151	E3
West Rd. Felt	TW14	98	B4
West Rd. Maid	SL6	39	F4
West Ridge. Bou E	SL8	3	D2
West Sq. Iver	SL0	44	C4
West St. Hen-O-T	RG9	15	E1
West St. Maid	SL6	39	F4
West St. Mar	SL7	1	B1
West St. Newb	RG14	104	C2
West St. Read	RG1	86	A4
West View. Felt	TW14	98	B4
West View. Pease	RG20	50	B4
West Way. Shepp	TW17	125	E2
Westacott Way. Bur G	SL6	38	B2
Westborough Ct. Maid	SL6	39	E3
Westborough Rd. Maid	SL6	39	E3
Westbourne Rd. Felt	TW13	98	C3
Westbourne Rd. Sand	GU15	150	C4
Westbourne Rd. Stai	TW18	97	D1
Westbourne Terr. Read	RG30	85	E4
Westbrook Cl. Hung	RG17	100	B3
Westbrook Gdns. Brac	RG12	118	B4
Westbrook Gn. Blew	OX11	11	F4
Westbrook. Holy	SL6	40	C1
Westbrook Rd. Read	RG30	58	B1
Westbrook Rd. Stai	TW18	96	C2
Westbrook St. Blew	OX11	11	F4
Westbury Cl. Crow	RG45	143	D3
Westbury Cl. Shepp	TW17	125	D2
Westbury La. Pur O T	RG8	57	D3
Westcombe Cl. Brac	RG12	118	C1
Westcote Rd. Read	RG30	85	E3
Westcotts Gn. New G	RG42	91	F1
Westcroft. Slough	SL2	22	A1
Westdene Cres. Caver	RG4	58	C2
Westerdale Dr. Camb	GU16	152	A2
Westerdale. That	RG19	106	B2
Western Ave. Chert	KT16	124	A3
Western Ave. Hen-O-T	RG9	35	F4
Western Ave. Newb	RG14	104	C2
Western Ave. Stai	TW20	123	D3
Western Ave. Wood	RG5	60	C1
Western Cl. Chert	KT16	124	A3
Western Dr. Bou E	HP10	3	F3
Western Dr. Shepp	TW17	125	E2
Western Elms Ave. Read	RG30	85	F4
Western End. Newb	RG14	104	C1
Western Oaks. Read	RG31	57	F1
Western Perimeter Rd. Harm	TW6	70	A2
Western Perimeter Rd. Stan	TW6	70	A2
Western Rd. Brac	RG12	117	F4
Western Rd. Hen-O-T	RG9	35	F4
Western Rd. Read	RG1	85	F3
Westfield Cotts. Medm	SL7	16	C3
Westfield Cres. Shipl	RG9	36	A2
Westfield Cres. That	RG18	106	A2
Westfield Rd. Camb	GU15	151	D1
Westfield Rd. Caver	RG4	59	D1
Westfield Rd. Chol	OX10	13	E4
Westfield Rd. Maid	SL6	39	D4
Westfield Rd. Slough	SL2	22	A1
Westfield Rd. That	RG18	106	A3
Westfield Rd. Winn	RG41	88	A1
Westfield Way. Newb	RG14	104	C1
Westfields. Comp	RG20	31	E2
Westgate Cres. Slough	SL1	41	F3
Westgate Rd. Newb	RG14	104	C1
Westhatch Cnr. New G	RG42	91	E3
Westhatch La. New G	RG42	91	E3
Westhope Rd. Mar	SL7	1	C2
Westland Cl. Stan	TW19	70	C1
Westland. That	RG18	106	A2
Westlands Ave. Read	RG2	86	C1
Westlands Ave. Slough	SL1	41	E4
Westlands Cl. Slough	SL1	41	E4
Westlands Rd. Newb	RG14	131	D4
Westley Mill. Binf	RG42	90	C4
Westley Mill. Holy	SL6	63	F1
Westlyn Rd. Silc	RG26	135	F1
Westmacott Dr. Felt	TW14	98	C4
Westmead Dr. Newb	RG14	130	C4
Westmead. Wind	SL4	67	D2
Westminster Way. Wood	RG6	87	E1
Westmorland Cl. Woki	RG41	115	E3
Westmorland Dr. Camb	GU15	152	A2
Westmorland Dr. New G	RG42	91	F1
Westmorland Rd. Maid	SL6	39	E3
Weston Gr. Bags	GU19	145	F1
Weston Rd. Slough	SL1	41	F4
Westonbirt Dr. Caver	RG4	58	C2
Westons. Beed	RG20	51	E4
Westridge Ave. Pur O T	RG8	57	E3
Westview Dr. Twyf	RG10	61	F3
Westward Rd. Woki	RG41	115	F4
Westwates Cl. Brac	RG12	118	B4
Westway. Gori	RG8	34	B4
Westwood Glen. Read	RG31	57	E1
Westwood Gn. Cook	SL6	19	F3
Westwood Rd. Mar	SL7	1	B1
Westwood Rd. Newb	RG14	105	E1
Westwood Rd. Read	RG31	57	E1
Westwood Rd. Windl	GU20	146	C3
Westwood Row. Read	RG31	57	E1
Wetherby Cl. Caver	RG4	59	E3
Wethered Dr. Burn	SL1	41	D4
Wethered Rd. Mar	SL7	1	B1
Wetton Pl. Eng G	TW20	96	A2
Wexham Park La. Iver H	SL3	23	E1
Wexham Park La. Sto P	SL3	23	E1
Wexham Rd. Slough	SL2	43	D3
Wexham St. Sto P	SL3	23	D2
Wexham Woods. Slough	SL3	43	E4
Wey Ave. Chert	KT16	124	A3
Wey Cl. Camb	GU15	151	D3
Weybridge Mead. Yate	GU17	149	F4
Weycrofts. Brac	RG42	90	C1
Weymead Cl. Chert	KT16	124	B1
Whaley Rd. Woki	RG40	116	B4
Wharf La. Bou E	SL8	3	D2
Wharf La. Hen-O-T	RG9	15	F1
Wharf Rd. Newb	RG14	105	D2
Wharf Rd. Wray	TW19	95	E4
Wharf St. Newb	RG14	105	D2
Wharf The. Newb	RG14	105	D2
Wharfedale Rd. Winn	RG41	88	A2
Wharfside. Padw	RG7	109	E2
Whatley Gn. Brac	RG12	118	A2
Whatmore Cl. Stan	TW19	70	A1
Wheatash Rd. Chert	KT16	124	A1
Wheatbutts Meadow. Eton	SL4	41	F1
Wheatfield Cl. Maid	SL6	39	D2
Wheatfields Rd. Shin	RG2	113	F3
Wheatlands Cl. Read	RG31	84	C2
Wheatlands La. Ham M	RG14	130	A3
Wheatlands Rd. Slough	SL3	43	E2
Wheatley. Brac	RG12	117	F2
Wheatley Cl. Read	RG2	86	C1
Wheatsheaf La. Newb	RG14	105	D2
Wheatsheaf La. Stai	TW18	96	C1
Wheble Dr. Wood	RG5	87	E4
Wheeler Cl. Bur C	RG7	111	D2
Wheelers Green Way. That	RG19	106	C1
Wheelton Cl. Winn	RG6	87	F2
Whins Cl. Camb	GU15	151	D2
Whins Dr. Camb	GU15	151	D2
Whinshill Park. Went	SL5	121	D1
Whistler Gr. Sand	GU15	150	B3
Whistlers La. Silc	RG7	136	A1
Whistley Cl. Brac	RG12	118	C3
Whitamore Row. Hen-O-T	RG9	35	F4
Whitby Dr. Read	RG1	86	B3
Whitby Gn. Caver	RG4	59	E3
Whitby Rd. Slough	SL1	42	B3
Whitchurch Cl. Maid	SL6	19	F2
Whitchurch Rd. Pangb	RG8	56	B3
White Bridge Cl. Felt	TW14	71	F1
White City. Crow	RG45	143	E3
White Cl. Herm	RG18	78	C3
White Cl. Slough	SL1	42	B3
White Gates. Wick	RG20	75	E3
White Hart Rd. Maid	SL6	39	F4
White Hart Rd. Slough	SL1	42	B2
White Hart Row. Chert	KT16	124	A1
White Hill. Beac	HP10	3	F4
White Hill. Rem H	RG9	16	A1
White Hill. Shipl	RG9	35	D3
White Hill. Windl	GU20	146	A3
White Hill. Woo G	HP10	3	F4
White Horse La. Finch	RG40	141	E3
White Horse Rd. Wind	SL4	66	B3
White House Gdns. Yate	GU17	149	E4
White Lilies Island. Wind	SL4	67	D4
White Lion Way. Yate	GU17	149	E4
White Lodge Cl. Suth	RG31	57	D2
White Lodge. Mar B	SL7	1	B3
White Paddock. Whi Wa	SL6	39	D1
White Rd. Chil	OX11	10	B4
White Rd. Sand	GU15	150	C3
White Rock. Maid	SL6	20	A1
White Shoot. Blew	OX11	12	A3
Whiteacres Dr. Holy	SL6	40	B1
Whitebeam Cl. Woki	RG41	115	E2
Whiteford Rd. Slough	SL2	42	C4
Whitegates La. Read	RG6	87	D4
Whitehall Dr. Arbo	RG2	140	C4
Whitehall Farm La. Vir W	GU25	122	C3
Whitehall La. Eng G	TW20	95	F1
Whitehall La. Wray	TW19	69	D1
Whitehill Cl. Mar B	SL7	1	B3
Whitehill Pl. Vir W	GU25	122	C2
Whitehill Rd. Camb	GU15	151	E4
Whitehills Gn. Gori	RG8	34	B3
Whiteknights Rd. Read	RG6	86	C3
Whitelands Dr. Burl	SL5	119	E4

185
Whitelands Rd. That
Wyatt Rd. Stai

Whitelands Rd. That RG18 106 B2
Whiteley. Wind SL4 66 C4
Whitemoor La. Upp B RG8 54 C3
Whitepit La. Fla H HP10 3 E4
Whites Hill. Sulhd RG7 110 C3
Whites La. Been RG7 109 D4
Whites La. Datch SL3 68 A4
Whitestone Cl. Winn RG6 87 F2
Whitewalls Cl. Comp RG20 31 F3
Whiteways Ct. Stai TW18 97 D1
Whitley Cl. Stan TW19 70 C1
Whitley Park La. Read RG2 86 B2
Whitley Rd. Yate GU17 149 E2
Whitley St. Read RG2 86 A3
Whitley Wood La. Read RG2 113 E4
Whitley Wood Rd. Read RG2 113 E4
Whitmoor Rd. Bags GU19 145 F1
Whitmore Cl. Sand GU15 143 E1
Whitmore La. Sunn SL5 121 D2
Whitstone Gdns. Read RG2 86 B1
Whittaker Rd. Slough SL2 21 F1
Whittenham Cl. Slough SL2 43 D3
Whittle Cl. Crow RG17 143 D1
Whittle Cl. Woki RG40 141 F4
Whittle Parkway. Slough SL1 41 E4
Whitton Cl. Winn RG6 87 E1
Whitton Rd. Brac RG6 118 C3
Whitworth Rd. Bark RG2 141 D4
Whurley Way. Maid SL6 19 F1
Whynstones Rd. Ascot SL5 120 A2
Whyteladyes La. Cook SL6 19 F3
Wick Hill La. Woki RG40 142 A3
Wick La. Eng G TW20 94 C1
Wick Rd. Eng G TW20 95 D1
Wickford Way. Read RG6 113 F4
Wickham Cl. Bags GU19 145 F3
Wickham La. Eng G TW20 96 A1
Wickham Rd. Camb GU15 151 F4
Wickham Rd. Winn RG6 87 F1
Wickham Vale. Brac RG12 117 F2
Wicks Gn. Binf RG42 90 A2
Widbrook Rd. Maid SL6 20 A2
Widecombe Pl. Read RG2 86 A1
Widecroft Rd. Iver SL0 44 C4
Widmere La. Mar B SL7 1 A4
Wield Ct. Winn RG6 87 F1
Wiggett Gr. Binf RG42 90 B1
Wigmore La. Read RG30 58 A1
Wigmore La. Read RG30 58 B1
Wigmore La. Thea RG7 83 E1
Wigmore Rd. Tad RG26 134 C1
Wilberforce Way. Brac RG12 118 B2
Wilcox Gdns. Stai TW17 124 C3
Wild Briar. Woki RG40 141 F4
Wild Cl. Winn RG6 114 B4
Wildcroft Dr. Woki RG40 116 A1
Wilder Ave. Pangb RG8 56 C3
Wilderness Ct. Read RG6 87 D2
Wilderness Rd. Camb GU16 151 F1
Wilderness Rd. Read RG6 87 D2
Wilders Cl. Brac RG42 91 D1
Wilders Cl. Camb GU16 151 F2
Wildgreen N. Slough SL3 44 A1
Wildgreen S. Slough SL3 44 A1
Wildridings Rd. Brac RG12 118 A3
Wildridings Sq. Brac RG12 118 A3
Wildwood Dr. Tad RG26 134 B1
Wildwood Gdns. Yate GU17 149 E2
Wilford Rd. Slough SL3 43 F1
Wilfred Way. That RG19 107 D2
Wilfrids Wood Cl. Bou E HP10 3 D3
Willats Cl. Chert KT16 124 A2
William Cl. That RG19 106 B1
William Ellis Cl. Old W SL4 68 A1
William Sim Wood. Burl RG42 92 A1
William St. Read RG1 85 F4
William St. Slough SL1 42 C3
William St. Wind SL4 67 E3
Williant Cl. Whi Wa SL6 38 C1
Willington Cl. Camb GU15 151 D3
Willis Cl. Herm RG18 79 D2
Willoners. Slough SL2 42 A4
Willoughby Rd. Brac RG12 117 F3
Willoughby Rd. Slough SL3 44 A2
Willow Cl. Bur C RG30 111 D3
Willow Cl. Fla H HP10 3 E3
Willow Cl. Iver SL3 69 E4
Willow Cl. Newb RG14 104 C1
Willow Court La. Moul OX10 13 F3
Willow Ct. Camb GU16 151 E1
Willow Dr. Brac RG12 118 B4
Willow Dr. Maid SL6 40 A1
Willow Dr. Twyf RG10 61 E3
Willow Gdns. Read RG2 86 C1
Willow Gdns. Read RG31 57 D1
Willow Gn. West E GU24 153 F3
Willow La. Black GU17 150 B2
Willow La. Warg RG10 36 B2
Willow Pk. Sto P SL2 23 D3
Willow Pl. Eton SL4 67 E4
Willow Rd. Newt RG20 131 F1
Willow Rd. Stan SL3 69 F3
Willow St. Read RG1 86 A3
Willow Tree Glade. Bur C RG31 84 B2
Willow Way. Sand GU17 142 C1
Willow Wlk. Chert KT16 124 A1
Willow Wlk. Eng G TW20 95 E2
Willowbrook. Eton SL4 42 B1
Willowbrook Rd. Stan TW19 97 F3
Willowdale. Woki RG40 141 F4
Willowford. Yate GU17 149 E3
Willowherb Cl. Woki RG40 116 C4
Willowmead Cl. Mar SL7 1 C2
Willowmead Cl. Newb RG14 130 B3
Willowmead Gdns. Mar SL7 1 C2
Willowmead Rd. Mar SL7 1 C2
Willowmead Sq. Mar SL7 1 C2
Willowmead. Stai TW18 124 A4
Willows End. Sand GU17 150 A4
Willows Rd. Bou E SL8 3 D2
Willows The. Caver RG4 59 D1
Willows The. Light GU18 146 B1
Willowside. Wood RG5 60 C1
Willson Rd. Eng G TW20 95 D2
Wilmington Cl. Wood RG5 87 F4
Wilmot Cl. Binf RG42 90 B1
Wilmot Rd. Burn SL1 21 D1
Wilmot Way. Camb GU15 151 F2
Wilmot Wlk. Newb RG14 130 B3
Wilmott Cl. Winn RG41 88 A1
Wilsford Cl. Read RG6 113 F4
Wilson Ave. Hen-O-T RG9 35 F4
Wilson Cl. Comp RG20 31 F2
Wilson Ct. Winn RG41 88 A1
Wilson Rd. Read RG30 85 E4
Wilton Cl. Harm UB7 70 B4
Wilton Cres. Wind SL4 66 B2
Wilton Rd. Camb GU15 151 D2
Wilton Rd. Read RG30 85 E4
Wiltshire Ave. Crow RG45 143 D3
Wiltshire Ave. Slough SL2 22 B1
Wiltshire Dr. Woki RG40 116 B4
Wiltshire Gr. New G RG42 91 F1
Wiltshire Rd. Mar SL7 1 C2
Wiltshire Rd. Woki RG40 116 B4
Wiltshire Wlk. Read RG31 84 A3
Wilwood Rd. Brac RG42 117 F4
Wilwyne Cl. Caver RG4 59 E2
Wimbledon Cl. Camb GU15 144 C1
Wimbledon Rd. Camb GU15 144 C1
Wimblington Dr. Winn RG6 114 B4
Wimbourne Gdns. Read RG30 58 A1
Wimbushes. Woki RG40 141 E3
Winbury Ct. Maid SL6 39 F4
Wincanton Rd. Read RG2 113 E4
Winch Cl. Binf RG42 90 B2
Winchbottom La. Lit M SL7 2 A3
Winchcombe Rd. Newb RG14 105 D1
Winchcombe Rd. Twyf RG10 61 F2
Winchester Cl. Stan SL3 69 F3
Winchester Dr. Maid SL6 39 D2
Winchester Rd. Harl UB7 71 F4
Winchester Rd. Read RG2 86 A2
Winchester Way. Black GU17 150 B3
Winchgrove Rd. Brac RG42 91 D1
Winchstone Cl. Stai TW17 124 C3
Wincroft Rd. Caver RG4 58 C3
Windermere Cl. Felt TW14 98 C4
Windermere Cl. Read RG41 88 B2
Windermere Cl. Stai TW20 96 A1
Windermere Rd. Light GU18 146 A1
Windermere Rd. Read RG2 86 B2
Windermere Way. Slough SL1 41 E4
Windermere Way. That RG19 106 A2
Winding Wood Dr. Camb GU15 152 A2
Windle Cl. Windl GU20 146 B2
Windlebrook Gn. Brac RG42 118 A4
Windlesham Ct. Windl GU20 146 B4
Windlesham Rd. Brac RG42 117 F4
Windlesham Rd. West E GU24 153 F4
Windmill Ave. Woki RG41 115 F4
Windmill Cl. Stai TW15 98 C1
Windmill Cl. Wind SL4 67 D3
Windmill Cl. Woki RG41 115 F4
Windmill Cnr. Mort RG7 137 D3
Windmill Field. Windl GU20 146 B2
Windmill La. Buck RG7 108 A3
Windmill La. Wool RG7 108 A3
Windmill Rd. Brac RG42 118 A4
Windmill Rd. Cook SL6 19 F3
Windmill Rd. Fulm SL3 23 E4
Windmill Rd. Mort RG7 137 D3
Windmill Rd. Slough SL1 42 B3
Windmill Rd. Stai TW16 125 F4
Windmill Rd W. Stai TW16 125 F4
Windrush Ave. Slough SL3 44 A2
Windrush Hts. Sand GU17 150 A4
Windrush Way. Maid SL6 39 F4
Windrush Way. Read RG30 85 D4
Windsor Dr. Ashf TW15 97 E2
Windsor Hill. Bou E HP10 3 F3
Windsor La. Burn SL1 21 E1
Windsor Park Rd. Harl UB7 71 F4
Windsor Rd. Ascot SL5 120 A4
Windsor Rd. Datch SL3 68 A4
Windsor Rd. Eng G TW20 & SL4 95 F3
Windsor Rd. Holy SL6 40 B1
Windsor Rd. Maid SL6 40 B1
Windsor Rd. Oak G SL4 66 A4
Windsor Rd. Slough SL1 & SL3 42 C2
Windsor Rd. Sto P SL2 23 D4
Windsor Rd. Wray TW19 68 C1
Windsor Ride. Woki RG40 142 A4
Windsor Rise. Newb RG14 131 E4
Windsor St. Chert KT16 124 A2
Windsor Way. Read RG31 84 A2
Wing Cl. Mar SL7 1 B1
Wingate Rd. Wood RG5 87 F3
Wingfield Gdns. Camb GU16 152 B2
Wingrove Rd. Read RG30 85 E3
Winkfield Cl. Woki RG41 116 A2
Winkfield La. Wink SL4 92 B4
Winkfield Rd. Ascot SL5 120 A4
Winkfield Row. Burl RG42 92 A2
Winkfield St. Burl SL4 92 B3
Winnersh Gate. Winn RG41 88 B1
Winnersh Gr. Winn RG41 88 B1
Winscombe. Brac RG12 117 F2
Winser Dr. Read RG30 85 E3
Winston Cl. Shin RG7 113 E1
Winston Way. Pur O T RG8 57 D3
Winston Way. That RG19 105 F2
Winter Hill. Cook SL6 2 B1
Winter Hill. Cook SL6 19 D2
Winter Hill. Cook SL6 19 D4
Winter Hill. Maid SL6 19 D2
Winterberry Way. Caver RG4 58 C3
Winterbourne Rd. Box RG20 76 C2
Winterbourne Rd. Wint RG20 76 C2
Winterton Dr. Newb RG14 104 B3
Winton Cres. Yate GU17 149 E3
Winton Rd. Read RG2 113 E4
Wintoun Path. Slough SL2 21 F1
Wintringham Way. Pur O T RG8 57 E3
Winvale. Slough SL1 42 C2
Winwood. Slough SL2 43 E4
Wises Firs. Sulhd RG7 110 B2
Wishmoor Cl. Camb GU15 151 F4
Wishmoor Rd. Camb GU15 151 F4
Wispington Cl. Winn RG6 87 E1
Wistaria La. Yate GU17 149 E3
Wisteria Cl. Woki RG41 115 F3
Wiston Terr. Read RG1 86 A4
Witcham Cl. Winn RG6 114 B4
Withey Cl. Wind SL4 66 C3
Witheygate Ave. Stai TW18 97 D1
Withy Cl. Light GU18 146 B1
Withy Cl. Read RG31 84 B3
Withy Croft. Slough SL3 43 F4
Withybed La. Kint RG17 101 F2
Wittenham Ave. Read RG31 57 D3
Wittenham Rd. Brac RG12 118 C4
Woburn Cl. Camb GU16 152 A1
Woburn Cl. Caver RG4 58 C2
Wokingham Rd. Brac RG12 & RG42 117 F4
Wokingham Rd. Hurst RG10 88 C4
Wokingham Rd. Read RG6 87 E2
Wokingham Rd. Sand GU17 142 C1
Wolf La. Wind SL4 66 C2
Wolseley St. Read RG1 86 A3
Wolsey Rd. Ashf TW15 97 F2
Wolsey Rd. Ashf TW15 98 C1
Wolsey Rd. Caver RG4 59 D1
Wolsingham Way. That RG19 106 B1
Wondesford Dale. Binf RG42 90 B2
Wooburn Manor Pk. Bou E HP10 3 F3
Wooburn Mews. Bou E HP10 3 F3
Wood Cl. Wind SL4 67 E2
Wood End. Crow RG45 142 C2
Wood Green Cl. Read RG30 85 F4
Wood La. Arbo RG41 114 C2
Wood La. Bee H RG7 138 C3
Wood La. Binf RG42 90 B1
Wood La. Iver SL0 44 B4
Wood La. Slough SL1 42 A2
Wood Moor. Finch RG40 141 F1
Wood Rd. Camb GU15 151 D1
Wood Rd. Stai TW17 125 D3
Wood Ridge. Newb RG14 130 C4
Woodberry Cl. Caver RG4 59 D2
Woodbine Cl. Sand GU17 150 B4
Woodbine Cl. Winn RG6 87 E1
Woodbine La. Newt RG20 130 C1
Woodbourne Cl. Yate GU17 149 E3
Woodbridge Rd. Black GU17 150 A3
Woodbridge Rd. Read RG31 84 A3
Woodbury. Lamb RG17 25 E1
Woodby Dr. Sunn SL5 120 C1
Woodcote. Maid SL6 39 E3
Woodcote Rd. Caver RG4 58 C2
Woodcote Rd. Sou S RG8 14 B2
Woodcote Way. Caver RG4 58 B3
Woodend Cl. Burl SL5 119 F4
Woodend Dr. Ascot SL5 120 A2
Woodenhill. Brac RG12 117 F1
Woodfield Dr. Maid SL6 39 D3
Woodfield Way. Thea RG7 83 F2
Woodford Cl. Caver RG4 58 C2
Woodford Gn. Brac RG12 118 C3
Woodford Way. Slough SL2 22 A1
Woodhall La. Windl SL5 146 C4
Woodhaw. Stai TW20 96 A2
Woodhouse La. Head RG19 133 E1
Woodhouse St. Binf RG42 90 C1
Woodhouse St. Brac RG42 117 F4
Woodhurst La. Woki RG41 115 F4
Woodhurst Rd. Maid SL6 20 A1
Woodies Cl. Binf RG42 90 B1
Woodland Ave. Slough SL1 42 B3
Woodland Ave. Wind SL4 66 C2
Woodland Ave. Woki RG41 115 F4
Woodland Cl. Mar SL7 1 C2
Woodland Cres. Brac RG42 91 E1
Woodland Dr. Read RG30 84 B4
Woodland Way. Mar SL7 1 C2
Woodlands Ave. Bur C RG7 111 D2
Woodlands Ave. Wood RG5 87 E4
Woodlands Busn Pk. Maid SL6 39 D1
Woodlands Cl. Ascot SL5 119 F2
Woodlands Cl. Black GU17 150 C1
Woodlands Cl. Herm RG18 78 C3
Woodlands Ct. Crow GU15 143 F1
Woodlands Gr. Caver RG4 59 F2
Woodlands La. Windl GU20 146 C2
Woodlands Parade. Ashf TW15 98 B1
Woodlands Park Ave. Whi Wa SL6 39 D1
Woodlands Park Rd. Maid SL6 39 D2
Woodlands Park Rd. Whi Wa SL6 39 D2
Woodlands Rd. Camb GU15 151 D3
Woodlands Rd E. Vir W GU25 122 B3
Woodlands Rd. Shipl RG9 35 F2
Woodlands Rd. Tad RG26 134 B1
Woodlands Rd. Vir W GU25 122 B3
Woodlands Rd W. Vir W GU25 122 B3
Woodlands Ride. Ascot SL5 120 A2
Woodlands The. Woki RG41 115 E2
Woodlands Wlk. Black GU17 150 C1
Woodlands. Yate GU17 149 E2
Woodlee Cl. Vir W GU25 122 B4
Woodley Gn. Wood RG5 87 F4
Woodman Cl. Read RG2 113 E3
Woodmancott Cl. Brac RG12 118 C2
Woodmans La. Bur C RG7 110 C2
Woodmere. Brac RG12 118 C3
Woodmere Cl. Read RG6 87 D1
Woodmoor End. Cook SL6 20 A4
Woodpecker Cl. Twyf RG10 61 F2
Woodridge Cl. Brac RG12 118 B3
Woodrow Dr. Woki RG40 116 C3
Woods Rd. Caver RG4 59 F2
Woodsend Cl. Read RG6 113 F4
Woodshore Cl. Vir W GU25 122 A4
Woodside Ave. Fla H HP10 3 E4
Woodside. Black GU17 150 B2
Woodside Cl. Buck RG7 107 E3
Woodside Cl. Woki RG40 141 F4
Woodside. Cold A RG18 79 E1
Woodside. Fla H HP10 3 E3
Woodside La. Wink SL4 93 E2
Woodside. Newb RG14 130 B4
Woodside Rd. Ascot SL4 93 D2
Woodside. Sand GU15 150 C4
Woodside Way. Read RG2 113 E4
Woodside Way. Vir W GU25 122 A3
Woodstock Ave. Slough SL3 43 E1
Woodstock Cl. Maid SL6 19 F1
Woodstock St. Read RG1 86 C4
Woodthorpe Rd. Ashf TW15 97 E2
Woodthorpe Rd. Stai TW15 97 E2
Woodview Rd. Pangb RG8 56 B3
Woodville Cl. Black GU17 150 A3
Woodward Cl. Winn RG41 88 B1
Woodway. Camb GU15 151 D3
Woodway Rd. Blew OX11 12 A4
Woodwaye. Wood RG5 87 E4
Woodyer Cl. Wood RG5 87 F3
Woolacombe Dr. Read RG6 86 C1
Woolford Cl. Burl RG42 92 B1
Woolhampton Hill. Wool RG7 108 B2
Woolhampton Way. Brac RG12 118 B2
Woolton Lodge Gdns. Ball H RG20 129 F1
Woosehill La. Woki RG41 115 F3
Woosehill La. Woki RG41 115 F4
Woosehill. Woki RG41 115 F3
Wootton Cl. Read RG31 84 B4
Wootton Dr. Woo G HP10 3 F4
Wootton Rd. Hen-O-T RG9 35 E4
Wootton Way. Maid SL6 39 E3
Worcester Cl. Maid SL6 39 E2
Worcester Cl. Read RG30 85 D3
Worcester Dr. Ashf TW15 98 A2
Worcester Gdns. Slough SL1 42 B2
Wordsworth Ave. Yate GU17 149 D2
Wordsworth. Brac RG12 117 F2
Wordsworth Ct. Caver RG4 59 E4
Wordsworth Rd. Slough SL2 21 E1
Wordsworth Rd. That RG18 106 B2
Worlds End Hill. Brac RG12 118 C2
Worple Ave. Stai TW18 97 D1
Worple Rd. Stai TW18 97 D1
Worple The. Wray TW19 68 C1
Worrall Way. Read RG6 113 F4
Worsley Pl. Thea RG7 83 F2
Worster Rd. Cook SL6 19 F3
Worton Dr. Read RG2 113 D4
Wrabness Way. Stai TW18 124 A4
Wraysbury Rd. Stai TW18 & TW19 96 B3
Wraysbury Rd. Wray TW18 & TW19 96 B3
Wren Cl. Bur C RG7 111 D2
Wren Cl. Woki RG41 115 F3
Wren Cl. Yate GU17 149 D3
Wren Ct. Slough SL3 44 A2
Wrenfield Dr. Caver RG4 58 C3
Wrens Ave. Ashf TW15 98 B2
Wrensfield. Mar SL7 1 B1
Wrenswood Cl. Read RG2 113 D4
Wright Cl. Wood RG5 88 A4
Wright. Oak G SL4 66 B2
Wroxham. Brac RG12 117 F2
Wroxham Rd. Wood RG5 87 E4
Wyatt Rd. Stai TW18 97 D2

Name	Code	Pg	Grid
Wyatt Rd. Wind	SL4	66	B2
Wychcotes. Caver	RG4	58	C2
Wychelm Rd. Light	GU18	153	E4
Wychelm Rd. Shin	RG2	113	F3
Wychwood Ave. Brac	RG12	118	C3
Wychwood Cl. Read	RG6	86	C1
Wychwood Cres. Read	RG6	86	C2
Wychwood Pl. Camb	GU15	145	D1
Wychwood Pl. Camb	GU15	152	A4
Wycombe La. Woo G	HP10	3	F4
Wycombe Rd. Mar	SL7	1	C2
Wycombe Rd. Mar B	SL7	1	C3
Wye Cl. Ashf	TW15	98	A2
Wye Cl. Read	RG30	84	C3
Wye Rd. Woo G	HP10	3	E4
Wykeham Cl. Harm	UB7	71	D4
Wykeham Rd. Read	RG6	87	D3
Wylam. Brac	RG12	117	F2
Wylands Rd. Slough	SL3	44	A1
Wyld Court Hill. Hamp N	RG18	53	E3
Wymers. Burn	SL1	21	D2
Wymers Wood Rd. Burn	SL1	21	D2
Wyncote Cl. Read	RG2	86	C1
Wyndale Cl. Hen-O-T	RG9	15	F1
Wyndham Cl. Yate	GU17	149	E4
Wyndham Cres. Burn	SL1	21	D2
Wyndham Cres. Wood	RG5	60	B1
Wyndham Rd. Newb	RG14	105	E3
Wynford Cl. Read	RG30	85	E2
Wynnstay Gdns. Mar B	SL7	1	C3
Wynsham Way. Windl	GU20	146	A3
Wyre Ct. Sulh	RG31	57	E2
Wyres Dale. Brac	RG12	118	C1
Wythe Mead. Binf	RG42	90	A1
Wyvern Cl. Brac	RG12	118	A3
Yale Cl. Crow	GU15	143	F1
Yard Mead. Eng G	TW20	96	A3
Yardley. Brac	RG12	117	F2
Yarmouth Rd. Slough	SL1	42	B3
Yarnold Cl. Woki	RG40	116	C4
Yarnton Cl. Caver	RG4	59	E3
Yateley Rd. Sand	GU17	149	F4
Yates Copse. Newb	RG14	105	F3
Yattendon La. Asham	RG8 & RG18	54	B1
Yattendon La. Yatt	RG8 & RG18	54	B1
Yattendon Rd. Herm	RG18	79	D4
Yaverland Dr. Bags	GU19	145	E1
Ye Meads. Tapl	SL6	40	C3
Yelverton Rd. Read	RG2	86	B2
Yeomans La. Newt	RG20	131	D1
Yeomans Way. Camb	GU15	151	F3
Yeosfield. Swal	RG7	139	E2
Yeoveney Cl. Stan	TW19	96	B3
Yeovil Rd. Burn	SL1	41	F4
Yeovil Rd. Sand	GU15	143	F1
Yew Cl. Woki	RG41	115	F3
Yew Gate. Newb	RG14	104	C3
Yew La. Read	RG1	85	F3
Yew Tree Cl. Maid	SL6	39	F4
Yew Tree Ct. Gori	RG8	34	B3
Yew Tree Rd. Slough	SL1	43	D2
Yew Tree Rise. Read	RG31	84	B3
Yew Tree Wlk. Camb	GU16	151	F1
Yewhurst Cl. Twyf	RG10	61	E3
Yewtrees. Stai	TW20	123	E3
Yield Hall La. Read	RG1	86	A4
Yield Hall Pl. Read	RG1	86	A4
Yockley Cl. Camb	GU15	152	B2
Yoreham Cl. Winn	RG6	87	F1
York Ave. Slough	SL1	42	B4
York Ave. Wind	SL4	67	D3
York Cl. Newb	RG14	105	D1
York Rd. Binf	RG42	90	B2
York Rd. Camb	GU15	151	E4
York Rd. Hen-O-T	RG9	15	E1
York Rd. Hung	RG17	100	B2
York Rd. Maid	SL6	40	A4
York Rd. Mar	SL7	1	B1
York Rd. Newb	RG14	105	D1
York Rd. Read	RG1	59	D1
York Rd. Wind	SL4	67	D3
York Town Ind Est. Camb	GU15	151	D2
York Way. Sand	GU17	150	A4
Yorktown Rd. Sand	GU17	150	B4
Youlden Cl. Camb	GU15	152	A3
Youlden Dr. Camb	GU15	152	A3
Youngs Ind Est. Alde	RG7	134	C2
Zealand Ave. Harm	UB7	70	C4
Zinnia Cl. Woki	RG41	115	E4
Zinzan St. Read	RG1	85	F4